Smoking and Pregnancy

Smoking and Pregnancy

The Politics of Fetal Protection

LAURY OAKS

RUTGERS UNIVERSITY PRESS
New Brunswick, New Jersey, and London

Library of Congress Cataloging-in-Publication Data

Oaks, Laury, 1967–
    Smoking and pregnancy : the politics of fetal protection / Laury Oaks.
      p. cm.
    Includes bibliographical references and index.
    ISBN 0–8135–2887–9 (alk. paper) — ISBN 0–8135–2888–7 (pbk. : alk. paper)
    1. Pregnant women—Tobacco use—Social aspects. 2. Fetus—Effect of Tobacco
on—Social aspects. 3. Tobacco—Physiological effect—Social aspects. 4. Pregnant
women—Physiology—Social aspects. 5. Smoking—Health aspects. I. Title.
RG627.6.T6 O25 2001
618.2'4—dc21

                                                    00–039036

British Cataloging-in-Publication data for this book is available from the British
Library

Manufactured in the United States of America

In memory of my grandmother
Eva Mary Lanktree, née Madden (1913–1991)

Contents

Acknowledgments

This book, although critical of pregnancy advice, has benefited from the advice generously offered by many. I thank all who have contributed to this book during its different stages.

The dissertation research on which this book is based was inspired by Constance Nathanson's intellectual interests and richly supported by her advising, mentoring, and friendship. I am grateful to the women and health professionals who shared their views with me; I have worked to represent with respect and fairness their perspectives and experiences. Constance Nathanson, Gillian Feeley-Harnik, Emily Martin, Doug English, Nora Jacobson, Janine Holc, Lisa Kim Davis, Karina Kielmann, Jennifer Hirsch, Lisa Handwerker, Tom Fricke, and Roddey Reid pushed me to broaden the scope of my research and to sharpen my arguments. Pamela Burdell's steadfast support and assistance with financial matters facilitated the research process. I was very fortunate to receive a dissertation grant from the Mellon Foundation through the joint Ph.D. program in Anthropology and Population Dynamics at Johns Hopkins University and a Woodrow Wilson–Johnson & Johnson Dissertation Grant in Women's Health Award.

The members of my dissertation committee—Constance Nathanson, Gillian Feeley-Harnik, Emily Martin, Toby Ditz, Antoinette Burton, and honorary member Dawn Misra—provided enthusiasm as well as suggestions for expanding and shaping the dissertation into a book. It is an honor to have been welcomed into the academic community by such vibrant and supportive scholars.

Colleagues in the women's studies program at the University of California, Santa Barbara, respected the time I devoted to this project and offered their encouragement. I thank the women's studies program for providing me with financial support for the book's production. At Rutgers University Press, I have had the pleasure of working with Martha Heller, David Myers, Amy Rashap, Brigitte Goldstein, and Kathryn Gohl. The book also reflects the recommendations of an anonymous reviewer.

I also thank those who commented on various chapters-in-progress: Barbara Herr Harthorn, Lynn Morgan, Jo Murphy-Lawless, Clarissa Hsu, Janine Holc, Constance Nathanson, Jonathan Inda, and Sabine Frühstuck. Nora Jacobson and Doug English read several drafts of each chapter and the full manuscript. The suggestions of these friends and colleagues helped me to significantly rework the book's themes. Laura Holliday offered expert editing and important insights at short notice. Vivian Barrera provided industrious research assistance and cheerfully took on the task of formatting the bibliography. Joanne Rondilla graciously volunteered her artistic eye and graphic design skills. Jay Stemmle kindly took on the indexing job.

The long-distance encouragement I received from my family and friends has been appreciated; I have not expressed this often enough. Special thanks are due Mike Dooley and Dave Oaks for their creative services, including photography and the design of the cover art, and Mary Kay Sheldon and Beth Midgley for their parts in assisting Kathleen Midgley's modeling of "smoke-free" fashion.

I again especially want to recognize and thank Nora Jacobson and Doug English. Nora's consistent advice about how to create order out of what I often saw as chaos, conversations about points large and small, and honest criticism enhanced the quality of the book and the meaningfulness of carrying out this work. Doug's close readings and suggestions strengthened the book at my innumerable requests; his influence is present on each page, and his presence has influenced every page.

Chapter 1

Confronting the Pregnant Smoker

"Precious Baby," read the T-shirt of the very pregnant
young woman in the Newark, New Jersey, airport. Yet
there she sat dragging luxuriously on a Virginia Slims,
supplying herself and her desired child-to-be with a dose
of nicotine, carbon monoxide, hydrogen cyanide, DDT,
and benzopyrene. No one screamed, "Stop!" or "Please
don't!" No one murmured, "Disgusting!" or "How
Sad." No one was discussing the contradiction between
her chosen wearing apparel and her cigarette. In fact, I
appeared to be the only one shaking my head in dismay
at this remarkably ironic behavior.

—Pediatrician Mary Ann Cromer,
New York State Journal of Medicine, 1983

OF THE MANY expectations about what women should and should not do during pregnancy, the imperative to abstain from drugs, alcohol, and tobacco has received particular attention in the United States since the late 1970s. Prenatal health messages have become omnipresent—displayed on billboards, posters at grocery and convenience stores, stickers in restrooms of restaurants and airplanes, labels on product containers, and advertisements in the media. Pregnant women are also confronted with health warnings offered by their doctors, neighbors, friends, and even strangers. Indeed, practically every pregnant woman is aware of the message that smoking, drinking, and doing drugs are "bad for the baby."

The subtext of health education campaigns argues that if women know about fetal health risks, they will choose not to smoke, drink, or take drugs. What, then, explains why some women ignore these warnings? Pregnancy advice books and public health campaigns portray these pregnant women as aggressively self-indulgent or as helpless victims of addiction. They are "bad mothers" because they do not put their baby-to-be's health first.[1] But such labeling disregards the factors that may lead pregnant women to substance use—factors such as stress, poverty, nicotine addiction, or a network of family and friends who are substance users. Moreover, it fails to take into account that until recently, moderate smoking and drinking during pregnancy were accepted by the medical profession as well as the general public. Today, pregnant women are instructed to disregard the advice that was offered their mothers, who were told by their doctors that half a pack of cigarettes a day and a cocktail before dinner were harmless. Such indulgences did not make these women bad mothers.[2]

The new rules of pregnancy take their authority from medical-scientific research and are supported by strong social, even legal, proscriptions against women who refuse to conform to them. Criminal charges brought against women who allegedly abuse their fetuses by not following health advice represent the most extreme form of health education. Since the mid-1980s, more than two hundred women in thirty states have been prosecuted for practices during pregnancy that were deemed dangerous to their fetuses, including drinking, taking illicit or over-the-counter drugs, and having sex (Daniels 1993; Terry 1996; Roberts 1997; Roth 2000). Prosecutors are more likely to identify and charge poor Black women for substance use during pregnancy,[3] yet media accounts of such fetal abuse cases warn all pregnant women that not following medical recommendations could have severe consequences, including prison time, court supervision, court-mandated use of birth control, and loss of child custody. Further, the publicized stories about fetal abuse reinforce and intensify the moral imperative that underlies health advice: to be a good mother, a woman must follow today's pregnancy rules.

Although pregnant women who have used drugs or alcohol or rejected their doctor's orders have faced criminal charges, those who have smoked cigarettes have not. Beginning in the late 1980s, however, child custody cases began to admit smoking as evidence of unfit parenting. Judges have revoked the custody rights of mothers and other guardians in order to protect children from dangerous smoke-filled homes (Action on Smoking and Health 1995).[4] Given the rise in fetal abuse cases and some antitobacco advocates' relentless drive to end cigarette smoking, it is realistic to expect that in the future, legal action could be taken to protect fetuses from women's "smoke-filled wombs."

The proliferation of medical, legal, and popular concerns over pregnant women's health behaviors emphasizes that pregnancy is not only a natural physical process but one imbued with cultural and moral expectations about motherhood. Women who do not demonstrate proper "maternal nature," or the supposedly innate qualities of nurturance and self-sacrifice, are popularly portrayed as deviant and therefore subject to social control. This book investigates the dynamics that have intensified cultural attention to how mothers-to-be must protect their babies-to-be and that have constructed the pregnant smoker as a dangerously irresponsible individual who deserves moral, perhaps even legal, censure. It seeks alternate ways of approaching both the problem of and the solution to cigarette smoking during pregnancy.

The category of fetal abuser and the social condemnation and legal punishment of disobedient pregnant women are products of our particular historical and cultural context, one in which the fetus has gained status as a person. In medicine, the fetus is an unborn patient. Technologies such as fetal ultrasound, neonatal intensive care units, and fetal surgery allow intervention into and even the "rescue" of fetal life (Kolata 1990; Casper 1994, 1998; Rapp 1988, 1990, 1997, 1999; Rothman 1986, 1989; Taylor 1998). Obstetricians have performed court-ordered cesarean sections and blood transfusions against a woman's will, justifying their actions by stating that treating the fetus—one of their two patients—was necessary to preserve its life or health (Gallagher 1987, 1989; Jordan and Irwin 1987; Kolder et al. 1987; McNulty 1988). In the political and legal arena, the antiabortion movement continues to press for legal recognition of the right to life of the "unborn" (Luker 1984; Petchesky 1985 [1984]; Ginsburg 1998 [1989]; Simonds 1996).[5] Claims put forward in state legislatures and in the courts to "protect fetal health" by punishing pregnant women deemed to have put their fetuses at risk support the notion of fetal rights symbolically if not legally (Johnsen 1986, 1987; Moss 1990; Pollitt 1990; Chavkin 1992; Daniels 1993; Roberts 1997; Gomez 1997; Roth 2000). Between 1973 and 1992, thirty-three states and the District of Columbia passed legislation on women's drug and alcohol use during pregnancy aimed at ensuring fetal health (Roth 2000, 163). State legislation has ranged from education and treatment programs to actions against women for child abuse and neglect based on their behavior during pregnancy. In 1996, the South Carolina Supreme Court ruled that viable fetuses (those that can live outside of a woman's womb) have the same legal status as children for the purposes of child abuse law. Health care professionals in South Carolina were required by law to report pregnant women who take drugs or who otherwise fail to comply with prenatal advice (Roberts 1997; Herbert 1998). In 1998, the U.S. Supreme Court let stand the South Carolina ruling (Roth 2000, 195).

These trends reveal ways of thinking about pregnancy and pregnant women's bodies that set limits on women's agency and autonomy at the same time that they accord the fetus agency and autonomy. Framing pregnancy as a potential conflict—in which a woman's rights, needs, or desires clash with those of her fetus—opens the maternal–fetal relationship to surveillance, regulation, and intervention. As physician Wendy Chavkin argues, the maternal–fetal conflict model of pregnancy posits "woman as protector of the fetus" at odds with "woman as adult decision-maker" (1992, 72; see also Gallagher 1989, 215). Within this model, when a pregnant woman does not follow prenatal health recommendations, both her capability to make rational choices and her ability to perform the duties of motherhood are subject to medical, legal, and social judgment. Cynthia Daniels, a feminist political scientist, points out that the ideal of motherhood promoted by advocates of fetal rights is that of selfless motherhood (1993, 136). Indeed, scholars have analyzed how pregnant women's selfhood appears to recede as the selfhood of the fetus is increasingly recognized (see Morgan and Michaels 1999). Emphasis on the fetus as a person can all too easily reduce women's bodies to "maternal environments."

It follows that scrutiny of pregnant women's health decisions is pervasive; in addition to receiving medical advice through public warnings, many pregnant women find themselves surrounded in their daily lives by perhaps well-meaning but often intrusive lay experts. As one pregnancy advice book warns, "the world is filled with people who feel it is their responsibility to monitor your performance . . . the Pregnancy Police" (Iovine 1995, 64). Given the experiences of the women I talked with who had smoked during pregnancy, it is likely that someone did approach the pregnant woman in the Newark airport and that others would approach a pregnant woman in an airport or elsewhere to remind her that she should not smoke.

All pregnant women are subject to pregnancy policing, or the judgment, criticism, and advice-giving of authoritative others. Indeed, pregnancy advice is an example of what Michel Foucault (1979) calls disciplinary technology. Dispersed through social institutions and everyday practices, advice enacts power not through bodily violence or force but by "establishing norms against which individuals and their behaviors and bodies are judged and against which they police themselves" (Sawicki 1991, 68). Pregnant and even "prepregnant" women are expected to learn the rules of pregnancy from expert information sources—public health campaigns, pregnancy advice books, and doctors—to ensure the best health possible for their babies-to-be. Widespread knowledge about prenatal health risks represents part of the medicalization of everyday life, in which an individual's pursuit of a healthy lifestyle is considered a moral and social good (see Crawford 1980).

Feminist scholars may lament the extent to which pregnant women discipline themselves by strictly conforming to pregnancy advice. Barbara Duden comments, "A pregnant colleague who came to my office asked me to extinguish a cigarette. Why? Because she thinks that for the next six months she is the ecosystem for a fetus" (1993, 7). Women's responses to pregnancy advice demand a more complex interpretation than this. We cannot label pregnant women's acceptance of expert advice as merely indicative of their uncritical belief in medical authority or unquestioned dedication to protecting the health of their babies-to-be. Pregnancy advice has significant value for women who want to understand the process of pregnancy and to learn about prenatal health. The pregnancy policing that such advice often promotes, however, implies that those women who fail to seek out and accede to experts' guidance are weak willed, selfish, and immoral risk-takers who threaten the social order and well-being of future generations. Women's failure to seek out and follow advice about caring for their babies-to-be, then, is represented by health experts as not only a health but a social problem.

The pregnant smoker as the object of pregnancy policing is a relatively recent invention in the United States, and the social stigma currently attached to smoking by pregnant women is the product of complex and converging trends. These include medical research on the risks of smoking; antitobacco lobbying for regulation of smoke-free environments; efforts by antiabortion advocates to define the fetus as a person with legal rights; the medical conceptualization of the fetus as a patient; and rising social, medical, and legal expectations about pregnant women's responsibilities to act on behalf of their babies-to-be. I analyze the power of these intersecting forces by examining how smoking by pregnant women is judged by pregnant and parenting women themselves, health educators, health care providers, health policy makers, prenatal health program directors, the mass media, antitobacco activists, and prochoice and prolife advocates.[6] I seek to understand why smoking during pregnancy is seen as a problem and what different representations of the problem mean for women as moral and legal subjects.

The 1980s marks the period of the highest public visibility of antismoking campaigns aimed at pregnant women. Antitobacco advocacy at this time motivated health organizations and agencies to sponsor "stop smoking during pregnancy" campaigns and led the U.S. government to require pregnancy-specific surgeon general's warnings on all cigarette packages and advertisements; meanwhile, state and local governments enacted antismoking ordinances (Brandt 1990, 1992; Nathanson 1996, 1997, 1999, n.d.). Moreover, by the 1980s, the antitobacco movement had turned public attention to "innocent victims," nonsmokers harmed by secondhand smoke and all smokers who were addicted to smoking. Although women who smoke as well as their babies-to-be can be viewed as innocent victims, the dominant image of the pregnant smoker characterizes her not as innocent but as negligent; her baby-to-be, trapped in her smoke-filled womb, is characterized as the truly innocent victim.

The 1980s also witnessed the increasing intensity of antiabortion activism in reaction to the 1973 *Roe v. Wade* U.S. Supreme Court decision that legalized abortion as a woman's constitutional right. The antiabortion movement contends that each human being has, from the moment of conception, the right to life and that the law should recognize this right. Antiabortion campaigns have publicized images of "unborn babies" on placards and billboards and lobbied legislators to ban abortion. The most radical antiabortion factions have advocated barricading of abortion clinics, destroying clinic property, intimidating clinic workers and their clients, and murdering abortion providers (Ginsburg 1998 [1989]; Simonds 1996; Hern 1998). In 1989, in *Webster v. Reproductive Health Services*, a Missouri case that presented a possible challenge to *Roe v. Wade*, the U.S. Supreme Court allowed that abortion remained legal as established in *Roe* but upheld the state of Missouri's right to declare that life begins at conception and to limit abortion services in Missouri public facilities (Kolbert 1989). This ruling, celebrated by antiabortion advocates, motivated other states to attempt to impose greater restrictions on abortion rights (Heriot 1996). Connected to this vigorous antiabortion activism, and starting in the mid-1980s, charges of fetal abuse were brought against pregnant women who used drugs during pregnancy or who disobeyed doctors' orders (Daniels 1993; Gomez 1997; Roberts 1997; Roth 2000). These sorts of attacks on women's reproductive choices—whether on abortion or on "pregnancy lifestyles"—focus on protecting the fetus as a person with rights that may supersede those of the pregnant woman.

In short, in the 1980s, the combination of medical warnings about the fetal health risks associated with pregnant women's smoking and the increased recognition of fetuses as persons who have rights gave meaning to smoking during pregnancy as a highly visible public health and social problem that demanded an urgent response from the public. Pregnancy policing has become a social, medical, and legal imperative.

What Exactly Is the Problem? The Public Health Perspective on Smoking during Pregnancy

The development of a public health problem entails the identification of a health-related phenomenon as worthy of study, the accumulation of scientific evidence deemed credible by medical professionals, an assessment that the problem has widespread and measurable significance in terms of its costs to society, official recognition by public health leaders, and efforts to raise public awareness of the problem. By definition, health professionals name and legitimize public health problems.[7] Public health practitioners' emphasis on an individual's responsibility to comply with health recommendations is based on the assumption and justification of the authority of medical professionals.[8] Practitioners expect that ideally the public will understand the problem in the way that a health education campaign directs them to and that individuals will follow advice about how to reduce or eliminate the problem.

Smoking has been named "probably the most important modifiable cause of poor pregnancy outcome among women in the United States" (U.S. Department of Health and Human Services 1990, vii), and the fetal health consequences of a pregnant woman's cigarette smoking is "one of the most-studied risk factors in contemporary obstetrics" (Floyd et al. 1993, 379). In their review essay of the medical and public health literature on smoking during pregnancy, Louise Floyd and colleagues argue that "the results of well-designed epidemiologic studies leave little doubt that smoking during pregnancy exerts an independent, adverse effect upon numerous reproductive outcomes" (1993, 381).[9] Medical professionals tend to separate the results of studies on the fetal and infant health effects of smoking during pregnancy into two broad categories: conclusive and suggestive. In other words, while some medical findings are considered convincing and well established due to the strength, quality, and consistency of the data across studies, others are seen as preliminary and controversial.[10]

Health professionals do not always agree on which research results warrant being placed in the conclusive category, yet there appears to be nearly consistent agreement that the association between smoking during pregnancy and the increased risk of low birthweight is well established.[11] Conditions that are also routinely referred to in medical and health education literature as associated with smoking during pregnancy include increased risk of miscarriage (spontaneous abortion), preterm delivery, perinatal death (stillbirths and deaths of newborns), sudden infant death syndrome, and respiratory and ear diseases (Lumley and Astbury 1989, 242–243; U.S. Department of Health and Human Services 1990; Charlton 1994; DiFranza and Lew 1995). Other evidence of the possible health consequences to fetuses, infants, and children that are related to smoking during pregnancy is less widely cited and better categorized as suggestive. This evidence includes findings on childhood cancers (*New York Times* 1996b; Action on Smoking and Health 1999; Klebanoff et al. 1996; Sasco and Vainio 1999), cleft palate (Lieff et al. 1999), mental retardation (*New York Times* 1996a), behavior problems (Action on Smoking and Health 1998c; Brook et al. 2000), the transmission of HIV during delivery (Action on Smoking and Health 1997a), and the increased probability that the daughters of pregnant smokers will smoke when they are teenagers (Kandel et al. 1994; Kandel and Udry 1999). Further, the evidence that exposure of a nonsmoking pregnant woman to environmental tobacco smoke will influence the baby's birthweight (Martinez et al. 1994; Chen and Petitti 1995; Eskenazi et al. 1995; Sadler et al. 1999) as well as the likelihood of childhood cancers (Sasco and Vainio 1999) and spontaneous abortion (Windham et al. 1999) is preliminary or inconsistent.[12] Regardless of the conclusive or suggestive nature of this medical data, continuous research on the fetal and infant health risks associated with smoking during pregnancy itself strengthens the imperative that something must be done and motivates public health professionals to respond to what they define as a significant problem.

All antismoking campaigns strongly emphasize that low birthweight is a risk associated with smoking during pregnancy; this emphasis reflects both this well-documented association and the importance of low birthweight as a health indicator. The relationship between smoking and low birthweight (labeled prematurity at the time) was first documented in 1957 by Winea Simpson, who found that babies born to smokers were twice as likely to be born low birthweight than were those born to nonsmokers. Low-birthweight infants (those born under 2,500 grams or 5.8 pounds) are at higher risk of death, and as they develop, they are more likely to have chronic handicaps, cerebral palsy, blindness, mental retardation, and learning disabilities (Curry 1987, v). Although a range of social and biological factors is associated with low birthweight, research has shown an association between smoking and low birthweight independent of maternal age, alcohol and drug use, education, employment, parity (the number of previous children), prenatal care, socioeconomic status, and maternal weight (DiFranza and Lew 1995, 388; see also Lumley and Astbury 1989; Floyd et al. 1993). Many studies conclude that the greater the number of cigarettes a pregnant woman smokes, the greater the risk that her baby will be born low birthweight. Findings vary on the occurrence of low birthweight in an infant in relation to the trimesters or weeks during which the pregnant woman smoked.[13]

The dominant public health message to pregnant women is that no level of smoking is safe and that quitting before pregnancy is the best course of action. In fact, an Institute of Medicine–National Academy of Sciences panel on preventing low birthweight concluded that "the most important action a pregnant woman can take [to reduce the risk of low birthweight] is to stop smoking" (New York Times 1985c). Although such attention to the connection between smoking during pregnancy and low birthweight seems justified by the medical data, the public health focus on low birthweight ought not escape critical analysis. Biomedical research has led public health practitioners to emphasize a change in individual health behavior without adequately attending to the social factors related both to low birthweight and smoking, such as lower class status, stress, low social support, and poor material conditions (Oakley 1992; see also Boone 1989). Public health professionals ought to attend not only to individual, medical risk factors in their evaluations of low birthweight and in their campaigns to prevent its occurrence.

Looking more closely at the significance and meaning of low birthweight, sociologist Ann Oakley's work on the historical construction of birthweight as a salient medical measurement in Great Britain and elsewhere—"weight at birth" was added to the Standard Certificate of Live Birth in the United States in 1949—illustrates how the "quantification of the infant body" is connected to judgments about a mother's role in ensuring the baby's normalcy (1992, 256). The label "low birthweight" carries negative stigma because it is defined by health professionals as a medical problem. Further, the use of low birthweight as such an important health indicator presupposes that low birthweight is "a biologically caused condition, a fault in the mechanism of the body correctable by the doctor-as-repair-man" (Oakley 1992, 9). The designation of low birthweight as a measurable entity, proposed in 1919 by a Finnish doctor working in Germany, was meant to aid the understanding of prematurity and its relationship to infant death. The definition of low birthweight as under 2,500 grams (the original definition was at or under 2,500 grams) is the international standard today, and although statistically low birthweight infants as a group have a higher risk of death and health problems, low birthweight itself should not necessarily be taken as a health problem.[14] Low-birthweight babies can be as healthy as normal-weight babies. This fact is not obvious in antismoking campaigns, which consistently emphasize the importance of having a normal-weight baby.[15]

Public health professionals reinforce their campaigns against smoking during pregnancy by citing national statistics on the number of fetuses and infants affected by pregnant women's smoking and by calculating the resultant health care costs. Antismoking campaigns aimed at pregnant women are predicated on the belief that reducing the rates of smoking will benefit an individual's physical health and the nation's fiscal health. A review of the medical literature on the health consequences of smoking during pregnancy, for example, reports that in the United States, "each year, use of tobacco products is responsible for an estimated 19,000 to 141,000 tobacco-induced abortions, 32,000 to 61,000 infants born with low birthweight, and 14,000 to 26,000 infants who require admission to neonatal intensive care units . . . 1,900 to 4,800 infant deaths resulting from perinatal disorders, and 1,200 to 2,200 deaths from sudden infant death syndrome" (DiFranza and Lew 1995). The authors conclude that "all pregnant women should be advised that smoking places their unborn children in danger." The seriousness of the problem has also been emphasized by health experts and antitobacco advocates in terms of the magnitude of national costs attributable to smoking during pregnancy range. Estimates vary, from $135 million to $167 million annually in one health research study (Adams and Melvin 1998, 212) to antitobacco advocates' estimate (drawing on other health research data) that $1.4 billion to $4 billion is spent annually to treat infant health and developmental problems caused by maternal smoking and by pregnant women's exposure to second-hand smoke (Campaign for Tobacco Free Kids 1999b).[16] Of course the higher the numbers, the more serious the problem appears. But the bottom line remains the same: the problem of smoking during pregnancy is of measurable public health significance and demands the response of health professionals.

In fact, the national rate of smoking by pregnant women, like that of smoking by adult women and men, has declined since 1964, when the first surgeon general's annual report on smoking and health prompted a dramatic increase in attention to the health risks of smoking. In 1989, the year that information on smoking during pregnancy was first recorded on birth certificates (in the section "information for medical and health use only"), nationally, 19.5 percent of pregnant women reportedly smoked, whereas data from 1998 show that nationally 12.9 percent of pregnant women smoked (Ventura et al. 2000).[17] The value of this measurement to health practitioners is not entirely clear. Health researchers believe that national statistics underrepresent the actual proportion of women who smoke, in part due to the medical censure and social stigma associated with smoking; pregnant women are increasingly unwilling to identify themselves as smokers (Ventura 1999). I examine how health educators respond to the discrepancy between these national statistics and the far higher rates of smoking found in many communities.

These national data conceal the way that smoking—particularly during pregnancy and near young children—serves as a significant marker of social class status today.[18] The social stigma associated with smoking during pregnancy is exacerbated in the case of low-income pregnant smokers because they are seen as part of an unhealthy underclass or a culture of smoking. The rates of smoking during pregnancy are highest among white women more than twenty years old who do not have a high school diploma (48 percent) and lowest among women who have four years or more of college (2 percent). A comparison of smoking among pregnant women who represent the three largest demographic racial and ethnic categories indicates that white women have the highest smoking rates during pregnancy (16.2 percent), followed by Black women (9.6 percent) and Hispanic women (4 percent) (Ventura et al. 2000, 54).[19] Keeping these statistics in mind, I explore how health professionals and everyday women represent and address women who smoke during pregnancy, attentive to the way that pregnant smokers are identified in terms of class, race, and ethnicity and to the consequences of these characterizations for judgments of mothers.

"Don't smoke when you're pregnant" campaigns designed by public heath experts—who are located in federal and state government health agencies, national health organizations (such as the American Cancer Society, the American Lung Association, and the March of Dimes), and hospitals or clinics—warn the public about the fetal health risks associated with smoking during pregnancy while simultaneously producing a negative image of the pregnant smoker. The public health problem of smoking during pregnancy contributes to the social problem of bad mothering. From this perspective, by disregarding advice about how to care for their babies-to-be, pregnant smokers transgress ideals about maternal nature. Even if their overt intent is to inform the public about the health risks of smoking during pregnancy and to offer advice on how to quit smoking, health education campaigns participate in the policing of motherhood.

The Science and Politics of Smoking during Pregnancy

Health professionals attempt to convince the public that smoking during pregnancy is an important problem by presenting as "objective fact" data on the fetal health risks associated with a woman's smoking during pregnancy and on the magnitude of the problem. However, the pursuit of medical knowledge and the public dissemination of risk warnings based on research findings are inescapably political processes. Political concerns drive medical research funding, and in turn, public policy makers look to research results to justify their responses to health issues (see Clarke 1990, 1999; Nelkin 1992; Maynard-Moody 1995). Further, as social scientists document, risk assessment is inseparable from contests over power (Luker 1978; Nelkin 1989; Nathanson 1991, 1996, 1999; Douglas 1992; Kaufert and O'Neil 1993; Handwerker 1994; Murphy-Lawless 1998; Jacobson 2000).

A news brief published in *JAMA*, journal of the American Medical Association, captures one medical–political drama surrounding research on the fetal health risks of smoking during pregnancy: "Smoking Cigarettes May Do Developing Fetus More Harm Than Ingesting Cocaine, Some Experts Say" (Cotton 1994). The article reports medical professionals' opposing positions. On one side, the American College of Obstetrics and Gynecology and the American Academy of Pediatrics contend that of the two substances, cocaine is the most harmful if used during pregnancy. This view is challenged by a researcher at Duke University School of Medicine and a growing number of other investigators who argue that "tobacco is being overshadowed by hyperbole in the so-called war on illegal drugs" (Cotton 1994, 576; see also Slotkin 1998). This group points out that the effects of cigarette use during pregnancy may be more damaging to fetal health than those associated with cocaine use. Further, these critics argue, the problem of smoking during pregnancy is substantially more serious because it is more widespread; a far greater number of pregnant women smoke cigarettes than use cocaine.

Comparison of the fetal health risks associated with tobacco and cocaine use makes sense within a politicized context in which research and drug treatment funding is fought over among medical researchers and directors of drug treatment and smoking cessation programs. The contention, backed by risk assessments, that tobacco is as or more dangerous to fetal health than cocaine may help to win funding for medical research on the health risks of cigarette smoking during pregnancy and for smoking cessation and prevention programs.

Another feature of the relationship between science and politics is the use of scientific findings by political lobbies to support their efforts. The antitobacco advocacy group Action on Smoking and Health (ASH) has capitalized on research showing that cigarette smoking is more damaging than cocaine use to fetal and infant health to admonish the federal government for its failure to pass comprehensive antismoking legislation. ASH pointed out the contradiction between many U.S. senators' prolife positions and their rejection of antismoking regulations, "which could have done so much to protect the life and health of the unborn" (Action on Smoking and Health 1998b).

Indeed, the tobacco–cocaine debate provides an example of how medical research on smoking during pregnancy is given meaning through broader political controversies, including arguments over abortion rights, tobacco control policies, and the treatment of women who give birth to "crack babies." The definition of public health problems is not a direct outcome of making research results public but rather the result of a complex process in which scientific health risk assessments are used by health advocates to speak to broader subjects of social and political concern.

Although I am critical of the concepts and language of risk as used in antismoking campaigns directed at pregnant women, I do not dispute that the health risks associated with smoking are real. I believe that cigarette smoking poses health risks to pregnant women who smoke and their babies-to-be. Borrowing from anthropologist Mary Douglas, I argue less about the reality of the dangers and more about the ways health risks are politicized and communicated to the public (1992, 29). For decades, media coverage of the debate between public health officials and tobacco company executives over whether smoking represents a health danger promoted the subject to political controversy. Since the 1960s, public health officials have widely publicized studies showing that smoking is hazardous, whereas until the 1990s, the politically powerful tobacco industry presented scientific studies showing it was not dangerous (Whelan 1984; Kluger 1996; Mother Jones 1996). The drama surrounding the tobacco industry's cover-up of scientific evidence on the risks of smoking is even the subject of the award-winning film *The Insider* (1999).

Another crucial dimension of the relationship between science and politics is one of the politics of risk: the meaning of medical scientific risk calculations and health professionals' reliance on these statistical measurements to help determine pregnant women's autonomy and even legal rights. Each pregnant woman is expected, without question, to comply with medical advice about risk reduction, despite uncertainty over whether her own risk-taking behaviors will harm her fetus's health. The "scientific facts" on the risks of smoking are population-based estimates and predictions that cannot be applied with precision to an individual's experiences. Medical experts cannot in good conscience tell any individual pregnant woman who smokes that her fetus or baby certainly will be adversely affected; they can only warn her of this chance. Although some health educators with whom I spoke believe that this detracts from the power of their message, risk assessments and warnings continue to serve as the basis of obstetric treatment management policies (Oakley 1984; Martin 1992 [1987]; Davis-Floyd 1992; Kaufert and O'Neil 1993; Handwerker 1994; Murphy-Lawless 1998). The use of risk assessments in health warnings can consolidate medical professionals' power over pregnant women's decision making and extend beyond the medical world and into the legal. Medical evidence of health risks powerfully influences judgments about a pregnant woman's liability for her baby-to-be's and infant's health.

An Ethnography of a Public Health and Social Problem

Following the work of feminist scholars, I have adopted a critical, ethnographic perspective to study the dynamics through which smoking during pregnancy has come to be seen as a public health and social problem.[20] The value of an ethnographic approach is that it allowed me to examine the ways in which both health experts and everyday women conceptualize the issue of smoking during pregnancy and act at the intersections of the multiple discourses and social processes that influence the representation and treatment of pregnant smokers (Yanagisako and Delaney 1995, 18). Conducting interviews and analyzing a range of written sources, I investigated the ways the issue of smoking during pregnancy is constructed by powerful and ever-changing social, legal, and medical expectations of pregnant women as well as technological advances in fetal medicine, antismoking campaigns and policies, and debates over abortion and fetal rights. Interviews with health experts and women enabled me to capture in detail varied perspectives on the problem and reactions to health warnings.

The theoretical basis of my research is informed by the work of interdisciplinary feminist scholars who seek to understand the politics of pregnancy, reproduction, and motherhood in response to intensified cultural, medical, and legal trends that emphasize a pregnant woman's separateness from her fetus and threaten to constrain all women's reproductive choices, rights, and actions.[21] This literature demonstrates that rights, responsibilities, and sentimental attachments to a baby-to-be are not simply natural. They are formed in relation to a complex web of cultural views, public health campaigns, media representations, and government policies that creates ideals about how mothers-to-be should think, feel, and act. I communicate this complexity by narrating the history of cigarette smoking during pregnancy in a way that magnifies the connections between social and cultural expectations about what it means to be a good mother in the United States and the experts' recognition of smoking during pregnancy as a public health problem.

I became interested in the issue of smoking during pregnancy while working as a research assistant on a study of health-related social movements, including the antitobacco movement (Nathanson 1996, 1997, 1999, n.d.). Sifting through hundreds of citations on smoking and health, I came across news stories and medical studies calling attention to how cigarette smoking harms the unborn. Having come to political consciousness in the 1980s, a period during which "the unborn" signaled an antiabortion position, I was intrigued and motivated to look deeper. This forced me to think back to my introduction in the mid-1970s to the health education message that smoking is dangerous. School-based antismoking campaigns at that time were high on shock value (including textbook photos of charred lungs and films of middle-aged adults who smoked cigarettes through tracheotomy holes after throat cancer surgery). I began to consider why I have never smoked regularly and why I believe much of the scientific evidence on the health risks of smoking.

Pondering my stance on the issue of smoking during pregnancy led me to ask several personal–political questions: I knew that my grandmother had been a smoker, but did she smoke when she was pregnant? Why, in the 1980s and 1990s, were women who drank alcohol or took drugs but not those who smoked cigarettes during pregnancy charged with fetal abuse? Given my assumption that it was in the best interest of women and their babies-to-be to avoid smoking, how unassailable was my feminist position that a pregnant woman should have the right to choose how to treat her body? These questions and the connections I began to make between the issue of smoking during pregnancy and my main interest—women's reproductive rights and fetal politics—led to the research on which much of this book is based.

When gathering material for this book, I cast a wide net that would allow insight into the historical and cultural development of smoking during pregnancy as a public health and social problem in the United States.[22] Between September 1995 and August 1996, I conducted interviews with more than thirty health experts and forty-two everyday women in the Baltimore–Washington, D.C., area. These interviews were designed to capture participants' views on smoking during pregnancy and related issues. (See appendix A for interview research methods and appendix B for profiles of research participants.) The category "health experts" includes health educators, obstetricians, a maternal–fetal health specialist, nurses, nurse-midwives, antitobacco policy advocates, and prenatal clinic directors. The label "everyday" woman refers to those who were pregnant or were mothers when I spoke with them. The categories "expert" and "everyday" are not fully satisfactory because individuals in both groups formed their perspectives by drawing on a combination of expert and everyday experience and information. The main distinction I made is that experts, by definition, occupy a position of authority due to their professional training and employment, whereas everyday women do not. Indeed, everyday women constitute the audience that health professionals seek to reach with their antismoking messages. The differences between each group's position of authority, I expected, would influence how the interview participants perceived the risks of smoking during pregnancy and pregnant smokers themselves.

In addition to interviews, I closely read news reports covering smoking during pregnancy, which I located in the *New York Times* by systematically coding relevant index entries and in other newspapers by less methodically keeping a clippings file of published stories. When analyzing this material, I looked for details about how the issue was framed as a problem and whether the stories carried moral themes about motherhood or referred to the abortion issue or to fetal abuse. I also read public health and medical studies on smoking during pregnancy; pregnancy advice books, magazines, and pamphlets; antismoking materials produced by health education and health advocacy organizations; and antiabortion and prochoice literature. My attention to how pregnant smokers were represented in these various materials was motivated by my desire to trace the discourses and practices that promote pregnancy policing of those women who create dangerous "smoke-filled wombs."

During my research, several encounters heightened my awareness of the strength of antismoking standards in the mid-1990s and challenged my personal response to a woman's choice to smoke. When I met Leslie Hollins for a lunchtime interview, one of her first questions was whether it was all right if we sat in the smoking section of the café. Although I generally avoid eating in the smoking section of any café or restaurant and felt it ironic given my research interests, I agreed. "Great!" she replied, "You've just made my day!" A few weeks later, as I sat at Angela Perry's kitchen table talking over coffee, she—in her own home!—asked if I minded if she smoked. I quickly smiled and said, "of course not," to which she responded with a long, drawn out "whew." Both women's reactions signaled that my willingness to accommodate their desire to smoke and my nonjudgmental attitude were unusual or an unexpected relief.

Had Leslie or Angela been pregnant, I would have found it more difficult to maintain my seemingly nonjudgmental but privately negative position on smoking.[23] Like the pediatrician who at the opening of this book described seeing the woman in an airport wearing a Precious Baby T-shirt and smoking, I too, when I see a pregnant woman smoking, list in my mind the possible negative health effects on the baby-to-be. But I do not think that rushing over to tell her "Stop!" or "Please don't!" or that whispering "Disgusting!" or "How Sad" and glaring disapprovingly would lead her to put out her cigarette and call it her last. My conviction is that smoking during pregnancy, like smoking in general, presents health risks best avoided; this vies with my desire to reject the public, moral labeling of pregnant smokers as fetal abusers and bad mothers. In part, this book looks at the pregnant smoker in ways that challenge the moral policing of pregnant women who smoke without downplaying the seriousness of the health risks that smoking poses to women and their babies-to-be.

This book explores the trend from condoning to condemning pregnant smokers and aims to encourage a health advocacy response to smoking during pregnancy that neither condones nor entirely condemns it. Each chapter takes up a dimension of this public health and social issue, which my analysis artificially separates for the sake of clarity. That the various threads of the issue are so intricately interwoven means that I treat several main components of the smoking during pregnancy problem in greater or lesser depth in each chapter.

Chapter 2 provides a broad frame by examining pregnancy advice literature to demonstrate how the medical and social expectations of pregnant women have become increasingly strict. As doctors have learned more about risks to fetal health, pregnant women have been instructed to follow more closely doctors' orders and to actively cultivate their maternal nature. One of the main lessons in pregnancy advice is a "healthist" one, enforced by pregnancy policing: women must attempt to protect the health of their babies-to-be by avoiding prenatal health risks. I close the chapter by discussing how women themselves respond to and participate in pregnancy policing.

Chapter 3 traces specifically the emergence of maternal smoking as a public health problem. I look at how medical assessments of fetal health risks and antitobacco advocacy brought smoking in general and pregnant women's smoking in particular to public attention. An analysis of medical texts and pregnancy advice literature beginning in the 1960s reveals the changing tone of antismoking warnings. A second emerging public health problem, paternal smoking, is the subject of the last section of the chapter. Unlike the antismoking advice that targets pregnant women, warnings aimed at men tend to be far less moralistic or strict. This disparity reflects not only the relative newness of the topic of the fetal health effects of men's smoking but also the differing social expectations faced by mothers- and fathers-to-be regarding their responsibilities to ensure fetal health.

Chapter 4 critically analyzes the strategies health educators use when counseling pregnant women about the fetal and infant health risks of smoking. While these health professionals see cigarette use as serious a risk as drug use, they encounter women who believe that smoking does not adversely affect fetal or infant health. Thus the health educators' job is to convince women to see the risks of smoking from the experts' point of view and to act on the chance that a baby born to a mother who smokes will be adversely affected. This creates conflicts over the authority of women's interpretations of their pregnancy experiences and highlights the moral component of health education messages. I argue that the uncertainty inherent in predicting risks to an individual pregnant woman and her baby-to-be leads health educators to bolster their health warnings with judgments about women as mothers.

In chapter 5, women respond to antismoking advice, offering a commentary on the limits of professional authority and providing a context for their own judgments of the fetal and infant health risks of smoking. This chapter reveals both differences and similarities between smokers' and nonsmokers' risk perceptions of smoking and secondhand smoke and their tolerance of pregnancy policing. Contextualizing women's ideas about prenatal health risks stresses the importance of public health professionals' valuing of women's "embodied knowledge" and women's decision-making abilities.

Chapter 6 revisits the themes discussed in chapters 3 and 4, adding a new, political layer of analysis. It explores how both antismoking and antiabortion campaigns mutually reinforce pregnancy policing and how we judge women who do not act on behalf of the interest of their babies-to-be. Drawing on visual depictions of the fetus as a person in antismoking and antiabortion literature, I analyze antismoking advocates' efforts to appeal to women's desires to be good mothers. Further, I investigate why neither prolife nor prochoice advocates have readily accepted the invitation from antitobacco advocates to join efforts to persuade pregnant women to abstain from smoking.

In chapter 7, I link concerns about the fetal health effects of smoking during pregnancy and debates over women's reproductive rights to charges of fetal abuse aimed at pregnant women who do not follow health advice. I address two different responses to fetal abuse: criminal justice and public health. Although pregnant smokers have not faced fetal abuse charges, some antismoking advocates and legal experts depict smoking during pregnancy or smoking near young children as child abuse, which suggests the possibility that fetal abuse charges could be brought against women who smoke when pregnant.

Chapter 8 offers a response to this threat to women's agency and autonomy by expanding on antitobacco advocates' most recent approaches to smoking in general. My analysis considers how these efforts influence representations of and health education campaigns directed toward pregnant smokers. I look to feminists and women's health advocates to participate more fully in attempts to move antismoking and other campaigns directed at pregnant women away from pregnancy policing and stigmatizing of some mothers-to-be as bad mothers. In conclusion, I suggest specific ways that those who believe strongly that pregnant women should abstain from smoking can collaborate with antitobacco efforts in ways that demonstrate caring about women and their babies-to-be.

By presenting a critical analysis of the medical, legal, and social trends that have produced and continue to support the idea that the pregnant smoker is a bad mother, I call for closer attention to what many readers may take for granted as good health advice: Don't smoke during pregnancy. As many women who smoke during pregnancy can attest, taking this advice is not that simple. Further, we cannot assume that giving such advice is simply "good." I argue that it is crucial for the defense of women's reproductive rights to scrutinize the dynamics that have promoted past and present antismoking advice.

Chapter 2

The New Rules of Pregnancy

The images which underlie the advice industry are threefold: the perfect child, the perfect mother, and the perfect birth. . . . In order to be a perfect mother and have the perfect birth, a pregnant woman is exhorted to lead a selfless, healthy life, uncontaminated by sex, cigarettes, alcohol, employment, or anxiety.

—Judith Lumley and Jill Astbury,
"Advice for Pregnancy," 1989

THE EXPECTATION THAT women should not smoke is part of a more general, fairly recent trend toward increasingly stringent "pregnancy rules." The idea that babies can, and therefore should, be "made" perfect underlies pregnancy advice and the medical and social policing of pregnant women's lifestyles. Pregnancy advice transmits information about what is "natural and normal" and tells women how to "do" pregnancy the right way, or the socially and medically acceptable way, in the name of creating a perfect (or near-perfect) child. Thus a perfect mother-to-be is produced, and women are taught to emulate her. The rules of pregnancy have changed substantially over time, partly as the result of the medical profession's changing understanding of fetal health and development. The discovery that women's reproductive biology fails to naturally protect the fetus has strengthened the idea that women's behavior while pregnant must be regulated and supervised by health professionals as well as by each pregnant woman herself. The pregnancy advice industry reinforces this belief and sustains the maternal–fetal conflict model of pregnancy by positing pregnant women and their babies-to-be as potentially antagonistic actors. This chapter's analysis of pregnancy advice provides insight into how dominant social ideologies about the health responsibilities of pregnant

women promote self-discipline by women and surveillance, or pregnancy policing, by others on behalf of their babies-to-be.[1]

Changing Expectations of the Expecting Woman

As strange as it may sound, health professionals recently have extended the
length of pregnancy, as one book's title makes clear: *The Twelve-Month Pregnancy: What You Need to Know before You Conceive to Ensure a Healthy Beginning for You and Your Baby* (Herman and Perry 1997). The authors contend
that "a healthy pregnancy really begins *before* you conceive. . . . By adopting
a healthy life-style as soon as you begin trying to conceive—no smoking, no
drinking, no unnecessary exposure to toxic chemicals, avoiding and treating
infections, consulting with your doctor before taking any medications, stay-
ing fit and eating well—you can give your baby a head start toward a healthy
life" (1997, 1; original emphasis). In this view, every woman should plan pregnancy carefully and "train" for pregnancy by acting as if she were already pregnant, living a risk-free lifestyle on behalf of a hoped-for healthy baby. This
expansion of pregnancy rules to "prepregnant" women extends the medical
gaze to all women of reproductive age and promotes the idea that women
should strive to be healthy as a sign of caring for their future, imagined babies-
to-be (see also Brooks Gardner 1994, 82). It also reinforces a woman's sense
of control: prepregnant women who follow health professionals' advice learn
to expect that they will have a healthy baby.

Although many women may not seek out or receive information about
pregnancy and health until they are certain that they are pregnant, health
professionals increasingly contend that advice should be sought much earlier
because it is during early pregnancy that the embryo and fetus are most susceptible to damage.[2] A nurse-midwife who taught a preconception care class
I attended emphatically agreed, citing the 1989 federal report "Caring for Our
Future": "The prepregnancy visit may be the single most important healthcare visit viewed in the context of its effect on pregnancy" (quoted in Schwarz
1995, 26).[3] An *American Baby* article explains that "prepregnancy care is vital because the most crucial stages in your fetus's development will occur before you may realize you're pregnant. . . . The first prenatal visit may take place
too late to prevent permanent damage to the fetus" (Schwarz 1995, 26). Such
warnings urge women to play an active role in creating a healthy baby by pre-
paring their bodies for pregnancy. Yet relatively little attention is paid to how
the health of the father-to-be influences fetal health; pregnancy is seen mainly
as a woman's project.

The views of health experts about a woman's role in pregnancy have varied over time. In contrast to current ideas, which emphasize the many ways a pregnant (or prepregnant) woman's behavior significantly affects her baby-to-be, an article published seventy years ago by *Parents' Magazine* declared: "No mother can any longer think of herself as overwhelmed by the task of 'making' her child; she must regard herself as the trustee of something far finer than she could possibly make single-handed. This change in point of view means that while the mother can no longer hope to produce a preacher by reading sermons, she need no longer fear that if frightened by a mouse or what not she will deposit a 'birthmark' in the shape of a mouse upon the child" (Wood and Carruthers 1930, 19). By debunking folk beliefs about influences on the baby-to-be, these authors redefine the pregnant woman's role from one of active maker to passive trustee. Any hopes of shaping the personality of the baby-to-be are dashed and fears of physically marking it dispelled. This trade-off is part of scientific progress: "as the mysteries of life, little by little, are being better understood and superstition is being gradually replaced by science, the emphasis has shifted from the mysticism of 'maternal impressions' to the practical knowledge of nutrition and hygiene" (1930, 19). Wood and Carruthers's vision of a future in which scientific views of prenatal influence would come to dominate other views has proven true, but they might be surprised that today, women's prenatal responsibilities continue to be informed by both folk and scientific beliefs.

Among those I interviewed, women of all ages recounted superstitions or old wives' tales concerning pregnancy, often with amusement. Beliefs about how to predict the sex of the baby-to-be were most common, but others involved warnings about how a woman might endanger the fetus. Luisah Croswell, who was pregnant in the mid-1980s, reported that her relatives, "country Carolina people," cautioned her, "Don't laugh at people, they'll harm your baby, [and] if you hear voices, don't answer because they might want to take your baby." Other women mentioned theories about fetal influence that contradict and reject experts' beliefs. Bernadette Ryan drank "a little red wine" when she was pregnant to "build up the baby's blood," and Sarah Leigh Snyder's mother claimed that smoking during pregnancy strengthened her baby's lungs.

Although the women who recounted these folk beliefs did not take them seriously, they, along with others, were not as quick to dismiss the more common stories women tell about how they attempt to assist their baby-to-be's intellectual development or shape its personality. Yet these often sound like modern-day superstitions. Sondra Thorton explained that when she was pregnant, she took certain precautions to avoid exposing her baby-to-be to negative things: "If I was watching TV and something violent came on, I'd turn away. I tried to think good things, positive things, you know: I changed my attitude and tried not to be exposed to certain things." When I asked Bernadette Ryan, who had her son in the 1970s, if she had communicated with her baby-to-be, she said she wished she had known more about how to be a positive influence on him: "Not like they know how now, but I'd talk to it, say 'mama's baby' and thangs. Not sit and read to it like now. If I'd known I could've done something, I would of. . . . To make him more intelligent, or like music. I'd use them earphones, anything. I believe music calms 'em, I do."[4] Sarah Leigh Snyder believes that reading aloud during pregnancy shaped her toddler's interests: "I talked to Emma. I read books to her, and now she walks aroun' with books, so I think maybe I helped her out!"

These actions represent the flip side of concerns about fetal protection: if women can inflict fetal harm, they can also promote fetal improvement. Women's observations, scientific research, the marketing of prenatal learning devices, and representations in popular culture of fetal development lend legitimacy to this possibility. A scene in the 1996 Hollywood film *Mr. Holland's Opus* shows a high school music teacher and his wife applying headphones to her pregnant stomach. *Parents Expecting*, a free magazine distributed at obstetric offices, advertises a FirstSounds Prenatal Listening Kit that features "a fetal monitor, headphones for personal listening, an instructional audio cassette in 5 languages, and a recording cable" (*Parents Expecting* 1996, 31).[5]

Critics of this phenomenon have voiced skepticism about the value of attempting to influence babies-to-be. Carla Mullinger explained, "I don't go crazy over that kind of stuff, but I talk a lot to them after they're born. I wouldn't just stand there and talk to it [when I was pregnant], but I did maybe rub my stomach, but nothing more." In his book on fetal development, Christopher Vaughan launches a strong critique, noting that "some people have used information about learning in the womb to sell what they call 'prenatal universities.' Expectant parents pay for courses that purport to teach their babies vocabulary in the womb. Scientists roundly scoff at these claims" (1996, 198). Still, regardless of the scientific merit of multilingual fetal education, the idea that the baby-to-be is significantly enhanced or endangered by a pregnant woman's behavior pervades pregnancy advice literature.

This has not always been the case. Until the 1960s, health experts described women's biology itself as protective of fetal health. A 1958 Public Affairs pamphlet titled "Will My Baby Be Born Normal?" is an example of this model. It assures women that, yes, almost every baby will be normal: "we are blessed that our children are so well protected from all that we swallow or inject into ourselves. Every child has a silent nurse, constantly on duty, protecting him from almost every kind of poison, and much better prepared than his mother to see to it that he receives precisely the right amount of food and oxygen. This nurse screens out almost everything in the mother's bloodstream that could harm the child, before it reaches him, and even manufactures the extra chemicals that he needs. That nurse is the placenta" (quoted in Marcus 1993, 135). The pregnant woman's body provides for and protects the health of her baby-to-be without need for her conscious intervention. Indeed, some women apparently still believe this model of pregnancy. Explaining the need for extensive antismoking education, Lucy Pratt, a nurse, commented, "It is surprising for some of our moms to learn how direct and severe the risk of smoking is. Some think that there is a barrier between what they do and the baby, and don't understand that there's a direct route from inhaling the substance to the baby."

Although some women may still think that their body is responsible for screening toxins before they reach the baby-to-be, health professionals have revised their theory. A pattern of birth defects called into question the idea that the placenta (the internal "silent nurse") is a reliable protector of prenatal health and "opened our eyes to the vulnerability of the unborn" (Jimenez 1980, 43). In the late 1950s and early 1960s, obstetricians discovered that some women who took thalidomide, a prescription sedative used to quell morning sickness, gave birth to babies with major physical deformities. More than ten thousand affected babies were born, mainly in Europe (the drug was not approved in the United States), and the problem attracted worldwide attention.

The thalidomide discovery, however, was not the first suggestion that the health of the baby-to-be could be harmed by a substance ingested by the mother. Reflecting medical ideologies prevalent in 1930, *Parents' Magazine* contended that "through [the pregnant woman's] blood . . . in spite of its protective mechanism, the unborn child may actually be poisoned by certain chemicals, including alcohol and lead and others, and by the toxins of certain diseases" (Wood and Carruthers 1930, 19). The knowledge that a woman's actions and her environment could harm the baby-to-be was commonplace, but the association of thalidomide with birth defects led scientists to radically rethink the function of the placenta.

The placental barrier, previously thought to block hazardous substances from fetal circulation, could no longer be considered a protective mechanism.[6] The thalidomide tragedy turned the attention of experts and the public to the fragility of fetal health. One pregnancy book summarized how this knowledge changed the way medical professionals regarded pregnant women's biology: "Until fairly recently the developing baby was considered to be at the same risk level as the mother, but unfortunate experience [discoveries about the dangers of thalidomide and German measles] has resulted in the changing of that opinion. We now know that the fetus must be considered separately from the mother as far as vulnerability is concerned" (Fried and Oxorn 1980, 109).[7] The cautionary thalidomide tale is often retold in pregnancy advice literature to mark the great divide between past and present knowledge: "From that time on, pregnant women were expected to be much more careful about what they put into their body" (Winthrop 1992, 10). In these narratives, more sophisticated medical knowledge created the need for more stringent pregnancy rules.

The thalidomide finding represented a particularly dramatic turning point because it revealed the vulnerability of medical knowledge; it "has become the shorthand for the nightmare dangers that may lurk behind modern pharmaceutical technology" (*New York Times* 1997b).[8] Thalidomide both produced new understanding of the placenta and pointed to the fallibility of medical experts: a doctor's orders might cause harm. But the message that doctors do not always know best was overshadowed by the idea that pregnant women must be more strictly supervised by medical experts because their bodies do not naturally protect the fetus. Just a decade after the discovery of the relationship between thalidomide and birth defects, obstetricians Nicholson Eastman and Keith Russell warned pregnant readers that "pregnancy should be a healthy, happy time. Childbearing is a natural process, the supreme physical function of womanhood; and no other event confers so much in deep-seated, abiding contentment. . . . But health and happiness are dependent in large measure upon proper guidance by a competent physician" (1970, vii). The expectation that pregnant women should seek prenatal care is so dominant that likely few women would disagree with the argument that it is important, even if they reject Eastman and Russell's other assumptions.

After the thalidomide discovery, pregnant women who were concerned about the safety of the medications they were taking sought their doctors' reassurance, as women continue to do today. Thus, the medical discrediting of the barrier theory of the placenta's function ironically bolstered the authority of the medical profession. It also shifted attention to the pregnant woman's responsibility to protect the health of her fetus; this notion continues to be a—if not the—dominant theme in pregnancy literature.

Where to Turn When You're Expecting: Proliferating Sources of Advice

Information gathering constitutes part of the pregnancy experience today (see Rothman 1986, 45, as cited in Georges and Mitchell 2000, 184; Brooks Gardner 1994, 81). Indeed, the cover of *What to Expect When You're Expect-*

ing declares, "This excellent book should be *required reading* . . . for expectant parents" (Eisenberg et al. 1991 [1984]; original emphasis). As an obstetrician and columnist for *American Baby* argues, gone are the days when a patient was expected to be passive and to rely only on a doctor's orders. Each woman must "be responsible for her own health and find out as much as possible about prenatal care, labor, delivery, and care of the newborn" (Gause, 1980). Remarking on this transition, health educator Josephine Dittman explained to me, "In my day, you didn't question the doctor. He was God. He answered all your questions. Now women are more self-reliant." Women with whom I spoke received information and advice from a variety of sources, including health care professionals, friends, relatives, and coworkers who had been pregnant recently as well as books, magazines, and the mass media. The proliferation of pregnancy advice means that information is readily available to those who want it but also that there is no escaping the constant barrage of pregnancy instructions. Health care providers, friends and acquaintances, and even strangers feel justified in giving information, even when it is not requested. Part of being a good mother-to-be is determining which advice is best and then following it.

Nearly all the women I interviewed seemed to believe that recommendations from doctors and women who had experienced pregnancy were the most reliable because these sources were the most knowledgeable and believable. In response to my questions, "If you had questions, who did you talk to?" and "Who did you ask for advice?" women stated:

I asked a doctor or nurse or older sister or somethin'. (Tricia Greene)

The doctor. And parentin' books. I still got some, and if I've nothin' to do at home, I sit and read 'em sometimes. (Andrea Sellers)

My gran'mother or mother. Most of the time, gran'mother. . . . She's just more open to talkin' 'bout things, you know. (LaVonda Serban)

My mother, mainly. Then my sister, because she's had a baby. So if I had a pain, like my uterus stretching, I'd ask her about it and then ask the doctor. . . . [I read] materials at the OB's [obstetrician's] office, but I got most of my information from the media. Listening to news shows like "20/20," readin' the newspaper . . . and I'd have conversations with friends about their experiences, like, 'Did you know that . . . ?' sort of thing. (Sondra Thorton)

If I was worried, I talked to my sister; she's a nurse with two kids. I guess a little to coworkers, or friends, but mainly I talked with my mom and sister, and, oh, my husband. (Jennifer Montelli)

Despite the fact that the thalidomide discovery revealed doctors' incomplete knowledge about pregnancy only a generation ago, I heard little criticism of doctors' ability to answer women's questions. No matter how well informed a woman is, a physician, by virtue of training and experience, is granted greater authority. For many, the doctor was the final or most reliable source of information, and she or he was consulted after other sources did not provide satisfactory answers or offered contradictory advice:

> I read books, can't remember the title of the one. I asked my sister lotsa questions—she had two kids. I'd call her a lot. And I asked stupid questions to the doctor. I said, "I know this is stupid and everyone asks you, but . . . " (Carol Zimmerman)

> I had *What to Expect When You're Expecting*; doesn't everyone have it? I talked to friends, a neighbor, and coworkers who've had babies recently. . . . But everyone has different advice, so if something really bothers me, I ask the doctor. (Katie Wolfe)

Doctors are not always respected as the best source of information. LaNeisha McDonald took her grandmother's advice over her doctor's because her grandmother had what LaNeisha considered greater knowledge through personal experience: "I take my gran'mother's advice more than the doctor though. 'Specially if it's a male doctor or one who hasn't had kids. . . . Like for when my daughter came out, she was allergic to milk when she's born. My grandmother said use Gatorade, so she's raised on it." Few doctors, or for that matter others, would agree that substituting Gatorade for milk was the best advice LaNeisha could receive. However, some women share her belief that some doctors are more trustworthy than others. In particular, doctors who have experienced pregnancy themselves are perceived to have more credibility than those who have not.

Taken together, women's stories about who they turn to for pregnancy advice reveal diverse networks of advice and information. Much of the sharing of pregnancy experiences is centered around female relatives (mothers, grandmothers, and sisters) and others who are part of a woman's social life (partners, friends, neighbors, and coworkers). Women's expectations and knowledge are built on hearing about others' practices, and they create or reinforce emotional connections between women. This sharing is not only a way to exchange information but also a strategy for defusing anxiety about pregnancy and birth.

The idea that knowledge builds confidence and reduces stress is evident in these responses to the question "What sorts of books did you consult?"[9]

The bible, *What to Expect When You're Expecting*. And I have to say in terms of meaningful advice that *What to Expect*, without doubt, was the best. I referred to it, lent it out, gave it to people as gifts. And maybe it was so useful is because it's real, you know, the risks are put into perspective, and also . . . practical issues, such as I'd wake up in the night with something and I'd look it up . . . and it says "in the seventh month you may experience this," and you realize that other people get this too. So immediately it reduces fear: a solution is presented. (Meredith Rodgers)

Other than the doctor? I talked to my mother. And read a lot. I was in an HMO [health maintenance organization] then and they gave me a ton of stuff—I still have some of it somewhere. I read incessantly— went to the library often. Actually, I felt more knowledgeable than most, until I brought the baby home, and then I felt inadequate. . . . There's lots of stuff out there, but lots isn't known because some people don't read or talk about it. With the first baby, the HMO literature meant I knew lots that others didn't.
   LO: Like what?
   Like don't color your hair, or take Nutrasweet, or caffeine. For all these things, the effect isn't known, so it's best to be wary. (Katherine Shaffer)

Other women reported an "information overload," and therefore they decided to seek out less advice than they believed other pregnant women did. Contradicting the recommendation in one pregnancy magazine to control stress and fear of the unknown by "reading more about pregnancy to set your mind at ease" (Winthrop 1995, 10), several women discussed how knowing too much could cause unnecessary anxiety:

I had kinda a problem with the first pregnancy and had some sonograms. I went to a specialist and either was cured or the doctor was too alarmist and there was never a problem. So I was reading books, a lot of books. Then I decided I shouldn't have been reading any, and I wished I'd never had a sonogram. Because if you know too much, you just go crazy . . . you know, all the books show the possible problems that happen. The less I know, the better off I am. Now that's what I think. (Carla Mullinger)

I didn't go to the library and research it like some do. I couldn't look at those books that have photos of the fetus at three months and all that. It was a deliberate act on my part, because it only raised my anxiety. (Leslie Hollins)

I read that *What to Expect When You're Expecting*, but I didn't read it in depth. I never sat there and read it cover to cover like some people do. I was sorta warned by a friend not to read too far ahead because it can kinda scare you, just from the things that could happen or not happen. (Mary Beth Shannon)

How much information is enough for a woman to be knowledgeable without knowing too much varies from woman to woman. This decision is but one of many that pregnant women confront.

Providing up-to-date information and addressing women's concerns without alarming them are the explicit goals of much pregnancy advice literature. A prime example of this approach is seen in the best-seller *What to Expect When You're Expecting*, the book that nearly every middle- and upper-class white woman I interviewed mentioned and that is distributed free to some health management organization clients.[10] The guide, which has been translated into twenty-one languages, is co-authored by Arlene Eisenberg, a freelance writer, and her two daughters in collaboration with a doctor who served as medical adviser (Mehren 1995). The authors' goal was "to bring reassurance to expectant parents . . . with the hope that [the book] will help fathers- and mothers-to-be worry less and enjoy their pregnancies more" (Eisenberg et al. 1991 [1984], xx, xxiii). *What to Expect* is premised on the assumption that pregnancy is a time filled with worries about the health of the baby-to-be and that information can decrease those and other pregnancy fears.

The value of pregnancy advice such as that given in *What to Expect*, for women who seek knowledge about what they can do to fulfill their desires and to understand their bodily and emotional experiences, should not be underestimated.[11] However, while prenatal health information, often delivered in the form of pregnancy rules, may be reassuring to some women, it can be oppressive or judgmental to others. Most pregnancy advice literature is socially exclusive. Perhaps reflecting this, none of the African American women or women I would identify as working class mentioned it or any other book by name (except for one African American woman, who reported that she had read "Dr. Spock–type books"). The model pregnant woman as described in most pregnancy guides is a particular type of woman: a middle- to high-income, married, white woman who is in good health and is pleased about being pregnant. Targeting prenatal information to this niche creates expectations of how pregnant women live or ought to aspire to live even as it mirrors only some women's realities.

A main purpose of publications aimed at pregnant women, such as the parenting magazines *Parents*, *American Baby*, and *Child*, is the marketing of consumer goods. Their many ads appeal to those with substantial disposable income.[12] Recommendations to participate in leisure activities that are associated with upper- and middle-class lifestyles indicate that books as well cater to this audience. For example, at one point the immensely popular *What to Expect When You're Expecting* mentions the costs of "quality child care, a business wardrobe, and commuting" as financial considerations to be taken into account when weighing whether a mother needs to return to work after her baby is born (Eisenberg et al. 1991 [1984], 417). A picture is painted of the reader as an upwardly mobile businesswoman, one who has a choice about whether to return to work. At another point, the book suggests replacing the pleasure experienced through cigarette smoking by seeking "pleasure in other pursuits . . . go to a movie, visit baby boutiques, tour a favorite museum, attend a concert or a play" (1991 [1984], 55). Few of these activities likely correlate with the interests or desires of a large number of women who smoke during pregnancy, many of whom statistics show have modest income levels. *What to Expect*'s authors are aware of the class bias in their book, so in 1995 they announced that they would write a book aimed at low-income women (Mehren 1995). As of May 2000, however, the book has yet to be published.

Pregnancy advice also conveys other assumptions about pregnant women and their lives. Although recent books and magazines may feature some images of people of color, the content of most advice literature is strikingly devoid of reference to racial or ethnic diversity or to alternative family forms.[13] Addressing the gap in pregnancy literature designed for women of color, *Mama's Little Baby* (Brown and Toussaint 1997) was published thirteen years after the first edition of *What to Expect* and billed as *What to Expect* for an African American audience. Most books presume a supportive, heterosexual, marital relationship, although in some, "partner" is used interchangeably with "mate," "husband," or "spouse" (Louden 1995). *What to Expect* anticipates criticism on this point and responds in marketing terms: "The many references to 'husband' and 'father-to-be' aren't meant to exclude you. Since the majority of our readers are in traditional families, it's just simpler to use these terms" (Eisenberg et al. 1991 [1984], 28). Books marketed to the nontraditional family target lesbian mothers (Pepper 1999) and single mothers (Tippins and Tippins 1996). Few books are directed specifically at men (cf. Ash and Brott 1995; Barron 1998; Mungeam 1998), but sections or chapters of most pregnancy guides specifically address fathers-to-be. Finally, most advice literature assumes that the pregnancy was planned and desired by both the mother- and father-to-be. *The Pregnant Woman's Comfort Book* gushes, "You and your partner have wanted a baby for so long" (Louden 1995, 1). The implication that couples diligently plan their pregnancies is not supported by surveys, however. An analysis of 1994 national data on pregnancy found that 49 percent of pregnancies were unintended (Henshaw 1998).

Market forces, not social discrimination, may drive advice literature's relentless depiction of a homogenous group of happily pregnant, financially comfortable, white women; nonetheless, it should not be overlooked that many types of women are repeatedly under-represented. While the meaning and experience of being pregnant vary for individual women and by social context, pregnancy advice—powerfully backed by scientific knowledge—issues a narrow set of lessons about proper pregnant lifestyles that all women are expected to follow. Pregnancy advice constructs an ideal mother-to-be—one who does not reflect the experiences of many women yet directs women to model themselves in her image.

Pregnancy Lessons: The Power of Mothers' Nature

The pregnancy advice industry painstakingly instructs women on nearly every detail of their lives in an effort to educate them about how to "do" pregnancy properly. Much advice is based on the idea that women must discipline their bodies to care for and protect fetal life. Although women experience pregnancy as a biological process over which they are, in many ways, powerless, a main theme in pregnancy advice is that women can and should try to exert control over the development of their babies-to-be. Pregnancy advice teaches women what is "natural": women must, pregnancy guides contend, learn how to make sense of what is called maternal nature—preprogrammed nurturant and self-sacrificing behavior—and how to participate with the biological processes that they experience (see also Georges and Mitchell 2000). Health experts instruct women about how to correctly interpret their bodily experiences and how to treat their bodies in ways that will ensure that they have healthy babies. Learning to follow this advice is represented in pregnancy literature as necessary for the good of the baby-to-be and for the training of the good mother-to-be. The emphasis on women's management of pregnancy highlights the maternal–fetal conflict model, in which the interests of the mother-to-be and fetus are divergent, so that a woman must redefine her interests as what she is told is best for the baby-to-be. Their biological connection does not ensure a nurturing relationship. In fact, pregnancy advice about women's biological nature suggests that women's bodies may be "against" the fetus. Therefore, women are assigned the task of consciously creating both a nurturing physical environment and a caring emotional bond with their baby-to-be.

One dominant message in advice literature asserts that pregnancy is natural and that to be good mothers, women must learn to follow their innate maternal nature. "It is only natural and right that the pregnant woman's thoughts be dominated by the unborn child," asserts a book devoted to advising pregnant women against smoking during pregnancy (Fried and Oxorn 1980, ix). In this statement, "natural and right" stands as a shorthand for "natural, therefore right" or "right, therefore natural"; a woman's primary concern for the baby-to-be is represented as a natural maternal instinct and a moral imperative. Recognizing this premise is important because it underwrites nearly all of the instructions pregnant women are given about doing (and not doing) particular things. The authors, both of whom are medical doctors, go on to state that just as a woman should be concerned about fetal health, she ought to perform protective and nurturing maternal actions.

Another theme in pregnancy advice is that women must actively learn how to interpret what their pregnant bodies are telling them about their pregnancy. Women's maternal nature (the instinct to protect the baby-to-be) is connected to their biological nature (the physical process of pregnancy). *The Girlfriends' Guide to Pregnancy: Or, Everything Your Doctor Won't Tell You*, irreverent in tone but otherwise traditional, implores, "It is time to really understand that your body was intended for more than just being a vehicle through which you amuse yourself, promote yourself or abuse yourself. It is designed to gestate a baby. Nature has wisely put you on automatic pilot because She knows that, if left to your own devices, you might mess the whole thing up" (Iovine 1995, 104). Offering a similar but more nuanced message, *The Pregnant Woman's Comfort Book* contends that "at perhaps no other time in your life will your body so clearly tell you what it needs. . . . Pregnancy turns your instincts on full alert. The trick is to quiet down and tune in to them, while using solid information as a comparison" (Louden 1995, 102). Bodily instincts, apparently, are not as solid as physicians' advice because women have not been medically trained to understand the messages sent out by their bodies.

Jennifer Louden, a mother who has authored other best-selling self-help books, further suggests that physical aspects of pregnancy naturally prepare a woman for motherhood: "Pregnancy is a time of upheaval, excitement, fear, ambivalence, unbridled joy, animal instinct, and love. The challenges of pregnancy seem perfectly designed to prepare us to be mothers. For example, getting up five times a night to pee correlates with getting up five times a night to feed" (Louden 1995, 3). Iovine's and Louden's advice reveals that women are expected to monitor their so-called maternal nature and conform to its demands. Women must discipline themselves by cooperating with their "automatic pilot" or bodily instincts or by following their doctor's orders. The consequence of not doing so is "messing the whole thing up," which means failing to give birth to a healthy baby.

Other guides instruct women to manipulate their biochemistry on behalf of their babies-to-be, reflecting an extreme version of the idea that what is natural is also right. Margie Profet, an evolutionary biologist and author of *Protecting Your Baby-to-Be: Preventing Birth Defects in the First Trimester*, focuses on the function of pregnancy sickness in early pregnancy (more commonly called morning sickness). According to Profet, women must tune in to how pregnancy sickness protects their babies-to-be. She denounces other popular advice literature as "not only seriously misinformed, but potentially dangerous" (1995, vi) because it "runs counter to what nature is telling" women about their pregnancy sickness (1995, 3). Profet's argument is simple and intuitively appealing: "pregnancy sickness helps protect the baby-to-be from birth defects by discouraging the first-trimester woman from eating foods with high levels of naturally occurring toxins" (1995, vi). The book provides no direct evidence of a causal link between a lack of sickness and the incidence of birth defects, but it claims that women who have no or mild sickness run about three times the risk of miscarriage as women who experience pregnancy sickness. Profet cautions those who do not experience this "natural protection" that "they are actually at greater risk of harming their embryos" and instructs them to mimic the diet of biochemically balanced pregnant women, who "should expect to be repulsed by many, if not most, foods, and to desire only non-pungent foods that are bland, sweet, or sour" in the first trimester of pregnancy (1995, 9–10). It does not matter if a woman is acting on her own nature or merely acting out an ideal pregnant woman's nature. All women ought to experience pregnancy sickness or behave as if they do. In this way, women with faulty biology can protect their babies-to-be.[14]

Meeting the demands of pregnancy—as instructed by biology and by pregnancy advice authors—is achieved through conscious maternal effort (see also Brooks Gardner 1994; Georges and Mitchell 2000). Pregnancy is "naturally" a hard job that requires unfailing attention. Profet asserts that many women misinterpret their experience of morning sickness: it may seem bad, but really it is good. Understanding this, a pregnant woman "will come to a fuller acceptance of pregnancy sickness and experience greater joy during pregnancy" (1995, 273); when others are unsympathetic, "she can proudly announce, 'Pregnancy sickness is something I'm doing for my baby'" (1995, 118). My conversations with pregnant women about how miserable pregnancy sickness can be suggest that this approach is overly optimistic and that it misleadingly implies that women have control over whether they experience sickness or not. Another pregnancy advice author, Christopher Vaughan, shares with Profet the idea that morning sickness is beneficial: it should be seen as "part of a master plan—even if nature's method drives you mad" (Vaughan 1996, 47). He dismisses women's own feelings about pregnancy sickness and condescendingly suggests that it encourages women to care better for their fetuses: "Pregnancy is not always a joyful celebration of life. . . . After all, from an evolutionary viewpoint, it doesn't matter if pregnancy is easy for the mother—as long as she survives it. In fact, a little discomfort may be just the ticket to get her attention" (1996, 71). Profet would agree; she goes further to insist that pregnant women as well as physicians are misinformed about the value of pregnancy sickness.

Although Profet and Vaughan base their arguments on what they see as important advances in scientific knowledge about pregnancy and biology, the ideology of motherhood they promote is highly traditional. Women are instructed to realize that pregnancy is a time of self-sacrifice and to welcome even unpleasant experiences for the baby-to-be's benefit. A woman's actions must unstintingly and selflessly focus on protecting and enhancing her fetus's health. Anything less would be bad mothering.

Disagreements over the function and meaning of morning sickness indicate that although advice givers often talk about pregnancy as a natural experience, their definitions of the nature of pregnancy differ. The critique of mainstream ideas about pregnancy sickness informs women that they cannot trust their bodies to "do" sickness right and that they cannot trust most health experts to know its true meaning. All pregnancy guides are devoted to instructing women about how to interpret (and, in Profet's case, even imitate) the signals that their maternal nature is sending them. Women are expected to choose one of the versions of pregnancy nature that health experts offer and follow its rules. Health experts simultaneously encourage women to be intelligent, rational, proactive decision makers and undermine women's agency though such messages as "Follow your doctor's orders!" and "Your biological nature determines your fate!" Pregnancy guides offer maddeningly contradictory perspectives, telling women that they have nearly complete yet nearly no control over pregnancy and fetal health.

Women are well aware of this contradiction. I was repeatedly told stories of unwanted pregnancies, unexpected pregnancies, the loss of desperately wanted pregnancies, and the pain of not being able to become pregnant. These experiences strengthen the idea that neither doctors nor women themselves can fully understand or direct "reproductive nature" in their favor. Yet this does not lessen the essential message in pregnancy advice, which is that women must try to control their pregnancies.

Comparing her experience with those of others, Mary Beth Shannon concluded that she was very lucky to have been able to have a baby at all. She described how her experience of pregnancy was colored by a friend's miscarriage:

> It was hard for me—that day my baby was born, because my good friend lost her baby when I was out to here [she put her hands out in front of her to illustrate she had a large pregnant belly]. Talk about disappointment, or heartbreak! It just shouldn't have happened to her. . . . I mean, I didn't know what she was gonna do when she saw me in the hospital. The hardest thing was tryin' to get past that [Mary Beth's eyes filled with tears]. She and her husband were in the waiting room, and when the nurses were wheeling me to the postpartum floor, we had to cross the waiting room, and they were standing there. And they had me in the wheelchair, and the baby goes by, and I could just see . . . and I was like, here I am with all my excitement . . . and I could just see the pain on her face. To this day it still . . . [inaudible as she started to cry].

For Mary Beth and other women I spoke with, the uncertainty of pregnancy, and particularly early pregnancy, emphasizes that reproductive nature is beyond individual control and fragile. This theme runs alongside pregnancy directives that hold women responsible for their pregnancies.

Being unable to control pregnancy does not undercut the imperative to try to do so, which leaves women in the position of trying to do everything right while knowing that even following all the rules might not be enough to ensure a healthy baby. Cynthia Phillips, who experienced two miscarriages before she had her baby, explained that she was "nervous the entire time" about whether she would miscarry again during her third pregnancy. The belief that she could not trust her body led her to worry "about everything" and to give up things she enjoyed, including her morning cup of coffee, because she had read studies about the possible negative effects of caffeine. She also seriously considered the safety of some medical interventions. She had had genetic counseling and wanted to have genetic testing, but decided against it in her third month because it carried a risk of miscarriage. However, "they saw something" during a routine ultrasound exam, and her obstetrician suggested she have an amniocentesis, a procedure that involves the extraction and genetic testing of amniotic fluid. Cynthia's fears increased substantially because she worried that either she would miscarry from the procedure or they would find "something really bad" and she would have to decide whether to terminate her pregnancy. Although she had to wait a "really traumatic" two weeks after the test, the results were negative; she concluded that "the amnio relieved the worries that were in the back of my mind." Cynthia's case is but one illustration of how pregnant women face numerous decisions about whether to trust their "nature," despite the idea communicated in pregnancy advice books that pregnancy is a natural process. In addition, they must decide whether to follow their doctor's suggestions. In Cynthia's case, doing so was traumatic but in the end helped her become more confident that her baby would be healthy.

Those women who had to contend with contradictory medical advice from different obstetricians carried a particularly heavy burden of decision. Luisah Croswell received conflicting advice about whether she would ever be able to carry a pregnancy. She did not know whose opinion to trust, so she chose to try to beat the odds: "When I was twenty, I had a miscarriage. And after that I started smokin' and drinkin.' It did somethin' to me. It was stillborn—six months. They told me I'd never have a baby—I had fibroid tumors and things, and they wanted to give me a hysterectomy at age twenty-two! But one said 'There's a one in a million chance it could work out,' so they didn't do it. Then I had my son." That Luisah and her doctor decided that she should aim for that "one in a million chance" emphasizes again that medical science cannot always provide precise predictions about a woman's reproductive future. Although ideally she would have liked to have had two children, Luisah was diagnosed with cervical cancer and had a hysterectomy when her son was eighteen months old. Comparing her difficulties with her mother's, she continued: "And all my mother's kids were preemies. And I had a twin, but she died. Together we only weighed five pounds! My uncle whittled a little casket and shellacked it. Gave her a satin pillow and all. Then they brought it to my mother because she couldn't make it to the funeral. [Several years] after she had my brother, she miscarried." Keeping this in mind, Luisah believed that throughout her life, she had been more fortunate than her doctors had predicted, from her own premature birth to her ability to have a son despite her health problems. Her doctors agreed that she was one of the lucky ones, and Luisah says that the birth of her son would never have happened if she had not met that one physician who allowed her to take that one in a million chance. A combination of faith in her own capacity to have a baby and a faith in what she called medical miracles backed her decision.

Such stories about long-shot successes or failed or difficult pregnancies are shared among women, but they are rarely referred to in pregnancy advice literature. Books downplay the possibility that a baby-to-be may be lost or born with birth defects by directing women to control their pregnancies: "During pregnancy you will be challenged to make intelligent decisions in dozens of situations, weighing risk against benefit. Almost every decision you make will impact on your chance of having a healthy baby" (Eisenberg et al. 1991 [1984], 78–79). But *What to Expect* also notes that women cannot actually control pregnancy—they can only have "an enhanced sense of control" (1991 [1984], 52). While the attempt in pregnancy literature to instill feelings of power in women may indeed confer psychological benefits to individuals, it may also give them a false sense of responsibility. The danger is that a woman may un-necessarily blame herself for a miscarriage, premature birth, or her infant's dis-abilities or poor health.[15] Pregnancy warnings that stress the message that women can control the health of their babies-to-be reinforce these feelings and justify others' blame of women who do not give birth to healthy babies. The social implication of the strong emphasis on the notion that women can exert power over the health of their babies-to-be is that women's behaviors are measured against the rules of pregnancy; women who have unhealthy ba-bies or pregnancy problems are suspected of breaking the rules (see Landsman 1998). In this way, pregnancy advice sustains the assumption that women and their fetuses are in a relationship that involves potential conflict and rein-forces the idea that fetuses need constant care and attention.

Women are also warned by health experts that birth defects and early mis-carriages are natural, meaning unpredictable and uncontrollable. One woman who had experienced early loss of a pregnancy admitted that she worried about the office building she worked in: "I know it's tested for all those things, like asbestos, but . . . when I lost the baby, I thought maybe some environmental factor had something to do with it, or whatever, but you don't really know. . . . They [the doctors] just said, you know, that's nature, and that's the way it goes." But she was not totally satisfied with this explanation and wondered whether she could have prevented the pregnancy loss if she had quit her job. In line with one dominant pregnancy discourse, she asserts that she could have taken individual action to change her lifestyle to minimize her exposure to envi-ronmental risk.

When pregnancy books address the chances of miscarriage and fetal health problems, they offer information on things that could go wrong yet urge women not to dwell on these possibilities. Profet concludes her book by fueling her reader's fears in an attempt to lessen them:

> [Genetic] malformations are bound to occur by chance in the
> development of some embryos because there are thousands of things
> that can go wrong during the formation of a fetus from a fertilized egg;
> one tiny perturbation in the developmental pattern may result in a
> serious defect. If a woman who learns that her fetus or infant is

malformed reviews her entire first trimester, she probably will be able to ferret out all kinds of possible culprits: the potatoes she ate at Christmas dinner; the antihistamine she took for hives after a hike; the long hot bath she took one evening; the X ray she got when she sprained her ankle; the four glasses of wine she drank at the New Year's party before she realized she was pregnant; the fumes she accidentally inhaled while pumping gas one day; the make-up she wore to conceal the fact she didn't feel well. But the real culprit may simply be fate.

If a pregnant woman realizes during the first trimester she ate some of the foods on the "sin" list, inadvertently took some medicine, came down with a cold, or was exposed to something "bad," she shouldn't panic. Most babies are born healthy, even though almost all first-trimester women are exposed to substances that, at some doses, are teratogens [agents that cause birth defects]. (1995, 271–272)

Although Profet offers only that "most babies are born healthy" and does not give any statistics, *What to Expect* indicates that "drugs and other environmental factors account for less than 1% of all birth defects—and birth defects affect only 3% to 4% of all newborns. . . . In spite of the dire warnings making headlines and highlighting news programs daily, never have the chances of having a healthy, normal baby been better" (Eisenberg et al. 1991 [1984], 77). (This statistic, if accurate, means that of the approximately four million babies born in the United States each year, between 120,000 and 160,000 will have birth defects. In fact, the March of Dimes Birth Defects Foundation states that birth defects affect more than 150,000 babies each year [1999b, 1].) An astounding implication is embedded in this advice, which is meant to be comforting but which may also alarm readers. According to these statistics, a pregnant woman's avoidance of teratogens, as emphasized in pregnancy literature, is not the most important factor for ensuring a healthy baby-to-be. Genetic birth defects appear to pose the greatest risk. Genetics represents a way in which another sort of nature—the "preprogramming" of bodies—is more responsible for a baby's health than is a pregnant woman's behavior.

Increasingly, however, technologies such as genetic testing and fetal surgery offer women and their doctors the possibility of intervening in the pregnancy process.[16] Pregnancy advice tells women to follow two sets of instructions: tune in to their bodies and their maternal nature, and also monitor the entire process of pregnancy so that if necessary, they can intervene on behalf of the baby-to-be. It both produces and reflects the cultural assumption that we can and should control our health through self-policing and making so-called responsible decisions.

Pregnancy Lifestyles and Healthism

Health professionals' emphasis on managing one's health is not confined to pregnancy. Broader social dynamics support this ideology. In the United States since the late 1970s, "concern with personal health has become a national occupation" as part of what sociologist Robert Crawford terms "healthism" (1980, 365). Healthism is a "preoccupation with personal health as a primary . . . focus for the definition and achievement of well-being" in which responsibility for health—seen as a moral responsibility—is attributed to individuals (1980, 368). Indeed, the arguments voiced by advocates of healthy lifestyles rest on the particularly middle- and upper-class assumption that health status can be controlled. The logic of healthism downplays the idea that nature (such as genetic predispositions) and social factors (such as poverty) influence or determine our health. It also makes it possible to judge individuals, and indeed whole subcultures (for example, working class, ethnic/racial, or urban/rural), as irresponsible because they neither value nor work to attain good health (see Balshem 1993).

Further, health professionals' advocacy of healthism contains a moral appeal to an individual's patriotic responsibility to boost the nation's health. In his foreword to *Healthy People 2000*, then Secretary of Health Louis Sullivan indicates that a belief in each individual's responsibility to prevent disease should pervade society: "Americans . . . are coming to realize the influence that they, themselves, can have on their own health destinies and on the overall health status of the Nation" (U.S. Department of Health and Human Services 1991, v). The idea that a nation itself has a health status is made possible through measurement and statistical assessment of health indicators (such as infant and maternal mortality, average age at death, health care costs, and workplace absenteeism and productivity). In turn, the media reports on the nation's health status (e.g., "Broad Gains Seen in American Health" [*New York Times* 1997c]), and public health officials appeal to each individual to be personally committed to improving national statistics, which by definition are collective and impersonal.

The relationship between an individual's health and that of the nation is not this simple. *Healthy People 2000*, like the 1979 *Healthy People* report that preceded it, recognized the social and cultural factors that influence health (see Neubauer and Pratt 1981). Secretary Sullivan contends that "our most vulnerable [poor, disadvantaged] populations" lack what he calls a culture of character, "which is to say a culture, or a way of thinking and being, that actively promotes responsible behavior and the adoption of lifestyles that are maximally conducive to good health. This is 'prevention' in the broadest sense. It is also an absolute necessity, both because we are a humane and caring society and because, if we are to remain a vital society, we cannot afford to waste human resources. Good health must be an equal opportunity, available to all Americans" (U.S. Department of Health and Human Services 1991, v). Sounding much like a Progressive era reformer, Sullivan contends that changes in the character of a culture will lead to changes in the character of individuals within that culture, to the benefit of an entire society.[17] Despite his humanitarian language of equal opportunity, these remarks are disturbing. The belief that some cultures are more responsible (read moral) than others and that the members of the most responsible cultures prove their superior status by "adopting lifestyles that are maximally conducive to good health" has negative consequences for some groups more than others. According to this logic, those "high-risk" cultures as well as individuals who do not "actively promote responsible behavior" exhibit not only poor health but weak moral character. Sullivan's attempt to refocus attention on the link between a culture and individuals' health reveals that locating "ill health as a social rather than an individual responsibility does not remove blame or moral judgment, it simply shifts blame from stigmatized individuals to the marginalized groups of which they are a member" (Lupton 1995, 105). In Sullivan's analysis, groups with poor "cultures of character" threaten the nation's health status.

Healthist discourse is intensified in relation to pregnancy because pregnant women have the triple responsibility of being healthy for their own good, for the sake of the baby-to-be, and for the greater good of the nation's future generations. Pregnant women who have a healthy lifestyle will, by healthist logic, have healthy children. In turn, healthy children will contribute to the upward mobility of society. As Maureen McNeil and Jacquelyn Litt (1992, 123) point out in their analysis of medical and social concerns about fetal alcohol syndrome in the United States, the assumption that a woman will have a healthy baby if she follows medical advice is particularly resonant for people who hold middle-class expectations about their ability to improve their own and their babies' lives. One preconception advice book states: "Your current way of life may make a real difference in the quality of your child's life. With some relatively simple changes on your part, plus a few basic precautions, you can help give your child the best possible start" (Herman and Perry 1997, 48). *What to Expect* extends the importance of preconceptive health to a woman's grandchildren: "your good prepregnancy care will benefit not only your own children but your children's children" (Eisenberg et al. 1991 [1984], 424). In these accounts, women's health choices threaten or enhance the future of individuals and of society.

But which, and how many, simple changes and basic precautions constitute enough health-seeking to be judged favorably in healthist terms? *What*

to Expect's recommendations for a healthy pregnancy lifestyle include "eliminating temptation. . . . No wine in the fridge; no liquor on top of the bar. No
cake mixes in the kitchen cupboard; no white bread in the bread box" (Eisenberg et al. 1991 [1984], 63). If a woman eats white bread, likely a staple in
many households, she can be accused of not doing everything possible for the
baby-to-be. Even more remarkable, these prohibitions challenge the message
of the recent past, that pregnant women's desires ought to be indulged, best
symbolized in the stereotype of the otherwise unusual craving for pickles and
ice cream. (Neither item is listed in *What to Expect*'s healthy diet suggestions.)

Put simply, given the expectation that pregnant women should control
their bodies to avoid fetal health risks, each action a pregnant, and even a
prepregnant, woman takes offers her two choices—to be the good mother-to-
be (who properly expresses maternal nature) or the bad mother-to-be (who
does not). Again, women are positioned as either harming or caring for their
fetus (or future fetus) based on their compliance with health advice. This invites moral judgments by others.

Another popular healthist theme that appears in prenatal advice literature is that "when you care for yourself, you care for your baby." But self-care
is not always pleasurable (for example, quitting smoking, avoiding coffee or
alcohol, giving up favorite junk foods, or maintaining bed rest). Further, when
they are not pregnant, women may engage in some self-care activities and interests that are off limits during pregnancy because they pose a threat to the
baby-to-be, for example, reducing stress by taking a hot bath, drinking a glass
of wine, or having a rigorous aerobic workout.

For some, many of the "healthy pregnancy lifestyle" recommendations are
only slight extensions of how they believe they should live, pregnant or not.
This includes the imperative to eat a well-balanced diet, get adequate rest,
drink plenty of water, exercise regularly, not smoke, and so forth. Given the
current value placed on health, pregnancy provides another reason and added
pressure to do all those things a woman already feels guilty about not doing.
Exercise was mentioned repeatedly by middle- and upper-class white women.
In fact, an entire magazine, *Fit Pregnancy*, is devoted to the subject of pregnancy and exercise. I interviewed two suburban white women who emphasized this self-criticism about not exercising: Betsy Michaels admitted, "I did
want to do exercise, but I haven't had time for that, so that hasn't changed
any"; and Katherine Shaffer explained in an exasperated tone, "I wish I
could've gotten exercise religiously, and I belong to a health club, but I never
really go. I just don't have the time!" Tricia Greene, an older, low-income
Black woman, stated that when she was pregnant, her doctor told her to exercise. Part of her daily activities involved walking, not as exercise per se but

as transportation: "They say ya just can't lay down and not do nothin.' I didn't like that, when it was so hot. I used to have to walk all the way down from 10th Street anyway." The differences in these women's experiences—from not getting to the health club often enough to walking to and from work in the hot summer—point to how the circumstances of women's lives influence the meaning of and women's ability to conform to pregnancy advice. Perhaps the issue of exercise was raised so often because it is an example of something that usually is good for you but can become bad for you when pregnant.

Concerns about exercise are related to another area of expert advice—stress reduction. Meredith Rodgers recalled, "I had to give up exercising, and that really was a problem in that I find it helpful in controlling stress"; and Clarice Singer reported, "They say don't get stressed out. Tune it out. Talk it out with somebody. Don't be lazy, but be laid back." Indeed, *What to Expect* directs its readers to "identify sources of stress in your job and in other areas of your life, and determine how they can be modified to reduce the stress . . . remember, your stress quotient is only going to increase once the baby is born; it makes sense to try to learn how to handle it now" (Eisenberg et al. 1991 [1984], 114–115). This lifestyle discourse comments on how an individual can control her surroundings, not on the ways in which financial status, relationships, neighborhood, or work environment may put women in stressful positions largely beyond their control. Each individual woman is to blame if she cannot escape stress in her life. Regardless of her social and economic circumstances, every pregnant woman is instructed to work to protect her physical and mental health on behalf of her baby-to-be, not for her own sake.

Overall, the healthist directive that pregnant women ought to devote energy to caring for themselves often sounds as limiting as the message that they ought to care assiduously for their fetuses. In a discussion of how women may feel pressured to keep up the pace of daily life even if they are feeling tired, advice writer Jennifer Louden scolds: "It is this core denial of our needs [proper rest, in this example] that sets us up to be the kind of mothers we don't want to be: selfless, bitter, controlling martyrs. It is also the kind of attitude that leads to burnout, pregnancy complications such as preterm labor, and a general lack of a good time" (1995, 103). Louden recognizes that her words sound stern, but she contends that this harsh message is necessary to counter the "insidious voice. . . pushing us when we need to slow down and be good to ourselves" (1995, 103). This advice implies that women's attitudes toward pregnancy and the way they live their day-to-day lives are both controllable and predictive of the type of mothers they will be. Louden warns women that stress can lead to health problems and that it can make them bad mothers. The imperative that pregnant women take care of themselves may appeal to an individual's desire for self-control and empowerment, but it is just as disciplining as the message that pregnant women should be devoted to caring for their baby-to-be.

As a result, when women fail to fulfill the long list of expectations dictated in pregnancy advice, they may experience anxiety, which itself is considered to be bad for the baby-to-be. April McGough says this is a standard problem shared by herself and her friends. April was surprised by how soon she became pregnant after she and her husband decided to start trying:

> I think, well, we were worried about health, because I was over thirty, and I wasn't high risk or anything, but you figure, your eggs are pretty old at that point, so you always worry about the health of the baby. But I felt like I'd taken pretty good care of myself, and I'd started on the prenatal vitamins. But I'd had—within that two weeks when I was pregnant and didn't know it—I'd had one margarita, and of course you always think "My God, that margarita! I hope . . ." you know. I was at a restaurant, and I thought, "Oh, I'll just get one." And later, I thought "My God I was like a week pregnant and I don't know if . . ." I've heard so many people say the same thing—"I had a beer or a glass of wine." And then you sit there and you think about that. Like, "is everything going to be okay?"

Andrea Sellers, who did not plan her first pregnancy, also worried: "I didn't know I's pregnant, an' I went out 'cause I turned twenty-one. I drank a lot that night." Asked if she worried about it, she replied, "Well, I'd sit and think about if it'd be bad when the baby was born, but I kept it to myself." These fears about alcohol use reflect the high visibility of warnings about drinking during pregnancy and media images of children who have fetal alcohol syndrome. Moreover, April's and Andrea's experiences support health professionals' healthist argument that pregnancy should be thought of as a twelve-month-long process: had they acted as if they were pregnant, abstaining from alcohol in compliance with health advice, they would not have felt anxious.

Although individuals may receive positive benefits by subscribing to the healthist approach of following pregnancy rules—benefits such as confidence— there are numerous negative individual, social, and political consequences to such heavy emphasis on individual health responsibility. Those who reject healthism may be criticized, and those who attempt to live healthy lifestyles but still give birth to less-than-perfect babies may feel inadequate or guilty. People and groups may be morally categorized by their health status, and efforts to foster health and well-being at a social level may be sidelined and defused (Crawford 1980; D'Onofrio 1992; Balshem 1993; Lupton 1995).

Today, consistent attention to the institutional or structural aspects of pregnant women's lives is missing from most current advice literature and from health education theories. But advice has not always been primarily focused on individual action. A 1929 editorial in *Children* magazine on the problem of infant mortality, for example, begins with a familiar individualist line: "Nothing would be too great, no sacrifice too hard for a mother to make if only she could increase the chance for her baby to live" (Crumbine 1929, 7). The author's suggestions for action, however, depart from the individual: he encourages parents to join together to pressure city and state governments for birth and death registration, to advocate for ordinances that will ensure that milk dealers supply safe milk, and to establish prenatal care and infant welfare training and education for women. All parents are obligated to participate in this effort, he contends, because "every baby has a better chance to live when the parents of the community and the state unite to protect him" (Crumbine 1929, 7). This focus is radically different from the one that dominates more recent literature, which places the burden of protection squarely on the pregnant woman's shoulders: "A prospective mother can determine to a large extent what will happen to her child" (Montagu 1964 [1961], 237) and "you have the chance . . . to come as close as possible to guaranteeing your baby not just good health, but excellent health—with every bite of food you put in your mouth" (Eisenberg et al. 1991 [1984], 80). Crumbine instead enlists social support from a variety of sources, including parents, local communities, and government agencies.

At the time Crumbine wrote his editorial, child welfare was prominent on the national agenda, and parenting magazines published articles and editorials about the "better parenthood movement," legislative action, and national conferences devoted to children's well-being. Today we face a different social and political scene, and the healthist approach to well-being places accountability less on government and social programs than on individuals.[18] As one public health professional whom I interviewed pointed out: "I think there was a time when we had more—there was more concern—morally, ethically, and financially, for issues during pregnancy, and I don't see that as much anymore. And I think that there was a time when you said 'women and children first' and I don't think we're quite there anymore. And I don't see that as good. There was a time when there was more respect and empathy and attention devoted to MCH [maternal and child health] issues, to public health issues in general."[19] This public health professional's advocacy work is devoted to urging the government to assume more responsibility for supporting health programs for women and children.

During times when institutional support for health and welfare services for pregnant women and children was stronger, the support was attacked on the grounds that it lessened the need for individual responsibility (Lesser 1985). A 1942 *Parents' Magazine* article on the rise of prenatal care services in the United States illustrates this argument. It observes, "Prenatal clinics sprang up everywhere. The merits were sung from the housetops. Probably no single medical subject was ever given wider general publicity" (Corbin 1942, 18). This is not surprising from today's standpoint, when prenatal care and even prepregnancy care is promoted as essential to the health of future generations. However, the author delivers a sound critique of professional prenatal care services. First, she notes that "all this hue and cry about *prenatal* care has tended to overshadow *total* maternity care. . . . It has divided up a mother's life into segments. . . . But mothers don't live in segments. The coming of a baby is related to all of living" (1942, 67; original emphasis). These statements show advocacy on behalf of women and attention to pregnancy as a social, not only a biological, experience. But Corbin goes on to harangue women for being too medically complacent and not taking an active role in their own pregnancy supervision. Then she criticizes the purveyors of the medicalized paradigm of prenatal care: "The stressing of prenatal care above total living for safe maternity has sown the idea that women can live as they please, breaking the laws of hygiene and sound living, and then when their babies are on the way, the doctor, by some medical magic, can cast a charm over pregnancy and labor" (1942, 67). Corbin argues that women should not depend on doctors to protect the health of their babies-to-be and contends that they must instead devote themselves to healthy lifestyles. Today, of course, pregnant women are expected to do it all: attend prenatal visits, follow pregnancy advice, and maintain healthy lifestyles.

These excerpts from parenting magazines, one from the 1920s and the other from the 1940s, are not wholly representative of dominant ideologies about pregnancy responsibilities and lifestyles. But they illustrate how the healthism concept that is so pervasive today both has a history (Corbin 1942) and can be challenged by other models of social action (Crumbine 1929). Recognition of these different models of pregnancy expectations demonstrates that the current preoccupation with pregnant women's lifestyles, as seen in advice literature, public health education campaigns, and health warnings on consumer goods (such as cigarettes and alcohol), must be analyzed within the current healthist social and medical context.

For many, the idea that pregnant women should significantly modify their lifestyles to benefit the baby-to-be is an assumption that need not be examined. Such lack of reflection about why health is deemed individually controllable contributes to a failure to see how pregnant women's lives are structured differently, for example, by age, race, ethnicity, marital status, social and economic position, access to health care services, and so on. The healthism promoted by pregnancy advice unfairly supports uniform social expectations, reinforces increasingly strict pregnancy rules by which all women are judged, and invites others to monitor pregnant women. Ultimately, a pregnant woman's decision making, which comes to stand for her devotion to her baby-to-be, is questioned at every turn.

Fetal Protection as a Public Duty and the Effects of Pregnancy Policing in Everyday Life

The expectation that a pregnant women will adopt a healthy lifestyle is not only voiced by health experts but is part of public culture. Pregnancy policing represents the social surveillance of pregnant women and the enforcement of healthist values. Pregnant women find themselves constantly surrounded by "expert" advisers due to the pervasiveness of healthist ideology and widespread knowledge of pregnancy rules. A woman's doctor, health experts, family, friends, and coworkers offer advice in private, while billboards, vocal strangers, and the mass media instruct her about pregnancy responsibilities. The public, not just medical experts, has assumed responsibility for protecting the next generation by educating and monitoring pregnant women.

Whether other persons, particularly strangers, have the social right or moral obligation to intervene in health-related pregnancy decisions is widely debated. A feature in *Child* magazine addressed this issue two months after an alcoholic Wisconsin woman who gave birth to a daughter with symptoms of fetal alcohol syndrome was criminally charged with attempted intentional homicide and reckless injury. The magazine asked readers whether they "would say something to a stranger who's pregnant and engaging in an obviously unhealthy activity, such as drinking and smoking" (*Child* 1996). The results show that almost half would say nothing, "stating that the presence of a pregnant belly does not grant strangers permission to give advice," whereas more than half claimed that saying something is important. (The number of respondents was not given, and when I contacted the editors, they would not release the information.) The almost evenly divided audience response to the question and the magazine's refusal to take a stand on the issue are themselves comments on the debatable nature of the subject of pregnancy policing.

Other advice literature, however, including that offered by health experts, explicitly advocates pregnancy policing. Obstetrician and fetologist Peter Nathanielsz poetically contends that "each of us, not just pregnant women, has a responsibility to generations as yet unborn, whose names we do not know and whose faces we have not seen, to ensure that their lives are as healthy and fulfilled as possible" (1999, x). As a practical strategy for encouraging the public protection of fetal health, he suggests that "perhaps all pregnant women should be issued with T-shirts inscribed 'Baby on Board—Don't Abuse.'" This T-shirt would aid the goal of making "every mother . . . aware that her lifestyle profoundly affects the development of her fetus" even in early pregnancy by publicizing her pregnancy status before she is showing (1996 [1992], 10). Nathanielsz's suggestion that pregnant women wear a "Baby On Board—Don't Abuse" slogan can be interpreted in two ways—as woman-centered (don't abuse the vehicle) or fetus-centered (don't abuse the passenger). Those who encountered a T-shirt-wearing woman could conclude that they should not abuse the woman herself. (Indeed, violence against pregnant women has become a public health concern.)[20] Nathanielsz, however, stresses the fetus-centered message. Above all, the shirt would be a warning and reminder to the pregnant woman that she must exercise self-discipline for the good of the baby-to-be. It would also be an invitation for the public to join the effort of protecting the fetal passenger. This effort stems from a different impulse than that represented by the early twentieth-century movement to support maternal and child health through collective community and government action. The 1990s healthist effort emphasizes the surveillance, not the support, of pregnant women.

Perhaps most importantly, while women are told by a variety of sources how to act when pregnant, they also discipline themselves and other pregnant women. Judy Levine, a mother, physician, and public health professional, suggested that women make healthist changes without any prompting: "We all know, well, everybody who's a mother understands, that when you become pregnant you are certainly motivated—everybody cleans up their act. I don't know anybody who when they're pregnant didn't start thinking, 'well, should I be eating this saccharine, or whatever?' You clean up your act—everybody does, to varying degrees." Although it may be true that most women question their health practices more seriously when they are pregnant and that they modify their activities and behaviors, there is little tolerance for the variety of women's pregnancy lifestyles.

Some women follow health advice to what even they see as extremes. These women act on the assumption that if their individual health practices conform to expert advice, they can reduce pregnancy risks and control the health of the baby-to-be. Such behavior is the result of what one woman's husband (a physician) termed "pregnancy paranoia." Jennifer Montelli, pregnant with her second child, told me that she "stays away from caffeine": "Not that it's a health risk really, and I was never a big coffee drinker, but I try to have only caffeine-free sodas. It's tough though because caffeine helps me stay awake in the afternoons." April McGough laughed about how careful she was: "I mean here I am pregnant, and I was careful driving. I was like—I'd drive in the slow lane all the time, even if everyone was going slow! I got over that after a while, but in the beginning, I was paranoid." Patricia Doyle, pregnant for the fourth time, told me, "I'm Catholic, and you know the Eucharist? Bread and wine? Well, I took it, and when I did I felt so guilty. So I went to priest and said, 'Sorry, I know it symbolizes blood, but it sure tastes like wine,' and he said to take the body was okay for now." Pressure to be extra-vigilant motivates some women to alter their usual routines to an extent that they know exceeds others' expectations. Pregnancy paranoia, the result of the combination of pregnancy advice and women's own desires to have a healthy baby, is perpetuated by broader social ideologies that place responsibility for health upon each individual's actions. It also shows how adept some women are at policing themselves.

Despite the flamboyant advice author Vicki Iovine's assertion that "there is only one thing I hate more than a Pregnancy Police person; and that is a MALE Pregnancy Police person (as if a person without a uterus, or at least a medical degree, has any right in this universe to comment on how a pregnant woman lives her life)" (Iovine 1995, 64; original emphasis), pregnancy policing is also likely, if not expected, from the father-to-be. He supposedly has a higher stake than health professionals or strangers in whether or not his baby is born healthy. [21] This excerpt from *American Baby* indicates that fathers-to-be have a moral right to reprimand their pregnant partners:

> Q: I have always enjoyed feeling independent, but ever since I became pregnant, my husband, Bill, has been watching me like a hawk. . . . I ordered a glass of wine—*one* glass! You'd have thought I committed a crime. He humiliated me and kept talking about deformed babies. . . . Besides, this is still my body, right?
> A: Well, yes and no. On the one hand, like every adult, you have the right and responsibility to make your own decisions. On the other hand, you are carrying a baby—his baby as well as yours. . . . He may be acting the only way he knows to assert his desire to protect his unborn child. (Stern 1992, 18; original emphasis)

Instead of taking a position on whether one glass of wine is appropriate during pregnancy (a controversial question), or the manner in which Bill communicated his disagreement, the expert addresses the importance of respecting a man's participation in pregnancy decisions, however limited his repertoire for doing so, as the phrase "the only way he knows" suggests. This illustrates how a woman's decision about whether to act in certain ways, such as drinking wine, is grounded in a larger cultural discourse about gender relations, power, and the apparent right of others to intervene in women's pregnancy decisions, despite the fact that only mothers-to-be experience pregnancy in an embodied way.

The prevailing message in pregnancy advice literature is that pregnancy is a women's project and that men have a far less direct effect on fetal health. But men are instructed (and women are told to teach their partners) to be encouraging and supportive of women's healthy pregnancy behaviors. *What to Expect* even suggests that men "act pregnant": "You don't have to show up for work in maternity clothes or start drinking a quart of milk a day. But you can do your wife's pregnancy exercise routine with her; give up junk food for nine months; quit smoking, if you are a smoker. And when someone offers you a drink, tell them, 'No thanks, we're pregnant'" (Eisenberg et al. 1991 [1984], 413). To capture women's perceptions of the role of the father-to-be in protecting fetal health, I asked women whether their husband or partner did anything differently when the couple was expecting a baby. I was particularly interested in whether women believed that their partners policed their behavior and how they felt about it; I wondered if this could be a site of intense social surveillance of and pressure on women to follow pregnancy rules. As it turned out, none of them followed *What to Expect*'s recommendations.

In part, women's remarks about their partner's participation in pregnancy comment on their attitudes toward changes in the practice of fatherhood. Women's fathers had been expected to have little to do with pregnancy, birth, and infant care, and some men today continue to follow that traditional approach. Melinda Zabrowski talked in an exasperated tone about how her partner treated her when she was pregnant: "He's a typical old-fashioned male! He'd go get that extra thing I wanted to eat if I asked. He told me not to do so much, but he wouldn't pick it up if I didn't, so I still did everything as usual. He wasn't there for any of the births either." Joselyn Behm said that her husband was always helpful with housework (adding that all of her friends think she is very lucky), and when she was pregnant he took over more housework than usual. However, he did not share her many worries about health risks. Other men participated in pregnancy in ways that exhibited their desire to help protect the baby-to-be. April McGough laughed as she admitted that "he did everything. I milked it for all I could. I hate putting gas in the car, and he didn't like me being near the fumes, so he'd fill my car up. Now I still try to get him to do that, he won't. . . . He'd do things around the house, like moving heavy things or vacuuming and stuff." April was pleased that her husband adopted this caretaking role and that he seemed as excited as she about having a baby. She indicated that now that the baby is born, they have a less-than-traditional division of parenting labor, and after April returned to work, they shared childcare equally.

For other women, however, some aspects of their husband's participation involved unpleasant pregnancy policing and stress. Mary Beth Shannon recalled how her eating preferences caused tension in her marriage and that her husband believed he had the right to ask her to change her diet. She worries that if she becomes pregnant again, the same trouble will arise:

> I'm a very picky eater. I love candy and cookies and stuff like that and sometimes I have no control, and I just eat. I don't like a lot of things, so I really had to start tryin' things and eatin' healthy, and my husband was on my back a lot. . . . My big thing is I love sodas; I'm addicted to them. I mean, that was a big thing, so I had to adjust what I drank. In the beginning I was careful, because that's the best time to really be careful, and I watched it and stuff more at the beginning and the end.
>
> LO: And your husband wasn't happy with that?
>
> No, just because I'm picky and I tend sometimes to eat the wrong things, and he didn't want me to do that. He'd just look at me when I put something in my mouth, or give me the evil eye, or just say "you shouldn't be eating that" or [she raises and deepens her voice] "you should watch what you eat!" He'd tell me what he thought, and I used to get mad.
>
> LO: That sounds rough.
>
> Sometimes it rolled off my back, but after a while it was just, like, "leave me alone. I'll take care of it, I'm doin' better." And I used to get upset, and I get upset easy when people do that to me, and I cry. And he didn't like that.

Mary Beth and her husband do not disagree about what a good diet is, but they have different ideas about what makes up a "good-enough" diet. Mary Beth made her own judgment about when during pregnancy it was most important to "be really careful." Part of her frustration was that although she felt she was making progress toward following a healthier diet, which took great self-control, her husband continued to scold her for not "doing it right" instead of supporting the changes she made. Mary Beth realized that she was not going to be the perfect pregnant woman her husband wanted her to be. Nor was he the constantly supportive and understanding husband she would have liked.

Among the women I interviewed, fathers-to-be were represented as changing their behavior very little (Melinda Zabrowski), acting to protect their baby-to-be in a supportive way by taking over more housework and taking care of the mother-to-be (Joselyn Behm and April McGough), or urging their partners to take better care of the baby-to-be (Mary Beth Shannon). Women saw themselves as the ones responsible for following pregnancy rules and saw expectant fathers as playing a supportive or pregnancy policing role.

Recounting experiences of pregnancy policing outside of their homes, women described in detail social situations in which their actions while pregnant were criticized, watched, or permitted. Drinking alcohol at social events was an often-repeated example. Katie Wolfe reported that she had a total of three glasses of wine when she was pregnant: on New Year's Eve, at a sister's wedding, and at a birthday celebration. I asked her if anyone commented on this, and she said that when they did, it was in a joking, not negative, way: "I was worried at the wedding if people were watching me and thinking I'd had more than one glass though. But my friends know I'm not a big drinker, and they were like, 'Go ahead!'" In contrast, *What to Expect* assumes that pregnant women will be pressured to drink and encourages them to abstain from even a sip. Women should "be polite but firm" when turning down a drink, for example, by saying "Thanks, but I'll toast your birthday with orange juice— my baby's underage" (Eisenberg et al. 1991 [1984], 63). With this response, a woman demonstrates that she is doing her job of protecting the health of her baby-to-be. Such advice implies that women must be ever-vigilant in disciplining themselves because those around them may be insensitive to or ignorant of the new rules of pregnancy, which stipulate that any alcohol intake is hazardous.

Indeed, Julia Panciera—who was pregnant when we spoke—observed that friends of her generation and younger, who had been raised with the health education message "Don't drink during pregnancy," were more controlling than older friends. She described two encounters involving alcohol:

> I was at some friends' house for dinner last week and their ten-year-old son told me I shouldn't drink when I'm pregnant. His mother was just shocked because she'd offered me a glass of wine. He said he'd read the warning label on the wine bottle. . . . I find that people my age and younger, not the older generations, get so upset by my choosing to have a glass of wine. They don't think I'm capable of making that decision, I guess. Once at a restaurant, a friend of mine put his hand over my glass when the waiter came, and said "She won't be having any." As though not only was the decision already made, but apparently I was unable to speak for myself!

Even when women do speak for themselves, their opinions and decisions may be challenged. In defense of her decision to drink a caffeinated soda once, Jennifer Montelli asserts that she made a conscious and justifiable decision. Jennifer did not appreciate what she saw as unfair judgment voiced by a neighbor: "You do feel some pressure—social pressure—to do everything just right. For example, caffeine. I really am very conscious, but once at a neighborhood party, there was no caffeine-free soda, so I had one with caffeine. A woman there just kinda joking noticed it and said something. And this woman doesn't even put her kid in the car seat properly! I was kinda surprised. What'd she think I should've done, had a beer? Then what'd she have said?" Jennifer implies that her neighbor's concern has little authority because she does not use a car seat properly, which constitutes a greater risk to a child's health than does drinking a caffeinated soda when pregnant. Each woman judged the other's mothering practices against standard expectations about pregnancy and maternal responsibilities. Even women who are subjected to pregnancy policing, perhaps indeed because they are, have high expectations of other pregnant women. As Patricia Doyle assertively put it in response to my question "Has it bothered you when strangers give you advice?" she is not a passive recipient of advice: "No, I listen to what I want. I'm the type to say things to strangers, really." When asked what sort of things, she replied, "Like 'you might not want this advice, but I'm givin' it to ya.' I *give* advice."

It is the delivery of such unsolicited advice that is most likely to carry a potentially offensive moral message, whether from a stranger, partner, friend, or doctor. I observed an exchange about weight gain and healthy eating that illustrates this dynamic well. Two acquaintances, both eight or nine months pregnant, sat next to each other at a prenatal care class. During a break, several people went to a hospital vending machine, and one of the women returned with a bag of M&Ms. As she sat down, her acquaintance, who was not eating anything, said with a disapproving tone, "Get to eat junk food now, eh?" The woman with the M&Ms casually explained that she had not gained too much weight, so she need not worry. "Oh," replied the other pointedly, "I have to eat a lot too, so I keep my tangerines and yogurt with me at the office." Clearly, she was making a statement about which foods are more appropriate, simultaneously praising her own behavior and criticizing that of her acquaintance. This sort of moral patrolling suggests that once pregnancy lessons are learned, women use their knowledge even beyond protecting their own babies-to-be. Pregnant women are socialized through the new rules of pregnancy to become fetal protection agents.

Some women do not mind being the subject of pregnancy policing and may ask others to keep them in line. Cynthia Phillips went as far as to say, "I guess I'm not sure if I got pregnant to give up things or if I gave up things because I got pregnant." Cynthia gave up cigarettes, beer, and coffee because she was concerned about her baby-to-be's health. Her husband, friends, co-workers, and family helped her make these changes: "I was really attached to my coffee, I'll tell you. But ask anyone. I didn't do anything bad." The recognition Cynthia received from what she called complying with health advice made her feel good about these changes. The difference between the positive judgment Cynthia felt and the negative judgment other pregnant women receive has to do with whether the expectations for pregnant women are shared by the pregnant woman and the advice giver. Cynthia did not feel that the members of her support network made moral judgments of her but that they supported her own judgments about how to care for her baby-to-be. Clearly she had a very different experience from that of women who are told they are putting their babies-to-be at risk.

The effect of the current rules of pregnancy is to hold pregnant women, and indeed, all women of reproductive age, responsible for creating the perfect child. New medical understandings of fetal health and development and the imperative that all individuals should strive to be healthy create moralistic lessons about what every pregnant woman has to do to be a good mother-to-be. This has serious consequences for women's everyday decision making and ultimately their reproductive rights. The next chapter turns from this analysis of the general pregnancy policing that women face to explore the specific subject that is the focus of the book, cigarette smoking during pregnancy.

The Emergence of Maternal Smoking as a Public Health Problem

Chapter 3

A~N~ EDITORIAL COMMENTARY in a 1929 issue of the *Journal of the American Medical Association*, playfully titled "Lady Nicotine and the Ladies," disputed the assertion that smoking during pregnancy was a health hazard, a claim that had recently been made in a newsletter of the Methodist Episcopal Church's Board of Temperance, Prohibition, and Public Morals. The controversy, which was publicized in the *New York Times*, began when the newsletter printed two stories citing evidence that the health of newborns and young children was harmed if their mothers had smoked while pregnant (1929a). One story described a New York maternity hospital ward in which forty babies "suffered from tobacco heart caused by the cigaret smoking of their mothers."[1] The other claimed that "sixty per cent of all babies born of cigaret-smoking mothers die before they reach the age of two, due primarily to nicotine poisoning" (quoted in *Journal of the American Medical Association* 1929, 123). The church board condemned the members of the American Tobacco Trust as "conscienceless baby-killers" who were leading a "lying murderous campaign" by "recommending cigarets to women."

The *Journal of the American Medical Association* attacked these stories as groundless. Its counterclaim was based on a review of medical literature by a doctor and member of the Committee to Study the Tobacco Problem and on the ad hominem argument that the doctor who had observed that nicotine poisoning was a serious danger was associated with a cult.[2] More research, the journal's editors announced, was necessary before the church board or anyone else could legitimately assert that smoking during pregnancy caused health problems in newborns or children. As for the church board's broader concerns about smoking as an immoral practice, the American Medical Association (AMA) intoned, "the morality of smoking by women is not a medical concern any more than the question as to whether or not they should go bare-headed into church."

This dispute was part of a larger cultural debate about the relationship between cigarettes, morality, and science. Beginning in the 1920s, when smoking was rapidly becoming socially acceptable for both men and women, opinion leaders and the mass media took issue with temperance leaders'—such as the church board's—condemnation of cigarettes and alcohol on either health or moral grounds (Burnham 1989, 12).[3] At the same time, physicians attempted to maintain their professionalism by distinguishing their science from the morally imbued research claims made by antitobacco fanatics.

Five decades later, prominent medical professionals and antitobacco advocates alike recognized smoking during pregnancy as an important public health problem. In contrast with the early assertion by the medical association that smoking should not be seen as a moral issue, the warnings against smoking during pregnancy that began to be issued in the late 1970s contained moral judgments of pregnant smokers. The expansion of medical evidence—captured in the statement many women made to me, "we know more now"—provides one explanation for why attitudes toward smoking by pregnant women have shifted over time. Another factor is the healthist ideology underlying general health advice, as discussed in the previous chapter. But stories of the emergence of maternal smoking—and also, in the 1990s, of paternal smoking—as a public health problem are more complex. Science, politics, and social trends shape the ways in which public health issues are defined, thought about, and acted on.[4]

Science, Antitobacco Advocacy, and Smoking as a Health Problem

During the first wave of the antitobacco movement, from the late 1800s to 1930, smoking by women was controversial and contested; opposition to it included policies against women smoking in public and even a proposed ban on the sale of cigarettes to women (Brandt 1996, 63).[5] Yet smoking during pregnancy received relatively little public or medical attention. Interest in smoking by pregnant women rose following a wave of heightened social concern in the early twentieth century over child health and the dramatic increase in the number of women smokers.[6] According to a 1935 *Fortune* magazine survey, 31 to 40 percent of women living in urban areas smoked cigarettes (Goodman 1993, 108). Medical researchers in the 1930s and 1940s investigated the health effects of smoking by pregnant women on fetal and infant health, following prominent obstetricians' earlier suggestions of its dangers.[7]

In the 1930s, laboratory animal studies and clinical investigations supported the hypothesis that smoking could influence fetal and infant health. One study found that when a pregnant woman smoked, the fetus's heart beat more rapidly (possibly associated with the newborn condition "tobacco heart" noted by the church board in 1929) (Sontag and Wallace 1935). Anticipating today's antismoking campaigns, the *New York Times* reported that this study had found that "unborn babies indirectly 'smoke' along with their mothers" (1935). The scientists submitted that more research was needed to determine whether smoking actually harmed the fetus, although they considered it "not improbable that maternal smoking during pregnancy may have permanently harmful effects on the child." Other researchers reported that heavy cigarette smoking led to "more difficulty during the course of pregnancy, parturition, and lactation" as a result of "chronic nicotine poisoning" (quoted in U.S. Department of Health, Education, and Welfare 1979a, 8–10). In the years after World War II, coincident with a steep rise in the rates of smoking by women, medical attention focused on whether smoking by breast-feeding women could damage infant health (Charlton 1994, 267). During this period, however, smoking remained noncontroversial, and smoking during pregnancy was not publicly perceived as an urgent health or moral problem.[8]

In fact, research on smoking during pregnancy did not gain prominence within the medical community until the late 1950s, and findings were not made widely public until the next decade. A study published by Winea Simpson in 1957 was crucial to the development of smoking during pregnancy as a health problem, setting off "a tidal wave of medical interest" on the subject (Oakley 1989, 314). Simpson's article, published in the esteemed *American Journal of Obstetrics and Gynecology*, began by noting a lack of consensus among medical experts about how pregnant women should be counseled regarding smoking. Simpson cited this as motivation for her study: "During the past four decades the incidence of cigarette smoking among women has increased so rapidly as to make this question worthy of a sound scientific answer" (1957, 808). She reported that smokers had twice the risk of delivering a premature baby than nonsmokers and that the greater the number of cigarettes smoked per day, the greater the risk of prematurity.[9] Such findings did not automatically mean that concern about smoking during pregnancy gained public notice, however. It would take the efforts of the second wave of the tobacco control movement to bring this and future studies on the health risks of smoking to national attention.[10]

The mid-1950s mark the beginning of the second wave of the antitobacco movement. At that time, a rapidly growing volume of research cited smoking as a major health danger that could cause lung cancer and perhaps heart disease, prompting health advocates to pressure the government to notify the public and to institute restrictions on tobacco advertising and marketing. In 1962, a coalition of national health organizations successfully lobbied President John F. Kennedy to take government action on what then was perceived as a low-priority issue (Diehl 1969, 168–169; Kluger 1996, 200–223).[11] Health advocates were well aware that raising the subject of the health risks of smoking was politically sensitive, as is seen in the language of their first letter urging President Kennedy to set up a national commission to seek "a solution to this health problem that would interfere least with the freedom of the industry or the happiness of individuals" (quoted in Kluger 1996, 222). The surgeon general's Advisory Committee on Smoking and Health established by Kennedy evaluated the international scientific evidence on smoking and illness. The release of the committee's report in 1964 represents the first concerted government effort to inform the U.S. public that cigarettes could cause serious disease. This news was not a total surprise; in 1953 and 1954, *Reader's Digest* had covered scientific findings on smoking and lung cancer, which had caused a brief health scare (Warner 1985, 387). The Advisory Committee's report was announced by Surgeon General Luther Terry at a press conference held on a Saturday to minimize the expected jolt to the stock market but also to maximize the number of people who would read about the risks of smoking in their Sunday newspapers (Kluger 1996, 259). This signaled the transformation of the surgeon general into a public figure who communicated with the public through the media (Brandt 1990, 166).

After the report was released, antitobacco activity surged. Public health officials, nongovernmental health associations, and grassroots organizations worked together and independently to lobby for federal regulation of packaging and advertising; to establish clean indoor air regulations; and to create and support national, state, and local antismoking programs. This second wave of the antitobacco movement had strong advantages over the first wave, which had relied on moral ideologies about temperance and had attempted to prove that smoking was a health danger with only anecdotal evidence and "a jumble of pseudoscientific jargon" (Whelan 1984, 45). In the 1960s, the tobacco control movement benefited from the development of epidemiology, more sophisticated understandings of basic science, and the government's willingness to publicize medical findings on the health risks of smoking.[12] The two campaigns shared a moral component, though, particularly in their efforts to stigmatize smokers. One strategy that both employed was renaming—labeling nicotine and other cigarette contents as drugs and calling smoking a pernicious habit or, in the later period, an addiction (see Troyer and Markle 1983; Whelan 1984; Nathanson 1997).[13]

Smoking gained status as a priority public health problem after the 1964 report, and it has retained this status. A provision in the 1965 federal Cigarette Labeling and Advertising Act mandated that the surgeon general's office provide annual reports to Congress on cigarette advertising and the health consequences of smoking. These reports were covered by the mass media and have helped maintain a sense of urgency about the smoking problem. In 1979, Joseph Califano, the Secretary of Health, Education, and Welfare, named smoking "Public Health Enemy Number One in America" (U.S. Department of Health, Education, and Welfare 1979a, ii). In 1982, Surgeon General C. Everett Koop declared cigarette smoking "the chief, single avoidable cause of death in our society and the most important public health issue of our time" (U.S. Department of Health and Human Services 1982, xi). In the 1990s, cigarette smoking remained, according to Surgeon General David Satcher, "the most preventable cause of death in America" (quoted in Stolberg 1998).

Although the 1964 report enormously increased the attention paid by the medical profession, the public, and the government to smoking in general, it was not until the 1970s that smoking by women and smoking during pregnancy figured significantly in antismoking public health efforts. The effect of smoking on women was hardly mentioned in the 1964 surgeon general's Advisory Committee's report on smoking and health (see Terry 1981, 7). The studies reviewed in the report were based almost exclusively on research with men, and a cursory section titled "Other Conditions" presented data indicating a steady increase in lung cancer among women. Only four paragraphs and ten references addressed smoking during pregnancy. The report did cite evidence that smoking when pregnant could result in "lower than average birthweight," but at the time this did not constitute a major concern because low birthweight itself was not known to have a negative effect on a newborn's health (Steinfeld 1983, 1257).[14] Smoking was not yet viewed as a prenatal health problem: although it was thought to affect the fetus, the effect was not considered hazardous. Indeed, publications to increase public awareness about the health hazards related to smoking, such as Diehl's *Tobacco and Your Health*, included smoking during pregnancy as a side issue; Diehl devotes one paragraph to the possible fetal health effects associated with smoking, including low birthweight, premature birth, and spontaneous abortion (miscarriage) (1969, 96).

Former Surgeon General Luther Terry and other public health experts have attributed the paucity of early attention to the consequences of women's smoking to a lack of scientific evidence (1981, 6). Medical experts could only generalize from the data they had on men to women. But a peak in the rates of smoking by women the year after the 1964 *Smoking and Health* report was published and the steep rise in the lung cancer death rates of women, which began in the mid-1960s, led medical researchers to concentrate directly on smoking and women's health as well as on smoking during pregnancy (Husten et al. 1996). Over the course of the next decade, as research results poured in, subsequent surgeon generals' reports included more data on the consequences of smoking on fetal and infant health. The 1969 report noted findings associating smoking during pregnancy with low birthweight, spontaneous abortion, stillbirth, and neonatal death, and short chapters on these fetal and infant health risks were included in the 1971 and 1973 summaries of research. This accumulation of research results served as the basis for public health efforts that would advise women against smoking during pregnancy.

By the end of the 1970s, both women's smoking and, more specifically, smoking during pregnancy had become visible public health issues.[15] In 1971, Surgeon General Steinfeld called for smoking cessation projects directed toward women (Schmeck 1971), and in the mid-1970s, health organizations such as the American Cancer Society and the American Lung Association designed education campaigns targeted at women (Jacobson 1986, 126).[16] The 1977 surgeon general's report concluded that smoking during pregnancy is associated with a number of conditions that carry high risk of the newborn's death, including abruptio placentae (premature separation of the placenta from the uterus), placenta previa (displacement of the placenta), bleeding during pregnancy, premature and prolonged rupture of the membranes (or bag of waters), and preterm delivery. The 1979 surgeon general's report contained a chapter on smoking during pregnancy, with more than two hundred references to medical studies; it also added the risk of sudden infant death syndrome to the list of the dangers incurred by women who smoked during pregnancy (Terry 1981, 7).

Not until 1980 did the issues of women's smoking and smoking during pregnancy assume official prominence. That year, the surgeon general's annual report was devoted to the health consequences of smoking for women; it featured as one of its four main themes the notion that "cigarette smoking is a major threat to the outcome of pregnancy and well-being of the newborn baby" (U.S. Department of Health and Human Services 1980, v). Since the emergence of smoking during pregnancy as a public health problem, information on the latest research has been carried regularly in newspapers, magazines, television news, and pregnancy advice literature. Although these medical findings vary in conclusiveness, they usually are presented as strengthening the message that women should quit smoking, and the earlier the better.

Indeed, smoking during pregnancy did not become a public health problem only as a result of accumulating medical data. Heightened attention to smoking during pregnancy in the 1960s and 1970s was contemporaneous with a time of social and economic upheaval—captured in the phrase "sexual revolution"—that had profound implications for women's reproductive and working lives across class, ethnic, and racial categories (see Petchesky 1985 [1984], chapter 3). That women must be socially and legally allowed to choose the timing and number of their pregnancies stands as one of the most significant ideologies promoted by feminists and women's health advocates. Issues related to women's self-determination gained status as public controversies in the 1960s, coincident with an overall fertility decline in the United States. Concern over who was choosing to have children, when, and in what economic and family circumstances reached the public health agenda in the early 1970s. Teen pregnancy was seen as a pervasive social problem, one linked to childbearing by single mothers on welfare and women of color (see Nathanson 1991). The Supreme Court's 1973 ruling legalizing abortion ignited further debate about women's reproductive decisions. The politicized context of the 1960s and 1970s, in which the role of motherhood in women's lives and the "quality" of future generations were at issue, certainly helped make smoking during pregnancy and its effects on fetal and infant health worthy of scientific and public attention.

Although the warnings about smoking that were designed in the late 1970s and early 1980s stressed the importance of quitting smoking based on the available scientific data, the moral imperative that smokers should quit was not always strong. Surgeon General Julius Richmond, for example, concluded the introduction to his report on smoking and women's health by stating, "Each individual woman must make her own decision about this significant issue . . . the role of the Government, and all responsible health professionals, is to assure that this decision is an informed one" (U.S. Department of Health and Human Services 1980, xi). Pregnancy advice literature on smoking was not always as respectful of women's choice to smoke.

Perhaps the most widely recognized effort to educate the public about the health risks of cigarette smoking has been the legislation mandating health warning labels on cigarette packs and advertisements. The drive "to increase public awareness of any adverse health effects of smoking," as the Comprehensive Smoking Education Act (1984) reads, assumed that once warned, each smoker would decide whether to incur the risks of smoking. The implicit hope was that rationality would win out and the consumer would choose not to smoke.

The first labels, legislated in 1965, read, "Warning: The Surgeon General

Has Determined that Cigarette Smoking May be Dangerous to Your Health." In 1969, additional legislation modified the wording from "may be" to "is" dangerous; it also instituted a ban on radio and television tobacco advertisements.[17] Legislators did not specifically address cigarettes and pregnancy until 1982, when they convened to debate a revision in the health warning labels. At this time, smoking during pregnancy had already been established as a public health problem; it became an issue in the policy debate.

During committee hearings in the House of Representatives, Democratic Congressman Henry Waxman (an ex-chain-smoker and vocal antitobacco advocate from Los Angeles) juxtaposed the image of the rough Marlboro-type man with that of the fragile fetus in his assault on the tobacco industry: "The [advertising] messages speak of rugged lifestyles but are silent about the risks to the fetus resulting from maternal smoking" (Waxman in U.S. House of Representatives 1983). Waxman's comments contrast the independent adult smoker who chooses smoking as part of an image and lifestyle with the vulnerable, dependent, innocent fetus subjected to the risks of smoking without choice by a woman lured into smoking by cigarette advertising. His attack recalls the church board's 1929 charge against the American Tobacco Trust; Waxman, it seems, would have agreed that tobacco companies should be characterized as "conscienceless baby-killers." Those who promoted pregnancy-specific health warning labels argued that the labels would improve the health of future Americans by giving pregnant women information about the fetal health risks of smoking that would motivate them to quit.[18]

Antitobacco advocates' arguments for pregnancy-specific warning labels succeeded. In 1984, Congress mandated four labels, which must be rotated quarterly. Two address pregnancy: "Smoking Causes Lung Cancer, Heart Disease, Emphysema, And May Complicate Pregnancy," and "Smoking By Pregnant Women May Result In Fetal Injury, Premature Birth, And Low Birth Weight."

Predictably, the effort to include these labels was heavily opposed by the tobacco industry. Tobacco companies historically have rejected antitobacco advocates' definition of smoking as a health problem, attempting through advertising, government lobbying, and public statements to dissuade people from believing that smoking is a serious health risk. When the labels were first proposed, tobacco lobbyists argued that health warnings on smoking and pregnancy were not conclusively backed by science and therefore had no legitimacy. Tobacco industry spokespersons, citing contradictory medical evidence, sought to disprove a body of evidence showing that women who smoked were more likely to give birth to low birthweight babies. One rebuttal asserted that low birthweight was related to lower weight gain by pregnant women who smoke: smoking itself was not the problem; women's weight was. Another maintained that smokers are individuals "who have a poor reproductive performance because of constitutional reasons" (Rao in U.S. House of Representatives 1982, 696). Women who smoked during pregnancy, in other words, did not "perform" well as a result of individual characteristics unrelated to smoking (such as age, race, ethnicity, number of children, and class status). Tobacco lobbyists argued that women who gave birth to low-birthweight babies would do so regardless of whether they smoked.

The tobacco industry also contended that even if the babies born to women smokers had lower birthweights than those born to nonsmokers, this was not necessarily a health problem; in fact, it could be beneficial. "The Cigarette Controversy," a pamphlet distributed by the Tobacco Institute, urged pregnant women to dismiss public health officials' interpretations of studies linking smoking with low birthweight: "You've become accustomed to seeing magazine and newspaper articles that say that smoking can harm your unborn child. Studies do show that smoking mothers, on the average, have slightly lighter weight babies. Yet with more women reportedly smoking, infant mortality rates keep reaching record lows. Some studies have shown that the lighter babies of smoking mothers actually have better survival rates than similar weight babies of nonsmokers" (quoted in Cromer 1983). The tobacco industry insisted that the public health establishment was spreading misinformation in their health warning campaigns.

The tobacco industry and antitobacco advocates at this time agreed on one point: medical evidence about the many factors associated with low birthweight made it difficult to come to an irrefutable conclusion about the effects of smoking during pregnancy. Those lobbyists who advocated increased public health measures, however, believed that action ought be taken to advise the public of possible fetal health risks, despite medical uncertainty. In their report in support of health warning labels submitted to a congressional subcommittee, the 1980 President's Advisory Committee for Women disputed the tobacco industry's contention that smoking could not be singled out as a cause of low birthweight. Repeating the position stated in the 1979 surgeon general's report, it stated, "Although these variations [maternal age, parity, socioeconomic status, and race/ethnicity] make the relationship subject to some controversy, the relationship is sufficiently strong" to conclude that smoking can be a direct cause of fetal or neonatal death (cited in U.S. House of Representatives 1983, 352). With the assumption that future evidence would strengthen the data available at the time, the President's Advisory Committee urged the government to put its force behind the warning.

The strength of the scientific evidence on the health risks of smoking was not the only subject at issue. During the legislative debates, some policy makers seemed satisfied with the medical evidence on the increased risk of "pregnancy complications" due to smoking, as the health warning label now states. But they questioned the need for government intervention in publicizing this information. Legislators attempted to determine how widespread was knowledge of the risks of smoking during pregnancy. Building a case that pregnancy-specific health warnings were needed, Assistant Secretary for Health Edward Brandt asserted that "people tend to be aware of the risk of lung cancer but not necessarily of heart disease, [and] certainly not of the risk to the unborn child from the mother smoking during pregnancy," but this statement was roundly criticized by some congressmen as not adequately supported by proof (U.S. House of Representatives 1983, 75). One legislator asked Brandt if he had "statistics or a marketing survey" to demonstrate which groups were unaware of the risks of smoking during pregnancy. In response, the legislators reviewed a 1980 poll showing that 47 percent—nearly half—of all women did not know that smoking during pregnancy increased the risk of miscarriage and stillbirth (1983, 302). But no one could offer data that surveyed pregnant women; thus the question, "What percentage of pregnant women know that smoking during pregnancy is a fetal health risk?" could not be answered to the satisfaction of the House committee. At this point in the developing awareness of smoking during pregnancy as a public health problem, public health decision makers voiced concern over the knowledge of both medical professionals and pregnant women about the fetal health risks related to smoking.

Subsequent medical research on smoking during pregnancy has continued to support the claims about fetal and infant health risks carried by cigarette warning labels. These labels notify the public about the general risks of smoking during pregnancy, yet some of the language is vague and nonspecific (smoking "may complicate pregnancy" and "may result in fetal injury"). Pregnant women have received more detailed antismoking health warnings from their physicians and pregnancy advice literature. Such warnings, however, are not simply objective statements about medical findings. It is in pregnancy advice that moral themes related to smoking and the pregnant woman's responsibility to protect her baby-to-be would become prominently featured.

Stop Smoking!—A Rule in Pregnancy Advice and a Moral Imperative

Pregnancy advice literature, along with public health campaigns, does the work of translating technical scientific information for practical use. In the 1960s, at the same time that public attention was being drawn by public health officials and antitobacco advocates to the general problem of the health risks of smoking, obstetrics textbooks and pregnancy advice guidebooks began to acknowledge smoking specifically as a pregnancy issue. Thus, medical research findings, public health officials' recognition of smoking during pregnancy as a problem, antitobacco advocates' pressure to create an antismoking social climate, doctors' willingness to counsel against smoking, and increasingly strict pregnancy rules have all shaped changes in the antismoking advice offered to pregnant women since the 1964 surgeon general's report.

Among health professionals, attention to advising pregnant women about the fetal and infant risks associated with smoking during pregnancy has been uneven. When the surgeon general's report was issued, the AMA did not advocate antismoking measures, and women's obstetricians themselves might have been smokers.[19] Although medical recommendations likely varied from doctor to doctor and case by case, medical textbooks offer insight into the ways obstetricians were instructed to advise their patients. The leading medical textbook, *Williams Obstetrics*, first published in 1903, did not mention smoking until its 1966 edition. By then, the thalidomide tragedy had heightened the awareness of both medical professionals and the public about how pregnant women's health practices might influence fetal health. But scientific evidence on the health risks of smoking during pregnancy was scarce. The book cites only three studies, offering obstetricians little data with which to support an antismoking message. *Williams Obstetrics* states that the evidence on the association of low birthweight with heavy smoking during pregnancy is strong but that low birthweight does not cause newborn death. Further, it cites a study that found no increased risk of "stillbirths, major fetal anomalies, or maternal complications" among pregnant smokers, and another that found that although smoking during pregnancy speeds fetal heartbeat, this effect is not harmful. The authors conclude, "It is, nevertheless, recommended that excessive smoking be avoided during pregnancy; 10 cigarettes or fewer per day during pregnancy are quite likely innocuous" (Eastman et al. 1966, 331).

This advice parallels the AMA's hesitant stand on the general risks of smoking. A May 1964 pamphlet, "Smoking: Facts You Should Know," distributed by the AMA in response to the surgeon general's report on smoking and health, cites several "suspected health hazards"; it concludes, "Smoke if you feel you should, but be moderate" (quoted in Wolinsky and Brune 1994, 151). This message reveals disagreement among medical professionals about the conclusiveness of scientific evidence on the health risks of smoking and the need to warn the public (indeed, the doctors on the surgeon general's committee felt that the available evidence was sufficient to issue a warning). But not only scientific concerns shaped the AMA's position. The organization's leadership took a mild stand on tobacco until the 1990s. This has been attributed to funding of AMA research by the tobacco industry and to the AMA's relationship with members of Congress from tobacco-growing states who would vote against proposals for government regulation of health care (see Burnham 1989; Wolinsky and Brune 1994; Kluger 1996).

In turn, doctors' moderate advice was influenced by both the AMA's political position on smoking and medical professionals' limited findings on the fetal and infant health hazards associated with smoking during pregnancy. The suggestion in *Williams Obstetrics* that pregnant smokers should do so only in moderation is offered by obstetricians Eastman (a coeditor of *Williams Obstetrics*) and Russell in their book *Expectant Motherhood* (1970), written for a general audience. In their short paragraph devoted to smoking, they note that the 1964 release of the surgeon general's *Smoking and Health* report brought increased scrutiny to smoking during pregnancy: "Current interest in the harmful effects of cigarette smoking, quite apart from pregnancy, has stirred new concern over the possible harmful effects of smoking by pregnant women on the well-being of the infant" (1970, 84). Eastman and Russell cautiously reported that studies indicated that babies of smokers tend to be lower birthweight than those of nonsmokers, "but whether this lower birth weight indicates an injurious effect has not been established. Regardless of these findings, most physicians recommend that smoking should be eliminated in pregnancy or at least curtailed to ten cigarettes or less a day" (1970, 84). Eastman and Russell's language suggests that their moderate message to quit or limit smoking when pregnant was driven not by existing evidence but by expected future findings.

Pregnant women also encountered advice about smoking beyond the doctor's office in pregnancy literature. The first reference to cigarettes in parenting magazines was in April 1964, after the release of the first report to the surgeon general by the Advisory Committee on Smoking and Health. An editorial by George Hecht, the publisher of *Parents' Magazine*, focused on parental responsibility to set proper role models for schoolchildren so that they would not take up smoking (Hecht 1964, 38). It also mentioned in passing that the committee's report "confirmed . . . that cigarette smoking by pregnant women affects adversely the birth weight of their babies." In stark contrast to the abstinence imperatives presented in pregnancy literature today, Hecht espoused that "in our democratic tradition of free choice, the decision to smoke or not to smoke is one which grown men and women must make for themselves." As a publisher, Hecht chose not to advertise cigarettes. Departing from the practice of many other magazines, including women's magazines (see Ernster 1985), neither of the parenting magazines I surveyed (*Parents' Maga-*

zine, published since 1926, and *American Baby*, in press since 1938) ever ran advertisements for tobacco products.[20]

Not all pregnancy advice on smoking in the period after the 1964 surgeon general's report was as mild as Hecht's. In his pregnancy guide *Life before Birth* (1964 [1961]), medical doctor and anthropologist Ashley Montagu takes a much stronger antismoking position. Montagu's strident stand against "poisonous" tobacco is based on his survey of medical studies published between 1935 and 1964. The studies he cites did not find conclusively that smoking causes fetal health problems. Montagu sets uncertainty aside, however, and asserts that there is "no question at all that smoking is harmful to a child before birth, and the implication is clear for a pregnant woman who is also a smoker: stop smoking" (1964 [1961], 100). The moral subtext of his stance is revealed when Montagu contends that the good mother-in-training will act on his expert knowledge: "A prospective mother who is genuinely interested in the welfare of her child does not wait for 'proof'; the bare possibility that she may be hurting her child is enough to give her a reason to stop smoking. Nor is she likely to say, 'It's worth it,' because in this case the price for a selfish pleasure is exorbitant" (1964 [1961], 101). According to Montagu, to be a good mother-to-be, a woman must take seriously even the slightest scientific hint that smoking may carry fetal and infant health risks. His warning contains the misleading assumption that all infants born to women who smoke will be harmed: "A prospective mother who is finding it difficult to give up smoking might consider this: her child's entire life is being decided" (1964 [1961], 115). In his translation of ostensibly objective scientific data to pregnant women, Montagu brings the weight of ideologies about motherhood and maternal responsibility to bear on this discussion of scientific advances.

The book's foreword anticipates that pregnant women will "be frightened" or "panic" after reading Montagu's health warnings, so another doctor provides a more conservative, reassuring second opinion: "Don't panic if circumstances or even your own weak will causes one of Dr. Montagu's admonitions to go unheeded. Perhaps you crave a cigarette so badly that you forget or you simply disobey. The chances for a few cigarettes to cause any obstetrical difficulty such as early labor are too remote to brood over" (Alan Guttmacher, in Montagu 1964 [1961], v).

The discrepancy in the tone of Guttmacher's and Montagu's advice reveals that in the 1960s, doctors themselves disagreed, even within the same volume, about the proper advice to give women on smoking during pregnancy. Medical professionals' lack of consensus on what causes fetal harm is also evident in Montagu's advice on drinking during pregnancy. Although Montagu believes women should abstain totally from smoking, he does not take the same stance on drinking. This is not due to a lack of scientific study on the subject. Instead, Montagu dismisses the many publications showing that pregnant alcoholic women have higher rates of bearing "idiots," "malformed children," and "retarded children" than nonalcoholic women (1964 [1961], 114). He calls the idea that alcohol leads to birth defects a myth: "it can now be stated categorically, after hundreds of studies covering many years, that no matter how great the amounts of alcohol taken by the mother—or by the father, for that matter—neither the germ cells nor the development of the child will be affected." He continues dramatically, "an amount of alcohol in the blood that would kill the mother is not even enough to irritate the tissues of the child" (1964 [1961], 114). As these remarks make clear, Montagu's passionate advice to pregnant women about smoking and drinking is grounded in an inconsistent assessment of research findings. He builds a strong antismoking argument based on inconclusive medical evidence presented in thirteen smoking studies, yet he does not express similar sentiments about alcohol, despite similarly contradictory evidence on the fetal health effects of alcohol.

Montagu's position is more characteristic of recent antismoking messages than of the advice offered to pregnant women by his contemporaries. Until the late 1970s, pregnancy advice mainly promoted the idea that smoking in moderation was acceptable, although quitting was most desirable. In response to increasing medical evidence and growing awareness of the health risks of smoking publicized by antitobacco advocates, a shift began away from recommendations to cut down on cigarettes and toward recommendations to quit smoking completely. This coincided with the rise of healthist ideologies supporting the moral obligation of each individual to maintain her or his health and with the further stigmatizing of smoking by antitobacco advocates who were lobbying for policies to protect nonsmokers from involuntary, or secondhand, smoke.

A 1980 *American Baby* article reveals the contradictory advice women received during the transition. First, the author offers a moderate line: "Obviously, say doctors, it's better to quit completely than just to cut down. . . . But if you *can't* quit completely, cutting down is a good idea" (Edmondson 1980, 38; original emphasis). This position, however, is overturned by a doctor who warns that cutting down is not enough for babies-to-be who are "susceptible to birth complications and health problems." He asserts, "For a baby who is compromised, even a single cigarette could be 'the straw that broke the camel's back'" (Manchester, quoted in Edmondson 1980, 38). The notion that a single cigarette might be responsible for a baby-to-be's poor health contradicts the idea that reducing cigarette consumption is acceptable. Although the single-cigarette theory applies only to a certain set of babies, those who are "compromised," it is not clear which pregnant women would be considered healthy enough to be told that they could risk cutting down instead of quitting entirely, or, for that matter, what compromised status is and how pregnant smokers or their doctors could identify it. This uneven advice, which highlights individual variation in susceptibility to health risks, leaves open the possibility that women could determine that light smoking is not terribly unsafe for the baby-to-be.

Smoking for Two: Cigarettes and Pregnancy, the first book devoted to the issue and published with the intent of making technical medical data more accessible to a popular audience, presents a strong case against all smoking during pregnancy (Fried and Oxorn 1980). The authors review recent findings about the adverse fetal health effects of smoking during pregnancy, arguing that no one can dispute that pregnant women should quit smoking. Revealing that the status of smoking as a public health problem was well established at the start of the 1980s, they point out that nearly everyone knew of the message that smoking is a serious health risk. Yet such knowledge does not necessarily lead to quitting. They conclude: "Virtually all adults are aware that smoking is not good for one's health, yet still more than one in three lights up regularly. So, for many women, knowing smoking is harmful is not sufficient motivation to stop. Now, if we add the argument to mothers-to-be or women thinking of having a child that smoking is a hazard to the baby's health we add a strong incentive for at no other time during a woman's life is there likely to be a greater sense of responsibility for another human life than during pregnancy" (1980, 113). This appeal combines the "quit smoking" health message with a moral directive about the demands of motherhood during, and even before, pregnancy that was commonly seen in antismoking advice throughout the 1980s and into the 1990s. The incentive message—that to care properly for one's baby-to-be, a woman should not smoke during pregnancy—represents pregnant smokers as irrational decision makers who need to be trained to take mothering more seriously.

Advice offered by Elizabeth Whelan, a physician and author of *A Smoking Gun: How the Tobacco Industry Gets away with Murder* (1984), is representative of the harsh antismoking messages that would dominate pregnancy literature. As a columnist for *American Baby*, Whelan has written extensively about smoking during pregnancy, nearly always taking a hard line. In a 1979 article "Taking Care of Yourself and Your Baby during Pregnancy," she argues that "pregnancy is a time when you are—or should be—really tuned in to health . . . it's time to think about breaking some undesirable old habits . . . and maximize your chances for a healthy pregnancy and a healthy baby" (Whelan 1979, 20). On smoking, she states, "Smoking isn't smart at any time, but during pregnancy, it's really unforgivable. Your unborn baby shouldn't have to share the assaults that cigarettes inflict on your body. . . . Do yourself and your baby both a favor and kick the habit now! (1979, 20)" The risks of negative health effects for the baby-to-be are far reaching according to Whelan, from the often-cited low birthweight, miscarriage, stillbirth, and sudden infant death syndrome to the radical claim, unsubstantiated in medical literature today, that "almost every kind of learning disability has been associated with the cigarette factor." Whelan's presentation of such findings as truths supports her conviction that smoking during pregnancy is "really unforgivable." This blunt, morally laden advice is supported by the healthist ideology that gained popularity in the 1980s and also by antismoking public health campaigns launched in the same period.

In pregnancy advice in the 1990s, warnings against smoking are pervasive and often delivered in the form of reporting new research that gives additional reasons that women should quit. The most repeated new messages directed at women in the 1990s emphasized that they should stop smoking before they try to conceive, that mothers should protect their children from smoky areas and secondhand smoke, and that pregnant women ought to avoid others' smoke. Fathers-to-be are also instructed to quit smoking. Reflecting the idea that pregnancy is a twelve-month endeavor, which health care professionals attempted to popularize in the late 1990s, an article on "Planning for Your Next Baby" stresses that "you should change potentially harmful habits, such as drinking alcohol and smoking, and reduce or eliminate caffeine from your diet. By making these changes before you attempt to conceive, you improve your odds of having a healthy baby" (Schwarz 1995, 26). Item four on a January 1991 New Year's list of "ten simple changes that will benefit you and your children" in *Parents* magazine reads: "Quit smoking. Mounting evidence shows that secondhand smoke causes respiratory ailments and, possibly, cancer in children" (Finkelstein 1991, 17). Further, *American Baby* reports that studies show that the babies of nonsmoking pregnant women exposed to environmental tobacco smoke by their partners and coworkers have a higher risk of intrauterine growth retardation, subtle learning and behavior deficits, and possibly some childhood cancers (Schwarz 1996, 8). Pregnant (and prepregnant) women should quit smoking and avoid exposure to others' smoke.

Antismoking advice reflects the outpouring of medical studies on the fetal and infant health hazards associated with smoking during pregnancy, and at times it reflects the general antismoking culture within which it was written. *What to Expect When You're Expecting*, for example, urges pregnant women to remain smoke free by imposing antismoking restraints on themselves modeled on the public antismoking policies that proliferated in the 1990s: "When you were a smoker, you couldn't smoke in a theater, subway, or department store, [or] even in some restaurants. That was that. Now you have to tell yourself that you can't smoke, period. That is that" (Eisenberg et al. 1991, 55). Indeed, the growing antismoking climate and restrictions on where smokers can light up provide constant support for the message that women should not smoke during pregnancy and that they should not be exposed to secondhand smoke.

All pregnancy advice literature now carries warnings about the fetal and infant health risks related to pregnant women's smoking. The dangers of smoking during pregnancy are presented in detail in pregnancy books and magazines, in short lists about "what do do/what not to do" when planning pregnancy and when pregnant, and in articles about pregnancy complications. But the message that smoking is bad for the baby and the negative stigma associated with pregnant smokers are practically inescapable.

In short, social, medical, and political trends influenced the emergence of smoking during pregnancy in the late 1970s as a public health problem. The development of increasingly restrictive antismoking advice for pregnant women since the 1960s reflects not only heightened medical attention to the fetal and infant health risks of smoking during pregnancy but also the success of the antitobacco movement in putting smoking in general on the public health agenda and keeping it in the public eye. Also important is the social context in which women's reproductive decisions became subjects of political and legal debate.

Paternal Smoking as an Emergent Public Health Problem

The issue of paternal smoking has received increased attention from reproductive scientists, medical professionals, and pregnancy advice authors in the early 1990s. The status of paternal smoking as a problem is influenced by scientific assessments of men's reproductive health risks and by gendered assumptions about parenting. Given that only women can be pregnant—they "contribute both genetic material and body-labor to procreation" (Daniels 1999, 90)—it seems logical that research on smoking and fetal health looks more thoroughly at women's smoking during pregnancy than at men's. The assumption that women's health status is primary has eclipsed both scientific and public attention to the effects of men's health practices on fetal well-being. In contrast to the advice women receive about the reproductive health risks of smoking, the messages men receive tend to be far less strict and moralistic. Fathers-to-be who smoke are generally not represented or perceived as bad fathers. Indeed, the wider topic of paternal prenatal lifestyle has not been explored extensively in medical or popular pregnancy literature. The implication is that men's reproductive nature allows them to be less directly accountable for fetal health than are women, an assertion with which many would agree.

However, a growing body of medical data suggests that men's health practices influence fetal health both directly and indirectly to a larger extent than has been previously assumed. Paternal cigarette smoking, along with use of other substances and chemical exposure, is emerging as a public health problem. Perhaps this focus will lift some of the responsibility for fetal health off the shoulders of the mother-to-be; however, it might instead heighten the pregnancy policing of the father-to-be.

Until recently, medical professionals have not paid significant attention to the fetal risks associated with men's health practices, including paternal smoking. Researchers who have explored the effect of smoking by the father-to-be—an effect caused primarily by exposing the pregnant woman to smoke—on fetal and infant health, for example, low birthweight, have not reached uniform conclusions (Eliopoulos et al. 1994; Martinez et al. 1994; Chen and Petitti 1995). Scientific research is also inconclusive about the effects that men's smoking before or around conception has on such male reproductive health issues as decreased sperm quality, impaired motility, and impotence (Rosenberg 1987; U.S. Department of Health and Human Services 1990, 404–409; Brody 1995; Vine 1996a, 1996b).[21] The uncertain nature of the medical evidence, however, is but one reason why the influence of paternal smoking on fetal health has not achieved higher visibility. Until the late 1980s, reproductive scientists assumed that defective sperm (damaged by smoking, drinking, drug use, or occupational toxin exposure) could not successfully penetrate an egg (Daniels 1997, 589). More recent studies, however, have found associations between birth defects and male lifestyle factors as well as occupational and wartime exposure to toxins (see Daniels 1997, 1999).

One reason for the slowness with which scientists have approached paternal health effects on the fetus and for the scant media coverage of research results is that science is strongly influenced by gender myths, feminist scholar Cynthia Daniels (1997) persuasively argues. The idea that only virile sperm succeed in penetration and fertilization of ova has been propagated by scientists who contend that sperm compete with each other in Darwinian fashion so that only the highest quality sperm fertilizes the passively receptive, undiscriminating egg. This virile sperm theory, which reflects cultural assumptions about men and women's gender roles—men are competitive and aggressive; women are passive and receptive (see Martin 1991)—has meant that traditionally, reproductive science did not focus on whether abnormal or damaged sperm could influence fetal health.

Public health professionals contend that the main barriers to obtaining information about fetal harm associated with men's health are strictly scientific. Epidemiological studies are often inconclusive because it is difficult to measure substance exposures, to obtain an adequate number of research participants, and to fully account for factors other than substance exposure that influence men's reproductive health. Daniels points out that these challenges also often face researchers who study women's reproductive health but that scientists recognize the problems differently: "For instance, studies of paternal effects are routinely criticized for not controlling for maternal exposures, while studies on women virtually never control for the exposures of fathers" (1997, 596). As long as the health behaviors of the mother-to-be are seen as having primary responsibility for fetal and infant health, women alone remain culpable when their baby-to-be is not healthy, and research on fathers-to-be remains less urgent. This has been the case with attitudes toward and research on maternal and paternal cigarette smoking.

Public opinion on who is most responsible for fetal health is shaped by media coverage on medical research. In their analysis of the gendered dynamics of news reporting on scientific research, Joan Bertin and Laurie Beck (1996) reveal that regardless of the scientific conclusiveness of the evidence, findings that confirmed social expectations were given front-page coverage and presented more definitively than those that challenged social expectations. Media reports on studies that show an association between paternal health risks and fetal health are in the latter category. Indeed, newspapers rarely carry stories on the paternal–fetal health connection, despite the recent association between birth defects and men's lifestyles. Daniels's survey of nine national daily newspapers between 1985 and 1997 found seventeen stories on the possibility that paternal exposure to hazardous substances influences fetal health: "five on chemical wartime exposures in Vietnam and the Persian Gulf, five on cocaine, four on smoking, two on workplace exposures, and one article covering all causes" (1997, 601). In the same time period, these papers ran more than two hundred stories on pregnant women and cocaine use alone. This imbalance both reflects and supports the public perception that women, not men, are to be held accountable for fetal health.

There is some indication that men's reproductive health will receive greater attention in the future, and concerns raised in the 1990s about smoking by fathers-to-be suggest that paternal smoking is emerging as a public health problem. According to an article in *American Baby* magazine, 1992 marks a turning point in medical awareness of how paternal health practices might affect the baby-to-be (Heins 1992). The article notes that use of alcohol, cigarettes, and certain drugs, along with exposure to lead, radiation, and industrial solvents, has been associated with an increased risk of stillbirth, birth defects, low birthweight, and childhood cancers. But the author, a special consultant to the March of Dimes Birth Defects Foundation, warns that the woman reader should not worry excessively about her partner's exposure to hazards because more data are needed before conclusions can be reached. Using hesitant language, the article states that a man should consider avoiding or limiting smoking and drinking when he and his partner plan to conceive.

Although research on the fetal and infant health consequences of the health behaviors of fathers-to-be is on the rise, in pregnancy advice literature, the moral responsibility of fathers-to-be to protect their babies-to-be is represented unevenly, and advice about the seriousness of men's smoking is contradictory. This contrasts with antismoking messages that uniformly direct mothers-to-be to quit smoking. At one extreme, a 1995 *American Baby* advice column instructs women to be sympathetic toward fathers-to-be who do not quit smoking:

> Q: My baby is due in three weeks, and my husband and I have one big problem we can't seem to resolve. He's a smoker, and I desperately want him to quit before the baby's born. After all I've read about second-hand smoke, it seems like a reasonable request. Am I wrong?

> A: This isn't a matter of right and wrong. But, hard as it is to fathom, it isn't a choice either. Your husband is addicted to cigarettes—and it's one of the toughest of all addictions to break. You might believe that if he cared enough about becoming a father and about you and your baby's health, he would quit. (Stern 1995)

The reasoning offered here, that a man's smoking—immediately identified as a difficult addiction—is neither right nor wrong, is not extended to pregnant women. Smoking by pregnant women, for any reason, is considered wrong. The advice continues: "Smokers smoke as a way to relieve stress, and becoming a father rates high on the stress scale. In other words his smoking is not a reflection of his commitment to you or the baby." While mothers are instructed that they should do everything they can to positively influence fetal health and that their health practices symbolize not only commitment to but also love for the baby-to-be—seen best in the American Lung Association's 1980s national campaign "Because you Love your Baby . . . There's Never been a Better Time to Quit"—fathers receive a different message.

Relying on conventional addiction recovery discourse, the article advises the reader that she must "gently and compassionately" express her desire for her husband to quit and then wait for him to want to quit: "Let him know that he has your complete support if and when he's ready." Stern undercuts the stop smoking strategies relied on by health educators when she contends that criticism, scare tactics, or antismoking pamphlets do not lead a father-to-be to give up smoking. Many of these strategies, however, have been and still are used to encourage pregnant women to quit smoking. Finally, the concerned mother-to-be is informed that she is powerless to control her husband's behavior and is urged to "remember, he's a good person with a bad habit that need not poison your joy and excitement about the new family you're about to become." This advice instructs not only about health but also about gender and marital roles. The pregnant woman should be a compassionate empathizer, gentle supporter, and patient and nondemanding wife. She is assigned the maternal responsibility of protecting the health of her baby-to-be and infant by negotiating "no smoking in your home, in the car, or around the baby."

Not all advice to pregnant women about how to instruct fathers-to-be suggests that women should be understanding or patient. In contrast to the *American Baby* article, *What to Expect* bluntly orders the woman reader to "get your husband to give up illicit drugs and reduce alcohol consumption" before trying to conceive, and to "quit smoking. Both of you" (Eisenberg et al. 1991 [1984], 428). With the same message, a medical researcher flatly asserts, "It's not enough for you not to smoke [when pregnant]. You should try to convince your husband, common-law [partner] or fellow worker not to smoke, or insist that they not smoke, because their smoke gets into the baby" (Koren, quoted in Stolberg 1994). These imperatives are clearly directed at women as the primary caretakers of their husband's and baby-to-be's health. Women who smoke are admonished to demonstrate maternal nurturance by abstaining from cigarettes when pregnant and by taking full responsibility for their baby-to-be's exposure to smoke.

Pregnancy advice directed at men also includes the "no smoking" message. Quitting is mentioned twice in *What to Expect*—in the slim chapter that encourages paternal involvement in pregnancy, "Fathers Are Expectant, Too," and in the section "Feeling Left Out," in which the father-to-be is encouraged to "act pregnant" (Eisenberg et al. 1991 [1984], 413). Further, to relieve his anxiety about the baby-to-be's health, the father-to-be ought to "make certain that [his pregnant partner] abstains from alcohol, drugs, and tobacco. Research shows that you can best help her do this by abstaining yourself, at least when you are with her. If you think this is a big sacrifice, consider all the sacrifices she's making to have your baby" (1991 [1984], 416). The primary concern here is not about men's influence on fetal health but about helping the pregnant partner follow health advice. While the suggestion that men ought to act pregnant may support a shift of some of the burden of responsibility and moral judgment onto men, it also promotes pregnancy policing of mothers-to-be by their partners.

Other antismoking messages specifically target improving the health and social support behaviors of the father-to-be. In 1993, the March of Dimes launched "Men Have Babies, Too," a national health education campaign designed to raise awareness of men's roles in the health of their pregnant partners and babies-to-be. The campaign included literature, a video, and television and radio public service announcements urging men to abstain from smoking, drinking, or drugs and to be supportive of the mother-to-be by encouraging good nutrition, attending prenatal visits with her, and helping with housework. Paternal influence on fetal health, the March of Dimes stressed, is both biological and social, and practicing healthy and supportive behaviors is a responsibility that comes with being a father-to-be. As with the advice that men act pregnant, this campaign sought to draw men into participating in pregnancy in positive ways, but it also indirectly supported men's intimate surveillance of and possible control over pregnant women's actions. This tension seems unavoidable as long as only women can be pregnant.

A 1998 television advertisement for Nicorette gum, a smoking cessation treatment, offers another comment on paternal smoking. The ad features a testimonial by a young, white couple (presumably married) dressed casually in blue jeans. The husband states that they both used Nicorette when they were thinking about having a baby. Appearing embarrassed, his wife admits that she was the heavy smoker and he was the light smoker. The audience learns that the couple has been smoke free for a year and that they are expecting a baby. At this point, the husband jokingly suggests to his wife that they name the baby Nicorette. She apparently rejects this by rolling her eyes. The commercial does not provide information on why this couple feels it was necessary to quit smoking before pregnancy; it simply assumes that viewers are aware that neither women nor men should smoke when they are planning a pregnancy. This is remarkable given that health advice about paternal smoking is not only recent but hesitant. Perhaps the father-to-be's motivation is more closely related to the idea that it is unhealthy for babies and children to be exposed to secondhand smoke. It might even reflect the father-to-be's decision to act pregnant, as *What to Expect When You're Expecting* recommends. In any case, the underlying message in the ad is that both parents-to-be have acted responsibly by planning pregnancy and protecting the health of their baby-to-be and that therefore they can expect a healthy baby.

Offering a more stark example of health education directed at men, Roddy Reid (1997) analyzed television ads sponsored in the 1990s by the California Department of Health Services that warned viewers about secondhand smoke. Reid demonstrates how male smokers of varied racial and ethnic groups and class status are represented as callously threatening the health and lives of their family members. Men are portrayed as aggressors and women, children, and fetuses as victims. One ad features an Asian American husband who smokes at the kitchen table as his pregnant wife sets it.[22] To illustrate that he is to blame for her being affected by his smoke, she coughs violently and smoke pours from her mouth and nose. But in Reid's analysis, this ad also holds the pregnant woman accountable for endangering their baby-to-be. The pregnant woman acts irresponsibly by failing to avoid her husband's smoke and (in keeping with racist stereotypes of Asian American women) is too subservient to her husband. She neither instructs her husband to smoke elsewhere nor leaves the room; thus "she puts her husband's pleasure before her health and that of her fetus" (Reid 1997, 561). This ad implies that the good father does not smoke and that the good mother protects herself and her baby-to-be from it.

Taken together, the antismoking and pregnancy advice of the 1990s points to the emergence of paternal smoking as a serious public health issue. However, the messages directed at fathers-to-be remain uneven, and the scientific data backing the suggestion that men can harm fetal health—particularly by smoking before or around the time of conception—are considered by health professionals to be inconclusive. In comparison with maternal smoking, research on and attention to paternal smoking is in its infancy. This is not to say that increasing evidence of the influence of men's smoking on fetal health can ever lead to medical certainty; health risks, by definition, are uncertain. Regardless, a major implication of the greater emphasis by public health experts on maternal smoking during pregnancy is that women are instructed to assume primary practical, emotional, moral, and even legal responsibility for fetal care. Further, wider social perceptions about the lesser role of men in the health of babies-to-be focus medical and public attention primarily on women's health practices.

Figure 4.1. An antismoking T-shirt distributed by the Maryland Department of Health and Mental Hygiene as part of the "Quit and Be Free!" smoking cessation program, modeled by Kathleen Midgley. (*Photo by Mike Dooley.*)

Chapter 4

Achieving the
Smoke-Free Baby

Over 100,000 Pregnant Women Quit Smoking Each Year. Far more pregnant women quit smoking than any other group of smokers! Why??? Because they have special reasons to quit. Mothers quit to keep themselves healthy during pregnancy and to help the baby be as healthy as possible when it is born.

—State of Maryland Department of Health and
  Mental Hygiene, "Quit and Be Free!" n.d.b

Health Education
and the Problem
of Risk

HEALTH EDUCATION MESSAGES carry both technical and scientific information, such as estimates of the number of pregnant women who quit smoking each year or the risk to fetal health posed by smoking during pregnancy, as well as social expectations and moral judgments about what it means in American society to be a good, healthy mother. The unstated implication in the words of "Quit and Be Free!" published in the late 1980s, is that mothers-to-be who smoke are not doing everything they can to promote their baby-to-be's health. They are not free from cigarettes or from the negative stigma "bad mother." Pregnant women who smoke reject health educators' warnings and undermine the public health goal of achieving "smoke-free babies."

From a health education perspective, knowledge should produce change in women's health behavior; the failure to change risky behavior is a moral problem. Making moral assessments about patients based on whether they comply with health recommendations is embedded in the work of being a health professional (see Trostle 1988). As Martha Balshem (1993) argues in her critical analysis of a cancer prevention program, an underlying assumption in health education is that professionals have moral authority over lay persons because their views are backed by scientific and medical research. Educational campaigns against smoking during pregnancy cite population-level statistics and risk assessments as proof that efforts must be taken to induce pregnant women not to smoke. For health educators, smoking during pregnancy is a serious yet avoidable risk to fetal and infant health and an urgent public health problem that can be eliminated if women follow health professionals' advice.

The basic objective of the health education profession is "to improve the public's health through education" about health risks and how to prevent illness and disease (D'Onofrio 1992, 394). These health specialists, employed by public and private hospitals and government-funded clinics, must vie for professional recognition; negotiate time, space, and authority with doctors and nurses; compete for grants to underwrite their projects; and counsel clients who are often resistant to their messages. Health educators, however, do more than educate. A major part of their work is persuading their pregnant clients that they can and should attempt to control the health of their babies-to-be by making the right lifestyle choices to reduce risks. As one health professional put it, "there's enough information out there—people must take responsibility now."

From the standpoint of public health professionals, individuals who make "healthy choices" contribute to their own health and a greater good—a healthy society. Health educators' warnings about the fetal health risks associated with smoking during pregnancy have a moral authority that stems from their sense of professional duty toward future generations in their campaign to urge women to have smoke-free babies. Campaigns against smoking during pregnancy, according to an American Lung Association pamphlet, ultimately endorse a larger goal: "When [the pregnant smoker] stops smoking, she shows that she wants to raise her baby in a smoke-free world" (American Lung Association 1994, 7).

The problem that health educators encounter is that some women do not perceive the risks of smoking to fetal health to be high enough to warrant quitting smoking and so do not comply with the experts' advice. I argue that health educators' use of risk and statistics in their efforts to motivate pregnant women to quit smoking promotes the assumption that pregnant women should unquestioningly comply with health advice, fails to adequately account for the important social factors that give meaning to risk and risky behaviors in women's lives, and too quickly justifies a negative characterization of pregnant women who smoke.

The Symbolic Power of Naming Smoking during Pregnancy and Its Risks

Before exploring how antismoking messages directed at pregnant women rely on the concept of risk and the language of statistics, it is necessary to consider how health professionals name what they see as the urgent public health problem of smoking during pregnancy and the fetal health risks associated with it. Given the widespread knowledge that smoking during pregnancy can cause fetal harm, it is remarkable that this public health problem has been resistant to any one label. The practice and politics of naming have both symbolic and concrete consequences. As feminist scholar Paula Treichler explains in her analysis of discourses on HIV/AIDS, "In part, the name constructs the illness and helps us make sense of it" (1988, 195; see also 1999; Sontag 1990 [1978, 1989]). When public health professionals name a public health problem, they heighten its visibility and instruct the public to make sense of it in ways defined by health experts. Arguments about the best way to label the interrelated problems of smoking during pregnancy and the adverse fetal and infant health effects associated with smoking during pregnancy reveal the power of categorizing social practices. Labels themselves are not merely reflections of reality but strategies for creating reality. In fact, some health professionals argue that a more specific name for the fetal health effects of smoking would bolster the antismoking message by making the problem more real.

Women who smoke during pregnancy and the possible consequences of their smoking for fetal and infant health have been labeled in varied ways. The two sets of terms emphasize, on the one hand, what health professionals see as the social and moral problem of pregnant women's failure to protect their babies-to-be from the risks of smoking and, on the other, the medical problem of the negative fetal and infant health effects associated with smoking during pregnancy. The nomenclature offers several descriptors for the first problem: women who smoke during pregnancy, pregnant smokers, and smoking moms. Health professionals also use the terms "maternal smoking" or "prenatal smoking." To identify the second problem, some doctors have recommended the term "fetal tobacco syndrome" to describe the effects of smoking on fetal health, but it has never been widely used. This is significant given the pervasiveness of public attention to fetal alcohol syndrome since the late 1970s and to "crack babies" since the 1980s. Why has there been no front-page news about fetal tobacco syndrome (FTS) or nicotine babies? The naming of the smoking-and-pregnancy problem has been contested within public health and medicine, and no consensus has been reached.

Differences in the use of names signal changes in the way public health experts have framed the problems of smoking during pregnancy and the fetal and infant health problems attributed to it. Although labels for the former issue have changed over time, I have found no public discussion of the best term, whereas labels for the latter have been explicitly proposed. An editorial published in the *American Journal of Public Health* in 1978, provocatively titled "The Pregnant Smoker," calls for intensified public health education efforts directed at pregnant women (Fielding and Yankauer 1978a). This article marks the first use of the label "pregnant smoker"; it reappears in the 1980 surgeon general's report (U.S. Department of Health and Human Services 1980, 336). But the term "pregnant smoker" is pejorative because it emphasizes smoking not simply as something a pregnant woman does but as something essential to her identity. By contrast, the label "women who smoke when pregnant" recognizes smoking as but one practice of many in which pregnant women may engage. It is unclear whether this sort of analysis has led to changes in naming women who smoke when pregnant, but the term "pregnant smoker" is absent from the 1990 surgeon general's report. "Women who smoke during pregnancy" or "maternal smoking" take its place (U.S. Department of Health and Human Services 1990, viii). In practice, public health educators and nurses I spoke with occasionally referred to "smoking moms" as a group and to "maternal smoking." These labels juxtapose the act of mothering with the act of smoking, which, from a health perspective, pull in contradictory directions. Moms are expected to exhibit maternal, or nurturing, caring, and protective behavior toward their fetuses and children, while smoking poses a threat to the health and life of the smoker herself and to her baby-to-be and children.

Recently, much of the public health literature on smoking and pregnancy employs the term "prenatal smoking," which parallels popular discourse about women's behavior during the "prenatal period" (see Floyd et al. 1993). But this term is awkward because it directs attention not to the woman's practice but to the effect of smoking on that which is prenatal—the fetus. In comparing the terms "maternal smoking" and "prenatal smoking," we see that the first can be interpreted as a practice that mothers engage in, while the latter implies that the fetus itself is smoking. This connotation may be intentional.

Just as there has not been a consistent label for women who smoke while they are pregnant, there has been no agreement about how to refer to the possible fetal or infant health consequences of prenatal smoking. A 1985 commentary in JAMA argues that FTS ought to be used as a case definition or descriptive diagnostic term (Nieburg et al. 1985).[1] The authors offer four reasons supporting the use of the label FTS: these cases will (1) bring clinicians' attention to these "high-risk pregnancies and children"; (2) allow for more accurate epidemiological study; (3) allow better evaluation of smoking cessation programs; and (4) "finally, the term fetal tobacco syndrome explicitly relates maternal behavior to an adverse outcome of pregnancy and appropriately focuses more public attention on this preventable cause of serious morbidity" (1985, 2998–2999). Interestingly, the first three points are directed at health care professionals, whereas the last point addresses the public. The authors assert that officially naming the condition will convince others of its seriousness and, in fact, its very existence. This parallels the common assumption made in the contemporary public health field that education is the key to changing behavior. Nieburg et al. (1985) contend that application of the concept FTS will educate both health care providers and their clients and thus help end the practice of smoking during pregnancy. Going even farther, Joe Tye of the Health Advocacy Center in California adds another reason for use of the FTS label. Obstetricians who are sued as a result of complications "caused by fetal cigarette poisoning" could use documentation of FTS in their defense (Tye 1986, 863). This points to the interconnectedness of the medical and legal definitions of risk.

The label FTS has not been popular. I encountered only one other reference to it—in a nursing journal (Alexander 1987, 167). It is curious that the term was suggested although not taken up. When I asked Edward Miller, an obstetrician, why he thought the name FTS has not stuck, he gave an explanation based on clinical terms: "It isn't enough of an entity to be a syndrome." As he described it, for a condition to be properly termed a syndrome, a doctor should be able to go to a room full of bassinets and pick out the babies affected, based on either their behavior or appearance. However, he contends that this is not possible with FTS: "If you see 100 babies, you can't pick out the smoking moms." FTS, therefore, is not an appropriate label. For him, the medical argument against introduction of the term outweighs the political argument for it.

Health experts' inability or unwillingness to give this medical problem a name points to competing medical and scientific views about consequences of naming the problem. Those in favor of the FTS label argue that naming will make the problem visible, more easily discussed, and therefore more real. This increased visibility, they imply, will reduce smoking during pregnancy because women will come to see smoking as a serious fetal health problem and make the choice to quit. However, because the FTS label has not been used, health professionals must rely on other ways of stressing the fetal health risks associated with smoking during pregnancy.

One strategy that antitobacco advocates have emphasized to raise awareness of the seriousness of smoking as a health problem is the designation of tobacco and/or nicotine as a drug. The trio of drugs, alcohol, and tobacco is repeated often in public health literature, which works to equate the seriousness of the three. Drug use is generally portrayed as dangerous, unhealthy, illegal, and immoral regardless of pregnancy, and categorizing cigarettes with drugs implies that they too should be seen this way.[2] For example, a pamphlet on women and smoking published by the American College of Obstetricians and Gynecologists relies on the concept of drug addiction as it tells pregnant women that "cigarette smoking is now the most serious and widespread form of addiction. . . . Nicotine is even more addictive than many hard drugs. If you crave cigarettes at least once every thirty minutes, you are addicted. You are dependent on cigarettes" (1991 [1986]). The smoker who reads this and realizes that she has an addiction that is more serious than addiction to "many hard drugs" is not advised to seek professional treatment but instead is instructed to "take responsibility for your smoking habit" and quit.

Antismoking education at the elementary school level may also emphasize that nicotine is a drug. Health educator Liz Kluzinski strongly criticized the insensitive use of this message as an educational tactic, relating this story: "My friend's daughter for three days in a row said she had a stomach ache and couldn't go to school. But her mother saw through this and asked her what was going on at school—why didn't she want to go. This poor little second grader said that the teacher said that all smokers are drug addicts and will die! Her father and her aunt smoked, so the kid was scared to death!" While education about a smoker's risk of death due to lung cancer or heart disease might itself frighten a child, the antismoking message that cigarette smokers are drug addicts can compound the child's fear; criminals, or "bad people," use drugs and are punished if caught. Indeed, children armed with antismoking education might resort to morally patrolling smokers in their homes (figure 4.2).

The notion that smoking is as bad as or worse than using drugs has been marketed not only to the public by health professionals but also to health professionals by their colleagues. Writing in a nursing journal, Linda Alexander argues that "nurses must consider cigarette smoking in pregnancy to be as serious a risk factor to maternal and infant health as drugs and infectious diseases . . . cigarette smoke contains more than 1,000 drugs" (1987, 172). Emphasizing this perspective, Lucy Pratt, a nurse and health educator, described an incident from a seminar she attended on cocaine and babies: "The physician running the session listed all kinds of negative side effects of an unnamed drug—all kinds—it was just amazing. Then she asked us [health educators] in the room, 'What would you do to a pregnant woman who was using this drug?' We all said 'hang her from the nearest tree'! Turns out, that drug was tobacco . . . Cigarettes are extremely dangerous. But because it is a legal drug, people think it is okay. You know, they think, 'well, the government hasn't made it illegal, so it must be okay.'"

This account shows how important naming is to shaping and reshaping the ways people conceptualize health risks, substance use, and punitive solu-

Figure 4.2. Daughter: "You're a weak, pathetic drug addict!!" Mother: "But they're only cigarettes." Daughter: "Whatever." (*I thank Jennifer Hirsch for sending me this postcard. Laird Mark Ehlert/Maid in the Shade.*)

tions to drug-related health problems. The physician's point is that if tobacco is considered a drug (or a combination of many drugs), then health educators and their clients will treat it more seriously. Extending that point further to how the public thinks about cigarettes, Lucy Pratt contends that our cultural understanding of the dangerousness of cigarettes is influenced particularly by the fact that cigarettes are legally sanctioned. In the future, if nicotine were allowed by Congress to be regulated by the Food and Drug Administration or another governmental agency, cigarette smoking might be classified as drug use and pregnant women who smoked criminalized on these grounds.[3] Nicotine addicts and their victimized nicotine babies could capture front-page attention, just as crack addicts and their crack babies did in the late 1980s.

Some antitobacco activists support the view that babies born to smokers themselves are addicted to nicotine. The web page of the advocacy group Action on Smoking and Health (ASH) announced that "newborns [are] passive smokers who suffer from withdrawal" (1997b). ASH reports on a study not cited that found that newborns of pregnant women who smoke "have the same nicotine level as adult smokers, and almost certainly spend the first days of life going through a difficult withdrawal from the addictive drug nicotine. . . . Approximately 15 percent of all pregnant women use cigarettes, and the study suggests that virtually all addict their unborn child to nicotine." What appears to be the same study was reported in the *New York Times* (1997a); the news story includes the following statement from one of the researchers: "The baby of a smoking mother should be considered to be an ex-smoker." The rhetoric used by ASH and quoted in the *New York Times* easily categorizes pregnant women who smoke as pregnant nicotine addicts. This label certainly intensifies the moral stigmatization of women who smoke and heightens the stakes of the symbolic politics of naming this health problem. Although the outcry of public health educators to "hang them from the trees" is overstated, the message is clear: women who smoke when pregnant deserve disciplining because they take a preventable health risk. This conclusion is in line with punitive legal actions that have been taken against pregnant women for drug or alcohol use or for not complying with their doctor's orders.

Even if they believe smoking is a serious issue, health professionals may not see cigarette smoking as a drug-related ("nicotine-delivery") activity. Catherine Woods-Tyler, a physician, thinks that cigarettes are in a group separate from other addictive substances: "If you smoke a quarter or a half pack a day, you probably aren't addicted. And we see differences in how people respond to cigarettes. Some just like the activity, while others are addicted." Trish Jackson, a public health nurse and tobacco control advocate, suggests that new ways of seeing the problem are needed: "The public should see and understand addiction. It is not the person, the smoker, that is the problem; they are the victim. It's sort of like alcohol and drinking now, but the tobacco industry will be in front of this—they can try to look at how the alcohol industry has dealt with it." She rightly points out that the tobacco industry itself is a powerful actor and that it plays an influential role in the politics of naming smoking and smokers.

Threatened by the possibility of bans on nicotine and controls on its profits, the tobacco industry is a main force against the government's classification of nicotine as a drug. Later I discuss the tobacco industry's position in greater depth, but here it is important to note that cigarette advertising is the most visible way that tobacco companies shape our images of smokers. Such advertising is premised on associating cigarettes with positive feelings, attractive body images, and pleasurable social activities (see O'Keefe and Pollay 1996). Cigarette ads actively promote the message that smokers do not look or act like drug addicts.

Health professionals fear that the conflicting portrayals of smokers (as healthy pleasure seekers versus unhealthy addicts) and the lack of specific names for women who smoke during pregnancy or those infants who are negatively affected decrease the power of health professionals' argument that all smokers are unhealthy and that all babies born to women who smoke are at risk of being unhealthy. From their perspective, the fetal health effects of smoking during pregnancy ideally would be identified with a name (like FTS) that would emphasize the seriousness of this public health problem. Given the lack of a publicly recognizable name, health educators must rely on the idea that smoking during pregnancy is a risk to fetal health; this strategy, they fear, does not carry the same sense of urgency.

Meanings of Risk in Public Health

The main message that health educators communicate to the smoking moms they counsel is that the risks of smoking to the health of their babies-to-be are simply too high to take a chance. The only possible good choice is the choice not to smoke. This emphasis on risk prevention is based on a broader ideology that pervades the health education field; risk assessments and warnings are fundamental components of health education messages and public health campaigns. The assumption that individuals should consciously weigh the risks that threaten their health and rationally choose to avoid them is essential to public health efforts (see Neubauer and Pratt 1981; Becker 1986; Lupton 1995). Drawing on the work of social scientists, I analyze risk not as a neutral, statistical calculation that measures the probability of an event or outcome but as a social construction that highlights the authority that health professionals bring to their relationships with clients and that forms social expectations about what constitutes responsible, or moral, living.[4] Risk assessment is a disciplinary technology in that it establishes norms, perpetuates reliance on medical experts, and seeks to motivate individuals to attempt to control risk.

Anthropologist Mary Douglas identifies risk as a "central [Western] cultural construct" in policy making and in individuals' thought, one that symbolizes social understandings of morality and danger (Douglas 1992). In popular usage and political debate, the meanings associated with risk have been extended beyond the probability theory that underlies it: "The risk that is a central concept for our policy debates has not got much to do with probability calculations. . . . the word *risk* now means danger; *high risk* means a lot of danger" (Douglas 1992, 24; original emphasis). But why, then, substitute the term "risk" for "danger"? Douglas suggests that "danger" is less powerful than "risk" in political contests because danger, unlike risk, cannot be measured. In public health, risk is expressed in terms of odds ratios and statistical rates that represent the calculation of the occurrence of disease and the identification of risk factors that may lead to disease. The assessment of risk itself contains a moral imperative to choose to avoid those risks that are subject to individual control.

The importance of the concept of risk in public health reflects a broader cultural obsession with the chances of danger and the desire to control its odds (Hacking 1990, 4) that is fueled by continuous news coverage about potential health hazards (see Nelkin 1989). Health education campaigns, backed by medical research and statistics, often suggest "that almost everything we consume, do, or interact with in our environment is dangerous" (Becker 1986, 18). Sociologist Ulrich Beck (1992, 1994, 1999) argues that pervasive, even incalculable, threats to the environment and an individual's health are associated with late capitalism and globalization. The condition of living with uncertainty in the "world risk society" means that people are "expected to live with a broad variety of different, mutually contradictory, global and personal risks" (1994, 7) and are held accountable for making decisions about risk taking without being able to know what the consequences of these decisions might be (1999, 78). These considerations focus primarily on risks that are external threats, dangers that are imposed upon the individual, not risks that are internal or the result of an individual's lifestyle. Although public health professionals study and issue warnings to the public about both external and internal risks, the latter conceptualization of risk is what Deborah Lupton calls "the mainstay of health promotional activities" (1995, 81).

To counter the ever-present risk of disease and death—to beat or change the statistical odds—health professionals urge the public to exert personal control over risk-taking behaviors that are internal, for example, by abstaining from smoking. Critics of the concept of risk associate the imperative to attempt to control risk with the rise of quantitative assessment as the basis of reasonable decision-making in the face of uncertainty that characterizes Enlightenment thinking (Daston 1988; Hacking 1990; Douglas 1992; Porter 1995). Today, the belief that smoking is unhealthy constitutes the only reasonable position, and smokers are seen as unenlightened risk-takers who knowingly engage in self-destructive behavior, as former Surgeon General Antonia Novello has stated (U.S. Department of Health and Human Services 1990, xii). Her statement reveals the assumption that smoking is a guarantee of a serious disease. The risk taking of smoking itself, because it represents noncompliance with health authorities' advice, is subject to moral censure.

Risk assessments and warnings have particularly significant implications for pregnant women, who are expected to comply with health advice on behalf of their babies-to-be. Risk as a medium through which medical authorities attempt to control pregnant women's actions has a long history. Sociologist Jo Murphy-Lawless documents how risk calculations became central to the management of pregnancy and childbirth by the end of the nineteenth century (1998, 171). In creating a population of pregnant women and establishing statistical norms for how women's bodies should progress through pregnancy, labor, and delivery, the medical profession "ceased to read the *individual body*" (1998, 171; original emphasis). One result of this shift has been the misperception that population-based data can accurately predict an individual's pregnancy outcome (referred to in public health as the ecological fallacy). Arguing this point in her research on medical practitioners' labeling of poor pregnant women as high risk, anthropologist Lisa Handwerker writes that the scientific language of "risk assessment makes it possible to talk about and seemingly control what is in fact an unknown medical event for a specific individual" (1994, 669). In the case of cigarette smoking during pregnancy, antismoking messages employ the language of risk to convince women that their babies-to-be are endangered by smoking and that quitting smoking practically eliminates the possibility of prenatal and infant health problems.

Risk does not only apply to health and medicine, of course; it informs decisions about activities in numerous areas of social life. The concept of risk has been traced from the Italian *risco* as far back as the sixteenth century and has been mainly associated with nineteenth-century development of the insurance business (Ewald 1991, 198). Actuarial rating continues to be based on the estimation of the probability of an occurrence (such as death, theft, or auto accident) associated with measurable characteristics of a group or individual (such as age, residential location, or driving record) (see Stone 1989, 608). Both actuarial science and the public health field of epidemiology, the study of disease patterns in populations, attempt to identify behaviors and characteristics that represent risk factors. Today, insurance companies use epidemiological studies and risk calculations when they screen potential policy holders and set rate premiums.

One epidemiologist goes so far as to suggest that health insurers ought to charge higher rates to policyholders who have so-called modifiable risk factors, such as smoking, drinking, high cholesterol levels, and hypertension (Stokes 1983, 394). Indeed, some health insurance companies, and even automobile insurance companies, charge higher rates for smokers than nonsmokers. While it is clear that health insurers are factoring in the cost of treating smoking-related illnesses, the logic behind the automobile insurers' decision is curious. How does smoking impair one's driving skills: one-handed driving? fire hazard? dirty windshields? The answer is none of these. Statistical studies show that a high proportion of smokers are drinkers, and drinking and driving increases the likelihood of auto accidents (1983, 393). Joseph Stokes argues that a health insurance system that holds individuals accountable for their health choices would work for the good of individuals and for the public good: in the first instance, to "encourage people to take more responsibility for their health," and in the second, "to control the escalating costs of health care" (1983, 395). This logic echoes that of health policy makers and health professionals who assert that individuals' health choices directly influence the nation's fiscal health and moral fitness.

Health policy historically has been influenced, if not directed, by economic concerns. Since social reformers' attempts to improve public health in early nineteenth-century England and the United States, a main political motive underlying health policy is the desire for economic efficiency. This is not to say that health care decision makers do not feel genuine humanitarian concern about helping others avoid illness and suffering; many do.[5] But the emphasis public health officials place on disease prevention stems from the belief that "prevention will save money for the state in the long run" (Stone 1989, 599; see also Lupton 1995).[6] The relationship between individuals' physical health and the nation's fiscal health is revealed when national health care expenditures are represented as the burden of every taxpaying citizen. Reports on the cost of medical care for low-birthweight babies born to women who smoke, for example, imply that the U.S. taxpayer loses if women smoke during pregnancy. In 1985, a medical economist estimated that low-birthweight babies born to women who smoke "cost Americans $152 million a year in medical expenses" (New York Times 1985a), and a 1990 study concluded that for every dollar invested in smoking cessation efforts aimed at pregnant women, about six dollars are saved in neonatal intensive care and long-term care costs for low-birthweight babies (Marks et al. 1990). Further, estimates of neonatal intensive care costs for low-birthweight babies whose mothers smoked cigarettes range from $12,104 to $30,935, resulting in a total annual cost of $164 million to $792 million (see DiFranza and Lew 1995, 389). Citing a much higher figure, an antitobacco advocacy group states that annual health care spending to treat infants for health and developmental problems as a result of maternal smoking or pregnant women exposed to secondhand smoke is $1.4 billion to $4 billion (Campaign for Tobacco Free Kids 1999b; see also Centers for Disease Control and Prevention 1997; Adams and Melvin 1998). These types of calculations—themselves subject, as are all research findings, to political contest—make clear to policy makers and taxpayers a direct link between risk avoidance, disease prevention, and economic efficiency.[7]

Given the pervasiveness of today's "choose a healthy lifestyle" message—from television public service announcements to breakfast cereal boxes—it is surprising that the notion that we ought to analyze our risk factors and modify our health behaviors to prevent disease is quite recent. It was not until the mid-1970s that health professionals turned their attention to individual and group lifestyle factors that place people at risk of illness and death, such as smoking, drinking, high-fat diet, sexual activity, and stress (Crawford 1980; Neubauer and Pratt 1981). This healthist focus on preventing illness and disease drives public health education aimed at providing information with which individuals can assess their risk factors and change those behaviors that put their health at risk.[8] Assessment of one's risks is an important part of the process of health behavior change.

The dominant health education theories assume that individuals are rational actors who make choices based on whether the benefits outweigh the costs of changing a health behavior (see Sobo 1995, 32; Lupton 1995, 56; Yoder 1997). Smoking cessation materials directed at pregnant women, for example, emphasize that the pros of smoking do not outweigh the cons of quitting. Moreover, they focus on the benefits that smokers will receive if they quit smoking: saving money to spend on the baby, giving "the gift of good health to your baby," and having more energy for delivery (Missouri Department of Health n.d.).[9] Health professionals contend that thinking through this dilemma will help motivate the smoker to see that the rational choice is to quit smoking.

Stress on the idea that each person can control her or his health by making rational choices severely limits attention to the relationship between individuals and the social conditions of their lives. Reinforcing the assumption that control over risk is both possible and a moral duty, one health professional explained to anthropologist Lisa Handwerker that pregnant women who are high risk "are responsible for everything. They should be able to control their life circumstances. If they decide to have a baby then it is their responsibility to take care of themselves" (quoted in Handwerker 1994, 671).[10] When health professionals assume this perspective, they fail to consider the ways in which social circumstances and structural factors, such as poverty, racism, domestic violence, and so on, do not allow women to control their lives. Consideration of the socioeconomic conditions of women's lives challenges the notion that each individual can control her health status by choice. Social inequalities, not just individual actions, contribute to or constrain health and well-being.

Health professionals are well aware of the significance of social context and know that an individual's health status is influenced by social and economic structures. For example, the rate of smoking by pregnant women with nine to eleven years of education was 26 percent, while the rate for women with four years or more of college was 2 percent in 1998 (Ventura et al. 2000, 11). But the health education field is based on models that focus on individual behavior change; health educators are directed to target individual behavior, not social inequalities. As Carol D'Onofrio writes, socially conscious public health educators are frustrated with this health education premise: "Since groups at high risk of health problems frequently suffer from societal stigmatization, discrimination, and exploitation, these practitioners are troubled that the field of health education lacks theories to explain the root causes of these problems and to indicate possible ways of preventing or ameliorating them" (1992, 399; see also Freudenberg 1981; Wallerstein and Bernstein 1988; Minkler 1989; Balshem 1993). The imbalanced focus on individual behaviors over social inequalities is but one way in which health education is depoliticized, despite many practitioners' personal dedication to social activism and advocacy (D'Onofrio 1992; Balshem 1993). Several of the health educators with whom I spoke are members of antitobacco advocacy groups that work against the advertising and marketing of cigarettes to women. Such volunteer work allows them to broaden their focus from individuals as targets to what many activists contend is the root of the problem—the tobacco industry. This antitobacco approach is becoming more popular in public health campaigns, yet pregnant women likely will continue to receive antismoking counseling during prenatal visits that focuses on instructing individuals to quit smoking.

Whether speaking directly to smokers or designing antismoking campaigns, health educators and antitobacco advocates face the challenge not only of changing individuals' perceptions about cigarettes but also of criticizing American personal choice ideology. The conflict over enforcement of health risk reduction and the moral judgments that health education messages carry are perhaps most clear on this point. Health professionals want individuals to control their health status by not smoking, yet smokers want to have control over and respect for their own health decisions. Since the 1964 report on smoking and health, the decline of the social acceptability of cigarettes, the growing number of policies about smoke-free environments, and the demonization of the tobacco industry have increased the negative stigma attached to smoking. Establishing policies that limit smokers' access to cigarettes or to smoking areas reflects a public health strategy "to make healthy choices easy choices" (Lumley and Astbury 1989, 247). This carries the assumption that it is reasonable and fair to make unhealthy choices difficult choices. But who should have the power to decide which choices are healthy or unhealthy? In essence, that is the challenge issued on a bumper sticker that threatens: "Harassing me about my smoking may be hazardous to your health."

Whether smoking ought to be respected publicly and morally as a personal choice has been debated at length among antitobacco leaders, public health professionals, and the tobacco industry. In a 1971 television interview, the head of Philip Morris was asked to respond to a study showing that smoking during pregnancy was linked to low birthweight. Having already asserted that cigarettes were not hazardous, he went on to state that "some women would prefer having smaller babies" (Joseph Cullman, cited in Dreyfuss 1996, 47). While this response may appear cavalier, Cullman's impression has some support today.[11] Cullman evaded the morally loaded question of whether smoking harms fetal health by neither denying nor agreeing that cigarette smoking is associated with low birthweight. Instead he stressed the issue of personal choice: pregnant women, like others, deserve the right to choose whether to smoke. This rhetoric appeals to the American ideology, which became particularly popular beginning in the 1960s, that individuals could choose their lifestyles.[12]

In opposition to the "personal choice" argument, pediatrician Mary Ann Cromer remarked in the *New York State Journal of Medicine* that "it is naive to suggest that smoking by a pregnant woman in 1983 is a choice made by an informed adult, when every effort is being made by cigarette companies to undermine knowledge about the adverse effects of smoking on the fetus and on the mother herself" (1983, 1292). Cromer and others contend that the tobacco industry's advertising, marketing, and promotion unfairly represents cigarettes as danger free. Cromer's position supports more vigorous antismoking health education efforts as the key to reducing the rates of smoking during pregnancy. She argues that if pregnant women believe the health risks of smoking, they will choose to quit; this, of course, is not always the case. On the other side of the debate, the tobacco industry continues to posit that no matter the health risks, an adult's choice to smoke should be legally and socially accepted. In the 1980s and 1990s, the industry funded smokers' rights groups to campaign against governmental infringement on the right to smoke cigarettes and, more broadly, against what they saw as attacks on personal freedom (see Gup 1996).

The argument that smoking is a personal choice becomes more complicated when environmental tobacco smoke, smoking during pregnancy, and national health care costs enter the picture. When an individual chooses to smoke a cigarette, according to studies on the health effects of secondhand smoke, she or he creates a dangerous, smoky environment that puts others at risk (U.S. Department of Health and Human Services 1986). This in fact is what some health education campaigns contend happens when a woman smokes during pregnancy: she creates a "smoke-filled womb." Health risk data on secondhand smoke are the basis for campaigns that urge pregnant women not to smoke and for smoke-free workplace and public space policies. Further, the costs of treating smokers and secondhand smokers for tobacco-related illnesses are not only the smoker's burden but society's as well. Indeed, antitobacco advocates who aim to hold the tobacco industry responsible for the costs associated with smoking brought a suit that led to a 1998 legal settlement between forty-six states and the tobacco industry that includes a provision for recovering the medical costs of ill smokers (Meier 1998d). Recent antitobacco campaigns aim to hold tobacco companies morally culpable and financially responsible for their endorsement of a smoker's "choice" and for their role in putting the lives of nonsmokers at risk as a result of secondhand smoke.

Ideological issues about personal choice and the moral responsibilities of citizens to avoid health risks are not always visible on the surface of public health campaigns, yet they underlie health educators' counseling and antismoking efforts. Health educators' work with pregnant women who smoke entails providing women with information about the health risks of smoking, advising them to make the choice to quit smoking in order to reduce the health risks to their babies-to-be, offering resources and encouragement that will help them quit, and providing follow-up support.[13] Health educators' arguments rely on teaching women the best way to perceive health risks and persuading smokers to quit by stressing that reducing health risks is not only a practical but a moral good. The public health approach toward women who smoke during pregnancy has perpetuated these tactics, despite the demonstrable ineffectiveness of challenging individuals' risk perceptions as a method to encourage smoking cessation or other health behavior change.[14]

Medical Knowledge and the Frustrating Uncertainty of Risk

When counseling smoking moms, health educators use the language of statistics and risk as an important tool. Whether in technical terms or translated into the more accessible daily language of chance, health professionals emphasize the prospect of danger to encourage women to modify their behavior. A technical message from a fact sheet for pregnant women on the risks of smoking during pregnancy, reads, "If a woman smokes less than [a] pack a day, the risk of LBW [low birth weight] is 53 percent, but if she smokes more than [a] pack a day, the risk of LBW jumps 130 percent higher. (The LBW rate for nonsmokers is 8.5 percent)" (UCSD Cancer Prevention and Control Unit and the California Department of Health Services n.d.). This appears to suggest that if a woman smokes more than a pack a day, she has a greater than 100 percent chance of having a low-birthweight baby.[15] This description of the risk of low birthweight may not be intuitive; a woman who smokes more than a pack a day has a 69 percent chance of having a low-birthweight baby (130 percent of 53 is about 69). In clearer, less technical terms, a stop smoking workbook for pregnant women tells the reader that "if you keep smoking you will . . . be more likely to miscarry [and] double your chances of having a small, sick baby that weighs 5 1/2 pounds or less" (State of Maryland Department of Health and Mental Hygiene n.d.b, 2). Using both scientific and everyday language, health educators seek to convince women who smoke about the fetal health risks of smoking during pregnancy. In both messages, having what health professionals define as a normal-weight baby is assumed to be a valuable goal in itself. The second message further implies that low birthweight is synonymous with being sick, although this is not always the case.

Statistical language is important to health educators because familiarity with official reports and the data raises a health educator's confidence and ability to converse with physicians and nurses. Based on her work as a health educator, anthropologist Martha Balshem contends that health educators seek professional legitimacy by adopting the worldview of scientific medicine (1993, 66–68). Indeed, in my experience, health educators often cited the conclusions of scientific research in the form of statistical summaries, or they apologized for being unable to do so. Statistics also provide ways of measuring and evaluating progress. The authority of medical science is both expressed through and reinforced by the statistical jargon that pervades the health profession.

Two additional aspects of Balshem's observation are particularly relevant to smoking cessation efforts. First, scientific data and statistical assessments support health educators' position that smoking is a public health problem. Biomedical research offers what health professionals see as ample proof that smoking during pregnancy entails serious health risks to a baby-to-be. Statistics—such as the relative risks of smoking for low birthweight and other conditions, prevalence rates, and measurement of the number of cigarettes a woman consumes—quantify and define the extent and magnitude of the problem in terms that make smoking during pregnancy a real and urgent problem. Second, smoking cessation efforts promote what Balshem calls the central tenet of biomedicine: individuals are responsible for personal health by making "health lifestyle choices" (1993, 5). This assumption underlies the concept of healthism and ignores the context within which individuals live. It further supports the misleading idea that individuals can control their health by reducing risks.

In line with the idea that knowledge of health risks motivates behavioral change, some health educators believe that presenting risk calculations to pregnant women is the most powerful method of informing them of the seriousness of fetal and infant health risks. Clinic counselor Kate Bell-Woodard particularly faulted physicians who do not use their authority to drive home health risk warnings. When I asked how she would improve antismoking messages, she replied, "Doctors need to be tougher on it. The message needs to hit home: 'Here are your risks.'" For Bell-Woodard, the problem does not lie with the uncertainty of the risk warning but with the emphatic delivery of the message.

Health professionals continue to debate which approach to smoking cessation is the most effective. Edward Miller, an obstetrician-gynecologist and medical researcher, believes it is not worthwhile to "get better data to beat on pregnant women with." He recognizes that there is a difference between burdening pregnant women with guilt if they do not quit smoking and positively encouraging pregnant women to make this difficult change. Miller contends that what is needed is greater consideration of the ethical dimensions and effectiveness of persuading, or indeed "beating on," women through the use of strict antismoking messages.

Faced with the problem of repeatedly watching pregnant women fail at quitting, some health educators call for "better" statistics and "more solid" medical scientific evidence to help them present convincing, statistically backed arguments to women who smoke. Maria Baker, a smoking cessation counselor who works for a hospital, asserted that risk statistics, not subjective information, will lead more women to quit. A doctor's simple warning is not enough: "Moms go to the doctor, and the doctor just says 'stop.' Frequently, they aren't given statistical information. Like the doctor uses an 'I know . . . ' [subjective] sort of argument which doesn't carry as much weight versus saying '95 percent of the time.' When educating people, the more statistics, the better." Baker criticizes doctors for not using risk calculations and the authority of medical science to urge pregnant women to change their behaviors. Although she calls for the use of more statistics in health education, what she really wants are stronger statistics. The closer the risk assessment to 100 percent, the more power the risk warning carries, because the higher the probability, the greater the predictive value for an individual case.

Maria Baker and other health practitioners voiced frustration that the authority of statistical and risk-based arguments is not stronger due to the lack of 100 percent proof that a woman's smoking will result in health problems for her baby. Baker continued to explain that for some women, the evidence of their own past experience is stronger than biomedical evidence: "In general, there's not much perception of this being a problem [from the clients' perspective], especially if the woman has already had other children." To counter that message, Baker tells women, "You were lucky that time." She finds this unsatisfying, however, and concludes that "unfortunately, there is so much we don't know—it is like trying to prove the negative case." Although Baker suggests that advances in medical science will make it possible to be better informed about fetal health risks, the problem she points to has less to do with the state of medical knowledge and more with using the concept of risk when counseling an individual pregnant woman.

Along the same lines, Josephine Dieter, also a prenatal health educator in a hospital, expressed frustration over the difficulty of presenting smoking as an uncertain fetal health hazard when she gives antismoking advice to pregnant women: "You also hear 'my mother smoked during hers, and they are fine.' Sad to say, but if they smoke and the baby is not low birthweight, this reinforces their smoking behavior. This sounds terrible, but we should sort of 'want' the baby to be low birthweight so that they'll believe that smoking is harmful. If you can say without a doubt, [the message would] have a better effect. But it is just a risk, and who thinks they'll be the one?" Dieter's sense that women who do not follow smoking cessation advice should have low-birthweight babies as a way to convince them that smoking is dangerous reflects her frustration with the fact that when a woman who smokes has a healthy baby, health educators' warnings are proven wrong. Health educators, of course, do not want babies to be born low birthweight, but they do desire a more powerful antismoking message that will be convincing to all women.

A main difficulty of the health educator's mission is that smoking is a risk to fetal health; by definition, the consequences of smoking are uncertain. Further, as Maria Baker and Josephine Dieter comment, risk assessments are based on the study of a population of pregnant women and cannot predict a medical event for an individual pregnant woman or her baby-to-be. The nature of risk means that health educators cannot present pregnant smokers with guarantees.

In response, health educators have looked for ways to counter the views of pregnant women who emphasize the positive side of uncertainty, or the chance that the baby will not be adversely affected. One way to challenge this optimistic bias has been to stress the idea of control. Advice to pregnant women about reducing the myriad health risks to their babies-to-be promotes the illusion that women can control or limit the risks of fetal death or injury if they follow all the rules. In warnings about the risks of smoking during pregnancy, the explicit or implicit message is that a woman can almost guarantee having a healthy baby by quitting. A Colorado Department of Health pamphlet provides an example of the explicit approach. It reads: "If you quit smoking . . . your baby will grow better; your baby will get more food and oxygen; your baby's lungs will work better; your pregnancy will be healthier; and you and your baby can leave the hospital together" (n.d.). The proposed contract

between health educator and pregnant patient represented here—"quit smoking like we say you should and you'll bring home a healthy baby"—cannot be
made. Quitting smoking does not ensure that a woman will have a baby that
is healthy enough to avoid an extended hospital stay. The message is misleading, as the health educators I talked to would admit. They clearly know, and
find their work confronted by, the reality that quitting does not reduce to zero
the risks to fetal health associated with smoking. Indeed, more commonly, antismoking messages are worded carefully so as not to state that quitting smoking will ensure a baby's good health. The dominant message is that quitting
reduces fetal and infant health risks, as illustrated in a March of Dimes pamphlet that tells the reader, "Your baby is more likely to be born healthy [if
you quit smoking]" (1994b, 2).

When they deliver this type of risk message, health educators face the
problem mentioned earlier—that some women contest the idea that their
babies-to-be are subject to the same risk assessments as other women's babies.
Women who calculate risk in an optimistic way tend to know (or to be)
women who have smoked during pregnancy and who have had healthy babies. In response, health educators resort to explaining that if a woman smokes
when she is pregnant and does not have a low-birthweight baby, it is only
luck. As Constance Nathanson's critical analysis (1991) of teenage pregnancy
shows, family planning nurses take a similar stance: a teenager who forgets to
take an oral contraceptive or who rejects contraception is considered lucky if
she has sex yet avoids pregnancy. Similarly, E. J. Sobo (1995) demonstrates
the extreme differences between safe-sex educators' and low-income black
women's perceptions about the risks of HIV transmission in sexual relationships with men. From the health education perspective, a woman who takes
these reproductive chances (smoking when pregnant, failing to use contraception, or practicing unsafe sex) is irrational because she does not attempt
to completely avoid the risk of an unwanted outcome. Therefore, she is labeled irresponsible (Nathanson 1991, 177; see also Luker 1978). Health professionals are trained to avoid recognizing the positive chances, for example,
that a smoker may have a healthy baby, that a woman may not conceive even
if she forgets her pills, and that a woman may have unprotected sex yet remain HIV negative. Their goal is to teach women to interpret risk the same
way that they do, and to convince women to act to eliminate entirely the
risks of unhealthy or undesirable outcomes. Of course, health educators know
that a risk-free status is unattainable, but striving to attain it becomes a moral
good in itself.

Health professionals' bias toward focusing on the negative risks of smoking during pregnancy is seen clearly in a *Nurse's Guide* for smoking cessation

counselors. The *Guide* offers suggestions for convincing a pregnant woman who smokes to focus on the probability that she will be unlucky, regardless of her previous experience or the experience of friends. It cues the health educator to explain the concept of risk in everyday language: "Sometimes [smoking] causes big problems and sometimes only small ones (e.g., reduced weight gain of 200 grams). This is an issue of odds, like gambling. Smoking doubles the odds against you [for low birthweight]. You (your friend) were lucky last time. The problem is we don't know if you will be so lucky this time. Your best bet is to quit" (State of Maryland Department of Health and Mental Hygiene n.d.a, ix).

This sort of message does not offer statistics on the risks of fetal and infant health problems and emphasizes that smokers who give birth to healthy babies are simply lucky. It also contains thinly veiled moral judgments. Gambling itself carries negative connotations, and gambling with your child's health is simply inexcusable.

Nancy Edwards, who conducts smoking cessation counseling at a rural clinic where she estimates that 60 percent of the obstetric and gynecology clients are smokers, uses the gambling metaphor when counseling pregnant smokers. When I asked her what she generally said to a woman who already had a healthy child and smoked during that pregnancy, she responded: "It's like Russian roulette. You just don't know. I ask them 'Do you want to take that chance?'" Using the same metaphor even more graphically, Jayne Dunn, a nurse at a rural maternity clinic, explained that she tells women who smoke that it is "like putting a gun to your head when you don't know if it's loaded. Do you want to take a chance with your baby like that?" It is not difficult to extend this image to one of a pregnant woman putting a gun to her baby's head, certainly a disturbing image. The Russian roulette metaphor is particularly severe because it implies that a woman makes life or death choices when she smokes. This stark opposition emphasizes the extreme end of health messages about smoking during pregnancy: fetal or infant death. The Russian roulette warning lacks health information and falls back on the moral argument that avoiding health risks is part of being a good mother-to-be.

In keeping with the idea that good mothers-to-be take all steps to protect the health of their fetuses, health education messages primarily—often solely—emphasize quitting, not cutting down on, smoking. The American Lung Association instructs that "the only way to really protect your unborn baby is to quit" and offers a confusing statement on risk reduction: "Cutting down is better than doing nothing but it may not make things much better for the baby" (1994, 3). Cutting down on smoking is evaluated as "good, but not good enough" because it fails to "really" reduce health risks to the baby-to-be; it is dismissed as a viable option. Only the greatest amount of control over risk—quitting smoking—is condoned.

In short, health educators attempt to teach women to view smoking from the health educators' biomedical perspective, supporting their arguments with moral appeals. The logic behind their health risk messages relies on the assumption that if risks are understood, individuals will emphasize the negative possibilities of risk taking and will rationally act to change their smoking practices. However, health educators find that often this is not the case. National statistics indicate that 12.9 percent of all pregnant women reported smoking in 1998; this rate was down by a substantial 35 percent from 1989 (Ventura et al. 2000, 10–11). Given the pervasiveness of the message that pregnant women should not smoke, the women who continue to smoke are likely well aware that smoking involves possible health risks to the baby-to-be. Knowledge, health professionals realize only too well, does not always lead to behavioral change. The perpetual recourse to the "stop smoking for your baby" argument serves less as an educational device used to inform pregnant women about risks than as a moral imperative used to separate good mothers from bad mothers. In the absence of medical guarantees that healthy lifestyles will ensure healthy babies, medical practitioners fall back on the moral argument that it is good to avoid health risks. For health educators, armed with the latest data on smoking during pregnancy and health risks, a woman's failure to control the uncertainty inherent in pregnancy is subject to escalating medical and social disapproval.

Health Educators Voice Uncertainty about Statistical Knowledge

In addition to using risk statistics when they counsel pregnant smokers, health educators rely on the statistical measurement of smoking rates to understand the extent of the problem of smoking during pregnancy and to determine how many fetuses are at risk. Notably, smoking during pregnancy may not continue to be seen as a priority public health problem if national statistics continue to show decreased rates of pregnant smokers. The Public Health Service's national objective for the year 2000 was to decrease the rate of pregnant smokers to 10 percent (U.S. Department of Health and Human Services 1991, 95). The most recent national data showing that 12.9 percent of pregnant women smoked in 1998 seem cause for optimism that the goal will be reached (Ventura et al. 2000). However, even if the year 2000 goal were met, the health educators I talked with would not celebrate a victory over the public health problem of smoking during pregnancy.

This pessimism is not only because they want that remaining 10 percent to quit but also because in their communities, the rates of smoking by pregnant women are much higher than the national average for pregnant women. This leads health educators to question the accuracy of some health statistics, including prevalence rates, while at the same time uncritically accepting others, such as calculations of the risks of fetal health problems associated with maternal smoking.[16]

Indeed, the health educators I spoke with believed that official statistics underreported the rates of smoking during pregnancy. While leading a training session at a rural Maryland health department, Anne Dewitt paused as she put up an overhead projection filled with the state's official statistics. She scanned the small audience of smoking cessation counselors (all women) and warned, "As you all know, the data don't always reflect the truth."[17] Smiles, laughter, and nods indicated a consensus in the room. According to the data, 19 to 22 percent of women who attend public clinics in Baltimore smoke throughout pregnancy. But Dewitt contends that the rate is actually around 80 percent.

The reason for this enormous inaccuracy, Dewitt hypothesizes, is that there are high rates of nondisclosure because pregnant women are aware that smoking is highly stigmatized. Women's reluctance to admit that they smoke, particularly after smoking cessation counseling, is verified by clinical studies (Kendrick et al. 1995; Mullen et al. 1991), by clinic staff observations ("Some come in smelling like smoke and say they've quit. We'll watch them get into their cars and light up—even though 'quit' is in their charts"), and by a number of women who told me that they lied to doctors or nurses about smoking. Dewitt went on to provide an insightful cultural-economic analysis, positing that the official statistical data may be more accurate in smaller towns or counties, particularly in tobacco-growing areas, where women are more willing to identify themselves as smokers.[18] Experts on smoking during pregnancy are concerned about the ways the growing stigma against smoking during pregnancy is influencing statistics and their ability to do research on the subject (see Ventura 1999). Health researcher Patricia Dolan Mullen has noted that "pregnant women's rate of non-disclosure about smoking has skyrocketed," making it difficult for researchers to find pregnant women who smoke to participate in research that evaluates the effectiveness of smoking cessation programs (Mullen 1999).

Anne Dewitt's introductory, "as you all know, the data don't always reflect the truth," and concluding statements, "regardless of the numbers, we all know smoking is a problem," imply that statistics are not the best indicators of the extent of a problem; rather, observation and experience are. Indeed, it is health educators who have contact with women who smoke, not

statisticians. They are at the front lines, where they see low-birthweight babies who are sick, console women who experience pregnancy loss, and visit
grieving families in their homes after an infant has died of sudden infant death
syndrome. Health educators associate these and other "pregnancy outcomes"
with smoking during pregnancy.

For health educators, the most important way that standard quantitative
understandings of smoking are called into question is through their personal
contact with clients. Health education practitioners have their own version
of the relative risks of smoking, and these differ from the relative risks calcu-
lated by medical scientists or epidemiologists.[19] Scientists attempt to isolate
smoking during pregnancy from other prenatal risk factors to estimate the
chance of specific pregnancy outcomes, yet they cannot adequately account
for the less easily measured risk factors in women's lives that also influence
fetal health, such as stress and social support (see Oakley 1992). Epidemiologists may conclude that living in a white working-class or low-income neighborhood or household is statistically associated with women's smoking, but
they cannot explain why this pattern exists. By contrast, health educators can
offer socially based explanations because, through relationships that develop
over time and through home visits, they learn about the place of cigarettes in
the social context of women's lives. They also are aware of the logic used by
women who smoke when pregnant. Josephine Dieter, a health educator, noted
that "women aren't always ready to do all the things you should. They say 'I
gave up alcohol,' or whatever, so they think cigarettes are okay." Although
Dieter does not agree with this justification for continuing to smoke, she re-
frains from blaming women who make this judgment. She believes that the
real problem is the addictive nature of nicotine.

Other health educators offered different explanations of why women
smoke during pregnancy. Janice Walinski, who does smoking cessation education in a tobacco-growing region of Maryland, observed that women who
smoke have a number of risks to contend with. She was more judgmental than
Dieter, adding that some women simply do not care about their babies' health:
"Women don't see smoking as a major risk because of all the other risks in
their lives: drugs, alcohol, low income, housing. It is difficult to get them to
see smoking as an important risk. They all know it is a health problem and
that it affects the baby, but they have other overwhelming issues in their lives.
Or they just don't care. . . . I think it's due to education; many just have a
high school education."

Numerous other health educators stated that in their experience, lower
class and educational status strongly influence pregnant women's smoking.[20]
Vivian Lemay, a community health worker and nurse, believes that cigarette

smoking is a major problem in a working-class white neighborhood in Baltimore in which she does outreach and community health education. She finds that about 80 percent of women in the neighborhood smoke (which correlates with Anne Dewitt's estimate) and that most continue to smoke throughout pregnancy. This high percentage is a result of the pervasiveness of smoking in the women's families and households: "They can't get away from it, and they start young." Penny Rutherford, a nurse, argues that smoking is the number one prenatal health risk at the rural prenatal clinic where she works. She figured that "half, no, actually three-quarters" of the clinic's patients smoke. She figures too that despite counseling and education programs on the health risks and the expense of smoking, it is too much to expect many women to quit: "that logic just doesn't work for them. . . . Maybe I'm just too much of a cynic," she admits, "but I just don't think you can change someone's whole life for the nine months [of pregnancy]." Her remark suggests that many low-income pregnant women lead such "high-risk" lives that changing just one aspect, such as smoking, does not sizably reduce their overall health risk status.

Rutherford went on to sketch the importance of smoking in the lives of the women she encounters. The vast majority are low income (75 to 80 percent of the clinic clients received state medical assistance) and have partners who smoke, or they come from families and households in which everyone smokes. They hang out in bars and restaurants that are smoky, so their social time is spent around cigarettes. Rutherford finds it ironic and distressing that some women come to the clinic because they are concerned that "working at the factory down the road is dangerous to the baby due to the chemicals there, but then they'll smoke two packs a day without even thinking about it." She realizes that the motivation for women's fears about the fetal health risks related to factory work is not merely scientific; women want medical leave from their jobs so that they can receive pay without working. "But still, the logic is contradictory," Rutherford concludes. When I asked her what her clients would say to that, she predicted they would give her the often-repeated claim that "they smoked during the last pregnancy, and it was fine, or that their mother, or girlfriend, or sister did."

Penny Rutherford's relative risk calculation differs greatly from that of some of the pregnant women she counsels. She is aware that for some women, quitting smoking would change their whole life, or conversely, that their whole life would have to change to make it possible for them to quit. A woman's ability to quit is seriously challenged if she lives within a context in which smoking is part of daily life—which increasingly means lower socioeconomic communities and households. This observation points to a perception posited not only by Penny Rutherford but by other health educators—that smokers' culture and ways of thinking differ from those of nonsmokers. Nonsmokers think and act "logically" about health risks or understand and accept health educators' rational, biomedical advice. Smokers simply do not. The not-so-subtle subtext about quitting smoking is about class: a woman can move out of the smokers' culture by thinking and acting like a middle-class nonsmoker. Health educators' ideas about healthy lifestyles reflect and reinforce healthist, middle-class norms.

Like the health educators, a medical researcher with whom I spoke considered smoking to be a problem embedded not only in an individual's lifestyle but also in the high-risk subculture of smoking. Anne Charlton argues that a circle or cycle of disadvantage is activated when a woman smokes during pregnancy (1996, 90).[20] First, a child's experiences in utero direct his or her future life and health. Low birthweight and short stature are "likely to affect children's self-esteem and impede their social development," and having a smaller head circumference indicates that a child's brain growth, and thus her or his intelligence and social skills, may be limited (1996, 97). Additional environmental factors assault the child of a woman who smokes. Charlton assumes that the baby's father also smokes; she argues that growing up in a smoking family means that the child is exposed to secondhand smoke and therefore prone to respiratory illnesses. Due to illness, the child repeatedly misses school. The depressing narrative continues:

> Motivation falls if the continuity of learning is frequently broken. It becomes difficult to keep up with the rest of the class, self-esteem or self-perception falls in this domain. It is well-known that those children who underachieve, who are "fed up" with school and who place little value on academic progress are the most likely to take up smoking. . . . Another link is then forged in the chain. . . . Not only has the children's health been harmed, they are now on their way to damaging their own health further. . . . The health effects as well as the family norms have conspired to make the "at risk" children more likely to be smokers. They leave [drop out of] school as early as possible, having failed to achieve their maximum potential, and they are likely to have early pregnancies. There is evidence that younger women with a lower educational attainment, working in unskilled jobs are most likely to smoke during pregnancy, as are their male partners. Thus the cycle is continued to the next generation of children. The "family circle" is complete. (1996, 99,102)

Charlton paints a picture of an underclass, at-risk smoking culture that perpetuates a series of social ills that threaten the nation's health: high health care costs for repeatedly sick children, low educational attainment, low-paying jobs, and teen parenting. By this account, an individual pregnant woman's decision to smoke—not unemployment, poor public education, or social inequalities such as classism and racism—is a major factor in the continuation of class inequalities and health-related social problems. Further, Charlton disregards the experience of previous generations, in which women smoked during pregnancy without knowledge of possible risks to fetal health; it is unclear whether the cycle existed during past decades, and if not, why not.[21]

A popular answer to this question in health education, and suggested earlier by Penny Rutherford, is that many people in low-income and disadvantaged communities do not make rational health choices in response to risk warnings. E. J. Sobo's research on why low-income, urban black women reject safer-sex, HIV-prevention messages points to women's perception that HIV is transmissible in so many ways (including condom failure, emergency blood transfusion, and purposeful exposure by an HIV-positive person) that attempts to avoid HIV risks are futile. The safer-sex health education message does little to address this conclusion. Martha Balshem (1991, 1993), in her ethnography on health education about cancer risks in a working-class Philadelphia neighborhood, analyzes how so-called working-class fatalism becomes part of the disease that health educators must fight. The fatalist ideology that the course of future events is beyond personal control provides Tannerstowners with justification for their disbelief that certain behaviors cause cancer. Some of the women I spoke with share this view. Anastasia Powers, a low-income woman who has two young children, complained that "some woman from the Health Department smoking class" told her to quit. Powers's reply? "If God's gonna let something happen, it will." The smoking cessation educator's guidebook does not provide a response to this resistance; fatalism confounds the rational-belief basis of antismoking messages.

Health educators' belief that women who smoke hold misplaced hope for the chance that a baby will be born healthy is related to this sort of fatalism. Although they may not directly tell clients to avoid fatalistic thinking, health educators urge women to change the way that they calculate the relative risks of smoking. Health practitioners judge smoking to be a very high-risk activity and view it as preventable, whereas many women who smoke evaluate it as one of a great number of everyday risks and one that they choose to assume. Put simply, from the health educator's point of view, smokers' risk perceptions as well as the sociocultural contexts of their lives are in need of treatment.

Health care professionals' contact with women from varied class and social contexts allows them to compare risk perceptions, challenging them to be flexible in their assessments of how important the risk of smoking is. Theresa

Stephens, a nurse-midwife, contrasted the health concerns of those she called her professional clients with the concerns of her low-income clients. In the preconception health classes she teaches, Stephens presents information on environmental risks, exercise, diet, and vitamins. Although she also discusses smoking, "most of the people who attend are healthy—or, if they are smokers, they aren't telling us that." (From her standpoint, smoking automatically means that one is unhealthy, a contention many smokers would challenge.) The preconception class participants tend to be middle-class professional couples, "the sort of people who have resources and seek out information." But in her midwifery practice, Stephens meets a number of low-income women for whom smoking cessation is not always the first treatment priority. Stephens refers women who are drug users, for example, to another clinic for substance abuse treatment where they generally do not deal with smoking. As she puts it, "you can only tackle so many things at once." Toni Fielder, an addiction counselor, verified that "in an addiction [treatment] environment, smoking is low on the priority list"; a physician, Louise Martinez-Cooper, echoed: "If women are also using drugs, who's gonna say 'don't smoke' first? No one."[22] The fact that health professionals' definitions of the seriousness of smoking during pregnancy compared with other fetal health risks vary emphasizes the contested nature of the concept of risk and risk perceptions.[23]

There is a distinct contradiction between health experts' use of their own experience to counter the supposed authority of official statistics and these same experts' dismissal of their clients' arguments about the seriousness of the fetal health risks of smoking based on their clients' personal experience. Competition between focusing on the negative risk that a smoker's baby-to-be will be unhealthy (health practitioners) versus the positive chance that it will be unharmed (pregnant clients) is a struggle over differing risk perceptions and interpretations of risk taking. Health educators study the scientific evidence of health risks and see low-birthweight babies, born to women who smoked during pregnancy, who are sick; they conclude that smoking is a negative occurrence that should be prevented. Clients have known women who smoked when pregnant yet who have had healthy babies, or clients do not see low birthweight itself as undesirable because "it runs in the family," or a smaller baby is "cuter," or a small baby is less painful to deliver (see Rajan and Oakley 1990). A comment by a midwife serves as an apt health professional's counterpoint to a smoker's assertion that "my mother smoked and I'm okay: . . . You know, I've just seen enough really low-birthweight babies to worry about something like this." Many women who smoke do not share this experience, or at least they do not share this conclusion.

The work of health educators combines instructing pregnant women on

why and how to quit smoking, using arguments based on inherently impre-
cise risk assessments, and making moral judgments of women if they do not
heed the warnings and quit. Health educators assess both the strength of the
data that point to smoking during pregnancy as a serious health risk and the
character of the pregnant smokers they counsel. Those women who do not
quit are seen as irrationally putting their babies-to-be at risk and therefore
are judged irresponsible mothers. But taking into account the contexts of
women's lives calls into question the value of health educators' focus on changing an individual's "rational thinking" processes.

	What Do They Know
Chapter 5	That We Don't?

Women Respond to Experts' Warnings about Smoking during Pregnancy

THIS CHAPTER OFFERS a rejoinder to the experts' warnings about the health risks of maternal smoking by considering women's assessments of and responses to these warnings. Pregnant women's understandings of fetal health risks in part reflect their relationships with medical authority. That women when discussing their experience of pregnancy often commented on the advice or predictions of health experts, whom they frequently referred to as "They,"[1] highlights what scholars have found about the powerful place of medical authority in women's reproductive lives: women experience pregnancy and childbirth as a period of more frequent medical contact, and often as a time of increased social control.[2]

The women with whom I spoke held diverse attitudes toward medical knowledge and experts' health warnings. Some found experts reassuring. Katherine Shaffer, for example, recalled worrying about miscarriage in the eighth month of her second pregnancy: "I fell while running down the sidewalk after my three-year-old and went to the emergency room. But They said the baby was all right." Others challenged the authority and knowledge of health professionals: "They said that she'd be small, but They were wrong," Sarah Leigh Snyder announced proudly. Most commonly, pregnant women maintained a complicated relationship with health practitioners' expert knowledge, simultaneously relying on and rejecting different areas of health expertise. This is indeed the case for smokers and nonsmokers alike and for their views on expert advice about quitting smoking and avoiding secondhand smoke during pregnancy.

A dominant theme in many women's remarks points to what I have shown health educators are concerned about: the inevitable incompleteness of expert knowledge and the uncertainty inherent in warnings about health risks. Even those who generally respect medical authority were well aware of and dissatisfied with how much medical professionals did not know. Rita Shaw cited a list of things she would "like more evidence on," including, "Do I need to deliver in a hospital? Is an episiotomy necessary? How much coffee can I still drink without worrying? What are the risks of having so many sonograms?" When considering the things they would have liked more information about, many women summed up with "I guess they just don't know." Some ended this statement with "yet," implying that medical science has the power to eventually know all. These comments point to two types of concerns: the desire to predict with certainty "what will happen to my baby-to-be if I fail to follow all health advice," and the lack of definitive medical knowledge about pregnancy-related health concerns.

Women who smoke during pregnancy form their perspectives on the potential harms of smoking for fetal health while knowing, just as health professionals do, that there is no medical "100 percent proof" that smoking causes infant health problems. As health educators noted with frustration in the previous chapter, pregnant smokers rely on their own experiences of beating the odds to show that antismoking advice and fetal health warnings are wrong.[3] Additional evidence from medical research will not change the ability of health professionals or women themselves to predict with certainty the health of an individual baby-to-be because the concept of risk inherently entails uncertainty.

The uncertain nature of health risk warnings about prenatal health problems leads some women to discount or reject scientific and medical knowledge and authority, whereas others are inclined to accept it. This has to do not only with their general attitudes toward health authority, but also with the circumstances of their lives. Like health educators, pregnant women calculate relative risks by making comparisons between risk-taking activities. Smokers and nonsmokers alike mentioned cigarettes, alcohol, and drugs (some added vigorous exercise and lifting or carrying heavy things) as things that all pregnant women know they should avoid. In their day-to-day decisions, however, women make practical, not ideal, determinations about what they should do for the baby-to-be and for themselves.

Contrary to the assumption promoted by the maternal–fetal conflict model of pregnancy and by pregnancy advice literature, failure to heed all health warnings does not automatically signal a woman's lack of caring about her baby-to-be. Women often rely on their own authoritative knowledge or embodied knowledge, gained from their experiences and the stories of others, when making health decisions during pregnancy.[4] This sort of knowledge is knowledge that counts for these women, even if it contradicts the advice they receive from medical professionals.

Drawing on feminist scholars' ethnographic research on the meaning of women's smoking, I argue that an analysis of pregnant women's risk assessments and health decisions that takes into account the complexities of their lives and perceptions reveals the inadequacy of judging mothers-to-be only on whether they comply with health experts' advice.

Assessing, Interpreting, and Acting on Warnings about Smoking

Despite the fact that health professionals identified smoking during pregnancy as an urgent public health problem in the late 1970s, women continue to hold varied interpretations of the seriousness of the fetal health risks of smoking during pregnancy and the moral meaning of pregnant women's smoking. Even so, few women offered interpretations of smoking and health risks that went beyond the bounds of medical knowledge. One folk interpretation, however, turned conventional advice on its head: smoking during pregnancy is beneficial because it "strengthens the baby's lungs." Sarah Leigh Snyder's mother, whom she called "a dragon lady" because she smokes so much, smoked cigarettes during both of her pregnancies. Sarah Leigh criticized her mother's interpretation of the risks of smoking while pregnant: "She says we came out fine. But I was preemie—due in February and came in November, so really it wasn't fine. She says I wouldn't have survived if she hadn't smoked; it made me stronger!" Sarah Leigh rolled her eyes, dismissing her mother's logic.

Later in my research, I overheard a medical student informally tell a similar story to a group of students: a pregnant woman at a university hospital had told him that she smoked to make the baby's lungs stronger. Hearing this, a few listeners gasped, and one argued that she thought some people really did not know that smoking during pregnancy is a risk factor. The subject quickly became a joke as a second medical student offered the hypothetical situation that "the baby'd come out with defects and malformed, but at least its lungs would be strong!" This "logical" outcome provoked laughter all around. The reaction of Sarah Leigh Snyder and these medical students suggests that the idea that smoking could be beneficial to a baby-to-be is too far fetched to be believable. Indeed, the constant presence of antismoking messages seems to prohibit this interpretation.

The ways in which smokers and nonsmokers discussed the health risks of smoking during and after pregnancy reflected their awareness of antismoking warnings, particularly those about the risks of low birthweight, miscarriage, and smoking near infants. Their comments also revealed that knowledge of and confidence in health messages do not necessarily lead to behavioral change. This challenges a fundamental aspect of the models of health behavior change that are used in health education, which predict that an individual's knowledge of health risks will motivate the rational choice to comply with health advice (see Yoder 1997). It is not the case that all women who smoke during pregnancy outright reject or fundamentally disbelieve health warnings, although some do. Many women expressed the view that quitting, cutting down, or switching to "light" cigarettes during pregnancy was a good idea.[5]

Those pregnant women who attempted to follow health professionals' recommendations to stop smoking described quitting in various ways, from it being a simple task to an extremely difficult one. Susan Donahue explained that she quit smoking when she found out she was pregnant: "Cold turkey. Easy. I smoked maybe six the entire pregnancy." Sondra Thorton also found it easy to quit, "I knew before going to the doctor that you shouldn't smoke while pregnant. Quitting wasn't hard though because I found that when I was pregnant it didn't taste right." However, Amy Bellinger's comments reveal a different experience: "My second pregnancy was rough [due to her conflicted relationship with the baby-to-be's father]. . . . I smoked then. I couldn't quit. I stopped three months before the end though." Unlike these smokers, Andrea Sellers, despite her concern that smoking might mean that her "baby'd be small, premature, or maybe have asthma," disregarded health professionals' advice to quit. She limited the amount of cigarettes she smoked to a pack a day or less (more if she was upset) during each of her four pregnancies. Further, the pamphlets her doctor gave her on secondhand smoke worried her. After she had her first baby, she decided to smoke at home only with the windows open and did not like it when people smoked while they held her baby.

In sum, each of these women assessed antismoking warnings in ways that motivated them to change their smoking practices. But none complied fully with the dominant message of antismoking advice—that every woman should stop smoking before becoming pregnant, refrain from smoking at all during pregnancy, and ensure that her infant is not exposed to secondhand smoke. Further, contrary to the moral messages embedded in antismoking advice, there is no correlation between full compliance and caring. Women who fail to fulfill the demands of public health recommendations as well as those who do not express concern about the health of their babies-to-be.

Carol Zimmerman pointed out the contradiction between what she feels she should do based on health advice and how she acts. Carol quit smoking intermittently during pregnancy but could not stop completely; then she went back to smoking after her daughter was born. She explained, "My daughter got alotta ear infections when she was six months old, and then they said smoking could lead to—not cause—ear infections. So when she was six or seven months old, I tried to smoke outside, unless it was cold or something. But you know [raising her voice], I smoked and stopped when I was pregnant. I knew it wasn't good for the baby. That's what I don't understand about myself. Why can't I quit now when I could quit then? I know it's still bad for her!" Carol expects herself to quit smoking for the good of her child's health, and she agrees with her pediatrician that she should not smoke in the house, even if smoking led to but did not actually cause her daughter's ear infections. But she has been unable to follow fully the health advice she believes. Again, in contrast to the representation of mothers who smoke as uncaring, Carol's attempts to avoid smoking around her infant and her effort to quit smoking during pregnancy demonstrate care for her daughter's health.

Another woman's interpretation of the information she had about fetal health risks reflects that she associated being a good mother with following health recommendations. However, she used pregnancy advice in an intentionally subversive way not intended by health professionals. Sixteen-year-old Sarah Leigh Snyder recounted, "I didn't do any smoking or drinking with the first. I was so worried; I wanted to be a good mother. With the second, at two months, I knew I was pregnant, but up to five months I smoked, drank, took drugs. I wasn't sure if I'd keep it or have an abortion." Sarah Leigh explained that she felt extreme family pressure to continue the pregnancy: "They said they'd disown me if I had an abortion." Reflecting back on that time, she confided that she did "all those things you're not supposed to do" because she thought maybe she would cause a miscarriage. In that case, she would not have been to blame because losing the pregnancy would have been an act of nature, not the result of an abortion. I asked Sarah Leigh whether her doctors said anything about "things going wrong." "Just maybe low birthweight—but she wasn't!" she answered smiling proudly, "And now I love her so." Although she purposely enacted bad mothering early in her pregnancy, Sarah Leigh was able to escape being labeled by health practitioners and others as a bad mother because her daughter was healthy.

Given the limits on her power over pregnancy—her decision to have an abortion required parental or court permission—Sarah Leigh used her knowledge of prenatal health messages to try to "naturally" end her unwanted pregnancy. Sarah Leigh's logic confounds the assumption underlying prenatal health messages: women should use their medical knowledge to protect the health of their babies-to-be. Her situation also illustrates that pregnant women do not always have the control over their reproductive lives that they might wish. Nor do they have uniform strategies for using their knowledge of pregnancy risk warnings.

Although these women voiced the opinion that smoking by a pregnant woman presents a health risk to her baby-to-be or to her young children, other women did not. A main consideration for women who overtly question the content of health warnings—and one that can lead them to discount these standards—is how expert opinion on pregnancy and smoking has changed over time. Women are conscious of the fact that some things once socially and medically acceptable are now stigmatized. Implicitly, critics of antismoking warnings ask how we can so easily discard the experiences of numerous women who smoked during pregnancy without fear of smoking-related fetal and infant health problems. Many of these women had children who apparently did not suffer adversely.

Defiant and Uninformed Ancestors

Although a large majority of pregnant women are aware of the message that smoking during pregnancy is considered a fetal health risk, some remain skeptical. Ironically, in fact, on smoking and other health issues, the confidence and certainty with which health professionals deliver health advice may stand in the way of some people's acceptance of the message. The health education premise that "we know what's best for you" is significantly undermined when the professionals' predictions do not come true or are contradicted by a person's past experience.

In her ethnography on health education and everyday perceptions of cancer in a white, working-class Philadelphia neighborhood, Martha Balshem (1993) tells of repeatedly listening to stories about relatives or friends who did all the things that health professionals warn may cause cancer but who nonetheless avoided disease and premature death. These tales, or defiant ancestor stories, suggest that cancer prevention activities are unimportant and that health warnings mislead: "The defiant ancestor, so goes the story, smoked two packs of cigarettes a day, ate nothing but lard and bread, never went to the doctor, and lived until the age of ninety-three" (1993, 81). Anastasia Powers, a woman I spoke with, invoked a defiant ancestor when she discussed the risks of smoking, adding her own hypothesis about the origin of cancer: "It's never been proven to me that cigarettes cause things. My grandfather was ninety-four and smoked, but his lungs were good when he died. My twenty-six-year-old uncle died of cancer, and he never smoked a day in his life. I think it's the chemicals people work in." Indeed, this conclusion is the same as that of many Tannerstowners interviewed by Balshem and is tenable.[6] Those who

tell defiant ancestor stories challenge medical experts to account for the discrepancy between health warnings and an individual's actual experience. As
Hilary Graham writes on smoking, some people think that health experts offer the wrong type of proof because it is "scientific rather than everyday, [and]
generalised and untestable rather than individual and observable" (1976, 402).
The defiant ancestor presents everyday, individual, and observable proof that
can persuasively undercut official health warnings.

Intrigued by Balshem's analysis of defiant ancestor stories, I realized that
women who dismiss the antismoking advice and wisdom offered by health educators have a pregnancy-specific correlate to the defiant ancestor: "My mother/
friend/relative never quit smoking, and all her babies were big and healthy."
Some women use the defiant ancestor argument to deny the legitimacy of
health messages; the defiant ancestor provides personal evidence that medical experts are wrong and gives smokers a good reason to reject warnings voiced
by health educators. Indeed, health educators are particularly frustrated "when
they give you that line." Further, defiant ancestors cannot be judged negatively, according to this logic, for they successfully evaded the dire predictions
made by today's medical authorities. By extension, women who now ignore
those predictions ought not be judged.

Meredith Rodgers, a nonsmoker and trained midwife who thinks that
smoking during pregnancy is a serious risk, offers a different interpretation:
"Then there's the old argument that 'My mother smoked when she was pregnant, and it made no difference.' Saying that makes it very much a question
of 'If she could get away with it, so can I.' Rather than 'what we know now.'"
She asserts that it is irresponsible to assess the risks of smoking on past experience instead of on current medical advice. Indeed, many people see new
medical understandings of the health risks of smoking as progress and agree
with Rodgers that women must use this information to make moral, rational
decisions about smoking during pregnancy. What this perspective overlooks,
though, is that it remains true that some pregnant smokers have healthy infants because, as in the past, the negative health effects associated with smoking during pregnancy are risks, not certainties. The idea that smoking during
pregnancy does not always cause fetal or infant health problems is not simply
an outdated one. It is also one of interpretation.

Meredith Rodgers's remarks introduce a second character from the past—
the uninformed ancestor. Women I spoke with repeatedly remarked on the
lack of scientific evidence in the past about the possible health consequences
of smoking. Their mothers, uninformed, had no reason to worry about cigarettes as a health risk. Unlike women who smoke during pregnancy today, pregnant women of the past are often considered exempt from negative appraisal

or blame because "they just didn't know better back then." (I interpret the "they" in this sentence to mean both medical experts and women themselves.) Further, and in stark contrast to defiant ancestors, uninformed ancestors are potential compliers with our current antismoking advice: if only she had known a fetal health risk existed, she would have quit for the good of the baby-to-be.

Comparing the past and present rules of pregnancy, a number of women stated that it was easier to be pregnant a generation or two ago, when women were uninformed about smoking and other fetal health risks. Some commented that at times they have been judged by older women (often their own mothers) as overly cautious and fearful during pregnancy. Responses to my questions about the differences between pregnant women's health concerns today and those of their mothers and grandmothers were animated:

> Things were so different then! My mother didn't smoke or anything, but I have a friend about my age and her mother, she smoked during her whole pregnancy. And her doctor said it was okay. I mean, they really didn't realize the links. . . . I don't know that my mother really worried about what she did and what effect it had on the child. And then they weren't encouraged to breast-feed, so they didn't even have to worry about what they ate after the child was born. . . . She just talks about how young and naive she was and like "well, I'm pregnant again, guess I'll have another one." I mean, it was just what a good Catholic family does—has lots of kids. (April McGough)

> I've actually talked with my mother [who smoked during each of her four pregnancies] about it a lot. My impression is that they assumed everything would be fine. She thinks we're all crazy, we worry so much. They just had babies back then. (Jennifer Montelli)

> In my mother's time, they drank, smoked, whatever. She doesn't really come out and say it, but my mom thinks I'm way too cautious, like not drinking soda with caffeine. (Katie Wolfe)

> They just didn't know stuff back in that time. So it was easier to be pregnant then than now, you know. (Johnna Miles)

The idea repeated in these women's observations—that women of past generations had less to worry about during pregnancy because the state of medical knowledge was more limited than it is today—combines a romanticization of the past with a comment on the pressures that pregnant women feel today to follow the new rules of pregnancy. In the past, they suggest, women did not "do" pregnancy, they just were pregnant. Of course, stories about the advice that pregnant women received are constantly reinterpreted in light of

new medical findings and social expectations about pregnancy. Each generation of pregnant women may indeed feel that their generation has it more
difficult than the last.

What explains why some women discard the stories they have heard about
the pregnancy experiences of past generations and replace them with medically authoritative views on health risks while other women do not? Women's
perceptions of both health advice and the medical authority that backs it seem
to contribute to their trust or distrust of pregnancy advice. Those women who
comply with health advice may be enacting the healthist expectations illustrated in chapter 2, responding to the message that "doing" pregnancy right
involves seeking out the latest health information and making choices about
one's actions based on what is best for the health of one's baby-to-be.

On the other hand, dismissal of experts' advice can be viewed as a form
of resistance to medical power and authority. Emily Martin (1992 [1987]) illustrates the ways race and class differences influence women's medical care
during childbirth, the reasons they might oppose that care, and the methods
of resistance available to them. More closely related to health education and
advice, an explanation attentive to class difference could follow Martha
Balshem's (1993), which points out that those at the lower end of the strati-
fied class structure distrust authorities who exert power over them or who attempt to do so. References to "They" by some of the women I interviewed
and by the Tannerstowners Balshem interviewed conjure up the image of a
powerful adversary who occupies a higher social and economic position than
the speaker. This division alone indicates conflict that can be summarized in
the attitude expressed through the challenge "Who do They think they are,
trying to tell Us what to do?"

Skepticism about expert knowledge crosses class lines as well, suggesting
that resistance to medical advice is not only a result of a lower social class.
Elizabeth Blackmund, a suburban woman whose family is very well off financially, complained in an exasperated tone: "It's just terrible now! You can't
do anything if you are pregnant because it all seems bad. It really wasn't like
that when I was pregnant [in the early 1980s]. Well, some things you knew
not to do, but not like today. . . . And now, the problem is you never know
what to believe anyway. All these facts they give us are different. Who can
you trust?" Elizabeth thinks that the rapid pace of change and the high volume of medical evidence now bombarding the public via newspapers and television news shows undermine expert authority. She also sees medical advice
as proscriptive, limiting one's range of guilt-free action. Katie Wolfe, a middle-
class woman, also doubts that all the medical advice she hears is true. She
recalled that early in her pregnancy, she read about a study that said eating

broccoli is bad and another that declared morning sickness is your body telling you what is good for you. Katie concluded: "But you know, I'm not really at all sure what's true." Anastasia Powers, who has a lower class position than either Elizabeth Blackmund or Katie Wolfe, came to a similar conclusion about expert knowledge: "First, they said smoking calms nerves, then you're told not to do it. They just don't know, that's what I think."

Clearly, expert opinion does not hold unquestioned authority in the eyes of the public. It remains less clear, however, just what the root of women's skepticism is, how widespread such views of medical warnings are, and how distrust of medical experts influences women's health perceptions and decisions.[7] One public health scholar argues that a main problem is that public health research findings are often disseminated by the media before health experts reach a conclusion about what sort of recommendations should be promoted. This leads to contradictory information, which can cause confusion and skepticism about the value of expert advice (Becker 1986). Perhaps of greatest importance is the ability of health professionals and those who comply with health recommendations to pass healthist judgments about the character of those individuals who do not comply with health advice.

Nonsmokers' Perceptions of Pregnant Smokers and Health Experts' Warnings

Nearly every woman I interviewed had seen or known a woman who had recently smoked during pregnancy. The contrast between nonsmokers' characterizations of smokers and the actual smokers I was meeting was particularly intriguing. Almost without exception, nonsmokers made different, moral evaluations about their uninformed ancestors, who lived at a time when risks from cigarettes were not widely known, than about women who smoke today but "ought to know better" due to public health warnings. With the expansion of medical knowledge, they argued, comes a greater ability to attribute blame to pregnant women who take medically known risks with their baby-to-be's health.

By talking to a range of women, I aimed to capture what sorts of stereotypes nonsmoking women form about women who smoke while pregnant. In general, nonsmokers seem to support health educators in believing the health risks of smoking and the idea that women who smoke during pregnancy should be judged morally (see also Graham 1976, 400). Like health educators' assumptions, those of nonsmokers' about why some pregnant women smoke included nicotine addiction, stressful life circumstances, self-centeredness, and lack of caring about their baby-to-be's health. Nonsmokers position themselves on the side of medical experts and tend to view smokers as different. But with increased attention to the fetal health risks of secondhand or environmental smoke, health educators are also targeting nonsmokers with their antismoking campaigns. Therefore, nonsmokers too must assess whether to follow experts' warnings on the risks of secondhand smoke, and they are subject to health professionals' disapproval if they do not comply with such advice.

Despite the recurrent, strong disapproval of pregnant smokers by non-smokers, some nonsmokers eased their judgment of women who smoke by stating that health education messages are not strong enough. Meredith Rodgers stated, "I think there's too much emphasis on alcohol and not enough on cigarettes, given the relative risks involved." Patty Doyle contended that They aren't as harsh about smoking as They are about drugs, which leads women to consider that smoking may not be a problem: "Some women are selfish—I hate that. They say 'Don't smoke crack,' but to light up and put a cigarette in her mouth is okay?! I hate that. I don't let anyone smoke around me." When I asked Patty what she tells friends who smoke when they are pregnant, she replied, "'You know how black the kid's lungs are? And it's not gettin' any oxygen. If it comes out sick, it's your own fault—don't tell me about it!' I tell 'em flat out." Patty thinks that health professionals should blame women for smoking and that women are fully at fault if they smoke during pregnancy.

Women are not considered as much to blame if nicotine is viewed as an addiction instead of a choice. When nicotine addiction is seen as the problem, smoking is not a rational decision; it is beyond a woman's control. Indeed, the view that addiction is what drives women to smoke places women smokers in the position of being powerless victims of their biochemistry. This may gain them sympathy. Vivian Compton has seen "young pregnant girls" smoking in her low-income Black neighborhood. When I asked her, "Why would you guess that they do it?" she quickly responded, "They're probably addicted. It's pretty well known that they shouldn't do it nowadays!" Betsy Michaels hesitantly agreed: "I guess it's a habit, and a lot of people just can't stop, or um, but I really don't understand why they continue to do it 'cause so much is known about it." Lena Ferro has personal experience with several women who smoked when they were pregnant. Why does she think they did it? "If they really could stop, they would. . . . It is a medical addiction." Several of Lena's friends from her high school days have smoked during pregnancy, and one even hid it from her own husband, she was so ashamed. Weighing on her mind when we talked was a woman she knew who was currently pregnant, smoking cigarettes, and doing drugs. Lena repeated several times, "I'm just sick for that baby," shaking her head with disapproval but also with compassion for the woman who, Lena believes, is addicted to cigarettes and drugs.

Other nonsmokers focused less on the issue of smokers' biochemical addiction. When thinking about why women would continue to smoke during pregnancy, two women recognized that smoking might be the result of stressful conditions in a woman's life. LaVonda Serban commented, "Probably bad nerves, or it's the only thing they can turn to," while Katherine Shaffer explained, "I had a coworker who started smoking when she got pregnant. . . . She was a Nervous Nellie, and foolish too—but she came from a broken home and she ended up in a difficult, abusive relationship situation. Quite a predicament. She didn't carry to full term." Acknowledgment of the broader circumstances of smokers' lives can temper judgments of their smoking during pregnancy.

Although LaVonda and Katherine expressed their disapproval with empathy, some of the women I spoke with revealed remarkably strong views. Joselyn Behm told me that she's seen pregnant women smoking, adding, "especially, uh, I don't want to make it sound bad, but, at country fairs, and things like that, where there's a whole different social-economic group." When I asked why she thinks they might be smokers while other types of women are not, she continued, "Well, I assume they just can't quit. Either they're addicted to it or they aren't concerned. I assume they are aware it isn't good." She associates pregnant women's smoking with a rural lifestyle and lower class status, and offers two characterizations of women who smoke during pregnancy: nicotine addicts or uncaring mothers-to-be. Other women were even less guarded in their judgments. Mary Beth Shannon offered this criticism of women who smoke during pregnancy: "I think people who smoke a lot don't care. But some people, if they're tryin' to get pregnant and they want a healthier baby, I think then they'll stay away from it. But people in the inner cities that get pregnant just for spite or because they want to have a baby; these kids, they just don't care. And it's sad. They might know its bad, but it's their lifestyle and they don't want to change."

Mary Beth's thinly veiled comments reveal that she sees smoking during pregnancy as connected to the highly publicized teenage pregnancy problem. The label "inner city" in Baltimore is a code for "poor, African American"; thus her criticism reveals both the power of smoking during pregnancy as a characteristic of bad mothers and the racist stereotype of low-income, Black teenagers as socially irresponsible.[8]

Other women offered strong antismoking views and commented on the moral character of smokers. Martha Voss explained that she regards negatively anyone who smokes, but she is particularly distressed by pregnant women who smoke:

I've always said to my husband that I don't think I could've married someone that smoked, you know. It was just, even now, you know someone and you think that they're a nice person and they pull out a cigarette, you think—well, I do—I have just a different opinion about them. But I guess it's just a habit like anything else.

LO: Have you ever seen a pregnant woman smoking?

Yes. I have an old friend who smoked.

LO: How did you react to that?

It bothered me quite a bit. But she's kind of a very headstrong person, so I don't think I'd ever confront her about it . . . she's a nurse too, and you can't believe she'd take those kinds of risks.

LO: What do you think her reasons would be?

It's such a strong thing in her life, and just a habit she won't give up. I mean for nobody will she give it up . . . I just, I don't know what she was thinking but you'd think she would know better. Thank God her babies turned out fine—I mean they really didn't have any problems. But I still worry about it because she smokes in the house and has three kids, and putting them through it is just sorta a terrible, selfish kind of thing, you know.

Both Mary Beth Shannon and Martha Voss assert that the main reason women do not give up smoking when they are pregnant is because they fail to put their baby-to-be's health ahead of their own desire to smoke. In short, they do not care enough to quit. Smoking during pregnancy is a problem of bad mothering.

On this same theme, Bernadette Ryan suggests that women who truly care about their babies-to-be will seek out information about health risks. She discussed smoking, drugs, and alcohol in the context of what she calls the projects, a low-income African American neighborhood in Baltimore, where she lives:

I seen 'em smokin', doin' drugs. They just don't care; don't think it'll harm the baby. I drank wine, a little—to build up the blood. But not lots like they's doin' now . . . If they has a drug baby, they deserves to go to jail. That baby not asked to be born like that. It's a sin and it should be the law. Why they's getting pregnant—just killin' a newborn baby. That's sick!

LO: Do you think it's because they're addicted?

More their upbringing—just followin' their mothers. . . . I say they need to do research when they's pregnant—get more knowledge. If you don't know somethin', it don't hurt ya, they think. The mind is a terrible thing to waste, as they say.

Although Bernadette believes that women who smoke during pregnancy do so as a result of their social life and upbringing by their mothers (with, notably, no mention of fathers), she shares the dominant public health view that stresses individual responsibility. In her opinion, women should make efforts to change their behavior by seeking out and adhering to health advice. When they do not, the law should step in.

In general, the views of these and other women reveal that nonsmokers have faith in health warnings about smoking during pregnancy. Even when nonsmokers knew of counterexamples, the idea that smoking poses a serious fetal health risk was not met with extreme skepticism or discredited. Martha Voss's old friend smoked when pregnant and had three children who "had no problems," yet Martha did not revise her opinion that smoking was a threat to their health. In fact, in my interviews with both smokers and nonsmokers, stories about exceptions to the rule that smoking harms babies outnumbered stories about babies who were ill as a result of women's smoking during pregnancy.

Stories about the "lucky ones," or babies who were healthy despite health warnings that predicted that they would not be, did not weaken nonsmokers' antismoking beliefs. Thinking about the pregnant women she knows, Clarice Singer, who was pregnant when we spoke, commented: "Yeah—lotta 'em still smoke! One girl, she smoked the whole time she's pregnant—the whole time! And her little son is so cute. Didn't stay sick a lot or nothin'. They say you can be lucky—but I'm not doin' that. Maybe not everybody's baby can take it." Bettelyn Montgomery shared a similar assessment regarding her friend who smoked during pregnancy: "Those babies came out fine, so I guess maybe they were the lucky ones." Indeed, this is one of the main messages health educators aim to get across to women who smoke to convince them to quit: women should not smoke because they might not be so lucky. An avid nonsmoker, Michelle Hart, explained that she admonished Jasmine, a friend who smoked cigarettes during pregnancy, saying, "All that stinky stuff's goin' down to the baby!" Jasmine told Michelle to mind her own business and continued to smoke throughout her pregnancy. In the end, the baby was normal size and healthy. Jasmine is still a smoker, and Michelle concludes that due to her experience, Jasmine wrongly believes that smoking is not high risk. Michelle, of course, describes the problem that health educators face when they attempt to convince a women that smoking during pregnancy is a serious fetal health risk: women's experience and medical warnings do not always mesh.

This theme was echoed in other women's opinions about smoking during pregnancy. April McGough described her frustration with a family member who disregards health advice:

> I mean you see things on TV—in the news. It's just things you think
> people all know. You hear stories about studies—especially smoking—

and about crack babies. They say they're getting more now [in the hospital]. It's sad. My third cousin, she's younger than me, and she was pregnant and she smoked. She'd just make me so angry, I'm thinking, "you know, you're just lucky to be carrying this child, and as far as you know it's healthy" and she had two healthy kids—not underweight or anything.

LO: Did you ever talk to her about it?

My sister'd come in when we were all together and say, "Did you see her out there, smokin' away?" I'd go, "Yeah, I know, I just want to smack her!" It makes me so angry, I mean, "You're so lucky—some people can't have kids and you're just smokin' away. Not even paying attention." I mean, both her parents smoked though, her father died of cancer. And it's like she's still continuing to do it and she's got two kids. I just can't stand seeing it around kids, so if it's while they're pregnant, it's just worse, you know. I feel like, they must know. And I've seen some who smoked and gave it up when they were pregnant, quite a few, actually, and I just think that's something that you need to do, you know.

LO: What do you think it is about those who don't?

Maybe they're just so—in a state of denial because they have such a nicotine addiction. They say it's worse than cocaine, that they are so addicted that they can't stop. I have a hard time believing that they don't know.

April thinks of pregnancy as a gift—something a woman is lucky to achieve—and that women should pay attention to health advice about how to care for the baby-to-be and make sacrifices such as quitting smoking. April's anger toward her cousin was not abated when her children were born healthy; her cousin was simply lucky. By April's account, pregnant women who smoke are not ignorant about fetal health risks; rather, they are nicotine addicts. But no matter what the reason for women's smoking—when pregnant or around children—April's tone makes clear that she believes it unfair and unjust for women to take such a risk with a child's health.

The views of the nonsmokers I spoke with are in line with public health warnings: pregnant women should not smoke because it presents unacceptable risks to fetal health. Further, nonsmokers can be particularly harsh judges of pregnant smokers, and the negative images they portray of pregnant women who smoke reveal that smoking is a highly stigmatized activity. This reaction is related in part to the expectation that pregnant women should follow health advice for the good of the baby-to-be. Most nonsmokers imply that pregnant women should know better than to take such a risk with their baby's health.

In contrast to their belief in and support of health warnings about smoking, these same nonsmokers did not take as seriously advice about the fetal health risks associated with pregnant women's exposure to secondhand smoke, or environmental tobacco smoke. Since the late 1980s, pregnancy guides and antitobacco campaigns have instructed mothers to keep their infants and young children away from smoke-filled environments and to avoid smoky areas when pregnant. Although more attention has been paid to the message that babies and infants should not be around smoke, pregnancy advice literature also emphasizes possible fetal health problems, such as low birthweight: "new studies show that if a woman's partner smokes near her during her pregnancy, there are added risks" (American Lung Association 1994, 3), "so stay away from rooms where people are smoking" (March of Dimes 1994b, 3). *What to Expect* strongly warns, "if your husband (or anyone else who lives in your home or works at the next desk) smokes, your baby's body is going to pick up nearly as much contamination from tobacco smoke by-products as if *you* were lighting up" (Eisenberg et al. 1991 [1984], 57; original emphasis). Although *What to Expect* suggests that smoking and environmental tobacco smoke exposure carry nearly the same level of risk to the fetus, pregnant nonsmokers generally do not draw this same conclusion.[9] A lack of urgency about environmental tobacco smoke as a serious health risk is reflected in a number of women's comments:

> I hate smoke. I didn't think about it being a problem when I's pregnant because most places had smoke-free policies anyway. (Michelle Hart)

> I'm infrequently around it—only if we're in a restaurant with bad ventilation. But if I was in smoky place, I wouldn't like it.
>   LO: Why not?
>   Just for my comfort I guess, I hadn't really thought about whether it'd harm the child. (Rita Shaw)

> I just don't like the smell, and heard it causes birth defects, but don't really know exactly which. At the doctor's office, there are signs everywhere, including one that says something like, "Don't start life under a cloud." The last time I was pregnant, I remember being trapped in my in-law's car while they were smoking. It was terrible because I had morning sickness, you know. So I rolled the window down and they got the message. (Joselyn Behm)

> LO: How did smokers react around you when you were pregnant?
>   Most were courteous, during the first pregnancy especially [three years ago]. . . . There are times when people smoked in front of me, and I just removed myself. Mainly because I just don't like the smell,

not because I was afraid of any problems with the baby. My husband
played in a band during the first pregnancy, and I went to bars a lot
that sometimes had thick, irritating smoke. (Lena Ferro)

These comments do not reflect the perspective offered in *What to Expect*.
Only one of these women, Joselyn Behm, specifically comments on antismoking health education campaigns (although the American Lung Association
slogan she cites targets women who smoke during pregnancy and predated
warnings about secondhand smoke in relation to pregnancy). Yet her concern
about risks to the baby-to-be was secondary to her physical discomfort of being in a smoky car while experiencing morning sickness. No one voiced a
strong opinion about exposure to smoky places on the grounds that such exposure may have fetal health consequences, although each woman expressed
a personal dislike of being around smoke. This suggests that women assessed
the risks to their babies-to-be based on their own intolerance of smoky places,
not on health warnings about pregnant women avoiding smoky areas for the
sake of the baby-to-be. Nonsmokers' evaluation of the risk of secondhand
smoke as low risk could be associated with the fact that their exposure to smoke
was only occasional; all of the nonsmokers I interviewed characterized their
exposure to smoke and smokers as limited (several attributed this to Maryland's
smoke-free laws regulating public spaces, workplaces, and restaurants).

Some women were explicitly skeptical of the need to avoid smoky places
to protect their baby-to-be's health. Like Lena Ferro, who said she went to
smoke-filled bars when she was pregnant yet did not worry about fetal health
risks, Julia Panciera questioned the public health advice to avoid smoke exposure entirely. Julia discovered that some of her friends were more worried
about cigarette smoke than she was. One incident in particular annoyed her:
"A friend asked me where we should go out for his birthday, and I said since
it was his birthday, he should choose. He wanted to know what kind of environment I felt okay in, and added 'of course, it should be smoke-free.' I said I
didn't care if I was around smoke now and then, and since he's a smoker we
should go someplace where he can enjoy a cigarette. He told me—in a very
forceful way—that he absolutely refused to smoke around me." Julia "didn't
worry at all" about secondhand smoke because she so rarely encountered it,
and she was frustrated that her friends refused to smoke around her to "protect the baby" when she herself had decided that the risk was so low that it
was not a problem. Overruling her judgment, she felt, was a form of disre-
spectful pregnancy policing: "I'd say, 'Go ahead, light up,' but they wouldn't.
So I'd argue with 'em, 'Have a goddamn cigarette!' but they just wouldn't."
(We both laughed at the idea of ordering someone to smoke.)

However, one nonsmoker, LaNeisha McDonald, explained that she became more worried about secondhand smoke when she was pregnant: "My grandmother died of cancer last year. She didn't smoke, but my step-grandfather did 'til she was very sick. So I just leave if there's smoke—try to be careful." LaNeisha's personal experience, not a public health campaign, influenced her assessment of the health risks of secondhand smoke exposure.

While some nonsmokers represent themselves as occupying the moral high ground because they respect health warnings about smoking, few took the same attitude about avoiding secondhand smoke. Michelle Hart's "I hate smoke" and Patty Doyle's "I don't let anyone smoke around me" were among the most adamant statements I encountered about being subjected to others' smoke. The message that exposure to environmental tobacco smoke is an important fetal health hazard does not seem to have the same status as the message that smoking during pregnancy puts the baby-to-be's health at risk. This is not because such messages are new: antitobacco activists have fought for smoke-free public areas since the 1970s; the 1986 surgeon general's report focused on the health risks to nonsmokers of "involuntary smoking"; public health campaigns on secondhand smoke have targeted pregnant women since the late 1980s; and numerous local, state, and national smoke-free regulations were passed in the 1990s.[10] Perhaps the relative lack of concern is related to the greater attention paid over time to the risks of environmental tobacco smoke to infants and children.

Nonsmokers' analyses of the importance of complying with antismoking advice reveal contradictions. Although nonsmokers I spoke with asserted that any amount of smoking by a pregnant woman is too dangerous a risk, nonsmokers also stated that occasional secondhand smoke exposure is an acceptable risk. This attitude reveals that nonsmokers are critical of public health warnings and may not fully comply with health experts' instructions on how to care for their babies-to-be. It also points to how easily nonsmokers could be identified as bad mothers. I argue that smokers and nonsmokers, although they may not follow all pregnancy rules, ought not be characterized simply as uncaring and irresponsible mothers-to-be.

Smokers' Perspectives on Warnings about Smoking during Pregnancy: Unwanted (and Unwarranted?) Advice

"They know smoking's bad for the baby, and for themselves too," Molly O'Neill, the coordinator of a smoking cessation program for pregnant women, reported. She added, "But then there's also the social influence—they think people are looking at them and saying 'That's terrible! Look at that pregnant woman over there smoking!'" O'Neill did not expect that women who smoke would feel this way: "I thought smokers kinda wrote this off. But it is very important to them." Although the women O'Neill spoke with said they felt guilty and embarrassed about smoking during pregnancy, I did not get this sense in my interviews. The women who had smoked during pregnancy were un-apologetic about their rejection of antismoking advice and angry about oth-ers' judgments of their actions and care for their babies-to-be.

Carrie Burdine, for example, who smoked one and a half to two packs of Marlboros a day during each of her two recent pregnancies, explained that despite the warnings she received from everyone, her children were born healthy:

> LO: Did anyone tell you you ought to cut down?
> Oh yeah, I heard that from everybody—the doctors, my mother, my friends.
> LO: What did you say to them?
> It's kinda hard to quit, you know, and hard to cut down. Just—I don't know why I smoked—not stress, I just set around and did nothin', so I smoked. At my job, I was always hearing that I should quit. But my babies were eight pounds somethin'—*not* low birthweight.

Christina Lee's experience also contradicted medical advice and height-ened her distrust of medical knowledge. Because Christina knows women who smoked during pregnancy whose babies had no problems, she finds it ironic and disturbing that although she quit smoking while pregnant, her baby was not healthy: "He [the doctor] didn't tell me not to [smoke], just said to cut down. But I stopped anyway. . . . I guess 'cause it's better for the baby, and my husband hates when I smoke. . . . But guess what? My daughter has asthma, and I'd stopped!"

Other women resented advice about their smoking practices, whether from health experts or strangers:

> LO: Did the doctors ever say anything to you about smoking?
> Every time. "Smokin' today, Andy?" He gave me all these papers about what it can do. . . . It kinda got on my nerves after a while—they keep sayin' it and sayin' it.
> LO: What did you say [to him]?
> "Just leave me alone! I know I can't do this and that, *but I'm the one decidin'.*" I wanted to choke the nurse sometimes! (Andrea Sellers)

> LO: What did you say to people who told you it was bad to smoke?
> It's my life, and my baby. If you want to raise my baby, go ahead.

At the mall once, a woman said "you shouldn't smoke, it'll harm the baby." I say, "God created it [smoking], so it can't hurt." People shouldn't be ignorant with me. (Anastasia Powers)

The way these women reacted to antismoking advice is similar in that they both were offended by others' questioning their decisions whether to smoke. But the grounds on which they made their decisions differ. Andrea accepted the claim that smoking during pregnancy is bad for the baby, whereas Anastasia challenged it. Each woman assessed both the medical evidence behind health warnings and the delivery of the warnings.

Offering more criticism of antismoking advice, two friends in their early twenties (who shared a rapidly empty pack of cigarettes while we talked) rejected doctors' authoritative, moral judgments and the idea that smoking is an equal risk for every pregnant woman's baby-to-be. Tessa Andrews argued, "It's your body. You know what's right and wrong for you. Doctors tell you, with the doctor way of sayin' it. Might not be best for you though. We're all different." Susan Donahue nodded vigorously in agreement. In their view, personal, subjective experience is more important than medical experts' knowledge and advice.

Women may particularly resent universal statements by health authorities not only because they offer unsolicited advice but because they do not take individual situations into account. In fact, Tessa and Susan's argument hinges on what anthropologists Carole Browner and Nancy Press (1996) refer to as embodied knowledge. In their study of women who received prenatal care at a California health maintenance organization, Browner and Press found that women drew on their subjective, bodily experience to assess and then accept or reject a range of prenatal health recommendations.

Relying on one's own embodied knowledge instead of on medical advice, however, leaves pregnant women vulnerable to criticism voiced by health professionals and others. Leslie Hollins—who smoked more than the four cigarettes a day her obstetrician advised but did not inhale the smoke—has particularly bitter memories about the unsolicited advice and harsh judgment she received. Although Leslie's doctor did not bother her much about smoking because she concealed how much she smoked, she painfully recalled that "all the men I worked with would yell at me" for smoking because it might harm the baby. Once she even burst into tears and left the office. At this point, Leslie leaned into the table, clearly still angry about the incident: "It was none of their damn business!" She felt it unfair to be criticized for not caring for her baby-to-be when in fact she had changed the way she smoked to reduce the health risks.

For other women, being told to quit smoking was bothersome, but it was more justified and tolerable when it concerned the baby. These women represented others' advice as unwanted yet in part warranted. For example, a woman might consider her husband's reprimands about smoking as an expression of caring about her and their baby-to-be and even refer to this as evidence of his dedication to fatherhood. Debra Williams recalled why she stopped smoking when she was pregnant: "My husband was leanin' on me. To keep the baby's health, it's a good cause. My husband took my cigarettes away and put 'em down the toilet. . . . I started again right after I had the baby. I just wanted to—I remember how I celebrated! I finished a pack in no time." Debra's tone implied that although giving up cigarettes was a hardship, she respected her husband's drastic actions and thought of them as an admirable part of his caring about the baby.

Rae Ann Dixon criticized her baby's father for his lack of attention to her worries about how smoking could affect her baby-to-be. Rae Ann did not mind antismoking advice and associated her own quitting with her love of kids in general: "It made sense . . . you can have a miscarriage [if you smoke during pregnancy.] I don't wanta do that. I love kids—I'm hopin' to have more kids. I'm just waitin' to get married." Rae Ann respected her doctor's advice, even though she could not totally quit smoking during her first pregnancy: "When I's first pregnant, with my first child, I smoked. I's told not to do that, but I'd sneak a few. With the second, I didn't and I still don't. The pediatrician said you'd mess up your kid's lungs 'n' stuff." However, she described her fiancé as unconcerned about the risks of smoking on fetal health: "When I got pregnant, smoking bothered me. I couldn't take it. I got asthma too. My second baby's father smokes a lot. I told him to go outside when I's pregnant. He didn't do it. That really irritated me." Rae Ann stresses how her efforts to comply with health warnings far exceeded the efforts of her fiancé, and thus she points out his lesser commitment to ensuring the health of their baby-to-be. She sees both antismoking advice and following such advice as signs of caring.

Angela Perry's description of how she reacted to antismoking advice when she was pregnant reveals both a dislike that others would tell her what to do and a respect for their concern for the health of her baby-to-be:

> It was back in '80s, ya know. They's sayin' stuff . . . said it's dangerous, low birthweight and all that. And I understand, but I needed that cigarette! It calms my nerves. I went from Kools to Lights though.
>
>   LO: How'd you feel about the things you were told you should or shouldn't do?

You can't tell somebody "don't do this." They'll just want to more.
LO: Did it bother you?
They're worryin' about my unborn child and my health. So I
didn't mind much.[11]

Part of Angela's message is that although she understood the antismoking campaigns, They (health experts) could not comprehend how necessary smoking
was to her life. She compromised by switching to a "light" brand, which was
her way of balancing care for her baby-to-be with her own needs.

Given that cigarette smoking in general has an increasingly negative connotation in the United States, it seems likely that this sort of care will be
overlooked as strict judgments of pregnant women who smoke intensify. As
Angela and others point out, pregnant smokers are aware that they are judged
morally. But judging smokers without considering their point of view or without acknowledging the compromises they make, such as cutting down or
switching to a less desired brand, can increase the resentment that smokers
feel toward those who give health advice. The underlying message carried in
antismoking messages is that nonsmokers know what is best for smokers. This
assumption can impede health educators' antismoking efforts and heighten
the antagonism that some people feel toward health experts. Recognizing this,
women's health advocates and feminist scholars argue that health education
campaigns can benefit from a deeper understanding of what smoking means
in women's lives and from less moralistic, more respectful antismoking
messages.

Changing the Focus of Antismoking Attention:
The Varied Meanings of Women's Smoking

Although health data provide useful statistical demographic and behavioral
information about women, pregnancy, and smoking,[12] more attention to the
microlevel or day-to-day aspects of women's smoking is needed to understand
the economic, cultural, and political significance of cigarette smoking during
pregnancy. Recent qualitative studies point to how smoking is embedded in
women's daily lives and how it plays a significant role in smokers' relationships with others (Graham 1976, 1987, 1993; Jacobson 1986; ASH Working
Group on Women and Smoking 1993; Greaves 1995, 1996). From this perspective, cigarette smoking is not simply a medical problem that can be solved
through health education. It is also a social issue that must be approached
with attention to women's social status, daily responsibilities, and gender roles.

To highlight the cultural specificity of the meanings associated with smoking and other tobacco use, the International Network of Women Against

Tobacco's Herstories Project conducted interviews with women in ten countries. In some countries (e.g., India), women's use of tobacco is considered traditional, whereas in others (e.g., Japan), women who smoke cigarettes challenge traditional cultural ideals (American Cancer Society 1994). But even within a society, contrasting images of women who smoke may coexist. Interviews with British nurse trainees and student teachers illustrate a tension between the unladylike and liberated meanings of women's smoking in the present and reflect how stereotypes about women and smoking have changed over time (Knopf Elkind 1985). Looking more deeply at what smoking means to women, sociologist Lorraine Greaves (1996) discovered five significant themes drawn from interviews with residents of domestic violence shelters and feminist activists in Canada and Australia: smoking organizes social relationships, creates an image, controls emotions, fosters a dependency, and creates an identity. Hilary Graham's (1976, 1987, 1993) work reveals that for white, low-income British mothers who are responsible for full-time care of their young children, smoking provides a way of "coping with caring-in-poverty." Finally, Bobbie Jacobson (1981, 1986), a feminist, physician, and antitobacco advocate, has published two books that include case studies of how British women have been victimized by the "ladykiller" tobacco industry and suggests how women can quit and fight back.

Each of these studies contains an explicit or implicit critique of cigarette use without negatively stigmatizing or blaming smokers. Designing antismoking campaigns using this approach might circumvent the resistance that smokers may have to heavy-handed, overly moral health education messages, a subject I pursue in this book's last chapter.

THE MEANING OF FIRST EXPERIENCES WITH SMOKING

To understand the broader picture of women's smoking during pregnancy, I asked women about their experiences with and feelings about smoking at different points in their lives. Smokers and nonsmokers told colorful stories about the first time they tried a cigarette (between the ages of eight and eighteen). Girlfriends, older siblings, and cousins were coconspirators in this activity that often but not always was hidden from adults. Indeed, in popular culture and in smokers' lives, smoking is associated with friendship, intimacy, and sexuality. Cultural narratives about cigarette smoking span from receiving a cigarette from a trusted friend after a harrowing experience, to provocatively asking an attractive boy for a light, to sharing postcoital cigarettes with a lover. Literary critic Richard Klein identifies the shared nature of cigarettes as central to their socialness: "The value of cigarettes, their use as a universal token of exchange, is linked to their insertion in a gift-giving economy. Cigarettes have the gift of giving—to the other, to oneself, to the beyond" (1993, 137). As do all gifts, cigarettes enmesh smokers in a network of relationships that can include their most intimate partners and the homeless stranger who asks not for money but for a cigarette or a light. Lorraine Greaves observes, "Sharing the experience of smoking, particularly in an anti-smoking environment, can solidify, mend, build or even create social relationships" (1996, 39).

Stories about smoking for the first time emphasize that smoking is a social activity, and some women attributed their early smoking to American cultural norms and the pervasiveness of smoking. For Bernadette Ryan and Bernice Johnson, smoking represented common teenage experimentation with adulthood. I asked Bernadette why she started smoking twenty years ago. She replied, "Just doin' somethin' everyone else was, I guess—just bein' eighteen in America at that time, you know. My cousin started when she's fifteen." Bernice recalled, "Sure, I tried it, but I couldn't smoke, no. Didn't know how to inhale, and I's blowin' smoke all over people! My cousin an' sister an' me went downtown and bought cigarettes—cost one cent for a cigarette those days [over forty years ago]. We'd walk the streets, and carry 'em up like this (hidden behind her hand) so older people couldn't see. We'd get killed for it if they did." When I asked April McGough if she ever smoked, she laughed, recalling: "In like eighth or ninth grade, I tried it. It made me sick. . . . It was what a bunch of neighborhood kids were doin' it to be cool. And I got in trouble for it. A neighbor stole them from her mother, then said we gave them to her. I got grounded for a week." Although the incident was difficult at the time, she now found it a humorous tale about growing up and an experience that influenced her to become a nonsmoking adult.

Angela Perry, who still smokes, was reluctant to admit to me with her children in the room that she began smoking at age thirteen. Angela's mother, a nonsmoker, did not object to her young teen's smoking after she tested Angela's physical capacity to handle it: "I tried it, and my mother said 'if you can drink a glass of water and then inhale [cigarette smoke], then drink a glass of water, you can smoke.' And I could do it." Angela was as curious as I was about why her mother chose this as the test, but she did not care at the time because she had met the challenge and gained the desired grown-up status that came with being a smoker.

Although none of these women's stories included attention to the health risks related to smoking, other women discussed how health problems led them to quit smoking after they had become regular smokers. Tricia Greene believes that young people mistakenly see smoking as acceptable. She implies that as a girl she was too naive to understand the long-term consequences of smoking. Years later, she gave up it up because "it jus' made me sick, an' I jus' stopped. I have asthma. Been off cigarettes seventeen years. . . . I prayed to the good Lord. The last cigarette I had was March 11, 1979." She quit because her doctors told her to give it up when she was in the hospital for shortness of breath. Now, her reflection on beginning to smoke contains criticism of it: "I's nine years old. . . . I's out with the boys 'n all, and girlfriends. Thinkin' it looks good and all. But then there's the coughin' and asthma." Tricia voiced regret that she became a smoker at such a young age and without a care for its long-term health risks.

Carla Mullinger remembers that she began smoking when she was a teenager, in spite of her mother's outspoken opposition. Her mother had quit smoking in her early forties due to health problems, and her father smoked sometimes, but "it was not a habit for him, and he'd never smoke in the house." Carla explained, "My friends smoked, and it was the cool thing to do. I did, occasionally, from when I was sixteen to twenty-two or so." Why did she quit? "Aw, I had bronchitis, and just decided, 'time to get rid of that habit.'" She laughed about how obvious this conclusion seems now.

Not every woman who tried smoking became a regular smoker. Some said they couldn't understand how others enjoyed it. LaVonda Serban reported, "Yeah, I tried it when I's eighteen or nineteen. But I didn't like the taste it left in my mouth. Others said it gave them a feeling—I didn't get no feelin' from it." Vivian Compton recalled that although her best girlfriend and sisters were smokers, she never took up the habit: "I tried it once and choked!" LaNeisha McDonald claimed that she has never even tried smoking. She cites her mother's strong antismoking attitude as the main influence on her decision not to smoke: "I was jus' scared, I guess . . . of my mother findin' out! I just never tried. Nor have I done drugs." For LaNeisha, cigarettes and drugs are in the same dangerous category, and abstaining entirely is the best course.

About the same time I was discussing with these women their early relationships with cigarettes, antitobacco advocates had stepped up a campaign directed at youths and teenagers in response to studies showing that many smokers try cigarettes around the age of thirteen or fourteen (Campaign for Tobacco-Free Kids 1995). One main focus of the campaign was how cigarette and smokeless tobacco advertising lures teenagers to become addicted. Although an analysis of the role of advertising in smokers' attraction to cigarettes is beyond the scope of this study, my research suggests that "trying it" is more importantly influenced by social relationships and willingness to experiment.

THE PLACE OF SMOKING IN RELATIONSHIPS WITH SIGNIFICANT
OTHERS, FAMILY, AND FRIENDS

Those women who tried cigarettes and became smokers described smoking in various ways: as relaxing, pleasurable, an addiction, and a way to celebrate or diffuse stress. For some, being a smoker constitutes a significant part of their identity, which is poignantly reflected in Angela Perry's comment: "I tell my kids I want a Pepsi and pack of Kools in my casket when I die!" Further, smokers explained how cigarettes became an integral part of social life and sharing (or conflict) between family and friends. Andrea Sellers complained that sharing cigarettes with her fiancé could be difficult:

> LO: Why do you think you smoke?
> Well, just somethin' to do.
> LO: When did you start?
> I's 16. If I have bad nerves, it calms me. An' my fiancé also smokes, but more than I do.
> LO: Yeah? How much?
> Two packs a day. He leaves with a pack and has one already he's into, an' he about snatches 'em from me in the morning. Then he comes back without any.

It is remarkable that while most of the nonsmoking women I interviewed stated that none or few of their friends use cigarettes and that they are rarely exposed to smoke, many smokers reported the opposite experience. Many women who smoke are involved in romantic relationships with partners who smoke and are surrounded by family and friends who are smokers. Sarah Leigh Snyder reported that most of the people she knows also smoke and then hesitated to correct herself, "no, everybody I know does." But Katherine Shaffer, who was never a regular smoker, commented on how little she comes in contact with people who smoke: "I remember once I was at an O's [Baltimore Orioles' baseball] game, before they banned smoking. A group in front of me was blowing smoke back at me—this is when I was pregnant the first time—and it really annoyed me. Now, none of my friends smoke. It's been a long time because I've been in a workplace that allowed smoking, and just in general I'm seldom around it now. When I go to other states I notice right away if they don't have same laws—in Pennsylvania, people smoke in the malls!"[13]

Indeed, health professionals and others have noted increasing social distance between smokers and nonsmokers as smoke-free policies have been implemented. Echoing then Surgeon General C. Everett Koop's 1985 prediction that in 1995 a smoker would have to "smoke alone or with other smokers" in a segregated area (*New York Times* 1985b), Maria Baker, a former smoker and health educator, commented: "They are becoming their own smoking society, really. A society of their own. And one that is protective of its numbers! They sabotage their own if one wants to decamp." Carol Zimmerman's mother, a smoker, "just couldn't take it" when Carol decided to stop smoking because she could no longer afford it. Carol recalled, "At one time I quit cold turkey because I was out of money. My husband worked only three weeks when I's pregnant. We hardly had any food. Only WIC [the Women, Infants, and Children food assistance program]—I's livin' off of egg sandwiches 'n' all. My mother went out and bought me a pack because she said I was being such a bitch though!" Antismoking advocates would cite this as a window of opportunity for quitting and disapprove of Carol's mother for sabotaging her daughter's forced attempt to quit.

Reflecting notions of the "segregated smoking society" that some health professionals identify as responsible for perpetuating smoking, several women reported that they failed to quit smoking because their friends or partners continued to smoke. Cynthia Phillips, a former smoker, says she quit each time she learned she was pregnant, but when she was not pregnant she would begin smoking again because she was "always around people who smoked."

Although smoking was described by women as pleasurable and part of social life, it was also discussed in the context of stressful events. Andrea Sellers, who wants to get a GED so she can find a better paying job, complained about how hard it would be to take the day-long exam: "I can't smoke there! I'll have to fit three cigarettes in maybe ten minutes. We only get two breaks." Tessa Andrews's long labor at a smoke-free hospital caused a problem for her husband, family, and friends who had accompanied her there: "At the hospital, I walked the halls. I went outside even, because my husband and everyone there wanted to smoke. So I'm jumpin' on and off the curb to start labor, like this!" While telling me this story, she reenacted her actions, cigarette in hand. Tessa did not remark on the irony of depicting a pregnant woman smoking a cigarette during labor or on how she had challenged health advice by being near secondhand smoke.

Carol Zimmerman talked at length about what smoking has meant to her and how it has been an influential aspect of her relationships with her mother, husband, coworkers, and daughter. "No friends or family smoke now," Carol stated. She paused, then confirmed, "Nope. My mom quit when I was nineteen. Now that my husband is gone, and I have a new workplace, nope. None. But I'm a real polite smoker. I never smoke in anyone's house, and in cars, I roll the windows down." Carol explained that when she was pregnant, she was around smokers at work and at home. This, along with financial stress and an abusive relationship, led her to smoke when she was pregnant five years ago, despite her intention not to:

> I stopped smoking when I was pregnant, eventually. I smoked one or one and a half packs. I'd intended to stop immediately, but it was hard. So I cut down, then stopped.
>
> LO: Why was it so hard?
>
> My husband smoked, and I had a small office and three cowork-ers smoked. . . . I quit smokin' but then when I was seven or eight months pregnant, I started again. The stress over money and every-thing was gettin' to me. Everyone around me was smoking anyway, so I thought "I'm gettin' all that secondhand smoke already anyway."

When thinking about her smoking during pregnancy, Carol is extremely self-critical:

> But the bad thing is that I started smoking a lot! I'd have a whole pack at work. I thought "Damn, that's way too much!" Most days, I don't have quite a pack a day. I's like "What-am-I-doin'?" When I brought the baby home from the hospital, I smoked only outside the house, unless it was cold out, then I'd stand by the door. I didn't think some smoke'd hurt her, just that a lot's not good. And I tried to ventilate the house. I have one strict rule though—I won't smoke if she's on my lap. I'm afraid she'll knock it and burn herself, you know. But now I say, "Honey, I can't hold you, I'm smoking." Or I go outside [her parents built a shelter outside her back door]—for her good—and she comes out and opens the door, like, "Mommy, you still smokin'?" and all the smoke goes in anyway!

Although Carol believed that smoking and secondhand smoke are health risks, she describes how ultimately she had little control over smoking due to her social situation. In fact, contrary to public health claims, Carol concluded that because she was exposed to so much smoke, her own smoking would not pose a great additional risk to her baby-to-be. This certainly is not the mes-sage pregnancy advice experts attempt to convey. Pregnant women are ex-pected not only to abstain from smoking but also to control their environment and the actions of smokers around them. Carol reveals that this is not always possible—she could not quit her job because she needed the money, and try-ing to convince her husband to abstain would strain a relationship already prone to violence. Like other smokers, given her social context, quitting would be a difficult process.

I have argued, as have other feminist health researchers, that women's daily lives must be taken into account when seeking to understand why they smoke. But an investigation into the meaning that smoking has in women's lives should not stop here. The reasons that women give for smoking reveal that in addition to social factors, biological factors may stand in the way of women who want to quit.

THE NATURE OF SMOKING: ADDICTION VERSUS CHOICE

Antismoking advice directed at pregnant women relies on several, often overlapping, messages. One main theme has to do with nicotine addiction, a biochemical condition that interferes with a smoker's ability to make healthy choices. For those who feel they are addicted to cigarettes, knowing the health risks of smoking does not necessarily facilitate quitting; this addiction undermines health professionals' emphasis on educating smokers about risk. But a countertheme to addiction is willpower: if nicotine addicts make the effort, they can quit. I address here the common assumption, made by health professionals and others, that pregnant women who smoke do so not because they choose to but because they are addicted. Health professionals' and smokers' conceptualizations of addiction and the choice to smoke contribute to different images of pregnant smokers.

Health experts' approaches to the problem of nicotine addiction vary widely, from seeing addiction as the main problem to ignoring it. Government reports on smoking first labeled nicotine as addictive in the 1980s, and research continues to emphasize its highly addictive properties.[14] Antismoking educators find their efforts frustrated by the nature of nicotine: "It's such a tough addiction, you know. If they're not ready [to quit], nothing in the world will make a difference" (Kate Bell-Woodard). Indeed, a medical text asserts that nicotine addiction must be treated "as a primary problem or disease in its own right" (Orleans and Slade 1993, ix). On the other hand, in response to pregnant women who say they cannot stop smoking because they are addicted, Maryland's Quit and Be Free! program stresses that quitting is a skill anyone can learn (State of Maryland Department of Health and Mental Hygiene n.d.b, 1), and *What to Expect When You're Expecting* (Eisenberg et al. 1991 [1984]) makes no mention of addiction in its antismoking advice. Representations of smoking focus on one of two themes: choice or addiction.

Although the rhetoric of choice implies that smokers have agency—the power of decision and action—the notion of addiction implies that a natural, biochemical process overrides that agency. If we see smokers as nicotine addicts who are controlled by their biochemistry, there is no room for their positive or conscious agency, such as the recognition that smokers may choose to smoke because it is a pleasurable, stress reducing, or a meaningful social activity. In fact, those health professionals and nonsmokers who believe that the risks of smoking outweigh any and all of its benefits might be most inclined to cite addiction as the reason women smoke. In this view, warnings about the health risks of smoking should lead smokers to the rational choice that they ought to quit. Addiction to nicotine intervenes in this process.

One effect of framing smoking as an addiction is that the smoker can be viewed as a victim of her biochemistry and therefore not to blame for continuing to smoke. Health educator Anne Dewitt thinks that the best line to take on smoking by pregnant women is "you have an addiction to nicotine," not "how could you do that to your baby?" She further explained, "It is not that women don't know that quitting smoking is good for the baby and for their own health. It is just very addictive and hard to give up. Many women cut down, but still need those three a day or whatever." Categorizing smoking as an addiction, as she sees it, is better than blaming the victim. This approach—identifying smokers as victims—emphasizes the opposite extreme of choice ideology. Health practitioners, as a result, argue that it is necessary to focus on helping smokers overcome the nicotine addiction that prohibits them from quitting.

But neither view of smokers—as individuals who have no choice over their behavior or as those who have total choice—seems to adequately represent their experience. Judy Levine, a physician and antitobacco policy advocate, contends that talking about addiction is tricky both because the issue of individual control is so important in American culture and because individual biochemistry is variable. She argues that "Americans are not, in my opinion, very comfortable with the idea of addiction—we don't like it, we don't understand it, we are more like 'if you really wanted to quit, you could.' And of course there's some truth in that, but there's a spectrum. There are people who, like my mother-in-law, decided one day to quit, and did. She probably wasn't very addicted. . . . other people try seven or eight times and can't. But we are uncomfortable with the idea that things control us."

Judy Levine's observation about the spectrum of addiction is reflected in other women's comments on their experiences. Anastasia Powers, who smoked during her first but not her second pregnancy, confided that her addiction to cigarettes has varied in intensity. But even when she is "more addicted," she is able to quit if she wants to. When I asked her how much she smoked when she was pregnant, Anastasia replied, "About five a day. The last eight weeks, I didn't smoke at all though. If I set my mind to quit, I can. Now, I'm more addicted, but it's all in the mind. I'm hyperactive, so I smoke. But I don't smoke in the house." Anastasia's cutting down from one and a half packs to five cigarettes a day and not smoking at home suggest that she takes seriously the warnings about how smoking might affect fetal and child health, even though she does not follow them perfectly. Her experience also challenges the idea that addiction is all controlling. Speaking to the same idea, Carol Zimmerman, a smoker who has found it very difficult to quit, explained that her relationship to cigarettes is more addictive than her mother's: "My mom still smokes an occasional cigarette. I don't understand how. If I had one, I'd have another." This again supports Judy Levine's contention that not all smokers are very addicted to nicotine.

Still other women recognized that addiction is one reason why they smoke but not the only reason. May Thomas both supported and dismissed the notion that addiction is the main obstacle to quitting smoking:

> LO: Did your doctors ever say anything about it [when you were pregnant]?
> Yeah—the doctors tell me to leave them cigarettes alone. That's tough though [she shakes her head]. I jus' couldn't stop.
> LO: Do you still see women who smoke while pregnant?
> Lotta 'em, the young ones too.
> LO: Why do you think they decide not to stop or cut back?
> I guess the nicotine's in the system, jus' like it's in mine. But it sure taste good after a good meal.

Although she acknowledged that she might be addicted to nicotine, May emphasized that the pleasure of smoking is a main factor in her inability to give up smoking. Angela Perry also pointed out that addiction is but one part of her experience of being a smoker. Like May, she enjoys smoking after a meal and also when she is out at a bar. But Angela's comments on why she smokes went one step farther, to attack antismoking policies, which she associates with the encroachment of authorities into even the smallest everyday choices:

> It's addictive—the companies know it. I'm addicted to smoking. I can go two–three–four hours, but then . . .
> LO: But you can't smoke at work, can you?
> No, but I do. And we get a fifteen-minute break, so we all go outside and smoke. Our cigarette break.
> LO: What do you think about the antismoking laws in Maryland now?
> Now they're tryin' to ban it in bars and restaurants! If they stop it there, then businesses are gonna close—you got a drink in one hand, cigarette in another. And after eatin', I gotta have that cigarette. I mean, I'm always sayin' "What're we gonna do in the year 2000? Walk aroun' like robots?" Or they'll say, "You can't sit in this chair, use that one?"

Angela's remarks reveal that although she feels controlled by her bodily response to nicotine, she is more angry about smoke-free policies than she is at cigarette companies that knowingly market an addictive product. She thinks that consumers deserve the right to smoke if they so choose. Angela has never wanted to quit smoking, but she cut down each time she was pregnant. Her addiction, then, neither victimizes nor completely controls her, and she both chooses to smoke and feels that she must. Angela's and other women's experiences contradict today's dominant images of smokers as agentless victims or addicts.

Although these characterizations also hold true for pregnant smokers, there is a further dimension to how pregnant smokers are represented and how they experience the desire to quit. Some authors of pregnancy advice books contend that pregnant women who smoke not only have a problem with addiction but experience an additional biochemical shortcoming—a deficient "maternal nature mechanism." In *Protecting Your Baby-to-Be*, Margie Profet contends that "pregnancy sickness alerts women to noxious 'burnt material' fumes, such as cigarette smoke, but long-term smoking thwarts this protective mechanism" (1995, 214). *What to Expect* claims that although a "natural aversion" to smoking may aid quitting, not all women share it: "For some smoking women, quitting will never be easier than in early pregnancy, when they develop a sudden distaste for cigarettes—probably the warning of an intuitive body. If you're not lucky enough to develop such a natural aversion, try quitting with . . . help" (Eisenberg et al. 1991 [1984], 56). The book does not explain why some women inherit a naturally intuitive body while others do not.

But do pregnant women themselves think that their relationship to smoking rests on their biology? Indeed, several women I met interpreted their or other women's responses to smoking as beyond their control. Amy Bellinger said that her body reacted differently to smoking during her two pregnancies: "The first pregnancy was a breeze. I was smoking before, but stopped because it made me sick. So I's smoking only when I didn't know I was pregnant, really. . . . The second pregnancy was rough. . . . I smoked then. I couldn't quit." When questioned about why she stopped during the first pregnancy but not the second, she responded, "I dunno—I just couldn't stop. It didn't make me sick—I's real surprised about that!" Contrary to the health educators' perspective, which would lead to the prediction that Amy's second baby, who was exposed to cigarette smoke throughout pregnancy, would have a greater risk of impaired health, Amy's first baby had "an air pocket or something in his lung and had to be in the NICU [neonatal intensive care unit]." Her second baby was healthy. Meredith Rodgers talked about her mother's "biological"

aversion to a number of substances, including cigarettes: "Both of her pregnancies, she didn't touch a cigarette or a drink, and then in the delivery room
after, she wanted both a cigarette and a drink [we laugh]. But she said defi-
nitely biologically she couldn't smoke, she couldn't drink, she couldn't drink
tea or coffee—couldn't touch caffeine." Meredith's mother was pregnant in
the 1950s, the period before health professionals warned women not to smoke,
drink, or ingest caffeine. She had what the authors of *What to Expect* refer to
as an intuitive pregnant body. Leslie Hollins, who smoked throughout pregnancy, thinks that her body's signals modified the way she smoked: "I believe
that the internal workings of the body repel bad things. When I was pregnant, I was really operating on habit, but then I only puffed cigarettes." Although she did not comply with antismoking advice to quit completely, Leslie
believed that smoking during pregnancy was a health risk. Further, Leslie implied that her natural impulse to not inhale as fully as she normally would
protected the health of her baby-to-be.

The three images of pregnant smokers I have discussed—nicotine addicts,
women who are incapable of making good health decisions, and women who
lack a natural aversion mechanism—do not reflect the complexity of women's
experiences with smoking. Representations of smokers as women who are influenced mainly by addiction or choice reinforce overly simplistic stereotypes
of the powerless victim, who should not be blamed, and the irresponsible bad
mother, who deserves blame. The third category of pregnant smokers, those
who have a natural aversion to cigarettes, are good mothers who are ruled by
positive biological influences; they evade blame because they quit smoking.
These three characterizations coexist but are not always given equal weight
in pregnancy advice literature and antismoking campaigns.

Indeed, in recent years, the dominant image of the pregnant smoker has
been that of the bad mother who fails to comply with medical advice about
making proper health decisions on behalf of her baby-to-be. This negative definition of women's power is an unsatisfactory basis for antismoking advice. It
reduces women's smoking activities to being the expression of personal, biological failure and provides little attention to the social structures and relationships in which women's smoking practices and their opinions about how
smoking affects fetal health are embedded.

The everyday women I talked with who smoke implied or stated that their
own interpretations of their smoking—their logic, decisions, and social relationships to cigarettes and to other smokers—were dismissed or undervalued
by health professionals and other pregnancy advice givers. Nearly every woman
agreed that quitting or cutting back on cigarettes and avoiding routine exposure to secondhand smoke were best for the baby-to-be, which means that

health warnings about smoking during pregnancy were taken seriously. Yet a number of women were angry about the ways health advice is delivered by health experts, friends, relatives, and strangers. Given that practically every woman has heard the message that she should not smoke during pregnancy, such advice is based less on health education and more on moral condemnation. Perpetuating the maternal–fetal conflict model of pregnancy, antismoking advice criticizes women's ability to be responsible decision makers, emphasizes that their primary duty is to protect fetal health, and questions their devotion to caring about their babies-to-be.

Chapter 6	"Because You Love Your Baby"

*Fetal Representations
in Antismoking and
Antiabortion Campaigns*

Fᴇᴍɪɴɪsᴛ sᴄʜᴏʟᴀʀs ʜᴀᴠᴇ explored the politics of pregnancy and reproductive health in response to intensified cultural, medical, and legal trends in the United States over the last three decades that emphasize a pregnant woman's separateness from her fetus and constrain the woman's choices, rights, and actions. Images depicting the fetus as autonomous threaten to overshadow the significance of pregnant women's bodies in the reproductive process, devalue the embodied relationship between pregnant women and their fetuses, and represent women as adversaries of their babies-to-be.[1] One particularly pressing feminist concern is the proliferation of fetal representations that establish the fetus as an actor who lives beyond the boundaries of a pregnant woman's body and inhabits a privileged place in the public imagination. Antiabortion advocates have publicized fetal images with the intent of cultivating the universal view that fetuses are babies. Yet, although some fetal images we see in public culture are sponsored by antiabortion organizations, others are not.

Public fetal representations—such as images in Hollywood films or in advertising—may not explicitly support the antiabortion cause; however, they indicate that fetuses are gaining symbolic status as persons in the United States (Petchesky 1987; Hartouni 1991; Taylor 1992, 1998; Morgan and Michaels 1999). Indeed, in her essay on the history of fetal imagery, Karen Newman notes that "there is no doubt that the media and new visual technologies have endowed the fetus with a public persona, a notoriety, even a star status" (1996, 25). The question of how fetuses should be defined is hotly contested in medicine, law, and popular culture, and as anthropologist Lynn Morgan writes, "the more we puzzle over fetuses, the more we legitimate the subject, and, by extension, the subjectivity, of the 'fetal person'" (1997, 324). A particular type of fetal person—coded as a vulnerable agent in need of, if not demanding, vigilant protection—is at the center of social policy, health policy, and legal debate.

Representations in popular culture, including antismoking campaigns, of the fetus as an autonomous and vulnerable individual have serious implications for public health policy, medical practice, cultural politics, and women's experiences of pregnancy and motherhood. This chapter explores connections between two seemingly separate areas of current social and political contest in the United States—antismoking education and antiabortion activism. It investigates how these campaigns increase the power of pregnancy advice and the stakes for women, who are measured against an ideal good mother. Health education efforts to convince pregnant women to quit smoking cigarettes and antiabortion drives to criminalize abortion reinforce fetal-centric medical, social, and moral expectations of women's reproductive responsibilities. At the same time that antiabortion and antismoking campaigns seek to change pregnant women's behaviors, they also reinforce specific ideas about how pregnant women must act to be good mothers-to-be. Antismoking and antiabortion messages rely on the maternal–fetal conflict theme in that they depict fetuses as vulnerable individuals and agents in need of maternal care and even public protection from their irresponsible mothers.

Fetal Imagery in Antiabortion and Antismoking Campaigns

The public introduction of fetal images is often traced to a 1965 *Life* magazine cover story, the "Drama of Life before Birth," which carried a series of photographs of developing fetuses taken by Lennart Nilsson (Franklin 1991, 195–196; Duden 1993; Stabile 1994, 74–83; Newman 1996,10–18; and Rapp 1997). These and later photos by Nilsson have been used repeatedly since the 1970s by the antiabortion movement in its literature and placards. In fact, abortion clinic protesters carried copies of a 1990 *Life* magazine featuring Nilsson's more recent work to try to discourage women from entering clinics in Rhode Island (see Stabile 1994, 83). From an antiabortion perspective, fetal photographs and sonograms present scientific evidence that developing fetuses are miniature humans. It follows that abortion constitutes the murder of a "preborn baby" and should be banned. Once women and policy makers come to see the fetus as a person, antiabortion advocates contend, abortion will be eradicated. As Rosalind Petchesky notes, publicizing fetal images is a central part of the antiabortion movement's campaign: "the strategy of antiabortionists [is] to make fetal personhood a self-fulfilling prophecy by making the fetus a public presence" (1987, 264). The many antiabortion representations of the fetus work to have this same effect of humanizing the fetus. Activists display fetal images on bumper stickers and "little feet" lapel pins as well as in media advertisements, pamphlets, posters, and billboards. The prolife tactic of presenting the visual image of the fetus as an independent miniature human supports the claim that the "unborn" deserve human rights.

Perhaps the most dramatic example of promoting the antiabortion cause through fetal imagery is the widely distributed National Right-to-Life Committee's 1984 video "The Silent Scream." The video claims to show via ultrasound the abortion of a ten-week-old fetus from the fetus's point of view (see Petchesky 1987; Hartouni 1992). The film aired on network television and was further publicized by media coverage of the debate that surrounded it. Images, music, and narrative work together to convince the viewer that what is seen is reality: abortion is violent, and the innocent child needs protection: "the ultrasound image is presented as a document testifying that the fetus is 'alive,' is 'human like you or me,' and 'senses pain'" (Petchesky 1987, 267). The idea behind "The Silent Scream" was sparked by antiabortion activists after a report in the New England Journal of Medicine suggested that women bond to their fetuses and recognize them as their own after seeing a sonogram (Petchesky 1987, 265). Physicians John Fletcher and Mark Evans cite two cases in which women stated that they would not opt for an abortion after having seen a sonogram. One woman claimed, 'It really made a difference to see that it was alive. . . . I am going all the way with the baby. I believe it is human'" (1983, 392). This is the conclusion that antiabortion advocates want viewers of "The Silent Scream" to carry with them.

At the same time that prolife activists have placed the fetal person in the public eye and medical professionals have increasingly come to see the fetus as a patient, health educators have paid greater attention to how pregnant women's practices—such as cigarette smoking, alcohol consumption, and drug use—negatively affect fetal health. Fetal rights advocates, pregnancy advice authors, and health professionals all voice concern about pregnant women's caretaking of their fetuses, often emphasizing how women might knowingly or unknowingly harm their babies-to-be.

Although antismoking materials aimed at pregnant women do not use the same methods to convince women to stop smoking, the baby's health is routinely presented as the ultimate reason women should quit. Using professional jargon, public health professionals refer to programs that promote health behavior change as interventions. Through smoking cessation campaigns, health educators attempt to intervene in the relationship between the pregnant woman and her fetus on behalf of the fetus's health. Indeed, the "don't smoke when you're pregnant" message must be read within a cultural-political context in which the so-called maternal–fetal relationship is increasingly constructed as one of potential conflict (see Chavkin 1992). Most health education campaigns are designed with the sincere intent to help women. However, the ways in which women are directed to quit smoking expose the micro-power of health policy and education over pregnant women's actions and reveal that moral discourses that label good and bad mothers are embedded in health campaigns. Antismoking and antiabortion campaigns draw on the symbolic concepts of rights, health, and maternal nurturance to produce powerful messages: babies-to-be are unique individuals who have rights to health and life; pregnant women are morally responsible for making healthy choices; and pregnant women must devote themselves to responding to the needs of their babies-to-be.

The use of fetal images in prenatal health and antiabortion campaigns promotes specific expectations about women's pregnancy practices and their perceptions of fetal life. Despite their differences, both campaigns rely on a combination of emotional and scientific arguments to demonstrate that fetuses are unique individuals who should have their rights to life and health protected. Sketches, cartoons, and narrative descriptions are presented to draw an emotional connection between the fetal image and the image of a dimpled, bouncing baby, while ultrasound imaging, lifelike models, and photography are employed to depict the biological realities of fetal life. These strategies promote specific ways of seeing the fetus and of defining how pregnant women should feel about and act toward their babies-to-be.

SMOKING DURING PREGNANCY AS A THREAT TO FETAL LIFE: APPEALS TO EMOTION

Only in the last three decades have health professionals sought to convince women that smoking is an intolerable fetal health risk, and the way they have presented fetal images has varied. In the late 1970s and early 1980s, two of the most visible health organizations, the American Cancer Society (ACS) and the American Lung Association (ALA), initiated national public education campaigns about the risks of smoking during pregnancy. Less publicly, these organizations also have been involved in national antitobacco coalitions and lobbying efforts (see Nathanson 1997). The earliest example of the use of fetal imagery for the antismoking cause is a 1974 poster produced by the ALA. The poster, whose title reads "Smoking Can Affect the Two of You," displays a drawing of a developing fetus, including placental matter (see figure 6.1). This poster is advertised in an ALA catalog as featuring a "startling

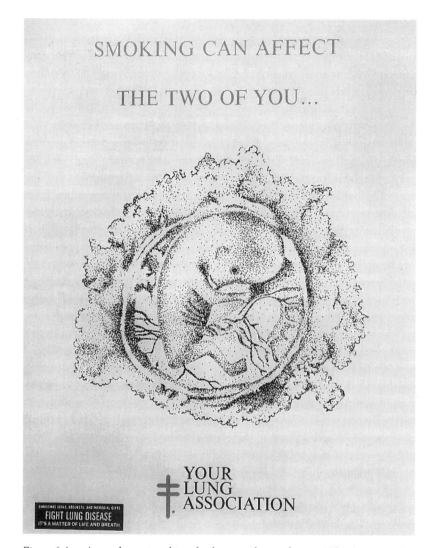

SMOKING CAN AFFECT

THE TWO OF YOU...

YOUR
LUNG
ASSOCIATION

CHRISTMAS SEALS, BEQUESTS, AND MEMORIAL GIFTS
FIGHT LUNG DISEASE
IT'S A MATTER OF LIFE AND BREATH

Figure 6.1. An early antismoking fetal image depicted on a 1974 American Lung Association poster. (*Copyright American Lung Association. Reprinted with permission.*)

but touching drawing of unborn child that is still in the mother's womb" (American Lung Association 1980, 21). Although the language of "unborn child" and "mother's womb" resonates with antiabortion discourse, the image contrasts with the publicized "miniature baby" fetuses promoted by the prolife movement. Most remarkably, the uterus and placenta are well detailed, and the fetus is early in its development and is fetal (not baby) looking. Antiabortion images generally do not include the pregnant woman's body and most often represent fetuses that look like babies.

Other antismoking materials do use fetal images that parallel those publicized by the antiabortion movement in an attempt to elicit an emotional attachment by a pregnant woman to her baby-to-be. The ALA's fetus poster was part of a "Smoking and Pregnancy" education program offered around 1980 that included a flip chart for health professionals and a take-home booklet for pregnant women. The cover drawing of both shows a transparent, pregnant white woman.[2] Both the woman and her fetus have cigarettes in their mouths, emphasizing that when the pregnant woman smokes, so does the baby-to-be. But the fetal images contained in these materials differ notably. In the flip chart, a diagram shows a fetus that resembles a tadpole more than a baby, with the subtext "Nicotine and carbon monoxide inhaled in cigarette smoke enter the mother's blood stream, cross the placenta, and enter the baby's blood stream. This cuts down on oxygen which is needed for normal weight gain and development" (American Lung Association of Maryland n.d.a, 1–2). The companion booklet designed for women to take home replaces this representation with a drawing of a miniature baby in utero sucking its thumb. Unlike the health professional's flip chart, the take-home booklet has a drawing of a fetus in a smoke-filled, Black woman's womb. The fetus's arms are crossed against its chest in a protective gesture, and it wears an angry expression. Its tongue sticks out as if it is choking or suffocating (n.d.b., 3), and its body language easily conveys the idea that a mother's smoking distresses her baby-to-be.

Indeed, many other, more recent warnings against smoking during pregnancy personify fetuses by featuring illustrations of thinking and talking fetuses that look like infants. The images with which some health educators want women to identify are stylized characterizations of the fetus as a baby, not scientific images showing the fetus as a developing human being. One theme emphasizes how a fetus attempts to communicate with the "pregnant mother," as seen in an ACS smoking cessation workbook's series of cartoons that asks "What would your baby say?" (American Cancer Society 1988, 5). One cartoon (figure 6.2) contrasts a model mother-to-be with an irresponsible mother-to-be. Two pregnant women stand facing each other, one eating a carrot, the other smoking a cigarette. The nonsmoker's smiling fetus says, "My mom's eating for both of us." The smoker's fetus is smaller, and its tongue hangs out the side of its mouth as it says, "My mom's smoking for both of us."[3] This simple illustration conveys expectations about pregnant women's eating and smoking. The choice of a carrot is not coincidental, for it provides

Figure 6.2.   Healthy baby-to-be: "My mom's eating for both of us." Sickly baby-to-be: "My mom's smoking for both of us." (*From American Cancer Society, "Special Delivery . . . . Smoke-Free," 1988. Reprinted with permission of the American Cancer Society, Inc.*)

a specific subtext: If cigarettes fulfill an oral fixation, eat a cigarette-shaped, nutritious vegetable instead of smoking so that your baby-to-be isn't harmed—or perhaps killed. The cartoon's caption reads: "If you smoke, there is more of a chance your baby won't 'make it' [survive] at all."

A second cartoon (figure 6.3), with a drawing of a fetus that wants to be born, illustrates the warning that "if you smoke, there is more of a chance that your baby will be born too soon." A smiling woman holds a lit cigarette in one hand and her pregnant stomach in the other while the fetus screams, "Get me out of here, quick!" This cartoon portrays an adversarial relationship between the woman and fetus: while she experiences pleasure from smoking, she is oblivious to her fetus's feelings and its attempts to communicate

Figure 6.3. Baby-to-be: "Get me out of here, quick!" (*From American Cancer Society, "Special Delivery. . . . Smoke-Free," 1988. Reprinted with permission of the American Cancer Society, Inc.*)

with her. Not only does she engage in an unhealthy practice, but she is self-absorbed and self-centered, qualities associated with neglectful mothering. The fetus's demand is the result of both "womb pollution" caused by smoking and a lack of emotional care.

Health educators' envisioning of what a baby-to-be is thinking, feeling, and saying is similar to that advanced by antiabortion activists. Prolife crisis pregnancy counselor Ellen Curro writes about trying to dissuade a woman from abortion in this way: "Even though I'm sitting listening and talking to this woman, it's as if I can 'see' the tiny baby inside her! The baby is facing me with a smile on its face, waving its arms as if cheering me on. The little one is saying to me, 'Keep talking to Mom, don't give up'" (1990, 18). Curro sees her job as some health educators see theirs: to inform the pregnant woman that she is ignoring her baby's attempt to communicate its needs. Similar advocacy on behalf of the fetus is demonstrated in a prenatal health pamphlet that instructs pregnant women to listen to an imaginary antismoking message from their babies-to-be: "'Mommy, please don't smoke!' That's what your unborn baby would say, if he or she could talk" (PennSAIC 1994 [1992], 2). Clearly, whether the intent is antismoking or antiabortion, the representation of fetuses as miniature individuals and pregnant women as neglectful mothers points to the connections between seemingly disparate discourses.

Although antismoking campaigns present examples of bad mothers, they also offer positive models of motherhood. Indeed, in many antismoking campaigns, quitting smoking is portrayed as a symbol of maternal love. The moral message of the health slogan publicized nationally by the ALA between 1983 and 1988, "Because you Love your Baby . . . There's Never been a Better Time to Quit," implies that women who do not quit smoking do not love their babies-to-be and that only nonsmokers are loving mothers. In 1986, the ALA launched a new campaign but retained the earlier fetal-centered theme: "I Quit Smoking: Because I Love My Baby." The ALA urges women to use their concern for their baby's health as justification for quitting and offers this slogan (on stickers and stand-up cards to replace ashtrays) as a way for women to announce that they have adopted proper mothering practices. In effect, the former smoker mimics the health professional's message, renounces her former bad mother identity, and declares that she has reformed to follow the medical and moral imperative to guard fetal health because that is what a good mother does. This form of self-congratulation not only publicizes the woman's reformation but implicitly instructs others to model the ex-smoker's self-discipline. These and other antismoking materials construct an ideal type of mother, one who is self-sacrificing, nurturing, and compliant with medical advice about how to care for the baby-to-be.

Although continually emphasizing how pregnant women ought to care for their babies-to-be, the antismoking themes of health educators have varied.[4] The ALA's smoking cessation efforts directed at pregnant women reveal the use of several overlapping messages and, over time, a shift in framing the issue away from the fetus and toward the family. In 1981, the ALA of Maryland produced a slide and tape presentation introducing the theme "Because you Love your Baby. . .There's Never been a Better Time to Quit." This campaign slogan was launched in a national ALA program introduced in 1983 and was included in ALA materials until 1988. In 1986, the ALA introduced a cessation program aimed at white and African American pregnant women called "Freedom from Smoking for You and Your Baby," but it retained the earlier fetal-centered theme until 1988 by distributing stickers, booklets, and stand-up cards stating "I Quit Smoking: Because I Love My Baby."

In 1988, after the release of new scientific data on the health risks of secondhand smoking to infants and young children, the ALA's health education materials were modified to emphasize abstinence from smoking during and after pregnancy. Pregnant women were offered a pin reading, "No Smoking PLEASE I'm Breathing for Two," and a new campaign, "A Healthy Beginning: The Smoke-Free Family Guide for New Parents," introduced the importance of a "smoke-free family." The idea of the smoke-free family removed some of the responsibility for "fetal smoking" from pregnant women and onto those around her. It also capitalized on the profamily discourse of conservative politicians, social movement leaders, and others who believed that the family as a foundational moral, social unit had been co-opted by nontraditional families formed by gays and lesbians, single mothers, and divorced/remarried parents (see Reid 1995).

The ACS has designed smoking cessation programs aimed at pregnant women that are similar to those of the ALA. In the late 1970s, the ACS took action on smoking and pregnancy. Its first smoking and pregnancy poster, "Why Start Life Under A Cloud?" was published in 1977 and features a profile photo of a pregnant woman who is smoking as plumes of smoke rise over her extended abdomen. Unlike later messages that refer to women's smoke-filled wombs, this visual representation emphasizes what is external to the woman's body—the cloud of smoke that rises from her cigarette. The slogan asks pregnant women to justify why they smoke, but it does not issue an imperative about quitting. The meaning of "starting life under a cloud" is unclear, but it seems to connote something sinister. Because both the pregnant woman and her fetus are under the cloud of cigarette smoke, the message points not only to fetal well-being but to a woman's health and the threat of her death.

None of the later ACS themes are as thought provoking, and they are far more directive. In 1988, the organization further encouraged each pregnant woman to "have a smoke-free baby" by producing a self-help smoking cessation program, "Special Delivery . . . Smoke-Free" (American Cancer Society 1988, 40). The activity book's introduction issues this challenge: "stopping smoking is a good idea. That's true at any time. But it's especially true now that you are going to have a baby. It's *your* choice to stop smoking—no one can do it for you" (American Cancer Society 1988, 1; original emphasis). This approach individualizes the practice of smoking and instructs women that fetal health is solely their responsibility. The ACS, however, is aware that women who smoke have partners, family members, and friends who smoke. Their workbook suggests that friends be enlisted in quitting efforts and provides cards for a woman to present to others to enlist their support here; for example, "Dear ____, My baby wants me to quit smoking—so I am! Please don't smoke near me or give me cigarettes" (1988, 21–22). The woman's request is initiated by the baby-to-be's desires, and in effect, she asks others to help her respond to her baby-to-be's "wishes." In doing so, she publicizes the strategically emotional and morally laden public health message that to be caring, protective mothers, pregnant women must not smoke cigarettes.

The ability of health educators to capitalize (consciously or not) on the prolife ideology of fetal personhood and to invoke fetal images as emotional symbols increases the power of these warnings against smoking during pregnancy. Drawing on emotional appeals, health educators often urge pregnant women to visualize the baby-to-be as a miniature infant at every developmental stage. The basic premise of prenatal smoking cessation messages is that "the fetus of a smoking mother also is an involuntary smoker. Although not actually inhaling ETS [environmental tobacco smoke], the baby is a captive recipient of tobacco chemicals passed across the placenta from the mother" (Charlton 1994, 267). Labeling the baby-to-be an involuntary smoker or captive recipient of tobacco chemicals re-creates him or her as an autonomous individual and victim who is unfairly put at risk by an insensitive and unhealthy smoker. Pregnant women are potentially either involuntary victim—if they are exposed to secondhand smoke—or aggressor—if they smoke, and health education materials mainly emphasize the latter role. One pregnancy advice book provides an extreme example, engaging its readers in a mental dialogue: "Would you blow a puff of smoke directly into your child's face? Would you deliberately surround your baby with carbon monoxide or cut off your child's oxygen supply? Of course you wouldn't. But every time you smoke . . . you could be exposing your fetus . . . to danger" (Herman and Perry 1997, 48; see figure 6.4).

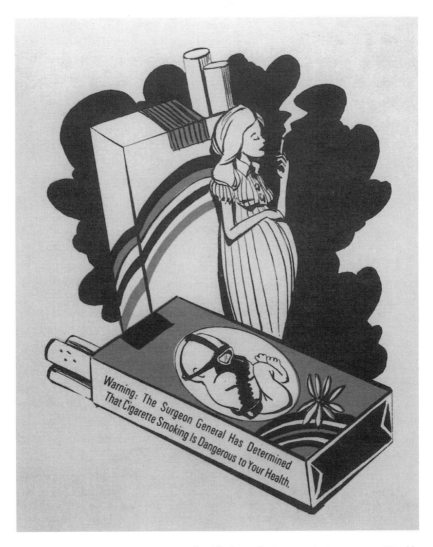

Figure 6.4. The fetus reacts to a smoke-filled womb. (*From U.S. Department of Health, Education, and Welfare,* Prenatal Care, *1973.*)

This warning offers strong social and moral messages but provides scant health information. Blowing smoke in anyone's face is a sign of disrespect and aggression, and surrounding a baby with carbon monoxide or cutting off his or her oxygen supply represents the intent to kill. Given this, the author asks the pregnant reader whether she intends to be a bad or even murderous mother. If she does not, then she must quit smoking. One antitobacco advocate and pregnancy advice columnist takes this moral argument a step further. She assures smokers that by quitting, "you'll be giving your unborn child what is justly his birthright: maximizing his or her chance to start life free from physical or mental disability" (Whelan 1980, 33). A woman who smokes when she is pregnant denies her baby-to-be's "right" to health.

Upbeat language and imagery are used by other antismoking advocates, but the argument about the meaning of smoking remains fundamentally the same: the fetus is an individual person in need of protection from its mother. A 1980 ALA antismoking pamphlet presents fetal life as a struggle that requires the pregnant woman's assistance: "Your baby-to-be, snuggled inside your womb, is silently engaged in a wonder-filled adventure: the struggle toward life. Your unborn baby needs all the help it can get in that struggle. Especially from you." The ALA further suggests that "when you quit smoking this minute, you'll be giving your unborn baby the smoke-free environment both of you need to be healthy. It's more than a gift. It's a matter of life and breath." This assertion—that a smoke-free womb is more than a gift—indicates that not smoking is a moral responsibility and that being born smoke free is an entitlement, not simply a privilege.[5]

In other antismoking literature, the phrase "smoke-filled womb," a play on "smoke-filled room," is used to conjure up the image of a miniature baby trapped in a smoky environment. The popular *What to Expect When You're Expecting* intones: "In effect, when you smoke, your baby is confined in a smoke-filled womb. His heartbeat speeds, he coughs and sputters, and worst of all, due to insufficient oxygen, he can't grow and thrive as he should" (Eisenberg et al. 1991 [1984], 56).[6] Although this statement describes what happens when a pregnant woman smokes and warns of the risk of low birthweight to the baby-to-be, the scientific content of the warning—that a lack of oxygen inhibits fetal growth—is overshadowed by the emotional image. The reader is invited to imagine an infant's reactions to being imprisoned in a smoky place and to envision the uterus as actually polluted with cigarette smoke.

DEMONSTRATING THE NEED FOR FETAL PROTECTION: APPEALS TO SCIENTIFIC AUTHORITY

Antismoking efforts rely not only on cartoonlike drawings and narrative descriptions of fetuses but also on real-time fetal images and "lifelike" fetal models. Visual access to fetal life through obstetric imaging technologies has been crucial to the social and medical definitions of the fetus as a patient and person,[7] and antismoking advocates support their claims about the dangerous effects of smoking on fetal health through scientific displays. This argument draws its power from a combination of the cultural association of science and medicine with truth or reality and the construction of the fetus as a vulnerable individual. It also parallels the antiabortion use of fetal sonogram images in "The Silent Scream," fetal photographs on billboards, and fetal models and preserved fetuses.

A 1977 film sponsored by the ACS uses fetal sonogram images to reinforce the message that pregnant women who smoke endanger fetal health.[8] The title of the film, "The Feminine Mistake," is an obvious play on the title of Betty Friedan's book *The Feminine Mystique* (1963). Whereas the book gives an analysis of the dissatisfaction of middle-class, college-educated, suburban housewives with their everyday lives and position in society, the film suggests that women have adopted the dangerous "male" practice of smoking in an attempt to be equal with men. Sit-com actress Bonnie Franklin, who hosts the film, announces that "the social equality women are achieving extends, it seems, all the way to self-destruction." In the film's conclusion, Franklin returns to this theme to inform women that if they quit, they will "feel more independent" and "in control" of their lives.

Throughout, the film both critiques and appropriates ideas about women's liberation. It warns women against "false equality," attempts to raise women's consciousness about the ways that cigarettes oppress them, and urges women to declare independence from smoking. By framing women's smoking this way, the ACS worked to reverse a set of cultural symbols that has been attached to women's smoking since the 1920s, when, after women's suffrage, some women's rights advocates and cigarette advertisers considered cigarette use by women to be a positive symbol of women's new status (Brandt 1996). Decades later, Philip Morris linked smoking with the changes brought about by the women's movement with its 1968 Virginia Slims slogan, "You've Come a Long Way, Baby!" (see O'Keefe and Pollay 1996).

The ACS's message is that smoking is not only self-destructive but harmful to "unborn children." One segment of the film devoted specifically to smoking during pregnancy begins with the image of a woman pushing a baby carriage down a busy city sidewalk. As she lights a cigarette, Bonnie Franklin intones, "One of the least publicized, but most insidious effects of cigarette smoke is upon the unborn child of a pregnant woman."[9] The only health statistic cited warns of a 30 to 60 percent increased risk of fetal and newborn death, and the remainder of the segment illustrates this risk through use of ultrasound technology. The central health education message is that the "unborn child" is "affected by each and every cigarette."

The scene cuts from the city street to a hospital, and the film introduces Dr. Frank Manning, who wears a white lab coat and who had published research on smoking and fetal activity (Manning and Feyerabend 1976). The camera focuses on an ultrasound monitor that is displaying vigorous pulses on the screen, which, the viewer is told, proves that the fetus is breathing. Manning explains that it is "immersed in fluid, but exercising the muscles it will depend on to survive." A pregnant woman, identified as Mrs. Delores Arrojo, lies in a hospital bed with her shiny belly exposed as a laboratory technician performs the ultrasound. The viewer is told that she has smoked one pack of cigarettes a day throughout the pregnancy. To demonstrate the effect of smoking on fetal movement, she smokes a cigarette. Manning then describes the change that has occurred in the sonogram image after a time lapse of thirty minutes: "no movements of the chest wall at all. This fetus is not breathing at all." Manning addresses Arrojo: "We've seen before your baby was breathing about 60 percent of the time. Now we see not at all. How do you feel about that?" Her eyes widen, she smiles slightly, and opens her mouth to speak when a voice-over preempts her response to announce: "Delores Arrojo has stopped smoking."

The unanswered question, "How do you feel about that?" lingers, as if directed to the audience to elicit an emotional response. The viewer, informed that Delores Arrojo quit smoking, is left with the impression that the experience of seeing her baby-to-be's ultrasound image and receiving health warnings convinced her to do so. Her own reasons for quitting are silenced, and she is portrayed as a compliant, reformed mother-to-be.

The antismoking argument in the film relies on the power associated with medical authority and the demonstration of scientific facts. The film attempts to establish that all fetuses will react to smoking as Delores Arrojo's baby-to-be did. In medical-statistical language, Manning points out that the fetus had been breathing 60 percent of the time, but the viewer has nothing to measure this against. Should babies-to-be, like infants, breathe 100 percent of the time? Manning explained that by "breathing" he means that the fetus is exercising the muscles that will later be used to breathe. But does a fetus take rests or stop "exercising"? The scene strategically evades such questions, and the strength of the message relies on the audience's assumption that not breathing is a threat to the fetus's life, just as it would be to an infant's.[10]

This demonstration was evidently judged effective by the ACS; it was revised and included in a second version of the film produced twelve years later. The 1989 update of "The Feminist Mistake," subtitled "The Next Generation," extends the section on smoking during pregnancy (hosted by a different TV mom, Meredith Baxter Birney).[11] The subject is first alluded to by a blonde teenager who ruminates about how smoking might influence her future life plans. She explains that she wants to have children one day but worries that "you can develop a really major addiction, like having three or four packs a day, and you become pregnant, and you're gonna have a kid and it's gonna affect your kids, and that's really scary." Smoking represents a dangerous threat to a "normal" woman's life course and to the health of her future, imagined fetuses and children.

Expanding on the addiction theme, the film uses the statement from the 1988 surgeon general's annual report on smoking and health that "cigarettes can be as addictive as cocaine" as the lead-in to the revised ultrasound segment. This statement suggests that smoking cigarettes is as dangerous and deviant as using illegal drugs. The film goes on to categorize pregnant women who smoke cigarettes as powerless addicts: "For people like Emma Parra, the craving is overwhelming even when another life is at stake." But Emma Parra does not only represent the addicted pregnant smoker. She also stands for the less-educated Latina woman, as does Delores Arrojo in the first film. The choice of these pregnant smokers is misleading: Latina women have significantly lower rates of smoking during pregnancy than do women of other racial/ethnic backgrounds. In 1998, 6 percent of pregnant Latina women smoked during pregnancy versus 9 percent of pregnant Black women and 16.2 percent of pregnant white women (Ventura et al. 2000, 54). The films suggest that less-educated Latina women are more likely than others to resist white, middle-class health norms and that therefore they deserve strict surveillance. Thus these antismoking messages underwrite the historical trend of disproportionate social and medical control over the reproductive experiences of low-income women and women of color (Davis 1983 [1981]; Petchesky 1985 [1984]; Roberts 1997).

The ultrasound scene begins as Dr. Andrew Chow of UCLA Medical Center identifies parts of Emma Parra's "baby," six weeks from its due date, on a sonogram screen. Baxter narrates: "[Dr. Chow] provides Emma a glimpse of her unborn child and cautions her against the danger of smoking." In contrast to the earlier film, the woman is in the foreground, and the doctor himself moves the transducer around her abdomen. While Delores Arrojo was passive and stared at the ceiling, Emma Parra holds herself up with one arm behind her head and is interested in watching the fetal image on the screen. The most striking difference is that while Delores's reaction to the sonogram image was edited out of the film, the audience listens as Emma, who speaks English with a Spanish accent, engages Chow in a conversation. She tells Chow: "I'm hooked on cigarettes. Does it go into the baby like [it goes] into my lungs?" He replies that "whatever enters your bloodstream does reach the baby to some degree." Chow's reply does not truly answer the question, and he fails to elaborate on the health dangers that face the fetus. Thus, little medical information is transmitted beyond the idea that smoking is "bad for the baby."

Suddenly the scene changes from the medical setting to a park. The camera zooms in on Emma Parra, who rests her hand on her pregnant belly while holding a cigarette. She comments, "It's a nice feeling when your baby moves. You'll feel it, but then I'll sit up there and I'll pick up a cigarette and then I won't feel it move for a while." The scene immediately shifts back to the hospital, where Emma's observations about her bodily sensations are demonstrated by the ultrasound. Chow now warns her about the fetal and infant risks of smoking, including low birthweight, impaired reading and writing ability, and poorer "performance in social relationships." She props herself up on her arms in the bed, nodding and biting her lip as she listens intently to the doctor's most powerful message: "You're in effect, with every cigarette you take, strangling and suffocating the baby for a little while." Chow's use of everyday language, "strangling and suffocating," instead of scientific language, such as "causing reduced blood-oxygen flow," more readily conjures up the image of intentional harm or even murder. As in the earlier film, the woman does not describe her reactions upon hearing this warning and seeing it demonstrated.

The film cuts back to the outdoor shot of Emma's hand resting on her belly and holding a cigarette. Outside the hospital and away from medical authority, she confesses that even after seeing the sonogram, she continues to smoke. In this camera frame, the spatial proximity of the cigarette to her baby-to-be signals the constant peril of fetal strangulation and suffocation, and suggests that she will smoke near her infant when it is born. In contrast to the 1977 film, in which Delores Arrojo quit smoking, Emma Parra stammers, as she explains, "If anything ever happened to, my, my, my kid, I think I would really really hate myself. But here I will not quit. . . . And it's a scary feeling wondering if this baby's gonna be affected by it." Emma admits that she is addicted to cigarettes, and she accepts the lack of control and guilt associated with being a pregnant smoker.

A later segment of the film suggests that Emma Parra's problem is not addiction but attitude. A white health educator leading an ACS-sponsored "Fresh Start" smoking cessation class (which Emma does not attend) declares: "You can totally adjust your attitude. It's a total choice on your part. . . . [It's an] empowering feeling, not letting that little cigarette run your life." Extended to pregnancy and smoking, and reflected in both ACS films, health experts state that pregnant women should let the "little fetus," not the "little cigarette," run their lives. This implies that the two compete for the woman's attention: if a woman smokes, her fetus loses.

In its sonogram demonstrations, the ACS presents smoking during pregnancy as a serious fetal health problem and exploits ultrasound technology to stress its status as a scientific reality. Notably, while the ultrasound images construct the fetus as a patient and a person who needs protection, the blame for women's baby-threatening smoking is placed differently in the two films. The 1977 version blames women, who are willingly participating in self-destruction, while the 1989 film points an accusing finger at the tobacco industry for hooking women on nicotine through slick advertising. Antitobacco advocate Virginia Ernster presents a critical analysis of cigarette ads to a high school audience in the 1989 video, stating, "I started getting really angry, not at women who smoke, but at what it was that was inducing women to smoke." This redirection of blame follows a paradigm shift in the public health approach to cigarette use, from antismoking activism to antitobacco advocacy. In the new framework, the smoker is a victim of the tobacco industry's advertising and marketing and deserves help (such as smoking cessation counseling or nicotine replacement therapy). But in either approach, messages about smoking during pregnancy remain fetal centered, and women are represented as either poor decision-makers because they choose to smoke or helpless addicts because they cannot quit.

The films also contain specific ideas about women's feelings toward their fetuses. The assumption behind the 1977 film is that if a woman sees her baby-to-be stop "breathing" when she smokes, she will quit smoking. This notion parallels the logic of prolife activists who argue that "if there were a window on a pregnant woman's stomach, there would be no more abortions" (quoted in Ginsburg 1998 [1989], 104) and the practice of some health professionals who show sonogram images to women to dissuade them from having abortions (Rapp 1990, 35; 1997, 47). Such visual tactics not only invoke assumptions about how women bond with their babies-to-be but also point to how the publicized visualization of fetal life can incite public protection of all fetuses. The 1989 film, however, confounds the bonding hypothesis because it portrays a woman who is worried about her baby's health but who does not quit smoking. While some viewers may be sympathetic to Emma Parra's plight, others likely are motivated by the idea that something must be done to stop nicotine addicts from smoking when pregnant (or perhaps even to stop them from becoming pregnant). In contrast to the 1977 film, in which Delores Arrojo complies with medical advice, the 1989 version portrays a noncompliant patient. It invites the audience to conclude that medical advice alone is not sufficient and that smoking during pregnancy is a social problem that everyone should do something about.

One action that the film's viewers are urged to take is to be critical of the tobacco industry's targeted marketing to women. However, framing smoking as a social problem in effect gives viewers, and the general public, license to intervene on behalf of the fetus. Telling a pregnant woman to stop smoking could be considered a way to help solve the problem. In fact, many of the women I talked with had been told to quit smoking when pregnant by family, friends, coworkers, and even strangers. Recall from the last chapter the anger Leslie Hollins still feels when she remembers how the men in her office harangued her when she smoked during her pregnancy. Her conclusion that "It was none of their damn business!" directly contradicts the message of the ACS's films, that smoking during pregnancy is everyone's business.

Although the modified and expanded version of the film is now more than ten years old, some health educators still find it a powerful educational tool. Maria Baker shows "The Feminine Mistake: The Next Generation" in her smoking cessation classes and believes that the scene with the fetal monitor and ultrasound showing how "the baby stops moving" is effective "even with low-education audiences."[12] This comment reveals that smokers who have "low-education" or lower class status are considered by public health professionals to be particularly resistant to antismoking messages. The strength of the film is that the audience, in Maria Baker's words, "gets to see reality."

There is little evidence that women react to the scientific evidence that smoking influences fetal activity by quitting smoking. Two clinical studies have tested the effectiveness of presenting a personalized fetal ultrasound image to pregnant women who smoke in hopes of reducing their smoking (Newnham 1993; LeFevre et al. 1995). The first study concluded that there was no decrease in smoking by women who experienced ultrasounds. The second found not only that women in the intervention group did not decrease their smoking more than women in the control group but that in fact they smoked a higher average number of cigarettes per day. The authors do not offer insight into why these experiments did not lead women to bond with their fetuses in ways that would result in quitting or reducing smoking.

The absence of a positive association between a woman's viewing a fetal sonogram and her protective health practices points to the diversity of ways women experience and think about pregnancy and fetal health risks. Despite the social and medical construction of the fetus as a person and medical patient, women's practices during pregnancy are not solely fetal centered. Emma Parra's statements stressed that she does indeed worry about her baby-to-be's health but that other things caused her to continue smoking. Contradicting the presumption made by some health professionals, a pregnant woman can disregard medical recommendations and still care about her baby-to-be. The simplistic formulations about smokers' feelings that are carried in antismoking materials do not reflect the complexities of women's experiences.

LIFELIKE FETUSES AND SMOKE-FILLED WOMBS

While the ACS's ultrasound demonstrations rely on real-time fetal imagery, other health education tools feature lifelike fetuses. Health educators and prolife activists present fetal models to mobilize the authority of science and to advance their cause. An ACS public service announcement and two health education models marketed by Health Edco represent fetuses in ways that are nearly indistinguishable from the fetal images used by antiabortion advocates. The scientific aspect of these images, which urges readers to think that "fetuses are really like this," is complemented by emotional and moral components that invoke the argument that fetuses are unique individuals who should have their rights to life and health protected.

In 1985 the ACS sponsored a thirty-second public service announcement that stunningly and intentionally exploits the fetal image, produced by antiabortion advocates, that some feminist scholars refer to as the "astronaut floating in space" (Oakley 1984, 174–175; Rothman 1986, 114). The spot opens with a close-up of the forehead of a babylike fetus (a puppet moved by invisible strings). A calm, warm ambiance is created as the fetus is bathed in yellow light against a black background and soothing synthesizer music is played. The sound of a heartbeat joins the music as the head of the fetus floats in from the left side of the screen. It sucks its thumb. The camera pans back to show the whole body of the fetus, now in a sitting position, grasping a cigarette in its fist. It takes its thumb out of its mouth and slowly raises the cigarette as a woman's voice-over asks: "Would you give a cigarette to your unborn child?" As she speaks, the cigarette reaches the fetus's mouth: "You do, every time you smoke while you're pregnant. Pregnant mothers, please, don't smoke." The camera retreats, and the fetus sits in a transparent bubble, an umbilical cord neatly resting at its feet. It exhales a stream of smoke and leans back against the bubble. The screen goes black except for the name and logo of the American Cancer Society; the heartbeat sound continues.

This health warning contains no direct medical information but visually reinforces the precept that when a pregnant woman smokes, her fetus, a miniature baby, also smokes. The fetus's activity is at first "natural" as it sucks its thumb but becomes "unnatural" when it holds a cigarette. This smoking fetus echoes prolife images of innocent fetal life, and its text echoes prolife discourses about the pregnant mother's responsibilities toward her unborn child. The end of this fetus's innocence, however, is not abortion but smoking.

The ACS's use of this fetal imagery sparked controversy. Two major networks, CBS and NBC, rejected the announcement because it might offend viewers (Broadcasting Magazine 1985, 190). Antismoking advocate Bobbie Jacobson noted that the antiabortion lobby loved the spot, while women's movement activists were outraged because it seemed to be part of an anti-abortionist conspiracy. Jacobson harshly criticized the ACS, charging, "It is hard to see how such a deliberately emotion-ridden and uninformative maneuver could have achieved anything other than alienating the women it sought to influence" (1986, 125). I contend, however, that the ACS's target was not solely pregnant mothers but the public in general. All viewers are implicitly urged to increase social pressure on pregnant women not to smoke.

The ACS vice president for public affairs claimed that the announcement was strictly "opportunistic advertising" and not indicative of an antiabortion position (Jacobson 1986, 125), but the ACS's fetal-centric themes certainly supported prolife ideology. Both antiabortion and antismoking campaigns explicitly seek to change women's actions during pregnancy by reinforcing ideas about how women must act to be good mothers-to-be. That both antiabortion and antismoking advocates have characterized fetuses as vulnerable, babylike actors in their fetal protection messages points to how the distinction between the fetal person and the infant has been erased significantly.

Although the ACS's smoking fetus spot represents the most explicit and conscious instance of the use of antiabortion fetal imagery to promote the antismoking message, another health education tactic that is remarkably similar to those employed by prolife activists is the use of fetal models in smoking cessation and prevention classes.[13] One model invokes the image of prolife activists carrying preserved fetuses in jars to clinic demonstrations to show that fetuses are preborn children: the Smokey Sue Smokes for Two doll featured in a 1996 Health Edco catalog with other models under the headline "Aversion Therapy Works! Nothing is as Gross as the Deadly Effects of a Cigarette" (Health Edco 1996, 4).[14] Smokey Sue is a Raggedy Ann– or Orphan Annie–looking doll that smokes cigarettes (figure 6.5). From the neck down, her body is a clear plastic jug filled with liquid and a model fetus. The sales pitch explains: "As Sue smokes, tars and nicotine pass through the water around the lifelike model of a seven-month fetus, mimicking the placenta. Collecting along the surface and in the darkened water, the tars and nicotine graphically show the pollutants reaching the developing baby" (Health Edco 1996, 4). The 1999 catalog adds that Smokey Sue "should be seen by all women of childbearing age" (1999b, 7).

The assumption behind this health education strategy is that women will associate the lifelike fetus floating in brown, polluted amniotic fluid with what really happens when they smoke and then determine to quit or to never start smoking. The doll's educational power lies in this imaginative leap. Smokey Sue may succeed in shocking smokers, but it does not impart biologically accurate information.

Figure 6.5.   Smokey Sue Smokes for Two. (*From Health Edco catalog, 1999b.* Reprinted with permission of Health Edco.")

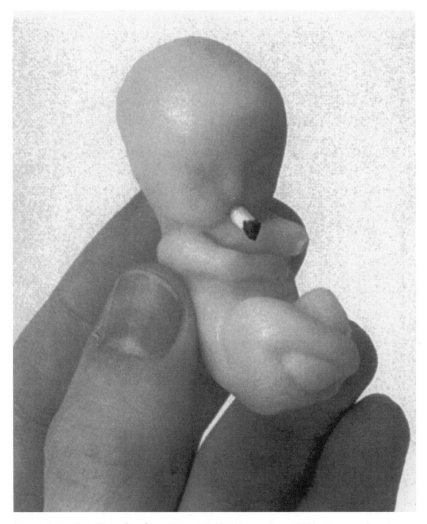

Figure 6.6.   Itty Bitty Smoker. (*From Health Edco catalog, 1999b.* Reprinted with permission of Health Edco.")

Health Edco offered a new antismoking model, the Itty Bitty Smoker, in 1997 (figure 6.6). The fetal model, the size of an adult thumb and made of pale-colored "BIOLIKE synthetic tissue," is not endearing but ugly. Its arms and legs are wrapped around its body in a protective pose, and it has a scowling facial expression. What sets it apart from other fetal models is the itty bitty (but not lifelike) plastic cigarette stuck in its mouth. The promotional catalog text reads: "Show who really winds up puffing on the 4,000–plus toxins in tobacco smoke. The model of a 10–week-old fetus, made of soft, realistic BIOLIKE, is a hard-hitting reminder that pregnant mothers have special responsibilities. Hand them out as a pregnancy health promotion, at health fairs, in smoking cessation classes—anywhere you need to get your health message across" (Health Edco 1997, 10; 1999b, 36).

Pushing the dramatic effect of this product even further, Health Edco currently markets the Itty Bitty Smoker as part of a model called the Womb of Doom (Health Edco 1999b, 48). The fetus rests in a cross-sectioned plastic uterus, as if lounging in a chair. The Womb of Doom combines the message that smoking by a pregnant woman creates a dangerous environment with the idea that when a pregnant woman smokes, her fetus smokes. Like the ACS's public service announcement and Smokey Sue, the smoking fetus model provides women with a tangible image that symbolizes the effect of smoking during pregnancy and the pregnant mother's special responsibilities.

An instruction card carries the Itty Bitty Smoker's purpose statement: "To demonstrate the fact that when a pregnant mother lights up, her baby also smokes. The harmful pollutants of cigarette smoke are absorbed by the infant." The card explains how to diligently care for the fetal model: "It can be damaged like real tissue. To ensure maximum life for the model, observe the following instructions carefully: 1. Wash gently with soap and water; pat dry. 2. Treat as sensitively as human flesh . . . [and] keep model in bag when not in use." The model combines an appeal to scientific reality by emphasizing its lifelike flesh with an appeal to emotion based on the shock value of imagining a fetus with a cigarette in its mouth.

Again, prolife discourse (whether intentional or not) is mimicked: the fetus is referred to as a baby and an infant, and correct care extends the fetal model's life. In fact, the Itty Bitty Smoker is much like the fetal models marketed and distributed by prolife advocates, such as Baby Hope, Young One, and Precious Preborn. For some, these models symbolize antiabortion extremism. In her book advocating prolife pregnancy counseling, Ellen Curro relates a story in which she sat next to a "pro-abortion" judge on an airplane: "He didn't figure out I was a prolifer until three-and-a-half hours into the discussion. That happened . . . when I reached into my purse for a tissue and accidentally pulled out 'Precious Preborn' (a model of a ten- to twelve-week-old preborn child). Jack had seen those models in a courtroom, and his immediate association was 'crazy, radical prolifer'" (1990, 12).

By pointing out the parallels between health educators' and prolife advocates' appeals to emotion and science through fetal images and models, I do not mean to imply a conscious collusion of political efforts. But given the current cultural-political status accorded to fetuses—mainly because of the prolife movement's promotion of fetal images—health education models do not stand outside of antiabortion discourse on fetal life and gender roles.[15] The health education tactic of combining emotional and scientific appeals to convince pregnant women to stop smoking draws on the prolife construction of the fetus as a vulnerable, babylike individual. Further, the emphasis in antismoking messages on good mothers as self-sacrificing, nurturing, and caring relies on the traditional American ideology of maternal nature that is supported by antiabortion advocates (see Luker 1984; Petchesky 1985 [1984]; Ginsburg 1998 [1989]). Within this framework, pregnancy confers motherhood and naturally carries the responsibility to protect and love unconditionally one's baby-to-be. While antiabortion activists attempt to convince women to continue their pregnancies on behalf of their fetus's life, antismoking advocates work to persuade women to quit smoking on behalf of their fetus's life and health. Those women who do not follow these admonitions are subject to moral judgment and are explicitly or implicitly labeled self-centered, uncaring, bad mothers. From a feminist perspective, this raises the question of whether there are positive ways to recognize the concerns that pregnant women have for their own fetus's health even when they do not (or cannot) follow all health directives.

Tobacco–Fetal Politics

Antismoking and antiabortion campaigns share the aim of educating the public about how pregnant women ought to behave; they also share the method of mobilizing strong national, state, and local political lobbies. Some critics, in fact, suggest that the two share common ground given their fetal protection concerns. However, as feminist philosopher Bonnie Steinbock notes, this is not the case: "There seem to be inconsistencies, both in morality and the law, in our treatment of the unborn. Some consider this evidence of confusion, or even hypocrisy. I once heard a politician dismiss an antismoking campaign that emphasized the effects of cigarette smoking on fetuses. With heavy sarcasm, he said, 'yet the anti-smoking lobby doesn't oppose abortion, which I suppose is also detrimental to fetal health'" (Steinbock 1992, 4). Although this sarcastic attack on the antismoking movement has not been elaborated, other critics also have pointed out the hypocrisy of both antiabortion and prochoice positions regarding the intersection of abortion politics and tobacco politics.

Since the mid-1990s, the stepped-up antitobacco movement has been working vigorously to stigmatize tobacco companies, and legislation and legal actions have begun to shake the industry's power. The tobacco industry has been under particularly harsh attack for not caring about the health of teenagers, who represent both prospective cigarette consumers and America's future. Antitobacco advocates charge that the industry has for years lured children and teenagers to become smokers and tobacco chewers through advertising (most flagrantly with the Joe Camel cartoon series; see Fischer et al. 1991) and sponsorship of sports and entertainment events that appeal to children and teens.[16] The portrayal of tobacco companies as a threat to children, who are vulnerable to advertising, and to the health of future generations heightens the rhetoric of the tobacco wars and is meant to appeal to politicians and policy makers (Meier 1998).[17] Within this context, some journalists and political lobbyists have highlighted the connection between the abortion conflict and the tobacco wars.

PROTECTING THE UNBORN AND TOBACCO INTERESTS:
CRITICISM OF ANTIABORTION ACTIVISM

The tobacco industry's allies have come under intense scrutiny as antitobacco advocates and the media continue to intensify the demonization of the tobacco industry. One target is the antiabortion lobby, which, according to some journalists and antitobacco advocates, is politically connected to the tobacco industry. From *Glamour* to *Mother Jones* to *USA Today*, journalists have publicized the ideological gap between prolife attempts to protect the unborn and prolife inaction on tobacco regulations (Saletan 1996, 1997; Estrich 1996). A decade earlier, antitobacco activists similarly criticized the relationship between the antiabortion movement and the tobacco industry (Whelan 1984, 210; Shear 1985). These two waves of criticism correlate with the mid-1980s campaigns both against smoking during pregnancy and for a Human Life Amendment, and the late 1990s campaigns to protect children and teens from the tobacco industry and to ban late-term (so-called partial birth) abortion. Although it may seem logical that prolife supporters would be vociferously against women's smoking during pregnancy because it endangers fetal life, antiabortion movement leaders have not taken an antitobacco position. The interests of tobacco, aligned with conservative politics, appear to override a political–moral conviction to save unborn babies from the peril of smoking during pregnancy.

Critics both within and outside the antiabortion movement argue that preventing smoking during pregnancy should be on the prolife agenda because smoking can result in what medical researchers DiFranza and Lew (1995) call tobacco-induced abortion. Revealing how medical science can directly influence political discourse, according to one journalist, DiFranza and Lew's article was used by ABC News to bait antiabortion leaders (Saletan 1996, 61). By the researchers' calculation, 3 percent (19,000) to 7.5 percent (141,000) of "clinically apparent" miscarriages annually are related to smoking.

Prolife activist Reverend Patrick Mahoney, executive director of the Christian Defense Fund, has unsuccessfully lobbied for an antitobacco position within the movement. It is unclear why Mahoney takes a strong antitobacco stance, but journalist William Saletan, who interviewed him, implies that Mahoney's motivation may be personal: his mother, a heavy smoker, died of cancer (Saletan 1996, 61). Mahoney dissects the political arguments that prolife leaders offer for not taking an antitobacco stand and challenges the antiabortion claim that other issues are more pressing. He claims that the prolife charge to ban late-term abortion procedures would apply only to approximately one thousand cases a year, a number that pales in comparison to the possible hundred thousand instances of tobacco-induced abortion. Further, prolife advocates have cited distrust of the Food and Drug Administration's regulatory role as another reason for their inaction on tobacco. Mahoney counters that antiabortion groups have petitioned the FDA to restrict RU-486, an abortifacient drug. As he put it, "Prolife people are already on record asking the FDA to intervene to protect unborn children from a drug. . . . So why not tobacco?" (quoted in Saletan 1996, 61).

The answer is not surprising: politics and money. Saletan, who has investigated the connection between the antiabortion movement and the tobacco industry, notes that conservative power lies in tobacco-growing states, where church-going, antiabortion constituents depend on the tobacco industry for their livelihood or remain sympathetic to tobacco company workers (Saletan 1996, 62). Additionally, funding by tobacco companies of prolife organizations is at stake, albeit indirectly. Campaign records reveal that of the millions of dollars the tobacco industry has donated to the Republican Party, thousands are distributed to antiabortion groups (Saletan 1997). Saletan provides no evidence, however, that the tobacco industry and prolife groups have a direct relationship.

Tobacco control advocates outside of the antiabortion movement also are aware of the discrepancy between prolife and protobacco positions. One tobacco control advocate and health educator I spoke with noted that "in [Maryland's] tobacco growing counties, pastors and preachers speak out against abortion, but not about smoking during pregnancy" (Anne Dewitt). At the national level, in 1994, antismoking advocate Scott Ballin, former chair of the Coalition on Smoking OR Health, issued a rhetorical challenge to the religious right. Ballin authored and distributed a "Contract for the Protection of America's Families and Children from Tobacco Use," modeled on the Republican "Contract with America" (Saletan 1996, 60). Ballin rewrote the Contract with America's sections on families, children, and ethics to focus on tobacco use and sent the contract to the prolife Christian Coalition along with a surgeon general's report and another study showing that smoking during pregnancy is associated with fetal health problems and miscarriage. But support for Ballin's contract was neither overwhelming nor predictable. The Christian Coalition's founder, Pat Robertson, signed the contract but declined to attend a press conference to unveil the antitobacco contract. The coalition's executive director at the time, Ralph Reed, however, continued to attack tobacco control initiatives. Saletan concludes that Reed, like other antiabortion advocates, sees the political danger in alienating conservative protobacco allies.

Although the conservative link between the antiabortion movement and the tobacco industry may explain antiabortion leaders' silence on the tobacco issue, an alternative explanation is that spontaneous miscarriage, whether the result of smoking during pregnancy or other factors, is simply not on the prolife agenda. In any case, those antiabortion and antitobacco activists who have sought to form a coalition between the two movements remain unsuccessful.

RELUCTANCE TO SPEAK OUT AGAINST WOMEN'S SMOKING: CRITICISM OF FEMINIST POLITICS

Antismoking advocates have directed their criticism not only at prolife advocates. Those both within and outside of the feminist movement have lobbied women's organizations to take a strong antitobacco position. In the 1980s, women's and feminist organizations were attacked by a surprising range of critics for not making eradication of smoking by women a priority. The lack of attention to smoking by feminist and women's movements has been criticized by feminists (Jacobson 1981, 1986; Shear 1985; Lerner 1996), medical experts (Steinfeld 1983), and public health officials (Terry 1981). Feminist groups' reluctance is in part related to the ideology of choice: if feminists argue that women's abortion choices should be respected, it follows that their choice to smoke should be respected. But feminist organizations have been latecomers to antitobacco advocacy also due to tobacco industry funding of women's organizations, sexism within the antitobacco movement, and disagreements with some antitobacco campaign tactics.

Much of the criticism of feminist inaction on smoking followed the 1980 surgeon general's report, *The Health Consequences of Smoking for Women.* In a 1981 speech to the National Conference on Smoking OR Health, former Surgeon General Luther Terry condemned women's activists: "I have always been curious why I have never seen criticism of this campaign [cigarette advertising directed at women] by leaders of the women's movement or rejection of this advertising by some of the media which purportedly stand for women's rights" (1981, 6–7). Although Terry overlooks the fact that in the 1970s, feminists rallied against cigarette advertising that was "offensive and/or insulting to women," it is true that they were not vocal about the health effects of smoking (Charlton 1970; see also Klemesrud 1971). The first women's group to publicly recognize the smoking issue was the President's Advisory Committee for Women. Unlike other organizations, this group issued a statement announcing that "smoking may well prove to be the major health problem facing women in the 1980s" (quoted in Whelan 1984, 207).

Bobbie Jacobson, a British antitobacco activist and feminist, wrote the first extensive critique of feminists' silence on smoking in *The Ladykillers: Why Smoking Is a Feminist Issue* (1981). The book, marketed to a feminist activist audience, includes a historical analysis of smoking and antitobacco activism in the United States, Great Britain, and Australia, self-help advice for smokers, and a mandate for antismoking advocacy that is relevant to women's lives. As is clear from her title, Jacobson argues that feminist organizations should put smoking on their agendas. The U.S. women's organizations she surveyed in the late 1970s neither saw smoking distinctly as a women's health issue nor felt responsible for addressing it, despite statistics showing that tobacco-related diseases killed more women than breast and cervical cancers combined. Indeed, the National Organization for Women's submission to the 1979 Kennedy hearings on women's health failed to mention smoking at all (Whelan 1984, 206). Women's health activists at the time failed to take up the issue of smoking in part because "the long-standing libertarian tradition of feminism tends to view antismoking campaigns as yet another manifestation of male 'experts' telling women what they can or can't do with their bodies" (Jacobson 1981, 80). But the position of women's groups was perhaps influenced more by material than ideological concerns.

Women-centered and feminist organizations have also been criticized for accepting tobacco company advertising and sponsorship. Marie Shear attacked *Ms.* magazine for running "almost 600 pages of tobacco ads" (1985, 6). This decision was connected to the issue of women's choice; *Ms.* defended its policy by arguing that readers could make an informed choice about tobacco consumption based on the health warnings contained in ads. The editors viewed women smokers not as powerless victims of tobacco advertising but as consumers who made a choice about the health risks they were willing to take. At the same time, however, the magazine was unwilling to criticize the tobacco industry; in the magazine's first ten years, it never carried an article on smoking and health (Whelan 1984, 206). *Ms.* later changed its policy on tobacco advertising, and since 1990 it has refused advertising of any kind. It also has published several articles on women and smoking.

One *Ms.* feature, clearly written from an antitobacco position, explores the question of why women's organizations accept funding by tobacco companies (Lerner 1996). While the author vigorously urges women's organizations to "kick the tobacco-money habit," she acknowledges the complexity of the situation. For some groups, the decision presents a moral conundrum, but for others, rejecting funding would ultimately do more practical harm than moral good. Some do not have the luxury of turning down tobacco funding because their activities would be curtailed without it. Tobacco companies most often fund organizations that promote women's business and political leadership, and for some groups, tobacco industry money makes up 5 to 10 percent of its annual funding (Williams 1991). Given the "perennial poverty of women's groups," some have decided to accept tobacco company funding and view it as a corporate donation, not as collusion with the tobacco industry.

Despite the silence of many women's organizations in the 1980s on tobacco in women's lives and in their organizations, other women's health advocates have worked hard for recognition within the antitobacco movement, which has not always been inviting. As a member of the International Network of Women Against Tobacco explained to me, part of the impetus for establishing the organization was that women found themselves at antitobacco conferences talking about women and smoking in the corridors and during breaks because the subject was not yet officially recognized. Bobbie Jacobson herself testifies that in 1983, at the Fifth World Conference on Smoking and Health, "to my surprise, I was invited to chair a session boldly entitled 'Smoking and Feminism.' Bob Wake, a professor of psychology and the conference programme chairman, warned me: 'You had better make it good. I've stuck my neck out on this one'" (1986, 128). Indeed, Jacobson has been acknowledged by other feminists for her dedication "to begin breaking down the sexism in the global movement dedicated to the effects of tobacco" (Greaves 1996, 7). A number of women-centered organizations were established in the 1990s, and the First International Conference on Women and Smoking convened in Northern Ireland in 1992.[18] In addition, feminists and women's organizations are members of antitobacco coalitions and lobbying efforts, diligently working to represent the interests of women and girls within the antitobacco movement. The designers of the Virginia Slims tag line likely never expected that women's organizing against tobacco would come such a long way.

Ultimately, despite the antiabortion movement's attention to fetal protection and the feminist movement's concerns about women's health issues, throughout the 1980s, neither prolife nor feminist groups used their political power to lobby against women's tobacco use. In the 1990s, feminist organizations began to do so, but antiabortion organizations remained silent. But even if those on opposite sides of the abortion issue came together in coalitions to support antitobacco politics, their strategies to prevent smoking during pregnancy would be predictably different. Prolife advocates likely would favor fetal-centric approaches to antismoking messages and the characterization of the pregnant woman who smokes as a "fetal abuser." Prochoice supporters might call for antismoking messages redesigned with a stronger emphasis on women's perspectives on fetal health and avoidance of themes that imply that pregnant women who smoke are bad mothers. The final two chapters address the consequences of these differing representations of pregnant smokers for legal and public health approaches to protecting fetal health.

Chapter 7

Cigarette Smoking as Fetal Abuse

ALTHOUGH SOME ANTITOBACCO advocates consider smoking during pregnancy to be child abuse, legal prosecutors have focused on pregnant women's drug and alcohol use; pregnant women's cigarette smoking has not yet been subject to criminal action. But medical and legal attention to the idea of maternal–fetal conflict and growing public antismoking sentiment suggest that in the future, criminal charges may be brought against pregnant smokers. In civil actions, mothers and other caretakers who smoke cigarettes have sometimes lost custody of their children as a result of keeping a "smoke-filled home" (Action on Smoking and Health 1995). It is conceivable that in the future, prosecutors will take legal action against women deemed as having "smoke-filled wombs."

Legal, medical, and feminist scholars offer different frameworks for dealing with the problem of the risks to fetal health that arise when women do not follow health advice. As with subjects such as drug use, violence against women, and gun violence, the protection of fetal health is seen by some as primarily a criminal justice issue, while others view it as a public health problem.[1] These approaches differ in their understanding of the problem, of who is to blame or be held responsible, and of which responses are most appropriate or effective. How the problem is framed significantly influences how law, medicine, and society judge pregnant smokers. Those who support legal action against pregnant women who commit fetal abuse perceive fetal abusers as threats to the social order and to the health of future generations. Those who are critical of fetal abuse charges see legal action as a threat to women's autonomy and reproductive rights.

Legal Actions against Women for Fetal Abuse

Although dominant criminal justice and public health approaches to fetal abuse are distinct, there are significant overlaps, beginning with the original identification of child abuse as a pervasive social problem. Across the nation, state legislators began to criminalize child abuse after a 1962 article in *JAMA*, the journal of the American Medical Association, introduced the new medical label of "battered child syndrome" (Kempe et al. 1962). Between 1962 and 1966, all fifty states established criminal legislation to punish child abusers (Pfohl 1977, 310), and mass media coverage of child abuse raised support for swift government action (Johnson 1989).[2] Such public attention established child abuse as a serious crime.

The antiabortion movement has tried to capitalize on public opposition to child abuse by equating fetuses with children, as seen in antiabortion placards and bumper stickers that read "Abortion—the ultimate child abuse." The continued drive against legal abortion since the late 1960s aims to protect unborn children through legal measures that would recognize fetal rights. Fetal abuse cases do not directly involve abortion; however, they extend the boundaries of the abortion issue because both abortion and fetal abuse transgress what antiabortion advocates see as fetal rights. In 1986, Harry Elias, the San Diego County deputy district attorney who initiated a nationally publicized fetal abuse case, phrased his media comments by using prolife rhetoric when he announced that parents have a duty to care for their children "from the moment of conception" (Schachter 1986, 6; see Gomez 1997, 42). Commenting on this case, the National Right to Life Committee furthered its claim that fetuses deserve rights, submitting that "just as born children can be subject to abuse and neglect, so can unborn children. . . . They have a right to be protected from that" (Schachter 1986, 6).[3] Prosecutors in many states, and some state legislatures, have agreed.

Fetal abuse cases fuse the authority of medical professionals with that of the state. Since the mid-1980s, more than two hundred women in more than thirty states have been prosecuted for health practices that medical and legal experts deemed dangerous to their fetuses (Center for Reproductive Law and Policy 1996a; Terry 1996; Roth 2000). In the 1999 legislative year alone, at least fourteen fetal protection statutes were proposed in various statehouses, and at least nine state legislatures proposed statutes that would punish women whose behavior might cause fetal harm (Center for Reproductive Law and Policy 1999, 1). Prosecutors have filed criminal charges mainly by extending child abuse, child neglect, and drug laws to cover the rights of the unborn child as a legal subject. As with child abuse legislation, actions against pregnant or parenting women combine the power of the legal and medical professions. Legislators and prosecutors rely on medical studies—for example, on the fetal health risks of cigarettes, drugs, or alcohol—and on health professionals' testimonies to back their arguments. Criminal prosecution of women for fetal abuse, neglect, or even attempted murder is justified by proponents as necessary to protect innocent fetuses from "preventable" harm and to hold pregnant women accountable for actions that might endanger fetal health. The prosecution of women for fetal abuse rests on the contention that punishment is appropriate for women who do not follow the pregnancy rules set out by health professionals.

The year 1977 marks the first reported case of a state's attempt to prosecute a woman for abusing her fetus; however, such legal action did not gain national attention until a decade later.[4] Although the majority of fetal abuse charges have been issued in extreme cases, such as those of excessive and repeated drug or alcohol use, women have been detained or charged on the basis of one-time drug or alcohol use. For example, in New Hampshire a legally drunk woman who was twelve weeks pregnant was charged with endangering the welfare of a child (Vigue 1996).[5] Women have faced criminal charges in cases in which the fetus or infant was harmed as well as in cases in which no harm was apparent. In 1987, Pamela Rae Stewart, a white, on-and-off homeless woman, was charged in San Diego in the death of her five-week-old son for failing to follow her physician's orders when she was pregnant. The prosecution contended that the infant's death was attributable to Stewart's failure to maintain bed rest; abstain from sex, methamphetamines, and marijuana; and get emergency care if she began bleeding (see Johnsen 1987; Gomez 1997, 42–46).[6] Two years later, in 1989, Jennifer Johnson, a Black woman in her twenties, was convicted in Florida on two charges of "delivering drugs to a minor" through her umbilical cord. Johnson had told hospital staff that she had used cocaine within twenty-four hours of giving birth to her son in 1987 and daughter in 1989. Neither newborn's health appeared impaired, although both tested positive for a cocaine metabolite (see Daniels 1993, chapter 4; Moss 1990, 280–284).

Although the cases against Stewart and Johnson were subsequently dropped, the movement to prosecute and convict women has continued in a number of states.[7] In addition to contesting women's control over their pregnancies, their bodies, and their children, the legal trend to hold women individually responsible for fetal health reflects a disregard for the social circumstances of women's lives. This is particularly well illustrated by a 1990 case in which a pregnant woman in Laramie, Wyoming, received medical treatment in a hospital emergency room after being beaten by her husband. Drunk at the time, she was arrested and charged with felony child abuse (see Roth 1993, 126), although there is no evidence that her husband was charged with abuse of his wife or the baby-to-be. A further and perhaps more shocking example of a lack of respect for women is represented in a Michigan narcotics officer's statement that "if the mother wants to smoke crack and kill herself, I don't care. . . . Let her die, but don't take that poor baby with her" (quoted in Hoffman 1990, 34). With the same hostility, the acting police chief who arrested the pregnant, drunk New Hampshire woman declared, "She can pickle herself all she wants, but that child doesn't have the opportunity to decide whether it's going to be retarded or not. . . . Somebody has to have responsibility for her unborn child" (quoted in Vigue 1996, B1). Although these men may voice extreme views, their comments demonstrate how concern for the fetus may be associated with a lack of concern for the pregnant woman.

In 1996, the prosecution of women for fetal abuse gained national attention when a district attorney's office in Wisconsin brought charges against Deborah Zimmerman for attempted murder of her fetus. Zimmerman, a white woman with a history of alcoholism, is the first woman to face such a charge. After drinking heavily at a bar during her eighth month of pregnancy, Zimmerman was driven to a hospital where she delivered a daughter who showed signs of fetal alcohol syndrome. The severity of the charge against Zimmerman stems not only from her allegedly repeated heavy bouts of drinking while pregnant but also from statements she made while intoxicated. Hospital staff testified that Zimmerman stated an intent to kill her baby-to-be. In a hearing on the case, Assistant District Attorney Joan Korb argued that the courts must "start holding women accountable for the harm they do to their unborn children" and that "sometimes it takes a prosecution to educate the public" (O'Neill et al. 1996, 53–54; see also Terry 1996).[8]

Although many women's health advocates would argue that this second aim is better carried out by public health campaigns, some states have established laws meant to punish women who might harm their fetuses and to warn other women to follow pregnancy advice. In the first judgment of its kind in the United States, the South Carolina Supreme Court ruled in 1996 that a viable fetus holds the same legal status as a person, and in 1998 the U.S. Supreme Court let stand this ruling. As a result, pregnant women who do not comply with health recommendations in that state can be charged with child abuse and imprisoned (Lewin 1997; Herbert 1998). Other states have reached different conclusions about whether criminal or health responses to pregnant women's risk taking are best (see Roth 2000). Fetal protection legislation efforts, part of the war on drugs, were strong in California in the mid-1980s, but the movement died after a decade (Gomez 1997). On the other hand,

South Dakota legislators instituted three laws aimed at reducing fetal alcohol syndrome cases: relatives or friends can commit a pregnant woman to a treatment center for up to two days; judges can order a pregnant woman to remain at a center for up to nine months; and pregnant women who drink can be prosecuted for child abuse (Aamot 1998). Although the treatment provision in the South Dakota legislation represents an improvement in this sort of legislation (including that of South Carolina), forcing women into mandatory alcohol abuse treatment is an unacceptable way to help women in that it rescinds their rights to privacy and bodily integrity (see Center for Reproductive Law and Policy 1996b). Such restrictions on pregnant women's freedom reveal how focusing on the fetus's well-being can lead to regarding pregnant women's bodies as baby containers.

Indeed, criminal fetal abuse charges and similar legislation, ostensibly justified as protecting fetal health, heighten the social surveillance of all women's pregnancy (and prepregnancy) decisions. Criminal sanctions serve the dual purpose of disciplining an individual for her wrongdoing—defined as not complying with medical advice to reduce the health risks to her baby-to-be—and warning all pregnant women that their health decisions may have legal consequences. The recent outpouring of concern over fetal abuse violates respect for women's autonomy by setting standards of pregnancy practice based on medical authority that all are expected to obey. Those who support fetal rights and fetal protection policies limit their attention to how the state can safeguard the "innocent" fetus with little regard for the rights of the "guilty" mother. Fetal rights claims give the fetus an individual identity, assert its equality with or even superiority over the woman, and establish its independent relationship with the state, bypassing the pregnant woman (Roth 1993, 118). The concepts of fetal rights and fetal abuse, backed by the ideology of maternal–fetal conflict, seriously threaten women's reproductive rights.

From Abortion Politics to Fetal Politics

Fetal abuse cases against pregnant women are grounded not only in the extension of child abuse law but also, some legal experts argue, in abortion law. Those legal analysts' interpretations of *Roe v. Wade* and the moral duties that they believe arise from the availability of legal abortion ironically support state intervention on behalf of fetuses. Writing in the *Virginia Law Review*, John Robertson contends that "the mother has, if she conceives and chooses not to abort, a legal and moral duty to bring the child into the world as healthy as is reasonably possible . . . the viable fetus acquires rights to have the mother conduct her life in ways that will not injure it" (1983, 405). This position might appeal to prochoice advocates because it recognizes that not all women want to continue their pregnancies and therefore that a right to legal abortion is essential. While some feminist philosophers and, in fact, the American Medical Association's Law and Medicine Board (Cole 1990, 2663) agree that pregnant women have a moral obligation to avoid health risks, they do not conclude with Robertson that this obligation should be legally binding (Steinbock 1992; Daniels 1999, 90).

The legal requirement that a pregnant woman must comply with medical advice if she chooses to continue a pregnancy not only undermines respect for women's bodily autonomy and health decisions but ignores the realities of many women's lives. Robertson's position too easily assumes that women have a real choice about whether to terminate a pregnancy. However, many lack access to abortion services for various reasons: financial constraints, the legal status of a minor, religious prohibition, social stigma, the distance to a clinic, waiting procedures, familial opposition, antiabortion protests and violence, and so forth (see Henshaw 1991; Scales and Chavkin 1996). Contrary to Robertson, for feminists and women's health advocates, assigning individual women the moral obligation for fetal care and backing that with legal pregnancy policing would be feasible only if these barriers to abortion did not exist and if women had full control over the conditions of their pregnancies (Daniels 1993, 138; 1999, 98).

Robertson nonetheless contends that prohibiting alcohol, drug, or tobacco use by pregnant women is feasible and constitutional. Statutes could be supported with a rational basis test because bans on the use of these substances would minimize risks to fetal health (1983, 442–443). The concept of risk, when used in the service of law, can be seen as a predictor of fetal and infant health outcomes. One legal scholar points out that restricting pregnant women from smoking or drinking alcohol could easily follow prohibitions on pregnant women's illegal drug use because "the harmful effect of these actions on the fetus is well established" (Moss 1990, 288). It goes unrecognized that pregnant women's risk taking does not necessarily lead to fetal or infant health problems and that health risks to individual babies-to-be cannot be predicted with 100 percent accuracy. In law, the assumption of the preventability of risk, regardless of the outcome of risk taking, is posed as punishable; risk taking itself becomes criminal.

Another legal scholar who agrees with Robertson's position goes further to advocate specific legal actions against pregnant women who do not comply with medical recommendations. Sam Balisy (1987) argues that *Roe v. Wade*'s reference to the state's compelling interest to "protect potential life" after fetal viability or during the third trimester of pregnancy allows legal action against a pregnant woman on behalf of her fetus. He suggests that there is a moral imperative and legal opportunity to force pregnant women to abstain from substances that carry fetal health risks, and he argues that health education has not and will not urge all women to quit smoking; thus, intervention by the criminal justice system is justifiable. Balisy's recommendations include criminal penalties "to deter women who abuse alcohol, drugs, or tobacco during pregnancy," mandatory reporting of fetal abuse by hospital and prenatal clinic staff, and confinement and rehabilitation (1987, 1235–1236).[9] Like Robertson, he leaves unanswered the important question of who determines what levels of substance use constitute abuse. That he uses the term "abuse" suggests that any use of tobacco, alcohol, or drugs should be subject to legal intervention. Abstinence is the only acceptable option.

This conclusion results perhaps from his sense of both the moral imperative that women must do everything possible to enhance fetal health and the legal reality that enforcement of substance use laws would be easiest if all use is banned. In Balisy's view, women who do not follow health advice are addicts, inadequate mothers, or individuals who are unable to make morally correct health decisions: "Public awareness campaigns are not always effective. In addition, there may be cases where the pregnant woman is fully aware of the potential effects of abusing harmful substances but either simply has no control to resist, doesn't care about the consequences, or has evaluated and accepted the risks inherent in continued substance abuse" (1987, 1235). Balisy's aim to hold all women to the same pregnancy rules disregards the diverse ways in which women negotiate fetal health risks. Noncompliance with medical advice is intolerable, and the only socially and legally acceptable mother-to-be is the ideal one—the one that pregnancy advice books instruct pregnant women to become.

Balisy's response to substance use by pregnant women assumes a cooperative relationship between the medical and criminal justice systems, a relationship that is fraught with tension. Fierce turf wars are waged between legal and public health experts over who can best define and address the problem (Johnsen 1987; Cole 1990; Gomez 1997; Roberts 1997; Roth 2000). The contrast between the criminal justice and public health approaches makes visible distinct presumptions about the root of the problem. Are pregnant women criminally neglectful and morally flawed, or are they unhealthy and in need of medical assistance (see Gomez 1997, 122)? The criminal justice approach maintains that pregnant women should be punished or subjected to the threat of punishment, whereas the public health approach supports education, prevention, and treatment services for pregnant women. Advocates for criminal justice action focus on worst-case examples and point out that public health campaigns cannot successfully avert all pregnant women's risk taking.

Although antismoking education has not resulted in all pregnant women quitting smoking, scholars disagree about the resort to legal sanctions. Feminist legal analyst Martha Field (1989) rejects both the focus on the fetus and the recourse to criminal justice measures promoted by fetal rights advocates. Field maintains that we must respect women's assessments of their health choices and their decisions to accept or reject medical advice. From this perspective, public health measures, not fetal abuse prosecutions, are the most appropriate response to concerns about fetal well-being: "If the real goal is not control of women but protection of the child-to-be and creation of as healthy a newborn population as possible, then appropriate means are education and persuasion, free prenatal care, and good substance abuse rehabilitation programs, available free of charge to pregnant women" (Field 1989, 125). Field's argument that public health strategies better respect women and can more effectively address prenatal health concerns than legal actions is certainly convincing. However, her recommendations read like a politically implausible wish list because they necessitate extensive changes in health care funding.

Other public health professionals and feminist scholars share Field's opposition to legal intervention in the lives of pregnant women. These women's health advocates predict that a social climate in which pregnant women fear criminal procedures will lead to setbacks in fetal and infant health. Wendy Mariner and colleagues argue that "prosecutions of drug-using pregnant women are based on an illusion, and a dangerous one at that. They foster the illusion that society is protecting its future generations. In reality, such prosecutions substitute punishment for protection" (Mariner et al. 1990, 37). The authors contend that the threat of criminal prosecution will deter women from seeking prenatal care, and thus a climate in which women fear fetal abuse charges has a counterproductive effect that punishes fetuses. This observation is contained in a report of the 1988 Institute of Medicine annual meeting: "Pregnant women who are aware that their life-styles risk their health and the health of their babies may also be afraid to seek care because they expect pressure to change such habits as heavy smoking, eating disorders, or the abuse of drugs or alcohol" (Wymelenberg 1990, 121; see also see also Gallagher 1989; Chavkin 1992). The risks associated with a criminal justice approach outweigh the fetal protection benefits it might possibly have.

Although the threat of criminal penalties may influence all women, poor women and women of color are the main targets of fetal abuse policies due to disparities in access to prenatal care and to racist and classist assumptions about dangerous mothers. Nearly all fetal harm cases have been brought against Black women (Daniels 1997a, 586; Roberts 1997, 175; Roth 2000).[10] In fact, a study of the Florida policy that requires reporting drug use by a pregnant woman found that African American women were ten times more likely than white women to be reported, despite the fact that both groups have similar drug-use rates (Chasnoff et al. 1990). In addition to racism being a significant factor in the surveillance of pregnant women, low-income women are monitored more closely than others by state agencies such as child protective services and government-funded prenatal clinics (Roberts 1997, 173). The women who might benefit most from prenatal care may be those who avoid medical institutions due to a (realistic) fear of medical and legal surveillance.[11] But it is not enough to simply encourage all women to seek prenatal care; action must be taken to reduce disparities in the quality of such care. The disproportionately high numbers of low-income women and women of color suspected of or charged with fetal abuse is part of a long history of social, medical, and political control over what has been represented as the "deviant sexual nature" of certain groups of women, particularly those socially marginalized due to their race, ethnicity, class, age, sexual identity, and mental or physical ability.[12]

Knowledge of fetal abuse charges is pervasive enough to be joked about to the middle-class audience of *What to Expect When You're Expecting*. In a parody of doctors' fears of lawsuits brought against them by pregnant women, the authors instruct women to protect themselves from malpractice claims. Here the definition of malpractice is a pregnant woman's rejection of her doctor's orders: "You needn't worry that you will have to pay your doctor a million dollars if you don't take the vitamins he or she prescribes. What you do need to worry about, however, if you are guilty of malpractice, is that you and your baby will pay the price in possibly more devastating ways—with health and even life being the cost." The book lists eight points that a woman should follow if she wants "to be a patient whom no one can charge with malpractice" (Eisenberg et al. 1991 [1984], 16). These include disclosing drug, alcohol, and cigarette use, following medical instructions carefully, never threatening or alarming a physician, and taking good care of herself. Ironically, given changes in the law since the book was first published, in some states, women who follow the advice to disclose drug and alcohol use may be inviting fetal abuse charges. Regardless of this gap, *What to Expect* offers more of a moral than a legal warning to its readers. In reality, women of color and low-income women bear the main burden of criminal prosecutions, but only ideal pregnant women can rest assured that they will not be symbolically charged with or held responsible for harming their babies-to-be.

Indeed, constructing noncompliance with medical advice by pregnant women as criminal has set a dangerous legal precedent that threatens the autonomy of all pregnant women. After the 1996 South Carolina Supreme Court ruling that allowed criminal child abuse charges against pregnant women whose actions might negatively affect their viable fetuses, reproductive rights attorney Lynn Paltrow emphasized that "there are not enough jail cells in South Carolina to hold the pregnant women who have a drug problem, drink a glass of wine with dinner, smoke cigarettes, fail to take prenatal vitamins, or decide to go to work despite their doctor's advice that they should stay in bed—all of whom could be guilty of the crime of child neglect as the result of [this] ruling" (Center for Reproductive Law and Policy 1996b, 1). Paltrow's point is not only that a slippery slope effect may result from fetal abuse laws such that pregnant women's actions that are high as well as low risk are de-fined as fetal abuse, but that women's autonomy is severely restricted when medical advice dictates legal rights.

This argument closes the symbolic distance between the high-profile "fetal abuser"—the crack user or alcoholic—and those pregnant women who repre-sent the vast majority—women who decide not to follow all pregnancy ad-vice yet who also demonstrate that they care about their babies-to-be. Paltrow and other women's rights advocates emphasize that actions against fetal abuse have broad implications for every woman's reproductive choices. Under fetal protection laws, even the distinction between pregnant, nonpregnant, or prepregnant women might be erased, and limits on women's health practices could extend to all women who are "potential future childbearers" (Field 1989). In fact, bars on women's employment in jobs that involve exposure to materials that may carry fetal health risks are currently in place as a result of this logic (see Daniels 1993; Samuels 1995). Such policies reflect the idea that women are not to be trusted with reproductive health decisions; others must step in on behalf of their fetuses.

Feminist critics demonstrate that while women are instructed to be ac-countable for all aspects of fetal health during pregnancy, health care and wel-fare services are increasingly restricted, substance use treatment programs are limited in number, and men are held less accountable than women for how their health practices influence fetal well-being (Rothman 1989, 96–97; Pollitt 1990; Daniels 1997, 1999).[13] Women and their (current or future) children are neglected by a government that does not provide adequate childcare ser-vices, child support for poor and single parents, or health care insurance. Public health policies that focus on the status of women and children in society, and not simply on the fetus, will be more effective in promoting children's well-being than will criminal justice measures.

In the early 1990s, in response to legal drives against fetal abuse, a num-ber of public health organizations and public advocacy groups issued position statements opposing punitive actions against pregnant women substance users (see Center for Reproductive Law and Policy 1996a, 11–12).[14] The American Medical Association itself has stated that physicians are rightly medical advisers and counselors, and it discourages doctors from resorting to legal action to change women's health behaviors (Cole 1990; see also Johnsen 1987). However, many prenatal health care providers disagree. A national survey of the heads of maternal–fetal medicine fellowship programs found that 47 percent believed that women who refuse medical advice when fetal health is endangered should be detained at hospitals or other institutions (Kolder et al. 1987). Although the criminal justice and the public health approaches to eliminating fetal health risks differ, there is no consensus within either group of professionals. This is not surprising given that like the ongoing debate over women's right to abortion, the question of how to treat pregnant women who do not comply with pregnancy advice remains highly contentious.

Cigarette Smoking as Fetal and Child Abuse

Although health advocacy organizations have come out against the prosecution of women for fetal abuse, some public health strategies—including antismoking campaigns—appear to support such measures. The emotion-driven campaigns that blame pregnant women who smoke for abusing their babies-to-be, designed by antismoking advocates in the mid-1980s, can still be found in prenatal clinics today. This suggests not only that some health professionals believe that scare tactics are appropriate and effective but that the professionals support punitive measures against pregnant smokers. Some antitobacco advocates support court cases that deny parents who smoke custody of their children on the grounds that subjecting a child to smoke is abusive and neglectful parenting.

One example of an antismoking campaign targeting pregnant smokers as child abusers is a 1986 American Cancer Society (ACS) poster that stood out among the many health education posters covering the walls of a state-funded prenatal clinic waiting room. The poster showed the shadowy profile of a woman's midsection; one raised hand holds a cigarette, and the other covers her very pregnant belly. The text reads: "Some people commit child abuse before the child is even born. According to the Surgeon General, smoking by a pregnant woman may result in a child's premature birth, low birthweight, and fetal injury. If that's not child abuse, then what is?" By framing the surgeon general's health warning (mandated in 1984 to be printed on cigarette packs and ads) with the assertion that smoking during pregnancy is child abuse, the ACS transforms the health warning into a legalistic comment about smoking during pregnancy.[15] The poster implies that smoking during pregnancy should carry criminal consequences, and it may mislead women into believing that it does.

The ACS is not the only organization that promotes the theme of fetal abuse in its antismoking campaigns. A 1987 American Heart Association poster declaring that "Some Kinds of Child Abuse Start Early" features the silhouette of a pregnant woman smoking. In small type, a caption states: "With each puff, your baby absorbs growth-reducing doses of nicotine, carbon monoxide, benzopyrene, ammonia and hydrogen cyanide. The results could be hard to live with. Quit smoking now" (cited in Condit 1996, 168). The connection that the ACS, the American Heart Association, and others make between smoking and child abuse implicitly condones the logic behind and possibly even the actual, legal prosecution of women who smoke during pregnancy.

The belief that smoking during pregnancy constitutes child abuse has been publicized in the New York Times, which reaches a broader audience than the relatively small one composed of pregnant women who see posters in prenatal clinics. Outspoken surgeon and antismoking advocate William Cahan, who worked as a volunteer for the ACS, has charged women who smoke during pregnancy with enacting "the most pervasive" form of child abuse in the United States (Cahan 1985). In an 1985 op-ed column in the New York Times, Cahan presents scientific evidence about the biological effects of smoking in sensational language: "Each cigarette puff" diminishes the "life-supporting flow" of placental blood vessels and causes "fetal distress"; over time, "the unborn's genetic material" becomes "deranged." This dire prediction implies that the babies of women who smoke are damaged in the worst possible, irreparable way—genetically. In fact, recent research supports this idea; the findings of a public health study suggest that heavy smoking during pregnancy can cause fetal genetic mutations that might increase a newborn's risk of cancer (Action on Smoking and Health 1999).

The solutions Cahan offers are twofold. First, women must quit smoking when pregnant: "what responsible woman can persist in a habit so threatening to her young? Using self-discipline, she can minimize the risk of a complicated pregnancy and imposing lifelong physical and mental handicaps upon her child." Second, "clergymen, educators, parent-teachers' associations and legislators" should lobby against tobacco "just as they do against alcohol, drugs, drunken driving, radioactive-waste disposal, dioxin and abortion" (Cahan 1985). Cahan's educational scare tactics seem intended not so much to convince women to quit smoking as to define smoking during pregnancy as a severe social and political problem. Given the venom with which he attacks pregnant smokers, Cahan's recruits to the antismoking movement might support extreme measures to punish pregnant women, similar to those meted out in more recent fetal abuse cases that entailed alcohol and drugs.

Pregnant smokers are not the only smokers subject to the charge of child abuse. In the late 1980s, attention to the question of whether smokers are good parents followed reports on the health risks of secondhand smoke or environmental tobacco smoke. Implying that the public cares more about the health consequences of smoking than do parents, a *Parents'* magazine article noted that despite the rise of antismoking ordinances, "one sizable group is still not protected: children whose parents smoke in the home." The author cites health experts' estimates that as many as half of all infants and children may be routinely exposed to environmental tobacco smoke, which can "damage a child's health even before birth" (Papazian 1991, 178). Warnings about the effect of environmental tobacco smoke on children focus mainly on how primary caregivers, most often mothers, endanger their children's health: "Infants at home with their mother are in an especially vulnerable position" (Charlton 1996, 98). If a mother smokes, the home is seen not as an ideal, safe space but as a polluted and unhealthy one in which a child's welfare is threatened. The images of the smoke-filled home and the smoke-filled womb signify improper mothering and invoke the question of the extent to which public regulation should control activities that take place in the privacy of an individual's home or body.

Action on Smoking and Health (ASH) has been at the forefront of an aggressive campaign to label as unfit those parents and caregivers who smoke near children. Established in 1967, ASH is a "national nonprofit legal action and educational organization fighting for the rights of nonsmokers against the many problems of smoking" (Action on Smoking and Health 1994). The organization's public relations style is upbeat and borders on hype. For example, its web site (http://ash.org) carries such news stories as "Mom's Smoking More Deadly Than Crack Use" (1998b); "Smoking Parents Are Killing Their Infants" (1996a); "Mother May Lose Custody over Smoking, Even in Kentucky" (1996b); and "Parents Are Deliberately Making Their Kids Sick, at What Point Does It Become Child Abuse or Endangerment?" (1996c). ASH offers legal assistance primarily to litigants who use smoking as evidence in child custody cases and seeks rulings that will set precedents about restrictions on environmental tobacco smoke even in smokers' homes.[16] Between 1988 and 1994, the organization assisted in twenty-three child custody cases and four child abuse or neglect cases involving the exposure of children in their homes to environmental tobacco smoke. Several cases received attention in the *New York Times* (1993a, 1993b), and one was covered by *Vogue* magazine (Fishman 1994). ASH literature also carries information about the health risks to fetuses of smoking during pregnancy, although there is no indication that it has acted on fetal abuse cases.[17]

A number of the smoking-related custody cases have involved extreme circumstances, such as a child's asthmatic or poor respiratory condition and households in which all members are smokers or smokers refuse to make compromises (such as only smoking outdoors). Even these serious cases, however, cannot justify this approach to antismoking advocacy. Emphasis on smoking as a significant factor in legal judgments of parenting ability is unacceptable because at its root is the objective of penalizing smokers. Feminist scholar and antitobacco advocate Lorraine Greaves suggests that this child custody strategy has caused divisions within the antitobacco movement, where some see it as lacking humanity (1996, 132).

The position ASH endorses levels the same charge against parents who smoke: smoking is inhumane because it threatens the health of children who cannot protect themselves. ASH defines exposure to secondhand smoke as child endangerment, based on the legal understanding that child abuse is "generally defined as any form of cruelty to a child's physical, moral, or mental well being" (1995, 7). That inflicting cigarette smoke on others is evidence of such cruelty may sound overly dramatic, but this line of reasoning has been central to many court cases and is supported by antismoking lobbyists who have successfully advocated public antismoking ordinances.

In the 1990s, several rulings on child custody specifically have associated a child's exposure to environmental tobacco smoke with child abuse or neglect. For example, a state circuit court judge in Jacksonville, Florida, awarded temporary custody of an asthmatic seven-year-old boy to his father to protect the boy from his stepfather's smoke, stating: "I'm not saying adults can't smoke. I'm just saying don't do it in front of a helpless child. Secondhand smoke is killing children and I think it's time for the courts of this country to help these children" (Judge Bill Parsons, quoted in *New York Times* 1993b). In 1994, an Oregon circuit court judge awarded custody of an infant to the state's Child Services Division, citing her hospitalization with pneumonia, asthma, bronchitis, and an inner ear infection allegedly caused by living in a smoke-filled home (Action on Smoking and Health 1995, 8). This case is particularly significant because it is the first to award custody of a child to the state to keep him or her away from a parent who smokes. That same year, a Fulton County, New York, family court judge ruled that custody of a twelve-year-old boy with asthma, allergies, and pulmonary disorders be awarded to his nonsmoking father and stepmother. The boy's mother was a smoker who, according to the court, failed to see smoking as a "serious threat" to her son. The court asserted that "we are at a point in time when, in the opinion of this judge, a parent or guardian could be prosecuted successfully for neglecting his or her child as a result of subjecting the infant to an atmosphere contaminated with health-destructive tobacco smoke" (Judge David E. Fang, quoted in Action on Smoking and Health 1995, 8–9). ASH applauded the precedent set by these and similar rulings, and has argued that equating smoking with child abuse is justified: "Any parent or guardian who voluntarily exposes a child to such a health risk . . . is inflicting as much, if not more, physical harm on a child as conduct more usually recognized as abusive or neglectful" (1995, 8). ASH is lobbying through the court system for the routine recognition of smoking near children as child abuse and neglect.

Antismoking advocates have claimed victory in some cases on the basis of a judge's statements rather than his or her ruling. William Cahan, for example, recalls becoming involved in one such smoking-related custody case (1992, 366). A lawyer reportedly remembered seeing Cahan's *New York Times* op-ed column on smoking as child abuse and called Cahan to discuss testifying on behalf of his client, the father of a six-year-old. The child's father had custody, and the mother had sued to regain it. In court, the father claimed that he had already quit smoking to protect his son's health, while the mother continued to smoke a pack and a half a day and to live with her parents, who also smoked. Testifying on behalf of the father, Cahan dramatically argued that the home should be "a refuge, a haven, not a hazard" and contended that "to rear a child in a smoke-laden environment is not unlike living in an asbestos-lined house or one built on radioactive soil. A child does not have to be beaten and bruised to be abused" (1992, 366–367). This logic, in which the definition of physical child abuse is expanded to include the act of smoking near a child, directly parallels that voiced by ASH. Cahan's efforts failed in this case; the judge, identified by Cahan as a heavy smoker, ruled in favor of the mother on the basis of "strong mitigating circumstances" that are not spelled out (1992, 367). The antitobacco lobby, however, claimed victory despite the outcome of this custody dispute; the judge issued a statement proclaiming that parental smoking "must be considered, as would alcohol consumption, for example, when viewing the suitability of a household environment in which a child is to be placed" (quoted in Action on Smoking and Health n.d., 7).

This "consideration" approach sounds reasonable, yet it has potentially negative material and symbolic effects, particularly for women. The custody cases described in ASH reports are disproportionately brought against mothers as primary caregivers. Of twenty-three suits listed in 1995, eleven were brought against a child's mother, three against a father, five against both parents, and four against others (Action on Smoking and Health 1995). A range of factors may create this imbalance; however, it is reasonable to question how social expectations about women's maternal nature play a role when custody is challenged on the grounds of a mother's cigarette smoking. One law professor suggests, for example, that judges may consciously or unconsciously judge women against the model mother who does not smoke because she wants to protect her children's health (in Fishman 1994, 210). Perhaps this is the case for fathers too, but so far more mothers than fathers have lost child custody battles due to smoking. Motherhood is more often on trial.

This appears to be an important factor in the case of Susan Tanner, who lost custody of her asthmatic daughter in part because Tanner was a cigarette smoker. Tanner, who denied that she had smoked near her daughter (*New York Times* 1993a), quit smoking. Yet even then she could not regain custody. The Tennessee judge in Tanner's case declared that "a belated cessation of smoking might evidence a desire for the custody of the child rather than concern for the welfare of the child" (quoted in Action on Smoking and Health n.d., 7). *Vogue* magazine offered a critical analysis of this judgment: "If she'd really been a good mother, the court seemed to say, she would have stopped earlier" (Fishman 1994, 210). This judge's ruling points to how antismoking sentiment works to reframe women's smoking so that it is increasingly seen, not only socially but legally, as conflicting with proper mothering and caregiving.

A Texas judge's admission that cigarette smoking was a significant factor in a case that had nothing to do with smoking points to the hostility toward mothers who are smokers and also to a punitive attitude toward poor mothers. In 1988, the judge (a former two-pack-a-day smoker) ordered a woman who had violated parole for stealing cattle in 1983 to quit smoking within thirty days (*New York Times* 1988). As reported in the *Times*, the judge explained, "She came to me pleading poverty and I don't know why, but I said, 'Do you smoke?' and she said 'Yes,' and I said, 'How in the world can you afford to? You said you don't have a job.'" He decided not to sentence her to prison for theft because she has five children. Instead, in his ruling he addressed what he saw as the drain on public welfare caused by her addiction to, and regular purchase of, cigarettes: "The Surgeon General said it's addictive, it's been publicly declared an addiction. The woman said she had no job. Why should the taxpaying public subsidize an addiction?" Not only does this judge's action imply that all smokers are deviant addicts, but it suggests that by quitting smoking the woman would become a more upstanding citizen and better mother.

The trend toward encouraging the public to see smoking mothers as bad mothers is further underscored if their actions are compared with those of ideal mothers, who go to great lengths to protect their children from health risks. Some women have used their authority as mothers, in combination with the power of antismoking advice and the increasingly strong antitobacco climate, to their child's benefit. In Connecticut, three women who have children with asthma filed law suits against McDonald's, Wendy's, and Burger King for violating their children's rights under the federal Americans with Disabilities Act by not maintaining smoke-free environments (Johnson 1993). In a similar vein, Lori Faley initiated a referendum to ban smoking in public areas in Greensboro, North Carolina (where the tobacco company Lorillard, Inc. is a major employer), after she had smoke blown in her face at a supermarket checkout line when she was pregnant (*New York Times* 1989). Faley and others founded GASP, Greensboro to Alleviate Smoking Pollution, which worked to support the smoke-free ordinance. The referendum passed by a slim 173 votes out of the 30,000 cast. Faley reportedly received threats in response to her activism and has since moved out of the state.

These are exceptional cases. Other women have not advocated for broadscale changes but have aggressively defended what they saw as their right to be in a smoke-free environment for the benefit of their babies-to-be. One woman I talked with said that her sister-in-law is a "fanatic" who will say to strangers, "put out your cigarette, please!" (Joselyn Behm). The most remarkable instance of a pregnant nonsmoker's attempt to avoid exposure to smoke on behalf of the health of her baby-to-be was related to me by a friend. Jane, who was in the first trimester of her first pregnancy, had attended a baseball game in a southwestern city. While standing in a designated smoking area near a concession stand, Jane asked a woman to put out her cigarette, explaining that she was pregnant. The smoker refused, and an argument ensued. Before others intervened, Jane slapped the smoker across the face. Despite the fact that they were in a place where smoking was legal, Jane felt she had the right as a pregnant woman to be in a smoke-free space to protect her fetus's health, and she strongly resented the smoker's lack of concern about the health of her baby-to-be. This episode reveals the strength of antismoking and fetal protection sentiment held by some and the fact that these feelings are not shared by everyone. Antitobacco advocates' campaigns, of course, encourage nonsmokers to feel entitled to smoke-free environments and may motivate pregnant women to take extreme actions to protect themselves and their babies-to-be from what they see as the dangers of environmental tobacco smoke.

Despite the antismoking campaigns initiated in the 1980s that equate pregnant smokers with child abusers and the healthist climate that promotes pregnancy policing, women who smoke during pregnancy have avoided legal fetal abuse charges. It remains unclear why fetal abuse charges have been brought against pregnant drinkers and drug users but not pregnant cigarette smokers. As suggested in chapter 4, the lack of a catchy phrase such as fetal tobacco syndrome or nicotine-addicted babies may contribute to a public understanding of smoking as less harmful during pregnancy than drinking or taking drugs. However, for pregnant women and for mothers who smoke, the public perception of the distance between cigarette smoking and the use of more stigmatized substances, like drugs and alcohol, appears to be rapidly closing. One antitobacco advocate I interviewed agreed that the increasingly strong antismoking sentiment has led to a growing middle-class hostility toward smokers, especially toward those who are pregnant: "My daughter had very nice lady nursery school teacher who had a couple children and got pregnant the year she taught my daughter. And she was a smoker. I knew it . . . but she was hiding it. I'm sure she was very ashamed of it. She was a nice middle-class teacher and, who knows, it might have even jeopardized her job. It's not impossible that they'd think 'if she'll take a chance with her own baby, what kind of nursery school teacher can she be?' It's not that far-fetched" (Judy Levine).

In Judy Levine's interpretation, the issue is not whether children will see their teacher—a role model—smoking and then emulate her behavior, or whether her students will be exposed to secondhand smoke, although those concerns may be important factors in people's opposition. Rather, the issue is the smoker's character and her ability to act responsibly. The woman's identity as a mother-to-be and a teacher clashes with her identity as a smoker. Although smoking during pregnancy has not been legally censured, it is certainly morally censured.

This chapter closes on a pessimistic note. Significant evidence indicates that, borrowing Judy Levine's words, it is not too far-fetched to predict that women who smoke during pregnancy may in the future be charged with fetal abuse. Such an outcome would be in keeping with previous cases brought against women for alcohol and drug use during pregnancy and the general trend toward holding women accountable for the health of their babies-to-be. But charging women with fetal abuse is an unacceptable way to express care for fetuses because it undermines women's agency and autonomy.

Chapter 8   From Smoke-Free Wombs to a Tobacco-Free Society

THE RISE OF FETAL abuse cases brought against women for not following pregnancy advice, the inclusion of smoking as a factor in child custody and neglect cases, and the increasing stigma surrounding smoking all point to the future regulation and punishment through the legal system of smoking by pregnant and parenting women. However, looking at recent efforts to encourage positive public health approaches to smoking, such pessimism may not be fully warranted. What antitobacco advocates describe as a recent paradigm shift in their fight against tobacco may lead to fewer fetal-centered messages that equate smoking during pregnancy with neglectful mothering or child abuse. Studies of smoking cessation programs support a move away from concern about fetal health as the main argument used to convince women to quit smoking and toward a broader approach to smoking and women's health. Indeed, feminist antitobacco advocates call for efforts that go beyond smoking itself to address the conditions in women's lives that lead them to take up cigarettes.

Still, closer attention must be paid to the question of whether current antitobacco frameworks adequately address smoking during pregnancy in ways that will change the direction of moralistic pregnancy-policing campaigns that instruct pregnant smokers to quit on behalf of their babies-to-be. Further, women's health advocates who are committed to retaining women's reproductive rights and to promoting pregnancy advice that is dedicated to women's health and the health of their babies-to-be must be more willing to participate in discussions about fetal care along with debates over fetal abuse (see Morgan and Michaels 1999). Toward this end, I offer an analysis of the latest antitobacco efforts aimed at ending smoking during pregnancy and propose future strategies.

Recent Approaches to Smoking during Pregnancy

Three areas of antitobacco efforts in the 1990s demonstrate how recent trends in antitobacco advocacy have influenced responses to smoking during pregnancy as a public health problem. I characterize these areas as advocacy against the tobacco industry, health education, and feminist antitobacco efforts. These efforts offer alternative strategies for confronting pregnant smokers without labeling them as fetal abusers or supporting criminal justice measures, as did a number of campaigns designed in the 1980s.

ADVOCACY AGAINST THE TOBACCO INDUSTRY

Although antitobacco advocates' efforts against the tobacco industry are not totally new—lobbying against tobacco advertising and for increased taxes and smoke-free public spaces began in the late 1960s and early 1970s—their work intensified and was substantially expanded in the mid-1990s. A comparison of public health advocates' antismoking strategies before and after the so-called paradigm shift in antitobacco advocacy reveals significant differences between previously dominant approaches and those that have recently gained popularity. When I refer to advocates against the tobacco industry, I include in this category government health agencies and officials, nongovernmental health organizations, and lobbying groups working specifically on tobacco control.

Five components characterize the paradigm shift (see figure 8.1). First, the definition of the problem has moved from tobacco use to tobacco distribution. This is significant because it means that health advocates are turning away from blaming the victim—the smoker—to blaming the tobacco industry for marketing and advertising a hazardous and addictive substance. In particular, advocates against the tobacco industry seek to prevent the illegal distribution of tobacco to youths with the hope that tobacco-free youths will become tobacco-free adults. Second, advocates' attention has moved from considering how tobacco use affects individuals to looking at how it influences society. Individual effects include the smoker's disease and addiction; societal effects include the risks that environmental tobacco smoke poses to nonsmokers and the costs of treating smoking-related illnesses. Third, public health advocates argue that long-term policy actions are more effective than short-term programs. An example of this difference at the local level is lobbying for smoke-free workplace regulations instead of sponsoring smoking cessation programs for a company's employees. Fourth, while in the past, the media has

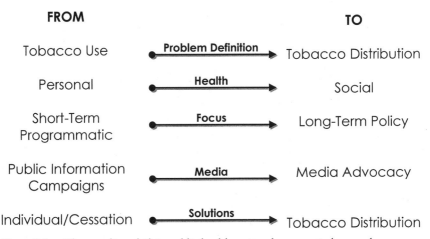

FROM   **TO**

Tobacco Use   •——**Problem Definition**——▸   Tobacco Distribution

Personal   •——**Health**——▸   Social

Short-Term   •——**Focus**——▸   Long-Term Policy
Programmatic

Public Information   •——**Media**——▸   Media Advocacy
Campaigns

Individual/Cessation   •——**Solutions**——▸   Tobacco Distribution

Figure 8.1. The paradigm shift in public health approaches to antitobacco advocacy.
(*I thank Wendy Rankin for providing this information.*)

disseminated health warnings through public information campaigns about the risks of smoking, the current trend is toward antitobacco media advocacy. Instead of endlessly repeating the "smoking is bad for you" message, media advocacy campaigns aim to motivate the public to take a stand against the tobacco industry by refusing to consume tobacco and by supporting antitobacco policies. Finally, in the old paradigm, solutions targeted the individual and focused on smoking cessation, whereas in the new paradigm, they are comprehensive and focus on creating an antitobacco environment. Comprehensive programs include lobbying for policy change, media advocacy, monitoring of tobacco law enforcement, and making smoking cessation resources easily available to smokers who want to quit (see Centers for Disease Control and Prevention 1999b; U.S. Department of Health and Human Services 2000). Efforts to create an antitobacco environment include working to establish or enforce tobacco policies at day-care centers, schools, the workplace, and public areas, and to promote tobacco-free communities and a tobacco-free society.[1]

Using these strategies, a reorganized and very vocal antitobacco movement has directed its energies at the tobacco industry. Underlying the legislative and regulatory struggles over tobacco is the issue of the industry's integrity. By focusing on the tobacco industry's false claims about the addictive nature of nicotine, the link between smoking and cancer, and the industry's efforts to market tobacco products to youths, antitobacco industry lobbyists have intensified their efforts to sway the public to the view that cigarette companies are corrupt (see Kluger 1996; Nathanson 1997, n.d.). For years, tobacco industry representatives fought the charge that smokers could become addicted to cigarettes. Although the industry continued to deny this claim, in 1994, two scientists formerly employed by Philip Morris testified before a congressional committee that the company hid evidence that they had documented in 1983 on the addictive nature of nicotine (Meier 1998b). Further, after decades of refuting evidence that smoking is linked to cancer, the industry recognized it as a health risk.[2] Yet, as former Food and Drug Administration commissioner and antitobacco advocate David Kessler notes, these changes have not resulted in a large step forward: "The tobacco C.E.O.s used to say that if somebody proved a link between cancer and cigarettes, they wouldn't sell them. So now they admit that it causes cancer, but they'll sell it anyway" (quoted in Goldberg 1998, 62). Finally, advocates point out that although industry representatives have contended that cigarette advertising is not meant to appeal to teens and youths, R. J. Reynolds's internal documents from the mid-1970s reveal that the company advocated targeting fourteen- to twenty-four-year-olds because they "represent tomorrow's cigarette business" (Meier 1998a). By exposing the ways the tobacco industry has withheld its knowledge about the addictive properties of nicotine as well as its ethically troubling strategic marketing techniques, antitobacco advocates have attempted to decrease the tobacco industry's authority and credibility, and to bolster their argument that tobacco products threaten individuals' health and the health of future generations.

In November 1998, after several years of negotiations, antitobacco activism resulted in a $246 billion legal settlement between forty-six state attorneys general and the tobacco industry. Settlement provisions include recovery of the cost of treating ill smokers, bans on tobacco billboards, limits on tobacco sponsorship of events, and funding to support a national foundation for antismoking advertising and research (Meier 1998d; Campaign for Tobacco-Free Kids 1999b).[3] Tobacco companies also face increasing numbers of class action and individual lawsuits brought by ill smokers and former smokers (Levin 1999a). Reducing youth smoking is a main priority of the 1998 multistate tobacco settlement, which reflects concern about the rising rates of cigarette smoking among youths and teens, the belief that lifelong smokers are those who begin when they are young, and the politically attractive goal of saving America's future generations. The highly publicized settlement agreement reinforces anti-industry advocates' contention that the tobacco industry must be held responsible for the consequences of the dangerous product it markets.

Despite this historic setback to the tobacco industry, antitobacco lobbyists are not fully satisfied. One main criticism is that the settlement money allocated to the states does not have to be spent on antitobacco programs (Levin 1999b). Further, while there is reason for advocates to celebrate the changing tide in the United States, their work is far from over if they are to hold tobacco companies accountable for their marketing not only at home but overseas.[4] Because of a reduction in consumption of cigarettes by the American public, among other reasons, the tobacco industry has pressed the U.S. government to support exportation of tobacco products. This intensified cigarette promotion in many less developed countries has resulted in increased consumption, smoking-related illness, and deaths (Crofton 1990; Stebbins 1990, 1991; Perlez 1997). The settlement agreement will not, as tobacco companies would wish, bring an end to antitobacco activism.

But how does the antitobacco industry influence the way the issue of smoking during pregnancy is seen? Antitobacco advocates do not place blame on individual smokers; instead they blame the tobacco industry, which knowingly markets a hazardous product that can addict many of its consumers and may cause serious illnesses. The trend toward vilifying the tobacco industry instead of pregnant smokers invites punitive action against the tobacco barons, not cigarette consumers, for putting fetal health at risk: "The conscience of the tobacco barons, if it exists, does not care about the harm they do, even to children as yet unborn. If they did, they would immediately cease and desist from making and marketing tobacco" (Nathanielsz 1999, 171). This attitude suggests that the tobacco industry, not pregnant smokers, should be charged with fetal abuse.

Antitobacco industry advocates also touch on the issue of smoking during pregnancy in their efforts to create a smoke-free society so that girls and young women—the next generation's pregnant women—never become cigarette smokers. The Campaign for Tobacco-Free Kids, launched in 1995 and composed of more than 130 organizations, is leading the new drive against the tobacco industry. The campaign aims to reduce youth smoking and secondhand smoke exposure by lobbying for federal, state, and local public policies to ban the sale and promotion of tobacco products to minors, to limit minors' access to tobacco products, to restrict tobacco advertising, and to create smoke-free public spaces (see Campaign for Tobacco-Free Kids 1999a). Further, it seeks to increase the number of organizations and individuals involved with antitobacco advocacy and to shape public opinion and action against the tobacco industry. A number of national organizations representing girls and women participate in the Campaign for Tobacco-Free Kids.[5] Their participation ought to ensure attention to how the tobacco industry specifically targets young women, for example, through advertising, sponsorship of events that appeal to girls, and marketing of cigarette brand merchandise and clothing.

Again, these efforts focus more on stopping the tobacco industry from creating consumers and less on the consumers themselves, taking the positive step of stigmatizing those who benefit from the tobacco business instead of those who smoke.

HEALTH EDUCATION: PREVENTION CAMPAIGNS AND SMOKING CESSATION PROGRAMS

Preventing young women from smoking is also the focus of health education campaigns that are not representative of new developments in antitobacco advocacy. Campaigns specifically aimed at girls have proliferated in the 1990s in reaction to alarming increases in the rate of smoking among teenage girls that contrasts with decreases in the rate of smoking among adult women. The rate of daily smoking by girls who are high school seniors rose from 17.9 percent in 1991 to 23.6 percent in 1997 (Centers for Disease Control and Prevention 1999a). The estimation that 80 percent of adult smokers started smoking before age eighteen provides further motivation to target girls with the antismoking message. Specific issues influence young women to smoke, including low self-esteem, depression and anxiety, weight consciousness, and glamorous cigarette advertising; thus, separate antismoking campaigns have been designed for young women (see Kaufman 1994; Patton et al. 1996; French and Perry 1996). To encourage young women not to start smoking, antitobacco advocates have embedded antismoking messages in health education campaigns that encourage them to make healthy, "empowered" choices.

This theme builds on the broader "girl power" trends in popular culture that have emerged in the late 1990s in entertainment and sports. The national not-for-profit organization Girls, Incorporated, for example, designed "the first website that encourages girls, young women, and the adults who care about them to become strong, smart, and bold about the dangers of smoking" (Girls Incorporated n.d.). Two national campaigns sponsored by the U.S. Department of Health and Human Services and aimed at young women also illustrate the empowerment theme.[6] "Girl Power!" launched in 1996, includes antitobacco education along with its public health messages about alcohol and illicit drug use, physical fitness, mental health, and teen pregnancy (U.S. Department of Health and Human Services n.d.). The "Smoke-Free Kids and Soccer" campaign, a collaborative effort between the Department of Health and Human Services and U.S. Soccer, features the U.S. women's soccer team. The campaign seeks to reach the more than seven million girls who play soccer by airing television and radio public service announcements and distributing antismoking literature to soccer programs and state and local health departments (U.S. Department of Health and Human Services, U.S. Women's

National Team, and U.S. Soccer 1999).[7] Its sponsors hope that the antismoking, pro-sports message will encourage girls to "resist pressures to smoke" and to "take up soccer and put down cigarettes."

Both of these national campaigns focus on instilling antismoking attitudes in girls through positive messages that link empowerment and well-being with being a nonsmoker; however, they build on health education tactics that do not correlate with the new paradigm in antitobacco industry efforts. Their reliance on the girl power theme is a healthist one that emphasizes the importance of taking individual control over one's health decisions. The unstated implication of these prevention strategies is that girls who choose to smoke make irresponsible decisions. This form of victim blaming is representative of the old models of antitobacco activism and supports a morally based antismoking message. This is contrary to advocates' actions that place blame on tobacco companies for luring young smokers, not on the smokers themselves.

The heavy emphasis on preventing young women from becoming regular smokers is welcomed by health educators who face the challenge of counseling pregnant women to quit smoking. Efforts to prevent young women from taking up smoking—whether new antitobacco policies or health education prevention campaigns—have not displaced antismoking programs aimed specifically at pregnant smokers. Statistics on women's smoking rates indicate that health educators will continue to see a need for smoking cessation programs. Based on the latest national data, from 1998, young women and women with low educational attainment have smoking rates that are far higher than the national average, which is 12.9 percent. White women ages eighteen and nineteen have the highest rates of smoking during pregnancy, 30.4 percent, and since 1994, the rate of pregnant teenagers who smoke has continued to rise (Ventura et al. 2000, 11). Among pregnant women over age twenty, those without a high school degree have a smoking rate of 29 percent, and white pregnant women who are not high school graduates have the highest smoking rate, 48 percent (Ventura et al. 2000, 11). Arguments for continuing smoking cessation programs for some groups of pregnant women, then, appear to have sufficient statistical justification.

What makes smoking during pregnancy a particular concern to health professionals, of course, is the added risk to the fetus that results from a woman's smoking during pregnancy. This, along with the fact that pregnant women have contact with health care providers during prenatal health visits, helps explain why programs targeting pregnant women will continue, despite the paradigm shift in antitobacco advocacy that is leading efforts away from convincing individual smokers to quit and toward policies that promote a tobacco-free society by restricting cigarette advertising and marketing. The danger is that programs for pregnant smokers will sustain the old antismoking moral messages that are focused on convincing women to be good mothers by quitting on behalf of their babies-to-be. Of further importance, programs for pregnant smokers advocate the healthist middle-class ideology as superior. Surveys reveal that a disproportionately high number of women who have low education levels (and, presumably, lower-class status) smoke during pregnancy. The alignment of smoking with lower-class status heightens the possibility of antagonism between antismoking health educators and their clients, and reinforces social stereotypes about lower-class women as neglectful mothers.

However, insights gained since the rise of "stop smoking during pregnancy" programs in the 1980s have altered some health educators' approaches. Public health intervention studies consistently find that smoking cessation programs for pregnant women are not very effective and that quitting is extremely complicated due to the many factors that influence women's smoking before, during, and after pregnancy. In a review article, Louise Floyd and colleagues conclude that smoking cessation programs for pregnant women have achieved only moderate success and that "a notable fact about prenatal smoking cessation trials as a whole is that even with the best results, the vast majority of women continue to smoke throughout pregnancy despite their knowledge of the increased risks of adverse consequences to themselves and to the developing fetus" (Floyd et al. 1993, 406). It has become clear that the moralistic messages "If you love your baby, you'll quit smoking" and "Don't risk your or your baby's health" are far too simplistic. But research shows that other, less negative antismoking strategies remain unsuccessful.

The Centers for Disease Control's Smoking Cessation in Pregnancy Demonstration and Research Project represents a turning point in public health professionals' understanding of the problems with antismoking programs for pregnant women. Between 1986 and 1991, the project sponsored smoking cessation programs for low-income women receiving prenatal care through Women, Infants and Children clinics and public prenatal clinics in Colorado, Maryland, and Missouri.[8] In each state, approximately 50 percent of clinic clients were regular smokers at the time they became pregnant. During prenatal health visits, women who participated in the study received supportive, encouraging antismoking counseling and pamphlets: "Becoming Smoke Free—Baby & Me" in Missouri, "Quit & Be Free!" in Maryland, and "Give a Gift to Your Baby" in Colorado. Participants were asked to report whether they had been smoking, and if so, how much. The researchers were discouraged to learn that although women in the study were more likely to report that they had quit smoking by the eighth month of pregnancy than women had who were not in the study, tests for cotinine (a nicotine metabolite) revealed that quit rates were not significantly different (Kendrick et al. 1995). Louise Martinez-Cooper, an antitobacco activist and public health professional, recounted these findings to me, concluding,

> It was a huge project and a big deal—lots of time and money—and it was a great disappointment. The achievement was only to have people learn to not tell us the truth.[9] The lesson [health professionals learned] was that it's not a simple problem. . . . First, there's addiction. It is not fully understood what it means. You can't just tell someone to quit smoking. Second, low-income women we see in the clinics are a less educated and highly stressed group. Almost universally they say that they know they shouldn't do it, but "smoking is the only pleasure for me. It is the only time I get five minutes to myself." They don't perceive smoking cessation as a priority. . . . So we learned that we must improve people's lives.

The results of the Smoking Cessation in Pregnancy project suggest that the issue of smoking during pregnancy itself is best redefined as an issue about women's well-being. As Martinez-Cooper points out, campaigns urging women to quit smoking (or to not start smoking) will be effective only if they also target women's low-education and low-income status, stress,[10] addiction, and social responsibilities and relationships. Broadening the scope of antismoking programs in these ways moves health education away from convincing individual women to choose to quit smoking toward, in Martinez-Cooper's words, "improv[ing] people's lives" so that they are less likely to take up and continue smoking.

Frustration with the traditional tools used in efforts to urge pregnant women to quit smoking—advice, smoking cessation self-help literature, and follow-up counseling and support—has led other health professionals to develop innovative approaches that replace the usual health warnings with the unusual positive incentive of monetary reward. To some extent, these strategies work to improve women's lives and move beyond stressing the moral imperative that women should quit smoking for their babies-to-be. In the mid-1980s, two physicians in suburban Philadelphia offered to deduct one hundred dollars or 9 percent of the prenatal care bill for those pregnant clients who signed a pledge and stopped smoking (*New York Times* 1986a). The doctors estimated that half of the 180 patients they saw each year were smokers and that 20 percent of them smoked heavily. The *New York Times* reported that "after years of nagging patients about the harmful effects of smoking on an unborn child, Dr. Mann said he and Dr. Haggerty 'finally figured we had to do something.'" The financial incentive achieved what the physicians called moderate success: during the program, of one hundred women who smoked, seventy-five pledged to quit and forty succeeded. (Women were on the honor system, and the report on this program does not state whether any of the participants misrepresented their quitting success.)

Although the strategy of providing financial reward to quitters is not widespread, it holds possibilities for other health professionals. But it also presents problems. Financially rewarding successful quitters may keep health professionals from nagging or repeatedly offering the same advice to women who are already aware that smoking is a fetal health risk, and it can contribute to women's economic well-being. However, the financial incentive approach places the responsibility for quitting on pregnant women, dismisses cutting down as a positive health behavior change, and expects women to quit without health professionals' assistance.

A more extensive project investigated this type of program in greater detail. Since 1996, Susan Prows and Rebecca Donatelle, professors in the Department of Public Health at Oregon State University, have tested a new approach to smoking cessation with the Significant-Other Supporter Program or SOS.[11] Their research program, like Mann and Haggerty's, relies on a strategy of incentives. Pregnant women in the program receive counseling and antismoking literature designed to help them quit, and those who are successful receive $50 a month in merchandise credit vouchers. But the SOS project goes a step further by also giving monthly rewards ($25 a month and $50 for the first and last months) to a "social supporter" if the pregnant woman she or he is supporting gives up cigarettes. These awards continue until the second month after the baby's birth. The study compares the quit rates of women in the SOS program with those of women who receive only a standard self-help smoking cessation booklet and counseling. Results show significant differences between the two groups: after the eighth month of pregnancy, 35 percent of the SOS participants and 9 percent of non-SOS participants still abstained from smoking, and two months after their baby's birth, 24 percent of SOS participants and 5 percent of non-SOS participants remained nonsmokers (O'Neill 1998). Demonstrating how difficult it is for many women to quit smoking, the SOS success rates are not very high, but they are indeed far higher than the non-SOS success rates.

When I met with Susan Prows to learn about this innovative intervention study, she explained that private funders who support antismoking efforts compose the financial component of the study. Therefore, the project simultaneously invites community participation while avoiding criticism that tax dollars are being spent irresponsibly on pregnant ex-smokers.[12] It is possible that some would oppose providing benefits to women who stop smoking, given the negative stigma surrounding pregnant women who smoke and the idea that good mothers simply quit smoking on their own. The project also seeks to sidestep being seen as a welfare handout, a predictable charge because the SOS study participants are low-income women who receive Women, Infants, and Children program assistance.

The researchers contend that by providing tangible, positive incentives, the program goes beyond giving moral antismoking messages about smoking during pregnancy, including those that equate smoking with fetal abuse. Prows notes that SOS also dispels the myth that "people will quit if you just tell them how bad it is for them" (quoted in O'Neill 1998). Offering incentives for a social supporter extends the responsibility for the effort beyond the pregnant woman, and the certificates for food, clothing, and household goods that successful quitters and their supporters receive potentially benefit the pregnant woman, her baby-to-be, and her family.

The risks of the SOS program, however, rest with its most novel aspect: the financial reward for the social supporter. In fact, participants are advised not to choose their partner or husband as their social supporter to reduce the chance of conflict, coercion, or perhaps even domestic violence that might occur if a pregnant woman continued to smoke. A related problem with the social support emphasis is that this strategy puts in place a "pregnancy police person," who potentially could use negative, stigmatizing antismoking messages in her or his attempt to persuade the pregnant SOS participant to quit. Further, from a social perspective, the program offers a quick fix without extending antismoking efforts to address the root causes of low-income pregnant women's smoking. Future results of the study, which will include an analysis of women's experience with the program, should offer insight into the extent of these shortcomings, which are embedded in the social supporter incentive model.

Another major drawback to widespread adoption of the SOS model might be its expense. The next stage in the research will be to assess the program's cost-effectiveness, and the researchers hope to demonstrate that the money spent to prevent women's smoking is offset by the money saved in health care costs. This may be the case; as Prows points out, smoking causes 20 percent of all low-birthweight deliveries, and each low-birthweight baby adds medical expenses of between four thousand and nine thousand dollars (O'Neill 1998). The SOS researchers also contend that they may find that social support, not the financial incentive, is the primary motivation behind women's quitting.

Changes in health education programs directed at pregnant smokers mainly reflect dissatisfaction with the low success rates of campaigns launched since the 1980s (see Floyd et al. 1993). Even the most successful programs rarely achieve quit rates higher than 20 percent (Robert Wood Johnson Foundation 1999a, 3). It should not be assumed, however, that the failure of antismoking efforts lies only with noncompliant pregnant women. Health practitioners may not consistently follow the professional recommendations for smoking cessation counseling, particularly in providing assistance and follow-up support to pregnant women who attempt to quit smoking (Zapka et al. 2000). Further, health professionals may not offer antismoking advice to their clients evenly. One study found that Black women were less likely than white women to receive such advice (Kogan et al. 1994). As they seek new ways to get their health messages across, health professionals must more closely investigate the consistency of their practices and the implications of social bias in their interactions with pregnant women.

Innovative efforts such as the SOS campaign are intriguing because they suggest that health educators can offer women who smoke during pregnancy practical resources without subjecting them to moral judgment. But feminist antitobacco advocates are motivated not only by the failure of past antismoking programs. Reaching beyond attempts to redesign smoking cessation programs, feminist antitobacco advocates envision efforts that address women's social status.

FEMINIST ANTITOBACCO ADVOCACY

The feminist antitobacco position represents a third dimension of recent antitobacco efforts. This stance was alluded to by Louise Martinez-Cooper when she stated that one of the lessons learned in the Smoking Cessation in Pregnancy project was that improving smokers' lives could contribute to decreased cigarette use. This is the central contention of feminist antitobacco advocates. Martinez-Cooper went on to say, "We must stop seeing pregnant women in isolation from the rest of their lives. We can start with teens and young women, and we must view women in context. Say, if they don't quit this pregnancy, maybe they can go on nicotine replacement after the birth so the baby isn't exposed.[13] Pregnancy is a very short period in a woman's life; it isn't realistic to expect so many changes. It just doesn't happen." From this perspective, the fact that a woman smokes at any time in her life is seen as the critical problem, and the focus is taken off the label "pregnant" and placed on "women's smoking."

This change in emphasis addresses feminist criticism of the ways antismoking campaigns have targeted pregnant women (see Graham 1976; Oakley 1989; Greaves 1996, 120–121). Indeed, from different perspectives—feminist antismoking activists drawing on theories from women's health advocates and antismoking health professionals looking at health studies that evaluated the effectiveness of smoking cessation programs—these two groups have arrived at the same conclusion: health professionals must see pregnant women's health as a continuation of their "nonpregnant" daily lives and attempt to understand how women's perspectives on fetal health risks are related to their personal experiences. The challenge is to appeal to women and girls who smoke by using methods that do not blame them. Instead, the method must reflect a broader view that considers the context within which the choice to smoke is made.

Judy Levine echoed the call to look more closely at the complexities of the lives of pregnant women who smoke and pointed out that some antitobacco advocates now stress explicitly the importance of working for social change: "The eleven-year-old girl who smokes is later the twenty-one-year-old pregnant woman, and we should look back and have a certain amount of empathy and say, 'this is where this came from.' So most of the people who do women-and-tobacco work try to look at pregnancy as part of the life spectrum. . . . There are women-and-tobacco folks who are interested in working on improving other issues in women's lives so that they don't feel the need to smoke. For example, poverty relief. Some feel that tobacco control should be more involved in other aspects [of women's lives]."

Framing smoking within the larger context of women's lives shifts the burden of blame from women to their social environments. It also offers the opportunity for antitobacco advocates to target community-based social change (e.g., poverty relief) instead of individual change (quitting smoking), which might alleviate the conditions that create the need to smoke felt by some women. This realization takes antitobacco activism a step forward by pointing out that the best antitobacco efforts cannot ignore other community concerns about the quality of life.[14] The benefit of this approach is that social, structural change helps communities and their members; the danger is that community-based antitobacco advocacy broadens the scope of public health policing from individuals to entire communities (see Balshem 1993; Lupton 1995). This is a tension inherent in community-based approaches that must be seriously considered.

Antitobacco advocates who focus on women's smoking, such as members of the International Network of Women Against Tobacco (INWAT), call attention to a complex range of issues that extend beyond the individual smoker to her social status and everyday well-being. These include issues addressed by the SOS program, such as the stressful effects of low-income and poverty status on women's lives and the influence of women's social support networks, as well as other issues, such as the strains of family life and motherhood, the images of women in cigarette advertising, niche marketing techniques that target young women, and the role of nicotine addiction in women's lives.[15] Dedicated to addressing tobacco as not only a health but a political issue with specific consequences for women's lives, INWAT points out that "women's tobacco use is sensitive to the interplay of political, social, economic, and cultural inequalities" (International Network of Women Against Tobacco 1998). Indeed, the global advocacy that INWAT promotes is particularly urgent because as tobacco profits decrease in North America, the industry continues to expand its markets overseas, where young women who do not smoke are a main target of their efforts.[16] Although the rate of smoking by women is expected to continue to drop in the United States, it is predicted that the rate will rise significantly in other regions of the world. International antitobacco networks such as INWAT seek to prevent women from taking up cigarettes by lobbying against the tobacco industry and its marketing tools and by involving greater numbers of women's health advocates in the antitobacco movement.

The work of INWAT and other feminist antitobacco advocates demonstrates how antitobacco efforts can stretch beyond a healthist approach that emphasizes individual responsibility to quit smoking toward an approach that considers society responsible for improving the quality of women's lives. The feminist antitobacco position advocates community-based action and social change beyond the smoking issue: "The solution to women's smoking will require nothing less than an improvement in women's lot" (Greaves 1996, 135; see also Graham 1976, 1987, 1993; Oakley 1989; Greaves 1995). Of central importance is alleviating the conditions that create the need or desire to smoke.[17] This way of reframing the problem of smoking is in line with the work of feminist health care advocates, who attend not only to the specific details of women's bodies, health, and lives but equally to promoting changes in the sociocultural, economic, and political contexts within which women's lives are shaped (see Boston Women's Health Book Collective 1998).

The call to connect antismoking efforts with social change may to some critics seem ineffective because it is out of political reach or overly ambitious. Designing antismoking messages and health education programs aimed at urging individuals to quit smoking may appear more feasible than promoting measures that encourage social and economic justice. The response to such criticism is twofold: first, statistics indicate that a far higher proportion of low-income (as measured by education level) women smoke during pregnancy; and, second, antismoking programs have not proven very effective. Given this, antitobacco advocates cannot contest the logic behind the argument that social change is vital to decreasing tobacco use.

The next step is translating the will for social change into public health practice. In his analysis of health movements based on social change models, which includes the women's health movement, Nicholas Freudenberg (1981) argues that the field of health education can support a social justice approach to health. His suggestions include the following: that health educators integrate social and economic analyses into their professional practice at all levels; that participation in labor organizations, civic groups, consumer organizations, and community associations be considered central to their jobs; and that health education training programs emphasize that social and economic change is essential to public health efforts. Health professionals devote the greater part of their time and energy to urging others to change, yet public health in the broadest sense stands to benefit if the field of public health changes its own approach, activities, and aims.

Smoking during pregnancy is not specifically on the new agenda of antitobacco advocates, which primarily seeks to challenge the tobacco industry. However, recent efforts to prevent smoking by young women, to restrict cigarette advertising and marketing that appeals to girls, and to focus on the social conditions that lead women to take up and continue smoking all indirectly address the issue of smoking during pregnancy without stigmatizing pregnant smokers. Women's health advocates must not ignore that smoking cessation programs aimed at pregnant women remain on the health education agenda. Some programs are indeed moving away from basing their arguments on fetal health, yet other efforts continue to instruct women in moral terms to quit smoking on behalf of their babies-to-be.

Although the most severe antismoking messages aimed at pregnant women were initiated in the mid-1980s, fetal-centric smoking cessation efforts have not disappeared, as demonstrated in this book's analysis of pregnancy advice literature, health educators' counseling strategies, and Health Edco's Itty Bitty Smoker, Womb of Doom, and Smokey Sue Smokes for Two models. Further, older antismoking messages that portray smoking as fetal abuse, such as the American Cancer Society's posters and videos, are still in use. Perhaps most important, the current healthist atmosphere surrounding a pregnant woman's responsibilities as well as the threat of fetal abuse charges promote pregnancy policing of women by others on behalf of their babies-to-be. Warnings against smoking during pregnancy can too easily slip from educating women about the health risks of smoking to conveying the message that pregnant women must quit smoking if they wish to be good mothers. Antismoking programs and messages directed at pregnant smokers demand constant critical attention from women's health advocates.

From Fetal Abuse to Fetal Care: Re-visioning
Feminist Theories on Fetal Identity

In this book, I have offered a critical feminist analysis of how smoking during pregnancy is seen by varied health experts and "everyday" women. My analysis points to the political significance of fetal-centered antismoking messages for women's reproductive freedom in relation to debates on abortion rights and fetal abuse prosecutions. In a time of varied assaults on women's reproductive rights, feminists and women's health advocates must participate more fully in debates on a wide range of fetal health issues. Cultural representations of fetuses as persons and patients are unlikely to fade given legal attempts to recognize fetal rights, the development of sophisticated medical treatment for fetuses, and the fact that many women experience and think of their babies-to-be as specific individuals. Feminists face the challenge of recognizing fetal identities without ceding the ground to those who seek legal limits on women's reproductive health practices aimed to protect fetuses (see Morgan and Michaels 1999).

Like other prenatal health issues such as drinking or drug use during pregnancy, smoking during pregnancy raises complicated questions for feminist politics and health advocacy. Extensive medical evidence indicates that smoking presents a potentially serious health risk for pregnant women, their babies-to-be, and their infants. But feminists' opposition to smoking by pregnant women entails political and social risks. Politically, how can a feminist argument support efforts to enhance fetal health without giving power to the prolife "fetal rights" ideology? Should a pregnant woman's "choice" to smoke be respected? Socially, can (and should) feminists hold an antismoking position without stigmatizing smokers as bad mothers? How can feminists and women's health activists lobby for a woman's right to abortion as well as for accessible prenatal care, safe prenatal testing, addiction treatment programs, workplace and environmental safety regulations, and a range of other measures that might benefit fetal health? Addressing these subjects involves closer scrutiny of feminists' current understandings of fetal identity.

Prochoice advocates have reacted to the antiabortion movement's mobilization of the fetus as its primary symbol by refusing to recognize the fetus as a subject or an agent. This approach leaves feminists vulnerable to the charge that they simply do not care about fetuses. Given the rise of legislation to protect fetal health and the criminal charges brought against women for fetal abuse and neglect, this vulnerability is increasingly problematic; reproductive rights arguments now pertain not only to women's abortion decisions but also to women's actions that pose a risk to fetal health. This expansion raises questions about the desirability of promoting prochoice language and avoiding reference to the fetus. Feminist journalist Katha Pollitt warns, "As the 'rights' of the fetus grow and respect for the capacities and rights of women declines, it becomes harder and harder to explain why drug addiction is a crime if it produces an addicted baby, but not if it produces a miscarriage, and why a woman can choose abortion but not vodka [or cigarettes]. And that is just what the 'prolifers' want" (1990, 414).

Pollitt points to the dangers of framing the abortion debate as a struggle between fetal rights and women's rights. This formulation leads to charges of hypocrisy, for example, if feminists support the right of a woman to choose abortion but disagree with a pregnant woman's choice to smoke or drink. As prolife lobbyists would have it, this stance is contradictory because respect for abortion rights is anti-fetus while attention to fetal health is pro-fetus: recognizing fetal health is the same as identifying the fetus as a person, which supports an antiabortion position. As Pollitt indicates, antiabortion advocates want to force feminists—indeed, the public—to regard fetuses as subjects.

The prochoice slogan "Pro-Family, Pro-Child, Pro-Choice" is one response to the antiabortion rights advocates' charge that prochoice advocates do not care about the well-being of children or families. But this tactic skirts the question of fetal identity: pro-child is not the same as pro-fetus. Such an erasure of the fetus may appear to be an inescapable part of feminist reproductive politics because seeing the fetus as a unique and independent subject automatically seems to support antiabortion politics.[18] An important consequence of the lack of recognition of fetal identity, however, is that it ignores the fact that many people do conceptualize particular fetuses as subjects and social beings, and refer to them as babies. Feminists risk losing support for the prochoice position by insisting that fetuses are not babies.[19]

To move beyond static, polarized prochoice and antiabortion arguments about whether fetuses are persons, prochoice advocates should attempt to recognize and publicize multiple representations of fetal identity. In fact, recent feminist approaches to fetal identity do not try to establish absolutes. Rather, they respect the social, contextual contingencies that define fetuses as persons or not (see Morgan 1996; Morgan and Michaels 1999). Given this approach, assuming that personhood is conferred when a fetus is conscious or sentient (see Petchesky 1985 [1984]; Steinbock 1992) becomes less meaningful than determining how different actors—pregnant women, health experts, policy makers, family and friends of a pregnant woman, and others—represent and construct fetal personhood. Anthropologist Lynn Morgan asserts that the search for a stable definition of fetal personhood is misdirected: "We cannot talk about 'the' fetus but rather need to talk about a diversity of situations and perspectives which carry with them many different meanings" (1996, 60).[20]

An important feminist strategy, then, involves demonstrating how fetal identities are variously understood in science, medicine, law, popular culture, and pregnant women's lives. Within this framework, analyzing cultural representations of fetal identity is more important than debating scientific proof about the true nature of fetal life or the real facts about fetal well-being. The definition of fetal life is constructed in multiple ways by different actors. Sociologist Monica Casper's ethnographic study of fetal surgery reveals that fetal identity is configured in varied ways within science and medicine itself, as "person, patient, research material, tool, therapeutic technology, and tissue source" (1994, 308; see also 1998; Maynard-Moody 1995). In the legal realm, although the South Carolina Supreme Court has ruled that the fetus is a person after viability (the ability to live outside the womb), courts in all other states have ruled that the fetus cannot be granted rights as a child or person (Center for Reproductive Law and Policy 1999, 2). Further, the use of fetal imagery and the portrayal of fetuses as subjects in contexts not intended to comment on abortion politics (including prenatal health education, Hollywood films, television and magazine ads, and memorials for miscarried fetuses) invite analysis of the multiple social and cultural constructions that "give life" to fetuses.

What demands significantly more attention still is how pregnant women, their partners and families, health care providers, health insurance companies, and health policy makers hold flexible, and at times conflicting, ideas about the conditions that constitute fetal personhood. In her work on women's, men's and genetic counselors' interpretations of fetal life in the context of amniocentesis testing, Rayna Rapp reports the words of one woman: "When we walked into the doctor's office, both my husband and I were crying. He looked up and said, 'What's wrong? Why are you in tears?' 'It's the baby, the baby is going to die,' I said. 'That isn't a baby,' he said firmly. 'It's a collection of cells that made a mistake'" (Rapp 1990, 28). Linda Layne's work on the "cultural denial of pregnancy loss" in the United States describes how the "realness" of a baby—felt by a pregnant woman when she abstains from coffee and wine, attends prenatal visits, and buys and receives gifts for the baby-to-be—is erased when a woman miscarries (1999a, 2000). These examples reveal that in some instances, women feel that there is not too much but rather too little emphasis on the fetus as a person.

Indeed, women's views on fetal identity vary widely. Despite the high visibility of the antiabortion movement's fetal images, debates over abortion and fetal abuse, and the widespread use of fetal sonograms, pregnant women (and others) do not think about or see fetuses in the way urged by prolife campaigns.[21] Contradicting the logic behind some antismoking and most antiabortion campaigns, the women I interviewed did not all identify fetal images as infantlike, independent babies. In response to sonogram images, some women felt reassured that their baby-to-be was real or healthy. Lena Ferro, a white executive assistant in her thirties who had difficulty becoming pregnant, said that her best memory of pregnancy was "just feeling the baby's moving, and the sonograms—seeing it's for real." But others interpreted the image as monstrous or could not think of the fetus as a baby until after it was born. Johanna Miles, a forty-year-old African American nursing assistant, remembered that her baby-to-be looked "like a big headed monster" in the ultrasound picture. Christina Lee, a working-class woman in her early twenties, explained that "I didn't have that bond, really. I couldn't think of it as a baby. I couldn't get the concept in my head 'I'm havin' a baby.'" When asked why not, she responded, "Well, you can't see it, so it's not really a baby, I thought. I had two sonograms and have the pictures still, but because I didn't see it all the time, you know, it wasn't really real."

Not only are there personal differences in the ways women see and think about babies-to-be, but feminist research documents variation within and between cultures. Cross-cultural studies reveal that the concern voiced in U.S. debates over fetal life about the "biological reality" of the fetus is not universal. In some cultures, ideas about fetuses are not primarily mediated by biotechnology; instead, they draw on cultural and religious traditions (Morgan 1989, 1996, 1998; Inhorn 1994; Oaks 1994, 1998, 1999; Conklin and Morgan 1996; Renne 1996; Hardacre 1997). It is clear that fetal identity is open to a variety of interpretations at the personal as well as social, cultural, religious, and political levels.

Given this situation, feminists and women's health advocates should increase efforts to expose the prolife fetus—which feeds fetal rights and fetal abuse ideologies—as just one of many versions of the fetus. At the same time, we must remain vigilant in our attention to how some fetal subjects may undermine attempts to secure and maintain women's reproductive rights. Health Edco's Itty Bitty Smoker, Smokey Sue Smokes for Two, and the Womb of Doom, for example, are marketed as antismoking education devices, yet they also invoke antiabortion politics. In effect, antismoking and antiabortion fetal models mutually reinforce similar notions of fetal personhood and of women's reproductive responsibilities; the fetus is a fragile, vulnerable being in need of a good mother's devotion and protection. Critical analyses of how notions of the fetus as person threaten to restrict women's agency and autonomy can redirect current ways of thinking about pregnancy in ways that detract from concerns about maternal–fetal conflict and heighten the acknowledgment of maternal–fetal care. This ought not be confined to academic discourses. Working against the grain in the spheres of law, health care, the media, and public culture, women's health advocates must continue lobbying and speaking out on behalf of women and their babies-to-be.

When I see a pregnant woman smoking, I feel concerned about the health problems her baby-to-be may experience as a consequence. But I do not think it is effective or acceptable to give her a "you're a bad mother" glare or approach her as a member of the pregnancy police to inform her that she is violating a pregnancy rule. Accosting women with the "don't smoke" message that they already know is not the answer. Yet we should not ignore that it is likely best for the woman and for her baby-to-be that she not smoke. A more appropriate approach to preventing smoking-related health problems and deaths is to support those public health practitioners and antitobacco advocates who have made a primary commitment to improving women's health and well-being. Actions to decrease the rate of women who smoke during pregnancy can be indirectly and productively addressed through antismoking advocacy and lobbying against the advertising and marketing of tobacco products.

Those who feel strongly that pregnant women ought not smoke can demonstrate caring about smokers and their babies-to-be by collaborating with antitobacco advocates to restrict tobacco advertising and marketing; to promote smoke-free environments; to monitor the smoking cessation messages, literature, and resources that women receive in prenatal clinics; and to insist that health providers and antitobacco advocates refrain from using negative, stigmatizing antismoking messages. Feminist antitobacco advocates ought to maintain a strong presence in local, national, and international antitobacco coalitions, ensuring that antitobacco groups critically consider how their actions affect women and girls (with critical attention to class, race, and ethnicity). These organizations provide the opportunity to collaborate with feminists and women's health advocates who are fighting against the tobacco industry.

Health practitioners, antitobacco advocates, legal experts, and policy makers must redirect their energy and resources away from a fetal-centered moral politics that implicates women who do not comply with health advice as bad mothers. Pregnancy advice literature ought to better reflect that women's health choices can be recognized as good even if they do not completely follow pregnancy rules instructing them to reduce risks to fetal health. Pregnant women actively negotiate their needs or desires with the perceived needs of their fetuses, and they do so in a variety of ways. The negotiated fetal care that women enact when they restrain their own desires on behalf of their baby-to-be's health—for example, by smoking half a pack of "lights" instead of a pack of favorite cigarettes a day—deserves greater positive attention.[22] The best smoking cessation programs today provide pregnant women with non-stigmatizing health information along with such resources as stress reduction techniques, noncoercive social support, and perhaps even financial incentives.

The redesign of antismoking campaigns aimed at pregnant women is particularly urgent. Mixing health advice with moral judgments against smoking during pregnancy supports the perception that public intervention in the maternal–fetal relationship on behalf of the fetus is socially, medically, and legally justified. The idea that pregnant women must sacrifice numerous desires as they strive to be good mothers is currently propagated through pregnancy advice literature; pregnancy policing by family members, friends, coworkers, and strangers; public health campaigns; and media coverage of the criminal prosecution of pregnant women for fetal abuse. But the solution to preventing fetal health risks does not lie in better surveillance, harsher moral judgment, or greater punishment of pregnant and parenting women. Rather, it requires turning serious attention toward women's perceptions of their babies-to-be, creating health education messages that neither blame nor scold, accepting fetal health risks in cases in which a woman does not fully quit smoking, and devoting greater resources to broad-scale social changes that alleviate the need to smoke. Transforming the assumption that all women can and must conform to model pregnancy practices or else face social, medical, and possibly legal censure demands a concerted and multidimensional effort.

Appendix A

Interview Research Methods

Drawing on recent trends in anthropological research, I used a multisited ethnographic approach to conduct interviews with health professionals and everyday women. Multisited ethnography involves the study of how a particular subject or issue is given meaning and acted upon by individuals and groups who inhabit different yet interconnected worlds (see Marcus 1995). By exploring the worlds of health experts and everyday women, I aimed to capture whether, how, and why these two groups' interpretations of the fetal health risks of smoking might differ.

Daily news coverage of the health policy "tobacco wars" and new smoke-free workplace regulations in Maryland, combined with the intense, on-going debates on abortion and fetal rights, led me to pay close attention to how I presented my research topic. When I contacted health experts, I stated that my focus was health professionals' approach to smoking during pregnancy; with everyday women, I couched the study in broader terms. The consent form explained that the research was meant to "understand a variety of people's views on health experiences and pregnancy, including cigarette smoking during pregnancy" and that participation would involve "an open-ended discussion of questions related to pregnancy, health, cigarette smoking, and other issues."

I was referred to many potential health expert participants by their coworkers or friends, and I contacted others by calling health advocacy organizations. In addition, I met several health professionals at prenatal or pre-conception care classes I observed. This component of the interviewing process meant that I visited the offices of physicians, health educators, and antitobacco advocates. All but three of these experts were women, and all but one were white. Interviews ranged from forty-five minutes to an hour and a half, and were compressed or stretched to fit the fast-paced and busy work schedules of most health experts. Several interviews were conducted by phone due to the distant location of the interviewee.

I contacted everyday women by tapping into social networks of friends, family members, and coworkers. I chose not to look for a statistically representative sample, as would be preferred in research that seeks to draw conclusions that can be generalized to larger populations. My convenience sample, however, includes women with diverse characteristics. This part of the research led me to kitchen tables and living room couches in urban and suburban homes, to workplace cafeterias, a parenting center and its summer picnic, prenatal clinic waiting rooms, and fast food restaurants. (Two interviewees deemed meeting there preferable and safer—for me as a white woman or for both of us, I'm not sure—than meeting in their homes "in the projects" of African American neighborhoods.)

The women I interviewed included smokers, ex-smokers, and nonsmokers of varied ages, races, and social class backgrounds. Age, race, and social class are significant when looking at smoking during pregnancy because national statistics indicate that young, white women who have lower educational attainment—and therefore likely lower economic status—are most likely to smoke. Talking with women from different generations was important because I hoped to capture women's perceptions about the changes over time in pregnancy advice in general and in regard to smoking. Those who had been pregnant before the rise of hard-line antismoking messages, I expected, would offer different opinions about the new rules of pregnancy than would those who had become pregnant after the increase in expectations about pregnant women's health behaviors. I limited participants to white and African American women because they represent the dominant racial groups in the Baltimore–Washington, D.C., area where I conducted the research. Finally, although I did not ask women to identify their socioeconomic status, I met participants at state-funded clinics, a parenting center for low-income women, and in their homes in neighborhoods or suburbs characterized by specific class identities; this assured me that I had reached women of diverse social and economic circumstances. Further, the jobs that women (and, where relevant, their partners) held provided insight into their social class status (see appendix B).

The interviews I conducted with everyday women ranged from fifty minutes to two hours, and all but two interviews were conducted face to face. Four women declined to speak with me, stating that they did not have time. At the end of an interview, I usually asked the participant if she knew of others I might talk with, using snowball sampling as a method of identifying further interviewees.

Because much of women's work, particularly in the home, goes unpaid, I offered everyday women fifteen dollars to participate; this was offered partly as an incentive and partly in recognition of the economic value of women's time (Hochschild 1989; Benn 1998). I did not offer payment to those I interviewed as health experts based on the (arguable) assumption that because we met during business hours and discussed a professional subject, the interview was considered a workday activity. Instead, I thanked them for donating their time to my study. A number of women voiced strong appreciation of the fifteen dollars. Most memorable was a woman I spoke with in a state-funded clinic waiting room who explained that she would go straight to McDonald's, eat lunch, and then drive to the hospital to deliver her fourth baby (knowing full well that it was against her doctor's orders to eat during labor). Before leaving, she loudly announced to the others in the waiting room, "Hey, this lady will give you fifteen dollars and all you have to do is sit and talk to her!" In another instance, a woman who was instrumental in introducing me to a group of lower-income women pointed out that I paid more than twice as much per hour as they made at their minimum-wage jobs. A few were not eager to accept the payment, however. When some women stated, "I don't need it," I explained that I believe all women's time is valuable and that I wanted her to accept the compensation; all then did accept it. Of course, I was on the richer end of the research relationship, because these health experts and everyday women shared with me the data that have made this book possible.

	Profiles of Interview
Appendix B	Participants

Each interview participant is listed in one of two categories—everyday women or health experts—based on the primary focus of our conversation. Participants have been given pseudonyms, and to further ensure anonymity, I have modified some of their biographical information.

Women Interviewed

I interviewed forty-six women, ranging in age from sixteen to sixty. Fourteen women were African American; thirty-two were white. Of the African American women, six had never smoked regularly, six were former smokers, two were current smokers, and two had smoked during pregnancy. Among the white women, thirteen had never smoked regularly, seven were former smokers, twelve were current smokers, and eight had smoked during pregnancy. In table A.1, women who had smoked cigarettes during pregnancy are also listed as previously or currently smoking.

Table A.1.
Women Smokers Interviewed by Race and Smoking Status

	Smoking			
Race	NEVER REGULARLY	PREVIOUSLY	CURRENTLY	WHILE PREGNANT
African American	6	6	2	2
White	13	7	12	8
TOTAL	18	13	14	9

TESSA ANDREWS is a white woman in her late teens who has three children. Tessa is married and works in a restaurant; her husband is a construction worker. She currently smokes but quit each time she was pregnant.

JOSELYN BEHM, a white woman in her early thirties, has a toddler and is pregnant. She has a college degree in economics and is not working outside the home so she can care for her children. Joselyn's husband is a financial analyst. Neither has smoked.

AMY BELLINGER is a nineteen-year-old white woman who has two young children. She is not in a romantic relationship and lives with her parents. Amy currently smokes and smoked during part of both pregnancies. Her ex-boyfriend and the babies' father is a smoker. Amy works at a restaurant.

ELIZABETH BLACKMUND, a white woman in her late forties, has three children. She has a college degree and does not work outside the home. Her husband is a corporate executive. Elizabeth smoked when she was in college but quit several years before trying to become pregnant. Her husband smokes heavily.

CARRIE BURDINE is a white woman in her mid-forties who has a teenager and an elementary school–aged child. Carrie smoked during both of her pregnancies but has since quit smoking. She is remarried, and her husband smokes. Carrie did computer training until the birth of her second child, and her husband works in the food service industry.

VIVIAN COMPTON is a fifty-three-year-old African American woman who had the first of six children at age seventeen. Vivian is separated from her husband of many years and does administrative work for a community-based organization. Neither she nor anyone in her household ever smoked.

LUISAH CROSWELL, an African American woman in her late thirties, is divorced and lives with her elementary school–aged child and her mother, who owns the house. Luisah works at a day-care center and used to smoke regularly, although she stopped smoking while she was pregnant. Her mother has never smoked.

JOSEPHINE DITTMAN is a married, white woman in her early forties who has two teenagers. Josephine works full time as a health educator, and her husband is an insurance company representative. She smoked as teen but quit before she was pregnant. Her husband has never smoked.

RAE ANN DIXON is a seventeen-year-old white woman who has two young children. She has never married and does not work outside the home. She smoked during her first but not her second pregnancy and currently smokes. The father of her children smokes.

SUSAN DONAHUE is a white woman in her early twenties. She is married and has a toddler. She does not work outside the home but would like to. Her husband is also seeking employment. Susan smokes, but she quit cold turkey when she learned she was pregnant and did not smoke for the duration of the pregnancy. Her husband smokes heavily.

PATRICIA DOYLE is a thirty-year-old white woman who has four children and is pregnant. Patricia used to smoke but quit during pregnancy. She is now an avid nonsmoker. Her husband does not smoke and works as a plumber. Patricia is not working outside of the home and considers herself a Domestic Goddess (a reference to the television show "Roseanne," which featured a strong working-class woman as its main character).

LENA FERRO, a white woman in her late thirties, is pregnant with her second child. She works full time as an executive assistant, and her husband works in the media industry. Lena used to smoke but quit before trying to become pregnant; her husband does not smoke. Lena's mother is a current smoker who smoked during pregnancy.

KERRY GILMARTIN is a white woman in her late twenties who has three children. She is divorced and does not work outside the home. She currently smokes but cut down during one pregnancy and stopped smoking during the others.

TRICIA GREENE, a fifty-five-year-old African American woman, is the mother of three children. She works as an office cleaner and is a former smoker who quit during each pregnancy. Her husband does not smoke.

MICHELLE HART is an African American woman in her mid-twenties who has a young child. Michelle has a longstanding relationship with the father of her baby and works as an administrative assistant. She and her boyfriend are nonsmokers, and she has never lived with anyone who has smoked.

LESLIE HOLLINS is a white woman in her early forties. She has one child and is divorced (her ex-husband never smoked). Leslie works as an executive assistant and writer. She cut down the number of cigarettes she smoked during pregnancy and was a smoker at the time of the interview. She later informed me that she had quit.

BERNICE JOHNSON, a sixty-year-old African American woman, has three adult children. She is a retired janitor who has never married. Bernice smoked regularly when she was young.

CHRISTINA LEE is a white woman in her early twenties. Christina currently smokes but quit smoking while she was pregnant. She is not working outside of the home, and her husband, a nonsmoker, is attending military school.

LANEISHA McDONALD is an African American woman in her early twenties who is pregnant with twins. She has one other child. LaNeisha, who provides childcare in her home, has had a long-term relationship with a man who is a printer. Neither of them has ever smoked.

SUE ANN McFADDEN is a thirty-two-year-old white woman who has a young child and an infant. Sue Ann works part time as a health educator, and her husband is a police officer. Neither has ever smoked.

APRIL McGOUGH, a white woman in her early thirties, has a young child. April works full time as a company's communications department director and holds an advanced degree. Her husband is a police officer, and neither has smoked regularly.

BETSY MICHAELS is a white woman in her late twenties who is pregnant with her first child. Betsy is a teacher, and her husband is an engineer. Neither has been a regular smoker, and Betsy's husband's parents smoked for many years but recently quit.

JOHNNA MILES is an African American woman in her late thirties. She has two children and had her first at age twenty-five. Johnna is a nursing assistant and is separated from her husband. She is a former smoker who gave up smoking when she learned she was pregnant.

JENNIFER MONTELLI is a white woman in her late twenties who is pregnant with her second child. Her mother has four children and smoked during each pregnancy. Jennifer has a college degree and plans to work outside the home only part time until her children are of school age. Her husband is an accountant. Neither has been a smoker.

BETTELYNN MONTGOMERY is a twenty-year-old African American woman who has one child. She works at a neighborhood center as an administrative assistant. Neither she nor any of her family members have smoked.

CARLA MULLINGER, a white woman in her late twenties, has two young children. She has a college degree and is not working outside the home in order to care for her children. Her husband is an engineer. Carla's mother smoked during pregnancy, and her father smoked occasionally but not in the house. Carla used to smoke but quit before she became pregnant. Her husband has never smoked.

JULIA PANCIERA is a white woman in her early thirties who was pregnant at the time of our interview. She is a graduate student, and her husband is a university professor. Neither has ever smoked regularly.

ANGELA PERRY is a white woman in her mid-thirties who had the first of her four children at age fourteen. Her mother, who had six children, did not smoke but allowed her children to. Angela works part time doing house-keeping, and her husband is irregularly employed. Both smoke. Angela cut down the number of cigarettes and switched to a lighter brand while she was pregnant.

CYNTHIA PHILLIPS is a white woman in her late thirties who has an infant. Cynthia works full time as a research assistant, and her husband is look-ing for full-time employment. Cynthia used to smoke and quit when she learned she was pregnant. Her husband quit smoking the third month she was pregnant, but after the baby was born he went back to it. He only smokes outside now.

ANASTASIA POWERS, a twenty-year-old white woman, has two young children. She receives government financial assistance and does not work outside the home so that she can raise her children. Anastasia does not currently smoke and smoked during one pregnancy but not the other. She is get-ting divorced, and her estranged husband is a mechanic who smoked two packs a day.

MEREDITH RODGERS is a white woman in her mid-thirties who has two young children. Her mother, who had the first of three children at age thirty-one, stopped smoking during pregnancy. Meredith is a nurse-midwife, holds an advanced degree, and works as a full-time researcher. Her hus-band is a physician. Neither has ever smoked.

BERNADETTE RYAN is a thirty-eight-year-old African American woman who is separated and has a teenager. Bernadette is a supervisor for a factory's cleaning staff, and her husband is a retired construction worker. She smoked while she was pregnant but no longer smokes.

LAVONDA SERBAN, an African American in her twenties, has two children. LaVonda does not work outside of the home, is not married, and lives in a multigenerational household. She has never smoked, and no one in her household smokes.

ANDREA SELLERS, a twenty-one-year-old white woman with four children, had her first at age seventeen. Andrea is studying to pass the GED and currently does not have a job outside the home. She is in the process of a divorce and plans to marry her boyfriend. She and her mother both smoke, and Andrea smoked during each pregnancy. (She is not sure if her mother did.) Her fiancé also smokes but more than she does. He works for a shipping company and does paving in the summers.

KATHERINE SHAFFER, a white woman in her mid-thirties, is married and has two young children. She has an advanced professional degree and a career in the computer industry. Her husband is employed part time and is also self-employed so that he can work at home and care for their children. Neither has been a regular smoker.

MARY BETH SHANNON is a white woman in her early thirties who has a young child. Her mother had the first of two children at age twenty-six and smoked during both pregnancies. She works as a part-time administrative assistant for a family business, and her husband is a computer scientist. Neither Mary Beth nor her husband has smoked, and her husband's parents smoked for many years but have quit.

RITA SHAW, a white woman in her early thirties, was pregnant with her first child at the time of the interview. Rita has an advanced degree and works as a research scientist. Her husband is a physician. Neither she nor her husband has smoked.

CLARICE SINGER is a twenty-year-old African American woman who is pregnant with her first child. Due to her pregnancy, she is not working outside the home, but she plans to attend a professional trade school. Clarice and her baby's father have a steady relationship. Both are nonsmokers and live in households in which no one smokes.

SARAH LEIGH SNYDER is a white sixteen-year-old who has two young children. She had her first at age fifteen, and her mother, who has two children, had Sarah when she was fourteen. Sarah does not work outside of the home and lives with her boyfriend, who works at a moving company. She smoked during one pregnancy but not the other and is a light smoker now. Sarah's mother smoked during pregnancy, and she and Sarah's boyfriend currently "smoke like chimneys."

MAY THOMAS is a forty-four-year-old African American woman who had her first of two children at age twenty-eight. May works part time as an office cleaner and has never married. She smoked during both pregnancies and is a regular smoker.

SONDRA THORTON is an African American woman in her early thirties who has two children. Sondra is a data archivist, and her husband works as a manager at a large corporation. She has been a regular smoker but quit each time she was pregnant. Neither she nor her husband currently smokes.

MARTHA VOSS is a thirty-year-old white woman who has a toddler. She works as a part-time researcher, and her husband is a computer programmer. Neither Martha nor her husband has ever been a smoker.

DEBRA WILLIAMS, an African American woman in her late thirties, had the first of two children in her mid-teens. Debra has been married for more than ten years to a nonsmoker who she says "forced her" to quit smoking while she was pregnant. She resumed smoking afterward and continues to smoke. She is a nursing assistant, and her husband is irregularly employed.

KATIE WOLFE is a white woman in her late twenties who is pregnant with her first. Katie is an administrative assistant and attends a professional school part time. Her husband recently finished trade school and works for a family-owned business. Neither has been a regular smoker.

MELINDA ZABROWSKI is a twenty-nine-year-old white woman who has four children. She is divorced and lives with her boyfriend, who works for a moving company. She works part time doing computer training. Melinda and her boyfriend smoke, and she quit during one pregnancy and cut down during the others.

CAROL ZIMMERMAN is a white woman in her late twenties who has one young child. She is in the process of divorce and works as both a part-time health educator and an administrative assistant. She currently smokes and quit smoking for part of her pregnancy. Her ex-husband was irregularly employed, and her family members are smokers.

Health Professionals and Antitobacco Advocates Interviewed

SUZANNE ASHMORE, 50s, health education program director

MARIA BAKER, 30s, nurse and smoking cessation counselor

KATE BELL-WOODARD, 30s, public health educator and antitobacco advocate

ISABEL BRADBURY, 40s, public health researcher and antitobacco advocate

TOM CREIGHTON, 40s, health education program director and smoking cessation counselor

ANNE DEWITT, 20s, health education program director

JAYNE DUNN, 40s, public health nurse

NANCY EDWARDS, 40s, health education counselor

TONI FIELDER, 30s, nurse and addiction counselor

GWEN FORREST, 30s, public health policy specialist and antitobacco advocate

PAULINE GAYTON, 30s, health education program director

TRISH JACKSON, 40s, public health nurse and smoking and health specialist

LIZ KLUZINSKI, 30s, smoking cessation counselor

VIVIAN LEMAY, 40s, nurse and health educator

JUDY LEVINE, 40s, physician and antitobacco advocate

FELICITY LUNDBERG, 50s, nurse and clinic director

LOUISE MARTINEZ-COOPER, 40s, physician and smoking and public health specialist

EDWARD MILLER, 60s, obstetrics and gynecology physician

MOLLY O'NEILL, 20s, smoking cessation program director

LUCY PRATT, 50s, nurse, clinic director, and smoking cessation counselor

PENNY RUTHERFORD, 50s, nurse

THERESA STEPHENS, 30s, nurse-midwife

ALLYSON WALKER, 30s, health education specialist and antitobacco advocate

JANICE WALINSKI, 40s, nurse and smoking cessation counselor

BILL WHITTMAN, 50s, smoking cessation counselor

MARJORIE WILCOX, 40s, antitobacco advocate and public health policy specialist

CATHERINE WOODS-TYLER, 40s, maternal–fetal medicine physician

Notes

Chapter 1 Confronting the Pregnant Smoker

1. I prefer the term "baby-to-be" over "baby" or "fetus," although I use all three. "Baby" blurs the boundary between pre- and postbirth status, whereas "fetus" sounds overly scientific or legal. Further, each term can signify antiabortion or prochoice discourse; antiabortion advocates have appropriated the everyday use of "baby," while prochoice advocates have avoided this term by using "fetus." Baby-to-be is not wholly adequate, however, because the term implies that every embryo or fetus will become a baby and emphasizes the product over the process of pregnancy. Despite these problems, I favor "baby-to-be" because it acknowledges that many pregnant women (and others) think, feel, and talk about the baby; yet the term also signals the political importance for women's reproductive rights of calling attention to how terminology invokes the on-going debates over the personhood and legal status of the fetus. For feminist scholarship that calls for increased recognition of multiple constructions of fetal personhood and simultaneous support of women's reproductive rights, see Rothman 1986, 1989; Morgan 1989, 1996, 1997, 1998; Taylor 1992; Casper 1994, 1997, 1998; Oaks 1994, 1998, 1999; Conklin and Morgan 1996; Layne 1997; and Morgan and Michaels 1999. I address these issues in chapter 8.
2. For analyses of the wide-ranging social and political uses of the label "bad mother" in the twentieth century, see Ladd-Taylor and Umansky 1998.
3. This discrepancy is not because more Black women than white women are substance users during pregnancy. It reflects the facts that poor Black women are more likely to be in contact with state agencies that will know of and report their drug use and that they are subject to biased assumptions about which types of pregnant women use drugs (Roberts 1997, 172).
4. Two recent studies found that numerous cases of infanticide are mistakenly attributed to sudden infant death syndrome (SIDS) (Hilts 1997). This is particularly alarming for women who smoke, because they may come under increased suspicion for murder; the babies of women who smoke during or after pregnancy are at increased risk for SIDS (DiFranza and Lew 1995; Klonoff-Cohen et al. 1995).
5. In September 1999, the U.S. House of Representatives passed the Unborn Victims

Violence Act, which would mandate the extension of federal criminal statues to cover the prosecution of those who cause death or injury to an "unborn child" while committing a federal crime (see Stryker 1999). Opponents of the bill argue that it promotes the status of the fetus to that of person and thus backs the fundamental premise of the antiabortion movement.

6. I use the labels "prolife" and "antiabortion" interchangeably. Although I believe the latter best describes the political cause, I include the former because it reflects activists' self-identification.

7. The naming and legitimation of public health problems by "officials" do not necessarily lead to the eradication of the problem. Constance Nathanson offers comparative analyses of the social and political factors that impede and facilitate the success of health-related social movements, focusing on gun control and tobacco control in the United States (1997, 1999) and maternal and infant health and tobacco control in the United States and France (1996).

8. Medical anthropologist James Trostle (1988) offers a critical analysis of the concept of medical compliance as it has been used by physicians and health researchers, calling attention to the concept as an ideology of authority, power, and control. More recently, health professionals have advocated replacing the term "compliance" with "adherence," meant to better "reflect the active role of the patient in self-management of treatment and the importance of cooperation between patient and provider" (Sumartojo 1993). But the underlying concept—that the health professional's perspective is the right one—remains largely unchanged.

9. Researchers have been unable to pinpoint the exact mechanism that causes adverse fetal and infant health effects because cigarette smoke contains more than four thousand compounds (Floyd et al. 1991).

10. Historian Allan Brandt (1990) analyzes the discussion among medical professionals in the early 1960s about ways to evaluate and present to the public epidemiological evidence on the health risks associated with smoking.

11. National data from 1998 indicate that 12 percent of infants born to smokers had a low birthweight compared with 7.2 percent of infants born to nonsmokers (Ventura et al. 2000, 11). The correlation between smoking and low birthweight holds for all racial and ethnic groups. It is theorized that the reason smoking reduces fetal growth is that carbon monoxide from cigarette smoke is transported into fetal blood, restricting the volume of oxygen that reaches the fetus, and that smoking causes constriction of the umbilical arteries, restricting blood flow to the fetus (U.S. Department of Health and Human Services 1990, 373).

12. Scientists have detected cotinine, a nicotine byproduct, in the hair of newborns born to nonsmoking women who were routinely exposed to secondhand smoke (*Washington Post* 1994), but it is unclear whether such exposure negatively affects fetal health.

13. Some studies show that a woman who stops smoking even as late as the eighth month prevents a low birthweight effect (Hebel et al. 1988), but others conclude that smoking cessation needs to occur earlier. MacArthur and Knox's (1988) data suggest that sixteen weeks is the low birthweight cut-off point, Lieberman et al. (1994) conclude that cessation before the third trimester reduces low birthweight risk, and Schell et al. (1994) have found that quitting by the end of the first trimester and the amount smoked in the first trimester were the most important factors associated with low birthweight. The implication for public health, they argue, is that women (especially heavy smokers) should be encouraged to quit before becoming pregnant.

14. The importance of low birthweight in medical studies is in part a result of its measurability. As the 1990 surgeon general's report on smoking explains, "Fetal, neo-

natal, and perinatal mortality are the most direct measures of pregnancy outcome. Mortality is relatively uncommon, and very large samples are needed for study. This has led to the widespread study of birthweight and the percentages of births that are low birthweight (< 2,500 g) as surrogates for the study of mortality. This strategy has been justified by the extremely strong associations between low birthweight and each of the measures of mortality. Equally important is weight at birth as a determinant of infant health" (U.S. Department of Health and Human Services 1990, 379). The category of low birthweight clearly serves numerous purposes.

15. Oakley further reveals that what may seem to be a systematic, objective measure—weight at birth—is subject to a variety of factors: "It matters how, when and in what manner babies are weighed, and it matters who does the weighing, what the nature of the weighing equipment is, and how the weight is both read and recorded" (1992, 260).

16. Adams and Melvin (1998) take into account research findings that are not widely publicized: smoking during pregnancy is associated with lower rates of pre-eclampsia (high blood pressure). As the rates of smoking during pregnancy decline, the costs of treating pre-eclampsia are expected to rise.

17. These statistics represent 80 percent of U.S. births. California, Indiana, South Dakota, and New York State (excluding New York City) do not include tobacco use on the birth certificate. Taking these exclusions into account, we find that the birth certificate data tend to show lower maternal smoking rates than those estimated based on data gathered from other national surveys (Ventura 1999, 72). Statistician Stephanie Ventura (1999) hypothesizes that this is mainly because birth certificate data are not detailed enough; the two questions ask only whether a woman smoked during pregnancy, and if so, how many cigarettes per day she smoked (see also Tolson et al. 1991, 7). Trends in smoking during pregnancy based on birth certificate data, however, are "generally consistent with those reported for recent years" in several national surveys (Ventura et al. 2000, 11).

18. The exposure of infants and children is a significant concern related to smoking during pregnancy. An estimated 70 percent of women who quit smoking during pregnancy take it up again within a year after their baby is born (Fingerhut et al. 1990). Researchers contend that this raises the possibility that the infant will be exposed to environmental tobacco smoke and that the woman may smoke during subsequent pregnancies.

19. The highest rates of smoking during pregnancy are found among American Indian (20.2 percent) and Hawaiian (16.8 percent) women (Ventura et al. 2000, 53); however, analysis of these groups is beyond the scope of this book. "White" and "black" represent the official categories—or "non-Hispanic white and "non-Hispanic black"—that are used in reporting national vital statistics (Ventura et al. 2000). I recognize that the naming of racial and ethnic categories is politically contested. The terms I use, "white" and "Black," or, interchangeably, "African American," reflect those used by the women I interviewed. When not reporting government statistics, I use the term "Latina" rather than "Hispanic" (see Martínez 1997, chapter 1).

20. A growing body of feminist ethnographic work on issues related to women and reproduction informs this book. I have relied particularly on scholarship by the following scholars: Emily Martin (1992 [1987]) and Robbie Davis-Floyd (1992) on pregnancy and childbirth; Anna Lowenhaupt Tsing (1990) on women charged with perinatal or neonatal endangerment; Kristin Luker (1978, 1984), Faye Ginsburg (1998 [1989]), and Wendy Simonds (1996) on abortion politics; Linda Layne (1990, 1999a, 1999b, 2000) on pregnancy loss; Constance Nathanson (1991) on teenage pregnancy; Monica Casper on fetal surgery (1998); Margaret Lock

(1993) on menopause; E. J. Sobo on women and HIV/AIDS (1995); Janelle Taylor (1998) on ultrasound imaging; Barbara Katz Rothman (1986), Rayna Rapp (1988, 1990, 1991, 1999), Carole Browner and Nancy Press (1995), and Susan Markens, Carole Browner, and Nancy Press (1997) on prenatal testing; Lynn Morgan (1989, 1996, 1997, 1998) on fetal personhood; and Margarete Sandelowski (1993), Helena Ragoné (1994), Marcia Inhorn (1994), and Sarah Franklin (1997) on infertility and reproductive technologies.

21. Some authors analyze the proliferation of fetal images in public culture, from literature, billboards, videos, and bus station signs sponsored by prolife organizations to Hollywood films, pregnancy-loss support groups, magazine and news stories, and automobile advertisements that are not directly related to political aims (Petchesky 1987; Condit 1990; Layne 1990, 1999a, 2000; Hartouni 1991; Duden 1993; Taylor 1992; Stabile 1994). Others examine the varied social construction of fetuses within medical science—a construction propelled by technological and imaging innovations (Franklin 1991; Casper 1994, 1998; Maynard-Moody 1995; Newman 1996). Further, feminist legal scholars critique the legal treatment of fetuses and the criminal charges brought against women who "abuse" their fetuses (McNulty 1988; Field 1989; Pollitt 1990; Daniels 1993, 1999; Center for Reproductive Law and Policy 1996a; Gomez 1997; Roberts 1997; Roth 2000).

22. My research benefited from critical, ethnographic work on women's smoking and smoking during pregnancy by sociologists Hilary Graham (1976, 1987, 1993) and Ann Oakley (1989) in Great Britain and Lorraine Greaves (1995, 1996) in Canada and Australia.

23. Throughout the book, I refer to "everyday" women by their first names and "health experts" by their last names for clarity in distinguishing between them.

Chapter 2   The New Rules of Pregnancy

1. Anthropologists Eugenia Georges and Lisa Mitchell (2000) note the paucity of feminist scholarship on recent pregnancy guidebooks. They provide an excellent comparative analysis of the leading pregnancy books of Canada and Greece, revealing significant differences in experts' constructions of mothers- and babies-to-be. Sociologist Carol Brooks Gardner (1994) addresses how the discourse of fetal endangerment between 1983 and 1993 in the parenting magazine *American Baby* is a form of social control. I pursue similar themes within a broader, ethnographic framework in this chapter.

2. Given this attention, I was surprised to hear from several women that their physicians would not see them until they were eight weeks pregnant. Mary Beth Shannon took a home pregnancy test that indicated she was pregnant. She commented, "I was a little iffy about it; I called my doctor, and she wouldn't see me until eight weeks because they can't really tell until at least you're that far." This reinforces the sense that women ought to educate themselves about health during pregnancy before they become pregnant and that they should live as if they were pregnant even before it is confirmed.

3. In Baltimore, several hospitals offer preconception care classes taught by health educators and nurse-midwives. The classes teach couples as well as women attending by themselves about health risks, financial planning, and the hospital's services to help women plan for a positive pregnancy experience.

4. To maintain the texture of the conversations I had with the people I interviewed, I have included many of the colloquial speech patterns they used in direct and paraphrased quotes based on the transcripts of notes I took during the interviews. I recognize that this attempt to reveal the communication styles of those I talked

with may be perceived by some readers as condescending; however, I have opted to allow women's voices to reflect some of the diversity of local language patterns.

5. This phenomenon is the subject of the 1992 French novel *The Divine Child: A Novel of Prenatal Rebellion*, which was translated into English in 1994. When the main character, Madeleine, learns she is pregnant, she decides to influence her twins immediately: "She would skip way ahead: instead of moronically waiting until her little shaver was six years old to send him to school, she would begin instructing him as of the earliest weeks of pregnancy. She had to act now, without procrastinating until birth; everything is clinched during the days, perhaps hours following conception. She would not put up with having a little good-for-nothing mooching inside her for nine months without doing anything. She would be both mother and tutor at once, transforming her interior into a classroom" (Bruckner 1994 [1992], 7–8).

6. Medical professionals now see the placenta as the center of endocrine functions and a communication system that transfers nutrients between the fetus and pregnant woman (Cunningham et al. 1989, 8). In *Simians, Cyborgs, and Women* (1991), Donna Haraway discusses the recent tendency in biomedical discourses such as immunology to focus on the body as composed of communication systems.

7. During 1964–1965, as the result of an outbreak of German measles, also known as rubella, more than twenty thousand babies were born with congenital abnormalities (March of Dimes Birth Defects Foundation 1999a). Further, an estimated ten thousand miscarriages and stillbirths have been attributed to the outbreak.

8. The specter of the so-called thalidomide babies has sparked recent national attention. In 1998, when the Food and Drug Administration approved thalidomide for leprosy patients, the move was considered highly controversial because it "raises fears that this infamous drug will create a new generation of babies born without limbs or eyes" (*New York Times* 1997b). One opponent of FDA approval even contended that "the existence of a single child malformed because of thalidomide outweighs any illnesses that thalidomide might alleviate" (Hoffmann 1997). To reduce the risks of fetal exposure to the drug, a number of regulations have been implemented: physicians and pharmacists must receive special training about prescribing it; women capable of bearing children must have a negative pregnancy test before receiving it, submit to monthly testing, and use two reliable forms of contraception; and men who take it must use condoms (Schwartz 1998). Enforcement of all contraceptive restrictions, of course, is not possible.

9. Two main types of authors write advice literature: the scientific medical expert and the friendly expert. Scientific expert advice is most often offered by an M.D. or Ph.D., who presents the technicalities of biological development and findings from medical studies. The friendly expert, on the other hand, is not usually an M.D. but may be a nurse and is a woman who has children. This second type of advice literature challenges the traditional medical genre by appealing to experience: "I've been there and can tell you what They don't." Despite their claim to oppositional authority, however, friendly experts direct women to their doctors for the final word on health-related matters.

10. *What to Expect When You're Expecting* is also a best-selling pregnancy book in Canada; see Georges and Mitchell (2000) for a critical analysis of it in the Canadian context.

11. I don't intend to belittle women's and men's desires to avoid having a child with disabilities. Several scholars discuss the stress of caring for a child with special needs, cultural ideas about quality of life, and the status of community and social services in the United States (Rapp 1988, 1991, 1999; Dorris 1989; Bérubé 1996; Landsman 1998).

12. *Parents* (P) identifies its audience profile as women aged 18–34 with growing children; *American Baby* (AB) markets to expectant and new mothers; and *Child's* (C) reader profile is made up of parents of children to age 12. In 1999, subscription prices ranged from $19.90 (P) to $12.97 (C) a year, and circulation from 812,000 (C) to 1.75 million (P). Special, free "expecting" editions of *American Baby* are distributed at physicians' offices and health clinics. Brooks Gardner (1994) provides further details about this magazine's audience.

13. Brochures and literature produced by state health departments and health voluntaries (such as the American Cancer Society, American Lung Association, and March of Dimes) better represent racial and ethnic diversity.

14. If a lack of pregnancy sickness is associated with miscarriage, and miscarriages are theorized to occur when the embryo is defective, then Profet encourages women to save embryos that may be defective and otherwise spontaneously aborted. Following this logic, Profet's message does not wholly support the aim of having a healthy baby.

15. One example is the guilt experienced by a woman who believed that working long hours on her dissertation, hunched over a keyboard, could have caused the spinal curvature that accompanied her son's Down syndrome (Bérubé 1996, 118). This woman holds a nursing degree and was well aware that this notion is medically unsubstantiated, yet still she felt there was some connection. Anthropologist Gail Landsman's (1998) excellent ethnographic study of motherhood and children with disabilities reveals that women who have disabled children routinely question "what they might have done wrong." Further, some struggle with feeling judged by others "as having done something improper such as using drugs or smoking cigarettes" and with their sense of injustice over the fact that that they "did everything right" yet had a disabled child. They are well aware that some women who fail to follow health advice have babies without disabilities (1998, 81).

16. This approach lends support to greater medical and technical intervention during pregnancy, which compounds the amount of advice and surveillance to which pregnant women are subject. See Rothman 1986, 1989, 1998; Browner and Press 1995, 1996; Casper 1998; and Rapp 1988, 1990, 1991, 1999.

17. The conceptualization of "culture" in public health is closely related to the history of the term "lifestyle." Although "life style" was not included in most dictionaries or in *Index Medicus* until the 1970s (Coreil et al. 1985, 427), the concept has a longer history. In the United States at the turn of the century, the idea, although not the term, was employed by social reformers who extolled the principles of "right living," meaning "living like the American middle class lived, or aspired to live" (Ehrenreich and English 1989 [1978], 170, 173). Slums were the target of these campaigns because health professionals thought that poverty and crowded living conditions created communistic thinking and thus endangered society as whole. More recently, however, this social interpretation of lifestyle has been overshadowed by an individualist concept, which has its roots in the 1920s, when lifestyle was adapted by Alfred Adler and the Adlerian psychoanalytic school. Their application of the term focused on individual life plans and behaviors, and not on social groups (Coreil et al. 1985). This definition of lifestyle was picked up in the 1960s in the United States and elsewhere, a time when high value was placed on the idea that individuals could choose their lifestyles. In this period, "alternative living" symbolized individual self-expression (Coreil and Levin 1985, 105–106). Health experts applied this notion of lifestyle to public health in the 1970s as part of a move toward focusing on individuals in the prevention of disease.

18. There are also child welfare advocates who support nonindividualist approaches, as is evident in the aphorism "It takes a village to raise a child" (Clinton 1996).

Policy actions, however, have moved the government away from institutional support for women and their children. The welfare system established in the 1930s was dismantled under the 1996 Personal Responsibility and Work Opportunity Reconciliation Act. The act's title indicates that the government's role is to encourage citizens to take personal responsibility. Another measure of a lack of institutional support is the failure of the mid-1990s drive for national health insurance. In 1998, 10.7 million children, or 15 percent of the population under the age of eighteen, were uninsured (U.S. Department of Health and Human Services 1998).

19. Feminist scholars Barbara Ehrenreich and Deirdre English (1989 [1978]) argue that there never was a "women and children first" era and that historically the government has made women responsible for children's health in the United States. Even public recognition of the child as an important social actor around the turn of the century did not lead to public responsibility. The child welfare movement was eclipsed by experts, who "had not material help to offer, but only a stream of advice, warnings, and instructions to be consumed by each woman in her [middle- and upper-class] isolation" (1989, 184). Indeed, these women were eager to embrace the science of child raising as a progressive, modern activity.

21. See Martin et al.'s (1996) public health study and Locker's (1996) popular press coverage.

20. Elsewhere in her book, Iovine does her share of harsh judging and strict pregnancy policing. On nutrition, she declares: "it should be understood that the baby's health is more important than any other consideration, and . . . any woman who starves herself or eats only trash foods should be permanently ostracized from the community of Girlfriends, if not from the universe" (Iovine 1995, 23).

Chapter 3 *Emergence of Maternal Smoking as a Public Health Problem*

1. The definition of "tobacco heart" is not given, but the condition may be related to "irritable heart circulation," a consequence of smoking listed in the medical journal *Lancet* in 1857 (cited in Whelan 1984, 38).

2. The Committee to Study the Tobacco Problem was established in 1918 by prominent physicians and scientists who conducted experiments on how tobacco affected "mental and physical efficiency" (Burnham 1989, 8). The report referred to by the *Journal of the American Medical Association*, "Tobacco and Physical Efficiency" (published in 1927), contains seventy pages of bibliography (1929, 123).

3. The increase in women's smoking had a substantial influence on the demand for domestic cigarette production, which doubled between 1921 and 1928 (*New York Times* 1929b). Rapid changes in women's social status, including their enfranchisement in 1920 and the easing of the strict separation of men's and women's social spheres, facilitated the controversial upward trend in women's smoking. Cigarette smoking was perceived by some as "a symbol of new roles and expectations of women's behavior" ushered in with women's suffrage, and debates on women's smoking provided a public forum for contests over changing gender ideologies (Brandt 1996, 64). Opponents argued that cigarette smoking was unladylike (see Greaves 1996, 20–21), and in 1922, the International Anti-Tobacco League contended that cigarettes jeopardized women's moral and maternal nature. The league warned that the increase in smoking "among women of respectability and among high school girls threatens the element of womanhood that must mother the American of tomorrow" (cited in Brandt 1996, 63). Notably, the league did not present smoking as a health threat but as a moral one. Knopf Elkind (1985) analyzes how in the 1980s, attitudes toward women's smoking continued to reflect early twentieth-century debates.

4. Social science scholarship has critiqued the ways in which science, which informs public health problems and medical practices, as a mode of knowledge production is inseparable from social politics. This is an enormous body of literature; see, for example, Harding 1986, 1991; Longino 1990; Haraway 1991, 1996; Nathanson 1991; Martin 1992 [1987], 1994; Nelkin 1992; Maynard-Mooney 1995; Downey and Dumit 1997; Casper 1998; Murphy-Lawless 1998; Clarke 1999; and Jacobson 2000.

5. On the first wave of antitobacco activism, see Troyer and Markle 1983; Whelan 1984; and Brandt 1992, 1996.

6. Viviana Zelizer (1985) demonstrates that between the 1870s and 1930s, the social status of children shifted radically. In a process culminating in the 1930s, compulsory education and child protection labor laws reshaped the U.S. work force, and good child health was seen as necessary to the future of the American nature. Medical and governmental institutions were established to safeguard maternal, infant, and child health. In 1881, the AMA founded its pediatrics section; in 1912, a federal statute established the U.S. Children's Bureau; and in 1920, the Maternity and Infancy (Sheppard-Towner) Act was passed.

7. J. W. Ballantyne, the Scottish pioneer of antenatal care, observed that women who worked in tobacco factories experienced an increased frequency of spontaneous abortion and death of their infants (Oakley 1989, 312–313; see also U.S. Department of Health, Education, and Welfare 1979a, 8–9). His views reached a professional audience through the medical text *Manual of Antenatal Pathology and Hygiene* (published in 1902) and a popular audience through *Expectant Motherhood* (published in 1914). Ballantyne was hesitant to conclude that tobacco use during pregnancy carried fetal health risks, but he was certain that it caused infant death: "While there is much doubt, therefore, regarding the evil effect of nicotism in cutting short antenatal life, there seems to be no shadow of doubt that there is a very large infantile mortality in postnatal life" (quoted in U.S. Department of Health, Education, and Welfare 1979a, 8–10).

8. During this period, however, Camel cigarette advertising—featuring doctors' endorsements—highlighted concern about throat irritation caused by smoking. That smoking was condoned by doctors was meant to signal that it was not considered a health hazard; concern over throat irritation could be categorized as concern over the pleasures, not the dangers, of smoking.

9. Simpson's definition of premature was birth weight under 2,500 grams. This is now referred to as low birthweight, whereas "premature" is used to designate babies born preterm, meaning before thirty-seven weeks of gestation.

10. On the history of the second wave of the antitobacco movement, see Gouin 1977; Schmidt 1977; Troyer and Markle 1983; Whelan 1984; Brandt 1992; and Nathanson 1997, 1999, n.d.; Kluger (1996) investigates the history of "the other side," the tobacco industry lobby.

11. Antismoking advocacy was initiated by the American Cancer Society (which in 1954 and 1957 published research concluding that smoking caused lung cancer), the National Tuberculosis and Respiratory Diseases Association (now the American Lung Association), the American Heart Association, and the American Public Health Association. The politically conservative AMA was notably absent from this movement. In fact, it did not endorse the surgeon general's 1964 report. At the time, the AMA collaborated with the Tobacco Institute to research the cancer–smoking link and "safer cigarettes"; later it opposed the regulation of tobacco advertising and the institution of health warning labels. Lobbying by AMA members for action against tobacco began to make inroads in the 1980s, and in the 1990s, the AMA has been an active member of antitobacco coalitions. See Burnham 1989, 24–25; and Wolinsky and Brune 1994, 144–173.

12. At the same time as epidemiologists charted statistical associations between smoking and disease based on what previously appeared to be isolated, individual cases of lung cancer and cardiovascular disease among male smokers, laboratory scientists developed innovative theories about the cellular mechanics of cancer. Combined, the evidence pointed to tobacco use as the main disease factor (Burnham 1989, 19–20).

13. The prominent anticigarette crusader Lucy Page Gaston—the founder of the Chicago Anti-Cigarette League in 1899 (Brandt 1996, 63) and the National Anti-Cigarette League in 1921—publicized the idea that there were twenty drugs in so-called coffin nails (Whelan 1984, 51). In 1995, the Food and Drug Administration, under the leadership of antitobacco advocate David Kessler, announced that nicotine is a drug and that cigarettes are drug delivery devices (see Nathanson 1997, n.d.).

14. Subsequent medical findings determined that low birthweight is associated with serious health problems and an increased risk of infant death. See the Institute of Medicine's *Preventing Low Birthweight* (1985).

15. Feminist sociologists Hilary Graham (1976, 1993) and Ann Oakley (1989) examine the history of the nearly parallel proliferation of the British government's antismoking warnings directed at women.

16. Some women's health advocates have criticized early campaigns for their lack of concern about women's health in general and their excessive attention to pregnant smokers as "receptacles for future generations" (Jacobson 1986, 125; Greaves 1996, 120–121). Although I agree with the second criticism, the evidence on the content of early antismoking campaigns indicates that messages that targeted smoking during pregnancy mostly followed or were concurrent with those aimed at educating women about the broader health risks of smoking.

17. The politics behind this legislation went beyond the issue of notifying the public of the dangers of smoking. Both versions of the health warning labels were far weaker than health advocates desired, and the legislation protected the tobacco industry from liability suits and from states enacting their own labeling legislation (Kluger 1996, 290–291; Nathanson 1997, 30–31).

18. In chapter 6, I argue that the legal and social debates over abortion, with their emphases on choice and fetal life and alluded to in Waxman's comments in 1983, surface repeatedly in antismoking campaigns.

19. One indication of this is a 1964 poll that found that 95 percent of physicians believed smoking was a health hazard but that 25 percent were still cigarette smokers (cited in Burnham 1989, 27).

20. The decision to reject tobacco advertising is highly significant. Public health advocates contend that public awareness of the hazards of smoking has been stifled by the financial power of the tobacco industry. In the late 1980s, the tobacco industry was the top spending advertiser in print media, the second highest in magazines, and the sixth in newspapers (O'Keefe and Pollay 1996, 67; see also Ernster 1985). The industry's enormous financial support of the media has meant that editors are hesitant or unwilling to run stories about the health risks of smoking. For example, in 1983, R. J. Reynolds pulled its advertising from an issue of *Newsweek* magazine when it learned the magazine planned to run a story on the nonsmokers' rights movement; this resulted in a loss of $1 million in advertising for that issue (Warner 1985, 386).

21. Health Edco's line of antismoking education tools includes only one that addresses men's reproductive health: a four-inch, drooping "impotent cigarette" (1999a, 36). Although the advertisement of this product proclaims that "for years, scientists have been warning that smoking can cause impotency," the surgeon general's 1990

report states that the link between men's smoking and "impaired sexual performance" has been publicized by the mass media but that medical evidence does not consistently support this message (U.S. Department of Health and Human Services 1990, 400). Yet a 1998 review of the literature refers to cigarette smoking as a "powerful predictor of erectile dysfunction" (Mikhailidis et al. 1998), and the *Digital Urology Journal* (2000) lists smoking as a common risk factor for erectile dysfunction.

22. The scope of the California campaign is remarkably more multicultural than most national or East Coast campaigns. Slogans were publicized in six languages (English, Spanish, Mandarin, Cantonese, Vietnamese, and Korean), and African American, Asian American, and Chicano/Latino audiences were the racial/ethnic groups specifically targeted. Reid suggests that this reflects California's demographics, its racial/ethnic and immigrant politics, and a symbolic "othering of people of color as unhealthy as opposed to a healthier white community" (1997, 551). It likely also reflects differences in the amount of state funding devoted to antismoking campaigns.

Chapter 4 *Achieving the Smoke-Free Baby*

1. This term follows the coining of fetal alcohol syndrome or FAS in 1978 (Fielding and Yankauer 1978b; Abramson 1981; Dorris 1989). The definition of FTS is composed of four criteria: (1) the pregnant woman has smoked five or more cigarettes a day; (2) the pregnant woman did not have hypertension during pregnancy; (3) the newborn has symmetrical growth retardation at full term; and (4) there is no other clear cause of growth retardation (Nieburg et al. 1985, 2999).

2. Advocates of the legalization of marijuana for medical use challenge the assumption that all illegal drugs are destructive and the reasoning behind the categorization of some drugs as legal and others illegal. See *Newsweek's* February 3, 1997, cover story.

3. In 1995, the Food and Drug Administration (FDA), led by antitobacco advocate David Kessler, contended that it had the authority to regulate nicotine as a drug and tobacco products as drug delivery devices. Antitobacco advocates, however, faced a setback in March 2000 when the U.S. Supreme Court ruled that the FDA did not have jurisdiction without congressional approval (Greenhouse 2000). This does not mean that the matter is settled; antitobacco advocates will continue to lobby Congress for more stringent nicotine and tobacco regulations and attempt to persuade the public that tobacco use is a type of drug use.

4. For critical analyses of the risk concept and its use, see Luker 1978; Douglas and Wildavsky 1982; Rapp 1988, 1990, 1991, 1999; Nelkin 1989; Brandt 1990; Hacking 1990; Beck 1992, 1994, 1999; Douglas 1992; Kaufert and O'Neil 1993; Handwerker 1994; Lupton 1995; Nathanson 1991, 1996, 1999; Lock 1998; Alexander 1998; Murphy-Lawless 1998; and Jacobson 2000.

5. In interviews with nonsmokers' rights advocates, Constance Nathanson found that many had experienced the loss of loved ones to tobacco use (1997, 73).

6. Corporate decisions about employee health services reflect this rationale. A March of Dimes' report urges companies to "invest in the future [because] today's babies are the work force of tomorrow. . . . Study after study, expert after expert, has echoed this prevention message over the past decade. And since you, as a United States employer, directly and indirectly foot the bill for unhealthy births, it is in your best interest to bring about change" (March of Dimes Birth Defects Foundation 1993, 1).

7. For policy reports reflecting this position, see the 1979 *Healthy People: The Sur-*

geon General's Report on Health Promotion and Disease Prevention (U.S. Department of Health, Education and Welfare 1979b) (modeled after a 1975 report by the Canadian minister of health, *A New Perspective on the Health of Canadians*) and the 1991 report *Healthy People 2000: National Health Promotion and Disease Prevention Objectives* (U.S. Department of Health and Human Services 1991). In fact, an even earlier framework for public health set the stage for focus on prevention and individual behaviors (Lupton 1995). In 1950, the American Public Health Association expanded the scope of public health practice, endorsing a shift in health care to primary prevention aimed at individuals (Coreil and Levin 1985, 106).

8. The history of HIV/AIDS education reveals how quickly definitions of risk factors and disease susceptibility can change. In the 1980s, health educators faced the challenge of changing public perception of who is at risk for HIV in response to new epidemiological evidence. The message of the early 1980s, that the populations at risk were in the 4-H group—homosexuals, hemophiliacs, heroin addicts, and Haitians—was discarded and replaced with the message that everyone is at risk and that "AIDS doesn't discriminate" (see Treichler 1988, 1999; Patton 1990, 1996). E. J. Sobo shows, however, that when people learn the new facts about HIV risks, they do not necessarily discard the old ones (1995, 25–27).

9. See anthropologist Linda Layne's *Transformative Motherhood* (1999c) for extended analyses of the prevalence of "the gift" as a theme in women's understandings and experiences of motherhood.

10. The label "high risk" is based on a health professional's assessment that the chance of adverse health conditions for a woman or her baby-to-be is greater than a statistically average risk (see Handwerker 1994).

11. See Rajan and Oakley 1990; Lawson 1994. Although none of the women I interviewed voiced this opinion, several health professionals told me that they counsel clients who desire small babies. These women believe that labor and delivery will be less painful and that smaller babies are cuter. Health educator Anne Dewitt characterized this as "really sick" and proposed that the way to counter such thinking is to convince women that a low-birthweight baby is an unhealthy baby.

12. Coreil and Levin (1985) analyze the risk of the concept of lifestyle and its application in public health in the 1970s as part of a move toward focusing on individuals in the prevention of disease.

13. The "best practice" model for smoking cessation counseling for pregnant patients instructs health care providers to follow four steps: ask, advise, assist, and arrange (see Robert Wood Johnson Foundation 1999b). Guidelines suggest that counseling sessions last five to fifteen minutes. Providers are instructed to ask patients whether and how much they smoke, advise them to quit, assist their quit attempt by emphasizing cessation skills and social support and offering pregnancy-specific, self-help smoking cessation materials, and arrange a follow-up contact.

14. For ethnographic studies on this point, see Martha Balshem (1993) on a community-based cancer prevention project, E. J. Sobo (1995) on an HIV/AIDS prevention program for low-income Black women, and Kristin Luker (1978) on abortion and unwanted pregnancy prevention efforts.

15. This description of the risk of low birthweight may not be intuitive; a woman who smokes more than a pack a day has a 69–percent chance of having a low-birthweight baby (130 percent of 53 is approximately 69).

16. Whereas women who smoke during pregnancy and dismiss health risk warnings are said to have an optimistic bias and are counseled to change their perspective, health professionals who hold beliefs that are not supported by science or statistical evidence legitimize their perspective by saying that they are "acting on their clinical experience" (Lumley and Astbury 1989, 243).

17. Not all health educators are critical of these statistics. Lucy Pratt, a nurse at a small county health department aimed at clients who are low income and people of color, told me that her "general, ballpark number" is that one-fourth of their pregnant clients smoke. She added, "If you want hard and fast numbers, get the official state data."

18. The question of how nondisclosure can be accounted for (or adjusted for, in biostatistical terms) has been broached by statisticians. According to Anne Dewitt, some researchers insert a 25 percent "fudge factor" in their calculations to correct for estimated underreporting. Quick addition, however, indicates that the fudge factor still would not bring the statistic reported for Baltimore even close to what she considers the accurate measure, 80 percent.

19. My use of relative risk plays on the biostatistical calculation of the same name.

20. Their perception is backed by national statistics, although, as I explained, health educators estimated the proportion of pregnant smokers in their communities to be much higher than national rates. Pregnant women who have nine to eleven years of education have a 26 percent rate of smoking, whereas those with four or more years of college have a 2 percent rate (Ventura et al. 2000, 11).

21. This combines the idea of the "culture of poverty" (associated with the work of anthropologist Oscar Lewis [1959] on how poor Mexican families adapted to their environments and popularized in the 1965 Moynihan report *The Negro Family: The Case for National Action*) with that of the "bio-underclass" (created by producing babies who are genetically disadvantaged; for example, as a result of a pregnant woman's crack use or, in Charlton's case, cigarette use). On the notion of the bio-underclass and the social control of women's reproduction, see Litt and McNeil 1994 and Roberts 1997, 19–21.

22. Marty Jessup's (1996) counterargument, aimed at the "addiction treatment community," points to several "unfounded concerns" held by health professionals who have kept nicotine addiction treatment separate from drug treatment. These concerns include the following: that nicotine addiction is not taken as seriously as addiction to other substances; that clients will avoid treatment if they know that quitting smoking is part of the treatment or if the center has a smoke-free policy; and that patients cannot quit. Jessup also notes that those treatment staff who smoke influence whether nicotine use becomes a treatment issue.

23. I discussed debates on the seriousness of smoking versus drug use during pregnancy in chapter 1.

Chapter 5   *What Do They Know That We Don't?*

1. I have capitalized "They" to convey the tone women used to discuss medical professionals. "They" connotes a body of professionals who share medical expertise and authority.

2. See Davis 1983 [1981]; Oakley 1984, 1992; Martin 1992 [1987]; Jordan and Irwin 1987; Rothman 1989; Davis-Floyd 1992; Browner and Press 1996; and Murphy-Lawless 1998.

3. Ethnographic studies in Great Britain of pregnant women who smoke, by Hilary Graham (1976, 1993) and Ann Oakley (1989), reveal similar themes.

4. See Graham 1976; Martin 1992 [1987]; Oakley 1992; Rapp 1999; Kaufert and O'Neil 1993; Davis-Floyd and Sargent 1996; Browner and Press 1996; and Markens et al. 1997.

5. Health educators caution, however, that "there is no safe cigarette" and do not condone the use of light cigarettes—those with lower nicotine or tar levels (State of Maryland Department of Health and Mental Hygiene n.d.a, ix).

6. Balshem's analysis goes further to trace the connections between defiant ancestors and Tannerstowners' ideas about causality and fate. Placing fate or God, not medicine or science, in control of disease asserts the moral authority of Tannerstowners' traditional foods, health beliefs, and work practices, all of which cancer prevention educators would like to modify (1993, 84).

7. Anthropologists have investigated how race, ethnicity, class, and culture shape pregnant women's attitudes toward health advice and their reactions to it, but they have not reached uniform conclusions. Work by Emily Martin (1992 [1987]) on childbirth experiences and Rayna Rapp (1990, 1991, 1999) on amniocentesis decisions, for example, demonstrates variation in women's attitudes and actions related to these social differences. Research on women's perceptions of and compliance with prenatal advice by Browner and Press (1996) and Markens et al. (1997), however, does not reveal significant differences.

8. Evidence suggests that the assumption that a high proportion of young Black women smoke cigarettes during pregnancy is not correct. National statistics reveal a smoking rate of 7 percent among pregnant Black teenagers ages 15 to 19 and 29.8 percent among pregnant white teenagers (Ventura et al. 2000, 11). Further, one study found that low-income Black teenagers who smoke are only half as likely as those who do not smoke to become pregnant and that smokers' first pregnancies occurred almost two years later than nonsmokers' (Fiscella et al. 1998).

9. Medical research on this question does not support the authors of *What to Expect*'s (Eisenberg et al. 1991 [1984]) assertion that a pregnant woman's secondhand smoke exposure is as dangerous to her fetus as her own smoking (see chapter 1, note 11).

10. Gwen Forrest, an antitobacco advocate and health policy specialist, noted that in Maryland's legislative debates on smoke-free workplace policies, women legislators addressed the risks for pregnant women of working in smoky environments and found that "jeopardizing pregnant women" was a good chord to play.

11. Although Angela did not suggest that smoking influenced her children's health, she related a story about her youngest child, Jamie. Jamie weighed five pounds two ounces and was eighteen inches long when she was born, but within a day, her weight dropped to four pounds seven ounces. Angela took Jamie's baby picture off the wall where it hung with numerous others to show me how baggy even her preemie sleeper was. As a newborn, Jamie had to stay in the hospital, and Angela cried because she had to go home without her: "She couldn't come home for three weeks! You should've seen her, when I brought her home she was so tiny." Health professionals and others, unlike Angela, might link Jamie's low birthweight with Angela's smoking during pregnancy.

12. See U.S. Department of Health and Human Services 1980; Kleinman and Kopstein 1987; Berman and Gritz 1988, 1993; Floyd et al. 1993; DiFranza and Lew 1995; *Journal of the American Women's Association* 1996; and Ventura et al. 2000.

13. The American Cancer Society posted signs asking patrons to comply with a voluntary ban on smoking that had been instituted in a mall near where I lived for a time in rural Pennsylvania. The request went unheeded by many types of smokers—teens, women with young children, and senior citizens—who gathered in the mall especially during the cold winter.

14. One study suggests that smoking during pregnancy alters the baby-to-be's brain so that it is susceptible to future cigarette addiction. Kandel et al. (1994) found that the teenage daughters of women who smoked during pregnancy are three times more likely to smoke than the teenage daughters of women who did not smoke during pregnancy. (The association was not as strong among sons.) They hypothesize that nicotine or other substances, including testosterone (see Kandel and Udry 1999), may "predispose the brain in a critical period of its development to the

subsequent addictive influence of nicotine consumed more than a decade later in life" (1994, 1407). Following this logic, women who smoke during pregnancy un-knowingly perpetuate a "cycle of addiction" within their families, not only through the bad example of keeping a smoke-filled home (see Charlton 1996) but also po-tentially through their biochemistry.

Chapter 6   *"Because You Love Your Baby"*

Some of the material in this chapter appeared in "Smoke-Filled Wombs and Frag-ile Fetuses: The Social Politics of Fetal Representation," *Signs: Journal of Women in Culture and Society,* Autumn 2000.

1. These points are analyzed in depth by Rothman 1989; Pollitt 1990; Tsing 1990; Hartouni 1991; Daniels 1993; Duden 1993; Stabile 1994; Oaks 1994, 1998, 1999; Morgan 1996; Roberts 1997, chapter 4; and Morgan and Michaels 1999.
2. The materials produced by health organizations generally depict white and Afri-can American characters, which contrasts with the nearly exclusive focus on white women of the popular advice literature, as discussed in chapter 2. For example, of the thirty-three photos featured in a 1986 ALA "quit kit," "23 depict white women in their late twenties to mid-thirties, either alone (18 pictures) or with a white male (3 pictures) or with a white infant (2 pictures). Fifteen of the 39 photographs depict an African American woman, either alone (12) or with an African Ameri-can man (2) or with an African American infant (1)" (Condit 1996, 170). Other materials present images of other people who represent racial and ethnic groups.
3. If the risk of secondhand smoke to the fetus were part of the campaign, neither woman would be an ideal mother because the carrot eater should not be in the presence of a smoker.
4. At times, antismoking themes clash when different audiences are targeted. For ex-ample, the ALA produces a "Smoke-Free Family" baby bib and newborn T-shirt, each inscribed with "I'm a Born Nonsmoker." This implies that some babies—those exposed to cigarette smoking in utero—are born smokers. But an American Non-smokers' Rights Foundation (n.d.) fundraising brochure for youth and teen anti-smoking education contradicts this idea. It asserts that "everyone is born a nonsmoker" and goes on to emphasize that children are taught to smoke by the tobacco industry.
5. See Layne 1999c for ethnographic approaches to the study of "the gift" and moth-ering.
6. The fetus is predominantly coded as male in prenatal health materials.
7. For analyses of the implications for pregnant women of imaging technologies, see Oakley 1984; Petchesky 1987; Franklin 1991, 1995, 1997; Stabile 1994; Casper 1994, 1998; Maynard-Moody 1995; Newman 1996; Rapp 1997; and Taylor 1998.
8. I've analyzed the ACS's films because the ACS is a highly visible, reputable, and authoritative national organization.
9. That the woman is smoking near her infant is not a concern because the film pre-dates the publicizing of research findings on the fetal health risks of secondhand, or environmental, tobacco smoke.
10. Ann Oakley cites research that found fetal breathing movements 31 percent (mean) of the time in fetuses of women without known pregnancy complications (1984, 167).
11. Although *Our Bodies, Ourselves* (1998), the women's health movement's "bible," lists this film as a resource on women and smoking, I would not endorse it as a woman-positive information source.

12. I did not specifically ask the women I interviewed if they had seen the ACS films, and none mentioned a film as a source of health information. It is, however, still available from the ACS.
13. This is remarkable given that models showing fetal development were first used in medical settings to demonstrate scientific facts and were appropriated by anti-abortion lobbyists to advance their political claims (see Newman 1996).
14. I became aware of Health Edco's Smokey Sue when reading Erma Jean Lawson's Ph.D. dissertation, which describes using the model in an antismoking interven-tion with low-income, pregnant teens (1990, 1994). Health Edco, which markets antismoking and other health education products, has an interesting history con-nected to antitobacco politics. Wayman R. Spence, a physician, designed a lung ashtray in 1969 as a "bit of black humor" and a "personal gesture of exasperation" when one of his patients rejected his advice to quit smoking (Health Edco 1999a). The ashtray featured a model pair of lungs, one clear and the other a "pukish yel-low brown," atop a black ashtray. Spence and John Banzhaf, who founded the radi-cal antismoking organization ASH (Action on Smoking and Health), presented lung ashtrays to all members of Congress before hearings on the 1969 Public Health Cigarette Act with the message "Don't Vote for Death." Ironically, Spence died in 1998 of lung cancer.
15. Fetal models, however, may be used in ways that directly contradict prolife aims, such as to explain an abortion procedure to a woman before surgery, or in ways that cannot be interpreted as supporting prolife politics, such as to memorialize a miscarried fetus (see Layne 1990).
16. In 1995, R. J. Reynolds Tobacco Company responded to criticism about market-ing to youths by sponsoring a "Right Decisions, Right Now" campaign to educate junior high and middle school students about illegal cigarette use. They also imple-mented a "Support the Law. It Works" program to discourage tobacco merchants from selling tobacco products to underage youth (R. J. Reynolds 1995). These ef-forts mimic the alcohol industry's attempts to discourage underage drinking. The company's Right Decisions campaign announcement includes a letter requesting that readers oppose government proposals to regulate underage smoking by writ-ing to the head of the Food and Drug Administration, their congressperson, and their senators. The heart of their political ideology is revealed in the letter's con-clusion: "Thank you for joining the efforts of people across the country in the fight for personal freedom in America." Beginning in 1999, as a condition of a 1998 multistate tobacco legal settlement, tobacco companies have sponsored media ads that urge youths not to smoke.
17. In the political arena, children's interests do not always prevail over tobacco in-terests. For example, after a seven-hour debate, the United States Senate, urged by President Clinton, defeated a proposal to increase cigarette taxes and use the funds to provide health care coverage for low-income children because passage threatened a budget resolution (Clymer 1997).
18. Organizations included the International Network of Women Against Tobacco (1990), the National Smoking Cessation Campaign for African-American Women (1991), Women and Girls Against Tobacco (1992), and the National Coalition FOR Women AGAINST Tobacco (1994). As of 1999, the National Smoking Ces-sation Campaign for African-American Women had changed its name and focus to the National Tobacco Independence Campaign, and Women and Girls Against Tobacco was no longer in existence.

Chapter 7 Cigarette Smoking as Fetal Abuse

1. I refer to medical and public health approaches interchangeably; more specifically, the medical approach focuses on the diagnosis and treatment of an individual's disease, whereas the public health approach concentrates on the prevention and understanding of disease within populations or subgroups.
2. Stephen Pfohl (1977) traces the changing societal definitions of acceptable discipline and parental authority over children since the early nineteenth century; he provides an excellent analysis of why child abuse became legally recognized in the 1960s. Barbara Nelson (1984) examines the historical process of instituting child abuse policies; she skillfully demonstrates how actors in government agencies and social movements have put "private deviance" in the public eye. Further, anthropological analyses emphasize how understandings of child abuse and neglect are culturally and historically variable (see Corbin 1981; Scheper-Hughes 1992).
3. While many antiabortion activists posit that fetuses should gain legal personhood status (Johnsen 1986, 611–612), the criminal prosecution of pregnant women on behalf of fetal health can actually work against antiabortion aims. If a woman is accused early in pregnancy, she may opt to abort. This reportedly occurred in 1992 when a pregnant woman obtained an abortion after she was charged with reckless endangerment for allegedly sniffing paint fumes (Center for Reproductive Law and Policy 1996a, 15, n. 27).
4. See McNulty 1988, 303. The 1977 case *People v. Reyes* was brought in California, a bellwether state after which other states often model their policies (Gomez 1997, 5).
5. The thirty-one-year-old woman was allowed to post $250 bail after she agreed to stop drinking, check in with the local police daily, and attend Alcoholics Anonymous meetings. She stated that she planned to have an abortion after she had saved enough money (Vigue 1996).
6. In a curious application of the law, the San Diego county district attorney charged Stewart under California's child support law, designed to enforce child support payments in divorce cases.
7. A local judge dropped the Stewart case on the grounds that laws applicable to children did not hold for fetuses (Gomez 1997, 43). The Florida Supreme Court threw out the Johnson case in 1992 on the grounds that drug delivery laws do not cover the delivery of drugs via an umbilical cord (Roberts 1997, 167).
8. In May 1999, the Wisconsin Court of Appeals rejected the case on the grounds that attempted intentional homicide and reckless injury laws do not refer to fetuses (Center for Reproductive Law and Policy 1999, 7).
9. Although most advocates of criminal or civil penalties against women focus on illicit drugs and alcohol but only briefly mention tobacco, Balisy includes tobacco throughout his discussion.
10. This is not the case for smoking during pregnancy. Pregnant white women have significantly higher smoking rates than do pregnant Black women (14.0 versus 9.5 percent) (Ventura et al. 2000, 58).
11. This is a significant concern, particularly when considering that prenatal care patterns differ by race and ethnicity. Women of color who historically have faced racial discrimination have lower rates of first trimester prenatal care and higher rates of late or no care. In 1998, 88.1 percent of white women, 82.4 percent of Asian or Pacific Islander women, 74.3 percent of Hispanic women, 73.3 percent of Black women, and 68.8 percent of Native American women sought care in the first trimester of pregnancy (Ventura 2000, 12, 53). The rate of late or no prenatal care was lowest among white women (2.3 percent), followed by Asian or Pacific Is-

lander (3.9 percent), Hispanic (5.1 percent), Black (7.0 percent), and American Indian (8.5 percent) women.

12. The reproductive surveillance and management of low-income women and women of color are most blatant in the historical instance of slavery (Davis 1983 [1981]; Roberts 1997). Today, reproductive discrimination is apparent in the unequal health care treatment that results from racist and classist views of health care providers and/or to a lack of health care insurance (see Nathanson 1991, chapters 3 and 9; Martin 1992 [1987]). It is also apparent in health policies that discriminate against specific categories of women, including lack of Medicaid funding for abortion for low-income women (see Petchesky 1985 [1984], 155–161; Roberts 1997, 229–232) and forced or coerced sterilization of and Norplant use for women of color and poor women (see Petchesky 1981; Davis 1983 [1981]; Lopez 1997; Roberts 1997; Shende 1997).

13. Notably, antiabortion advocate and lawyer Patrick Murphy (1996) has argued that men must be held accountable for their reproductive actions. He maintains that women and men who parent HIV-infected or drug-exposed children should "face the same mandatory counseling and probation or jail sentence as women convicted of abusing their unborn baby" when they do not follow medical recommendations. This represents a minority view.

14. These include the American Academy of Pediatrics, the American Medical Association, the American Public Health Association, the March of Dimes, and numerous others.

15. The calming effect that some women experience from smoking a cigarette complicates the claim that smoking is fetal/child abuse. Women may defuse tense situations—often associated with the burden of caring for others within the restrictions of limited material resources—by smoking, thus restraining themselves from becoming angry or abusive. A woman interviewed as part of a British study on low-income women smokers reported that she most wants to smoke "when I'm tired and worn out or when the children get a bit stroppy. When I'm violently mad and about to throttle them" (quoted in Graham 1993, 86). Of course, women who use smoking to dispel anger could turn to other outlets. My point is that the possible positive aspects of women's smoking should not be ignored in the rush to stigmatize smoking as indicative of neglectful mothering.

16. A 1921 child custody case filed with the Supreme Court of Brooklyn, New York, considered the issue of smoking by a guardian. In an attempt to win custody of her five-year-old son, who was in the custody of his paternal grandmother, a cigarette smoker, his mother stated, "I do not wish my boy to be brought up in such an atmosphere and to have him early in life contact the very pernicious habit of smoking cigarettes" (*New York Times* 1921). The mother's concern was not about her son's immediate health but instead about the possibility that he might follow his grandmother's example.

17. One member I spoke with briefly admitted that cigarette smoking during pregnancy had not "made it to trial" yet, but she had once heard about the makings of a case on the West Coast. A pregnant woman who smoked had miscarried, and her fetus, as my informant understood it, was "calcified." Some medical doctors apparently said that this was due to tobacco smoke and related to the fetus not getting adequate oxygen during pregnancy, but a legal case never materialized.

Chapter 8   *From Smoke-Free Wombs to a Tobacco-Free Society*

1. The Multnomah County (Oregon) Tobacco Prevention Coalition provides an example of this approach. The coalition was formed in 1995 to "promote projects

that prevent and reduce tobacco use through advocacy and education" and to work toward a "tobacco-free community" (Multnomah County [Oregon] Tobacco Prevention Coalition n.d.). The more than twenty-four coalition member organizations represent diverse constituencies. Member organizations include governmental and nongovernmental health organizations, the Portland public schools, several hospitals, the northwest Portland area Indian Health Board, the Medical Society of Metro Portland, and the Police Activities League. The coalition's four main goals are reducing tobacco availability to minors; reducing exposure to secondhand smoke through smoke-free policies; reducing exposure to tobacco advertising and promotion by banning advertising and urging event organizers to reject tobacco funding; and providing linkage to smoking cessation programs in the workplace and clinics.

2. The 1999 film *The Insider*, directed by Michael Mann, offers a dramatic portrait of the demise of the tobacco industry's cover-up. Internal industry documents reveal that tobacco-funded research discovered the adverse health effects of smoking cigarettes during the 1950s (Kluger 1996). In 1996, advancing the case against the tobacco industry, researchers identified more specifically a "direct scientific link between smoking and lung cancer." Cell biologists have found that a chemical in cigarette smoke causes genetic damage in lung cells that is seen in many malignant lung tumors (Stout 1996, 1).

3. The settlement involves forty-six states, the District of Columbia, and U.S. territories. Florida, Mississippi, Minnesota, and Texas settled with the tobacco companies before the agreement was signed.

4. The largest tobacco manufacturer, Philip Morris, experienced an 80 percent increase in overseas sales in the 1990s compared with an increase of less than 5 percent in the United States (Perlez 1997, 1). Although the rates of smoking by women vary widely cross-nationally, the practice is increasing in a number of countries, particularly among young women (Crofton 1990, 165; Mackay 1996). Thus, the issue of smoking during pregnancy is likely to gain increased significance worldwide. Despite the fact that the reduction and prevention of cigarette smoking have been central goals of U.S. public health policy since the 1960s, the government's trade policy has historically endorsed opening foreign markets to the importation and promotion of U.S. tobacco products (Barry 1991; Stebbins 1991). In so doing, the government has repeatedly moved "in favor of wealth and against health" (Araya and Laranjeira 1991, 255). A 1990 speech by former Vice President Dan Quayle in the tobacco state of North Carolina reveals this way of thinking: "Tobacco exports should be expanded aggressively because Americans are smoking less. . . . We're not going to back away from what public health officials say and what reports say. But on the other hand, we're not going to deny a country an export from our country because of that policy" (quoted in Kluger 1996, 714).

5. Participating organizations include the American Medical Women's Association, Boston Women's Health Book Collective, Center for Women Policy Studies, Girl Scouts of the USA, Girls Incorporated, National Association of Women Lawyers, National Partnership for Women and Family, National Women's Law Center, Society for the Advancement of Women's Health Research, and the YWCA of the U.S.A.

6. At the national level, since 1991, attention to women's health has been instituted through the U.S. Public Health Service's Office on Women's Health, which monitors the success of the Health Service's objectives to reduce women's and girls' smoking. The National Women's Health Information Center offers smoking cessation tips and resources (1–800–994–WOMAN and http://www.4woman.gov/nwhic).

7. A sense of this upbeat campaign, which coincided with the 1999 Women's World Cup hosted (and won) by the United States, is captured in a quotation by team co-captain Julie Foudy: "We'd much rather smoke a defender than a cigarette."

8. The Women, Infants, and Children program provides nutrition education and food certificates to low-income pregnant and breastfeeding women and their young children.

9. One doctor, Edward Miller, thinks it would be possible to monitor the smoking patterns of each patient as a way around this situation. He suggests that a carbon monoxide test be part of the other routine procedures at prenatal visits: "We could get a reading, and then say 'I see you're still smoking.' Otherwise, you're asking her to tell you a lie." Following his suggestion, however, would increase the already close surveillance of pregnant women and could aid in the prosecution of pregnant smokers.

10. Indeed, addressing stress may be gaining legitimacy in smoking cessation education. The Maryland State Health Department's smoking "quit kit," distributed to pregnant women at public clinics, includes a cassette tape that teaches women stress reduction techniques.

11. This research is one of ten intervention studies funded in 1995 by the Robert Wood Johnson Foundation's initiative "Smoke-Free Families: Innovations to Stop Smoking during and beyond Pregnancy."

12. Funders include Regence BlueCross and BlueShield of Oregon and HMO Oregon, Epitope Inc., Fred Meyer Corp., Good Samaritan Hospital in Corvallis, Albany General Hospital, and the March of Dimes (O'Neill 1998).

13. One recent, major change in smoking cessation practices is the high visibility of quitting aids, mainly nicotine replacement therapies that self-motivated smokers can obtain over the counter. Nicorette, a nicotine gum, was approved by the Food and Drug Administration in 1984 as a smoking cessation aid and was authorized to be marketed over the counter in 1996. Nicotine patches were introduced in 1992 and are now available without a prescription. Despite the fact that the FDA has moved nicotine replacement products out of the contraindicated category for pregnant women, medical experts debate the therapy's risks and benefits (see Lando and Gritz 1996). The controversy centers on which is more potentially harmful to fetal health, smoking or nicotine replacement, and guidelines do not exist for evaluating the risks and benefits of pregnant women's nicotine replacement therapy use (Zapka et al. 2000). That nicotine replacement is not considered a safe solution for many pregnant women strengthens the idea that women should quit before they become pregnant.

14. An excellent example of a community-based antitobacco advocacy approach is "Pathways to Freedom: Winning the Fight against Tobacco," a guide written by and for African Americans about how individuals can quit smoking and organize community opposition to tobacco advertising and marketing in Black neighborhoods (Fox Chase Cancer Center 1992).

15. INWAT is a coalition of more than six hundred antitobacco advocates from fifty-four countries; it was established in 1990 by women who were leaders in the antitobacco movement (see International Network of Women Against Tobacco 1998).

16. See Stebbins 1990, 1991; Crofton 1990; Connolly 1992; Mackay 1996; and Perlez 1997.

17. Of course, the feminist antitobacco position, like all other antitobacco efforts, fails to recognize the opinion of those who smoke occasionally but who identify as non-smokers and who attest that it is simply pleasurable to smoke, that cigarettes are not—for them—addictive, and that an occasional cigarette is not an appreciable health risk. One response to this position could be to acknowledge that indeed

occasional smoking may for some not carry a sizable threat of addiction or illness and to maintain that this is the case for only a small proportion of the population.

18. Morgan (1996) provides a compelling anthropological critique of several feminist philosophers' attempts to uphold a woman's right to abortion through moral theories of fetal personhood.

19. Feminist journalist Naomi Wolf (1995) argues this same point. However, I take issue with her contention that abortion is properly seen as a morally upsetting, negative experience (see also Morgan and Michaels 1999, 3–4).

20. See contributions in Morgan and Michaels's (1999) volume for feminist explications of this approach.

21. Feminist scholars have explored women's feelings toward their fetuses in relation to coping with infertility (Sandelowski 1993), experiencing pregnancy as a surrogate mother (Ragoné 1994, 1998), dealing with pregnancy loss (Layne 1990, 1999a, 1999b, 2000), choosing experimental fetal surgery to correct a fetal health problem (Casper 1998), and viewing fetal sonogram images (Rapp 1997; Taylor 1998).

22. Smoking cessation counselors who rely on the "stages of change" model of smoking cessation perhaps are more likely than others to support this approach (Prochaska and DiClemente 1992). The model posits six stages, from pre-contemplation to relapse, and the counselor is urged to praise any positive steps the smoker takes toward quitting.

References

Aamot, Gregg. 1998. "Judges Can Order Alcoholism Care." *Santa Barbara News-Press*, May 24, A6.

Abramson, Fredric D. 1981. "Policy Decisions in Prenatal Diagnosis: The Example of Action on Smoking and Health (ASH). 1994. "Allow Us to Introduce You to ASH." November. Washington, D.C. Pamphlet.

———. 1995. "Environmental Tobacco Smoke (ETS) as a Factor in Child Custody and Child Abuse and Neglect Cases." November. Washington, D.C. Pamphlet.

———. 1996a. "Smoking Parents Are Killing Their Infants." http://ash.org/kids/parents.html.

———. 1996b. "Mother May Lose Custody over Smoking, Even in Kentucky." http://ash.org/kids/kentucky.html.

———. 1996c. "Parents Are Deliberately Making Their Kids Sick, at What Point Does It Become Child Abuse or Endangerment? Help Protect Your Neighbors' Children." http://ash.org/kids/parents.html.

———. 1997a. "Smoking by Mom Boosts Baby's HIV Risk [05/02]." http://ash.org/may97/5-2-97-1.html.

———. 1997b. "Newborns Passive Smokers Who Suffer from Withdrawal." April 15. http://ash.org/.

———. 1998a. "Smoking Moms Cause Genetic Damage to Babies [04/03-2]." http://ash.org/april98/04-03-98-2.html.

———. 1998b. "Mom's Smoking More Deadly Than Crack Use [06/25-3]." http://ash.org/june98/06-25-98-3.html.

———. 1998c. "Prenatal Smoking Linked to Hyperactivity [08/02-3]." http://ash.org/sept98/09-02-98-3.html.

———. 1999. "Smoking Derived Cancer-Causing Agent Found in Newborns [03/03-3]." Excerpts from "Tobacco Carcinogen Found in Newborn Smokers," Reuters, March 2. http://ash.org/march99/03-03-99-3.html.

———. N.d. "Involuntary Smoking: The Factual Basis for Action." Special issue of ASH *Smoking and Health Review*. Washington, D.C.

Fetal Alcohol Syndrome." In *The Custom-Made Child? Women-Centered Perspectives*, ed. H. B. Holmes, B. B. Hoskins, and M. Gross, 89–93. Clifton, N.J.: Humana Press.

Adams, M. M., D. J. Brogan, J. S. Kendrick, H. B. Schulman, S. C. Zahniser, and F. C. Bruce. 1992. "Smoking, Pregnancy, and Source of Prenatal Care: Results from the Pregnancy Risk Assessment Monitoring System Working Group." *Obstetrics and Gynecology* 80(5): 738–744.

Adams, E. Kathleen, and Cathy L. Melvin. 1998. "Costs of Maternal Conditions Attributable to Smoking during Pregnancy." *American Journal of Preventive Medicine* 15(3): 212–219.

Alexander, Linda L. 1987. "The Pregnant Smoker: Nursing Implications." *Journal of Obstetric, Gynecological, and Neonatal Nursing* 16(3): 167–173.

Alexander, Jacqui. 1988. "The Ideological Construction of Risk: An Analysis of Corporate Health Promotion Programs in the 1980s." *Social Science and Medicine* 26(5): 559–567.

American Baby. 1983. "Medical Update: Smoking and Pregnancy." March 9.

———. 1995. "Smoke-Free Day Care." February 24.

American Cancer Society. 1988. "Special Delivery . . . Smoke-Free." Atlanta, Ga. Pamphlet.

———. 1994. "Herstories." *World Smoking and Health* 19(2). Special issue.

American College of Obstetricians and Gynecologists. 1991 [1986]. "Smoking and Women." Rev. ed. Washington, D.C. Pamphlet.

American Lung Association. 1980. "1980–81 Catalog." New York.

———. 1986. "Freedom from Smoking for You and Your Baby: A 10–Day Quit Smoking Program for Pregnant Women." ALA/HCHP Foundation. New York. Booklet.

———. 1994. "Facts about . . . Smoking and Pregnancy." Pamphlet.

American Lung Association of Maryland, n.d.a. "Smoking during Pregnancy." Baltimore, Md. Flip chart.

———. N.d.b. "Smoking during Pregnancy." Baltimore, Md. Booklet.

American Nonsmokers' Rights Foundation, n.d. "Everyone Is Born a Nonsmoker." Berkeley, Calif. Pamphlet.

Araya, Ricardo I., and Ronaldo Laranjeira. 1991. "Tobacco Epidemic or Bonanza? The Global Connection." *Journal of Addiction* 86(3): 253–255.

Ash, Jennifer, and Armin Brott. 1995. *The Expectant Father: Facts, Tips, and Advice for Dads-to-Be.* New York: Abbeville Press.

ASH Working Group on Women and Smoking. 1993. *Her Share of Misfortune: An Expert Report.* London: Action on Smoking and Health.

Balisy, Sam S. 1987. "Maternal Substance Abuse: The Need to Provide Legal Protection for the Fetus." *Southern California Law Review* 60:1209–1238.

Balshem, Martha. 1991. "Cancer, Control, and Causality: Talking about Cancer in a Working-Class Community." *American Ethnologist* 18(1): 152–172.

———. 1993. *Cancer in the Community: Class and Medical Authority.* Washington, D.C.: Smithsonian Institution Press.

Barron, James Douglas. 1998. *She's Having a Baby—and I'm Having a Breakdown: What Every Man Needs to Know—and Do—When the Woman He Loves Is Pregnant.* New York: William Morrow and Co.

Barry, Michele. 1991. "The Influence of the U.S. Tobacco Industry on the Health, Economy, and Environment of Developing Countries." *New England Journal of Medicine* 324(13): 917–919.

Beck, Ulrich. 1992. *Risk Society: Towards a New Modernity.* London: Sage.

———. 1994. "The Reinvention of Politics: Towards a Theory of Reflexive Modernization." In *Reflexive Modernization: Politics, Tradition, and Aesthetics in the Modern Social Order,* ed. Ulrich Beck, Anthony Giddens, and Scott Lash, 1–55. Stanford, Calif.: Stanford University Press.

————. 1999. *World Risk Society*. London: Polity Press.

Becker, Marshall H. 1986. "The Tyranny of Health Promotion." *Public Health Reviews* 14:15–25.

Benn, Melissa. 1998. *Madonna and Child: Towards a New Politics of Motherhood*. London: Jonathan Cape.

Berman, Barbara A., and Ellen R. Gritz. 1988. "Smoking and Pregnancy: Present and Future Challenges." *Wellness Perspectives* 4:19–26.

————. 1993. "Women and Smoking: Toward the Year 2000." In *Women and Substance Abuse*, ed. E. S. Lisanky Gombert and T. D. Nirenberg, 258–285. Norwood, N.J.: Ablex Publishing Corporation.

Bertin, Joan E., and Laurie R. Beck. 1996. "Of Headlines and Hypotheses: The Role of Gender in Popular Press Coverage of Women's Health and Biology." In *Man-Made Medicine: Women's Health, Public Policy, and Reform*, ed. Kary L. Moss, 36–56. Durham, N.C.: Duke University Press.

Bérubé, Michael. 1996. *Life as We Know It: A Father, a Family, and an Exceptional Child*. New York: Pantheon Books.

Boone, Margaret S. 1989. *Capital Crime: Black Infant Mortality in America*. Newbury Park, Calif.: Sage Publications.

Boston Women's Health Book Collective. 1998. *Our Bodies, Ourselves for the New Century*. New York: Touchstone.

Brandt, Allan M. 1990. "The Cigarette, Risk, and American Culture." *Daedalus: Journal of the American Academy of Arts and Sciences* 119(4): 155–176.

————. 1992. "The Rise and Fall of the Cigarette: A Brief History of the Antismoking Movement in the United States: In *Advancing Health in Developing Countries: The Role of Social Research*, ed. Lincoln C. Chen, Arthur Kleinman, and Norma C. Ware, 59–77. New York: Auburn House.

————. 1996. "Recruiting Women Smokers: The Engineering of Consent." *JAMWA* 51(1–2): 63–66.

Broadcasting Magazine. 1985. "'Smoking Fetus' PSA Proves Hot Topic." January 14, 190–191.

Broder, John M. 1997a. "Major Concessions: Industry Would Pay for the Costs of Treating Smoking Diseases." *New York Times*, June 21, A1, 8.

————. 1997b. "Clinton's Tobacco Demands Leave Bitter Taste for Some." *Oregonian*, September 18, A15.

Brody, Jane E. 1995. "Health Watch: Impotent Smokers." *New York Times*, January 4, C8.

Brook, J. S., D. W. Brook, and M. Whiteman. 2000. "The Influence of Maternal Smoking during Pregnancy on the Toddler's Negativity." *Archives of Pediatrics and Adolescent Medicine* 15(4): 381–385.

Brooks Gardner, Carol. 1994. "Little Strangers: Pregnancy Conduct and the Twentieth-Century Rhetoric of Endangerment." In *Troubling Children: Studies of Children and Social Problems*, ed. Joel Best, 69–92. New York: Aldine de Gruyter.

Brown, Dennis, and Pamela A. Toussaint. 1997. *Mama's Little Baby: The Black Woman's Guide to Pregnancy, Childbirth, and Baby's First Year*. Bergenfield, N.J.: Dutton Books.

Browner, Carole H., and Nancy Ann Press. 1995. "The Normalization of Prenatal Diagnostic Screening." In *Conceiving the New World Order: The Global Politics of Reproduction*, ed. Faye D. Ginsburg and Rayna Rapp, 307–323. New York: Routledge.

————. 1996. "The Production of Authoritative Knowledge in American Prenatal Care." *Medical Anthropology Quarterly* 10(2): 141–156.

Bruckner, Pascal. 1994 [1992]. *The Divine Child: A Novel of Prenatal Rebellion*. Translated by Joachim Neugroschel. Boston: Little, Brown and Company.

Burnham, John C. 1989. "American Physicians and Tobacco Use: Two Surgeons General, 1929 and 1964." *Bulletin of the History of Medicine* 63:1–31.

Bustan, Muhammad N., and Ann L. Coker. 1994. "Maternal Attitude toward Pregnancy and the Risk of Neonatal Death." *American Journal of Public Health* 84(3): 411–414.

Cahan, William G. 1985. "Abusing Children by Smoking." *New York Times*, March 9, A23.

———. 1992. *No Stranger to Tears: A Surgeon's Story*. New York: Random House.

Callard, Felicity. 1994. "'Just One More': The Circulation of Cigarettes in Advertisements Appearing in 'The Illustrated London News,' 1914–1915." Seminar paper, Department of Geography and Environmental Engineering, Johns Hopkins University.

Campaign for Tobacco-Free Kids. 1995. "Action Kit." Washington, D.C.

———. 1999a. "Homepage." http://www.tobaccofreekids.org.

———. 1999b. "The Toll of Tobacco in the United States since the Multistate Settlement Agreement Was Signed (from November 23, 1998 through April 5, 1999)." April 5. http://www.tobaccofreekids.org/html/usa_toll_clock.html.

Carroll, Jerry. 1996. "Killing Us Softly." *San Francisco Chronicle*, September 1, 1, 4.

Casper, Monica. 1994. "At the Margins of Humanity: Fetal Positions in Science and Medicine." *Science, Technology, and Human Values* 19(3): 307–323.

———. 1997. "Feminist Politics and Fetal Surgery: Adventures of a Research Cowgirl on the Reproductive Frontier." *Feminist Studies* 23(2): 233–262.

———. 1998. *The Making of the Unborn Patient: A Social Anatomy of Fetal Surgery*. New Brunswick, N.J.: Rutgers University Press.

Centers for Disease Control and Prevention. 1997. "Medical Care Expenditures Attributable to Cigarette Smoking during Pregnancy." *Morbidity and Mortality Weekly Report* 46(44): 1048–1050.

———. 1999a. "TIPS: Tobacco Control Information and Prevention Source." http://www.cdc.gov/tobacco/index.htm.

———. 1999b. "Best Practices for Comprehensive Tobacco Control Programs–August 1999." Atlanta, Ga.: U.S. Department of Health and Human Resources, Centers for Disease Control and Prevention, National Center for Chronic Disease Prevention and Health Promotion, Office on Smoking and Health.

Center for Reproductive Law and Policy. 1996a. "Punishing Women for their Behavior during Pregnancy: An Approach That Undermines Women's Health and Children's Interests." *Reproductive Freedom in Focus* 14 (February): 1–20.

———. 1996b. "South Carolina Supreme Court Issues Unprecedented Ruling Reinstating Conviction for Behavior during Pregnancy." Center for Reproductive Law and Policy. Pamphlet.

———. 1999. "Cases Highlight Dilemma of Women Charged with Crimes." *Reproductive Freedom News* 8(6): 1–3.

Charlton, Anne. 1994. "Children and Passive Smoking: A Review." *Journal of Family Practice* 38(3): 267–277.

———. 1996. "Children and Smoking: The Family Circle." *British Medical Bulletin* 52(1): 90–107.

Charlton, Linda. 1970. "Women Seeking Equality March on 5th Avenue Today." *New York Times*, August 26, 44.

Chasnoff, J., H. Landers, and M. Barrett. 1990. "The Prevalence of Illicit-Drug or Alcohol Use during Pregnancy and Discrepancies in Mandatory Reporting in Pinellas County, Florida." *New England Journal of Medicine* 322(17): 1202, 1204.

Chavkin, Wendy. 1992. "Women and the Fetus: The Social Construction of a Conflict." In *The Criminalization of a Woman's Body: Part II*, ed. Clarice Feinman, 71–80. New York: Haworth Press.

Chen, Lucia H., and Diana B. Petitti. 1995. "Case-Control Study of Passive Smoking and the Risk of Small-for-Gestational-Age at Term." *American Journal of Epidemiology* 142(2): 158–165.

Cherry, Sheldon H. 1992 [1973]. *Understanding Pregnancy and Childbirth.* 3rd ed. New York: Collier Books.

Child Magazine. 1996. "What Do You Think?" May, 15.

Clarke, Adele E. 1990. "Controversy and the Development of Reproductive Sciences." *Social Problems* 37(1): 18–37.

———. 1999. *Disciplining Reproduction: Modernity, American Life Sciences, and the Problems of Sex.* Berkeley: University of California Press.

Clinton, Hillary Rodham. 1996. *It Takes a Village: And Other Lessons Children Teach Us.* New York: Simon and Schuster.

Clymer, Adam. 1997. "Clinton Helps Kill Proposal to Raise Tax on Cigarettes." *New York Times,* May 22, A1, 26.

Cole, Helene M. 1990. "Law and Medicine Board of Trustees Report: Legal Interventions during Pregnancy." *JAMA* 264(20): 2663–2670.

Colorado Department of Health, Family and Community Health Services, n.d. "Give a Gift to Your Baby." Reprinted by the U.S. Department of Health and Human Services, Public Health Service. Pamphlet.

Condit, Celeste Michelle. 1990. *Decoding Abortion Rhetoric: Communicating Social Change.* Urbana and Chicago: University of Illinois Press.

Condit, Deirdre M. 1996. "Tugging at Pregnant Consumers." In *Evaluating Women's Health Messages: A Resource Book,* ed. Roxanne Louiselle Parrott and Celeste Michelle Condit, 154–174. Thousand Oaks, Calif: Sage Publications.

Conklin, Beth A., and Lynn M. Morgan. 1996. "Babies, Bodies, and the Production of Personhood in North America and a Native Amazonian Society." *Ethos* 24(4): 657–694.

Connolly, Gregory N. 1992. "Worldwide Expansion of Transnational Tobacco Industry." *Journal of the National Cancer Institute Monographs* 12:29–35.

Corbin, Hazel. 1942. "Before the Baby Comes." *Parents' Magazine,* October, 18, 67, 71.

Corbin, Jill E., ed. 1981. *Child Abuse And Neglect: Cross-Cultural Perspectives.* Berkeley: University of California Press.

Coreil, Jeannine, and Jeffrey S. Levin. 1985. "A Critique of the Life Style Concept in Public Health Education." *International Quarterly of Community Health Education* 5(2): 103–114.

Coreil, Jeannine, Jeffrey S. Levin, and E. Gartly Jaco. 1985. "Life Style–An Emergent Concept in the Sociomedical Sciences." *Culture, Medicine, and Psychiatry* 9:423–437.

Cosmopolitan. 1997. "Cosmo Controversy: 'Should a Pregnant Woman Who Abuses Drugs or Alcohol Be Locked up in Rehab?'" August, 72.

Cotton, Paul. 1994. "Smoking Cigarettes May Do Developing Fetus More Harm Than Ingesting Cocaine, Some Experts Say." *JAMA* 271(8): 576–577.

Crawford, Robert. 1980. "Healthism and the Medicalization of Everyday Life." *International Journal of Health Services* 19(3): 365–388.

Crofton, John. 1990. "Tobacco and the Third World." *Thorax* 45:164–169.

Cromer, Mary Ann. 1983. "'Precious Baby'." *New York State Journal of Medicine.* 83(13): 1292.

Crumbine, S. J. 1929. "Your Baby's Chance to Live." *Child,* January, 7.

Cunningham, F. G., P. C. MacDonald, and N. F. Gant. 1989. *Williams Obstetrics.* 18th ed. New York: Appleton-Century-Crofts.

Curro, Ellen. 1990. *Caring Enough to Help: Counseling at a Crisis Pregnancy Center.* Grand Rapids, Mich.: Baker Book House.

Curry, Mary Ann. 1987. *Access to Prenatal Care: Key to Preventing Low Birthweight.* Kansas City, Mo.: American Nurses' Association

Daniels, Cynthia R. 1993. *At Women's Expense: State Power and the Politics of Fetal Rights.* Cambridge: Harvard University Press.

———. 1997. "Between Fathers and Fetuses: The Social Construction of Male Reproduction and the Politics of Fetal Harm." *Signs: Journal of Women in Culture and Society* 22(3): 579–615.

———. 1999. "Fathers, Mothers, and Fetal Harm: Rethinking Gender Difference and Reproductive Responsibility." In *Fetal Subjects, Feminist Positions*, ed. Lynn M. Morgan and Meredith W. Michaels, 83–98. Philadelphia: University of Pennsylvania Press.

Daston, Lorraine J. 1988. *Classical Probability in the Enlightenment.* Princeton, N.J.: Princeton University Press.

Davis, Angela Y. 1983 [1981]. *Women, Race, and Class.* New York: Random House.

Davis-Floyd, Robbie E. 1992. *Birth as an American Rite of Passage.* Berkeley: University of California Press.

Davis-Floyd, Robbie, and Carolyn Sargent, eds. 1996. "The Social Production of Authoritative Knowledge in Pregnancy and Childbirth." *Medical Anthropology Quarterly* 10(2): 111–120.

Diehl, Harold S. 1969. *Tobacco and Your Health.* New York: McGraw-Hill.

DiFranza, Joseph R., and Robert A. Lew. 1995. "Effect of Maternal Cigarette Smoking on Pregnancy Complications and Sudden Infant Death Syndrome." *Journal of Family Practice* 40(4): 385–394.

Digital Urology Journal. 2000. "Erectile Dysfunction." http://www.duj.com/erectile.html.

D'Onofrio, Carol N. 1992. "Theory and Empowerment of Health Education Practitioners." *Health Education Quarterly* 19(3): 385–403.

Dorris, Michael. 1989. *The Broken Cord.* New York: HarperPerennial.

Douglas, Mary. 1992. *Risk and Blame: Essays in Cultural Theory.* London: Routledge.

Douglas, Mary, and Aaron Wildavsky. 1982. *Risk and Culture: An Essay on the Selection of Technological and Environmental Dangers.* Berkeley: University of California Press.

Downey, Gary Lee, and Joseph Dumit, eds. 1997. *Cyborgs and Citadels: Anthropological Interventions on the Borderlands of Technoscience.* Santa Fe, N.M.: School of American Research Press.

Duden, Barbara. 1993. *Disembodying Women: Perspectives on Pregnancy and the Unborn.* Cambridge: Harvard University Press.

Dreyfuss, Robert. 1996. "Tobacco Enemy Number 1." *Mother Jones,* May/June, 42–49.

Eastman, N. J., L. M. Hellman, and J. A. Pritchard. 1966. *Williams Obstetrics.* 13th ed. New York: Appleton-Century-Crofts.

Eastman, Nicholson J., and Keith P. Russell. 1970. *Expectant Motherhood.* 5th revised ed. Boston: Little, Brown.

Edmondson, Nelly. 1980. "A Health Alert: Smoking and Pregnancy." *American Baby,* 22, 38.

Ehrenreich, Barbara, and Deirdre English. 1989 [1978]. *For Her Own Good: 150 Years of Experts' Advice to Women.* Reprint. New York: Anchor Books.

Eisenberg, Arlene, Heidi E. Murkhoff, and Sandee E. Hathaway. 1991 [1984]. *What to Expect When You're Expecting.* 2nd revised ed. New York: Workman Publishing.

Eliopoulos, C., J. Klein, M. K. Phan, B. Knie, M. Greenwald, D. Chitayat, and G. Koren. 1994. "Hair Concentrations of Nicotine and Cotinine in Women and Their Newborn Infants." *JAMA* 271(8): 621–623.

Ernster, Virginia. 1985. "Mixed Messages for Women: A Social History of Cigarette Smoking and Advertising." *New York State Journal of Medicine* 85:335–340.

Eskenazi, Brenda, Angela W. Prehn, and Roberta E. Christianson. 1995. "Passive and Active Maternal Smoking as Measured by Serum Cotinine: The Effect on Birthweight." *American Journal of Public Health* 85(3): 395–398.

Estrich, Susan. 1996. "When Tobacco, Abortion Converge." *USA Today*, April 25, 13A.

Ewald, François. 1991. "Insurance and Risk." In *The Foucault Effect: Studies in Governmentality*, ed. Graham Burchell, Colin Gordon, and Peter Miller, 197–210. Chicago: University of Chicago Press.

"The Feminine Mistake." 1977. Dave Bell and Associates in cooperation with the American Cancer Society. Videocassette.

"The Feminine Mistake: The Next Generation."1989. David Bell Associates with Pyramid Film and Video. Videocassette.

Field, Martha A. 1989. "Controlling the Woman to Protect the Fetus." *Law, Medicine and Health Care* 17(2): 114–129.

Fielding, Jonathan, and Alfred Yankauer. 1978a. "The Pregnant Smoker." *American Journal of Public Health* 68(9): 835–836.

———. 1978b. "The Pregnant Drinker." *American Journal of Public Health* 68(9): 836–837.

Fingerhut, L. A., J. C. Kleinman, and J. S. Kendrick. 1990. "Smoking before, during, and after Pregnancy." *American Journal of Public Health* 80:541–544.

Finkelstein, Alix. 1991. "A Happy, Healthy, and Safe New Year!" *Parents' Magazine*, Janury, 17.

Fiscella, K., H. J. Kitzman, R. E. Cole, K. Sidora, and D. Olds. 1998. "Delayed First Pregnancy among African-American Adolescent Smokers." *Journal of Adolescent Health* 23(4): 232–237.

Fischer, P. M., M. P. Schwartz, J. W. Richards, Jr., A. O. Goldstein, and T. H. Rojas. 1991. "Brand Logo Recognition by Children Aged 3 to 6 Years: Mickey Mouse and Old Joe the Camel." *JAMA* 266(22): 3145–3148.

Fishman, Steve. 1994. "A Smoker's Tale." *Vogue*, May, 200ff.

Fletcher, John C., and Mark I. Evans. 1983. "Maternal Bonding in Early Fetal Ultrasound Examinations." *New England Journal of Medicine* 308(7): 392–393.

Floyd, R. Louise, S. Christine Zahniser, Eillen P. Gunter, and Juliette S. Kendrick. 1991. "Smoking during Pregnancy: Prevalence, Effects, and Intervention Strategies." *Birth* 18(1): 48–53.

Floyd, R., Louise, Barbara L. Rimer, Gary A. Giovino, Patricia D. Mullen, and Susan E. Sullivan. 1993. "A Review of Smoking in Pregnancy: Effects on Pregnancy Outcomes and Cessation Efforts." *Annual Review of Public Health* 14:379–411.

Foucault, Michel. 1979. *Discipline and Punish*. New York: Vintage Books.

Fox Chase Cancer Center. 1992. "Pathways to Freedom: Winning the Fight against Tobacco." Philadelphia: Fox Chase Cancer Center. Booklet.

Franklin, Sarah. 1991. "Fetal Fascinations: New Dimensions to the Medical-Scientific Construction of Fetal Personhood." In *Off-Centre: Feminism and Cultural Studies*, ed. Celia Lury, Sarah Franklin, and Jackie Stacey, 191–205. London: Harper-Collins.

———. 1995. "Postmodern Procreation: A Cultural Account of Assisted Reproduction." In *Conceiving the New World Order: The Global Politics of Reproduction*, ed. Faye D. Ginsburg and Rayna Rapp, 323–345. Berkeley: University of California Press.

———. 1997. *Embodied Progress: A Cultural Account of Assisted Reproduction*. London and New York: Routledge.

French, Simone A., and Cheryl L. Perry. 1996. "Smoking among Adolescent Girls: Prevalence and Etiology." *JAMWA* 51(1–2): 25–28.

Freudenberg, Nicholas. 1981. "Health Education for Social Change: A Strategy for Public Health in the US." *International Journal of Health Education* 24:138–145.

Fried, Peter A., and Harry Oxorn. 1980. *Smoking for Two: Cigarettes and Pregnancy.* New York: Free Press.

Friedan, Betty. 1963. *The Feminine Mystique.* New York: Dell.

Gallagher, Janet. 1987. "Prenatal Invasions and Interventions: What's Wrong with Fetal Rights." *Harvard Women's Law Journal* 10:9–58.

———. 1989. "Fetus as Patient." In *Reproductive Laws for the 1990s*, ed. Sherrill Cohen and Nadine Taub, 185–235. Clifton, N.J.: Humana Press.

Gause, Ralph W. 1980. "Dear Doctor." *American Baby*, August, 12.

Georges, Eugenia, and Lisa Mitchell. 2000."Baby Talk: The Rhetorical Production of Maternal and Fetal Selves." In *Body Talk: Rhetoric, Technology and Reproduction*, ed. Mary M. Lay, Laura J. Gurak, Clare Bravon, and Cynthia Myntti, 184–203. Madison: University of Wisconsin Press.

Ginsburg, Faye D. 1998 [1989]. *Contested Lives: The Abortion Debate in an American Community.* Berkeley: University of California Press.

Girls Incorporated. N.d. "Stamp Out Smoking." http://www.girlsinc.org/sos/.

Goldberg, Jeffrey. 1998. "Big Tobacco Won't Quit." *New York Times Magazine*, June 21.

Gomez, Laura E. 1997. *Misconceiving Mothers: Legislators, Prosecutors, and the Politics of Prenatal Drug Exposure.* Philadelphia: Temple University Press.

Goodman, Jordan. 1993. *Tobacco in History: The Cultures of Dependence.* London and New York: Routledge.

Gouin, Clara L. 1977. "Non-Smokers and Social Action." In *Smoking and Health II: Proceedings of the ACS/NCI Conference* [held in 1975], ed. Department of Education, U.S. Department of Health and Welfare, 353–356. Washington, D.C.: Government Printing Office.

Graham, Hilary. 1976. "Smoking in Pregnancy: The Attitudes of Expectant Mothers." *Social Science and Medicine* 10:399–405.

———. 1987. "Women's Smoking and Family Health." *Social Science and Medicine* 25(1): 47–56.

———. 1993. *When Life's a Drag: Women, Smoking and Disadvantage.* London: Department of Health.

Greaves, Lorraine. 1995. "Women and Health: A Feminist Perspective on Tobacco Control." In *Changing Methods: Feminists Transforming Practice*, ed. Sandra Burt and Lorraine Code, 195–214. Orchard Park, N.Y.: Broadview Press.

———. 1996. *Smoke Screen: Women's Smoking and Social Control.* London: Scarlet Press.

Greenhouse, Linda. 2000. "High Court Holds F.D.A. Can't Impose Rules on Tobacco." *New York Times*, March 22, A1, A23.

Grobstein, Clifford. 1988. *Science and the Unborn: Choosing Human Futures.* New York: Basic Books.

Gup, Ted. 1996. "Fakin' It." *Mother Jones*, May/June, 53–54.

Hacking, Ian. 1990. *The Taming of Chance.* Cambridge: Cambridge University Press.

Handwerker, Lisa. 1994. "Medical Risk: Implicating Poor Pregnant Women." *Social Science and Medicine* 38(5): 665–675.

Haraway, Donna. 1991. *Simians, Cyborgs, and Women.* New York: Routledge.

———. 1996. *Modest_Witness@Second_Millennium.FemaleMan© Meets Onco-Mouse™: Feminism and Technoscience.* New York: Routledge.

Hardacre, Helen. 1997. *Marketing the Menacing Fetus in Japan.* Berkeley: University of California Press.

Harding, Sandra. 1986. *The Science Question in Feminism.* Ithaca, N.Y.: Cornell University Press.

———. 1991. *Whose Science? Whose Knowledge? Thinking from Women's Lives.* Ithaca, N.Y.: Cornell University Press.

Hartouni, Valerie. 1991. "Containing Women: Reproductive Discourse in the 1980s." In *Technoculture*, ed. Andrew Ross and Constance Penley, 27–56. Minneapolis: University of Minnesota Press.

———. 1992. "Fetal Exposures: Abortion Politics and the Optics of Allusion." *Camera Obscura* 29:131–150.

———. 1997. *Cultural Conceptions: On Reproductive Technologies and the Remaking of Life*. Minneapolis: University of Minnesota Press.

Health Edco. 1996. "Answering the Health Education Challenge." WRS Group, Inc. Health Edco catalog. 3rd ed. Waco, Tex.: Health Edco by WRS Group, Inc.

———. 1997. "Health Edco Catalog: Lifestyle Health Education." Waco, Tex.: Health Edco, a Division of WRS Group, Inc.

———. 1999a. "WRS Health Education 1999 Catalog." Waco, Tex.: Health Edco by WRS.

———. 1999b. "1999 Catalog, 2nd edition: Bringing Health Education to Life." Waco, Tex.: Health Edco by WRS.

Hebel, J. R., N. L. Fox, and M. Sexton. 1988. "Dose–Response of Birth Weight to Various Measures of Maternal Smoking during Pregnancy." *Journal of Clinical Epidemiology* 41(5): 483–489.

Hecht, George J. 1964. "Stop Smoking . . . " *Parents' Magazine*, April, 38.

Heins, Henry C. 1992. "The Father's Role in Having a Healthy Baby." *American Baby*, October, 14, 36.

Henshaw, Stanley K. 1991. "The Accessibility of Abortion Services in the United States." *Family Planning Perspectives* 23(5): 246–263.

———. 1998. "Unintended Pregnancy in the United States." *Family Planning Perspectives* 30(1): 24–30.

Herbert, Bob. 1998. "Pregnancy and Addiction: South Carolina's Misguided Law." *New York Times*, June 11, A 27.

Heriot, M. Jean. 1996. "Fetal Rights versus the Female Body: Contested Domains." *Medical Anthropology Quarterly* 10(2): 176–294.

Herman, Barry, and Susan K. Perry. 1997. *The Twelve-Month Pregnancy: What You Need to Know Before You Conceive to Ensure a Healthy Beginning for You and Your Baby*. 2nd revised ed. Los Angeles: Lowell House.

Hern, Warren M. 1998. "Life on the Front Lines." In *Abortion Wars: A Half Century of Struggle*, 1950–2000, ed. Rickie Solinger, 307–319. Berkeley: University of California Press.

Hilts, Philip J. 1997. "Misdiagnoses Are Said to Mask Lethal Abuse." *New York Times*, November 11, A10.

Hochschild, Arlie Russell. 1989. *The Second Shift: Working Parents and the Revolution at Home*. New York: Viking.

Hoffman, Jan. 1990. "Pregnant, Addicted—and Guilty?" *New York Times Magazine*, August 19, 32ff.

Hoffmann, Roald. 1997. "Thalidomide, at What Price?" *New York Times*, September 25, A19.

Husten, Corinne G., Jeffrey H. Chrisman, and Murli N. Reddy. 1996. "Trends and Effects of Cigarette Smoking among Girls and Women in the United States, 1965–1993." *JAMWA* 51(1–2): 11–18.

Inhorn, Marcia. 1994. *Quest for Conception: Gender, Infertility, and Egyptian Medical Traditions*. Philadelphia: University of Pennsylvania Press.

Institute of Medicine. 1985. *Preventing Low Birthweight*. Washington, D.C.: National Academy Press.

International Network of Women Against Tobacco. 1998. "International Network of Women against Tobacco." http://www.inwat.org/.

Iovine, Vicki. 1995. *The Girlfriends' Guide to Pregnancy: Or, Everything Your Doctor Won't Tell You.* New York: Pocket Books.

Jacobson, Bobbie. 1981. *The Ladykillers: Why Smoking Is a Feminist Issue.* London: Pluto Press.

———. 1986. *Beating the Ladykillers: Women and Smoking.* London: Pluto Press.

Jacobson, Nora. 2000. *Cleavage: Technology, Controversy, and the Ironies of the Man-Made Breast.* New Brunswick, N.J.: Rutgers University Press.

JAMWA (*Journal of the American Medical Women's Association*). 1996. "Special Issue: Smoking and Women's Health," 51(1–2).

Jessup, Marty. 1996. "Nicotine: A Gateway Drug?" *JAMWA* 51(1–2): 21.

Jimenez, Sherry Lynn Mims. 1980. "How to Protect Your Unborn Baby." *American Baby*, November, 43.

Johnsen, Dawn. 1986. "The Creations of Fetal Rights: Conflicts with Women's Constitutional Rights to Liberty, Privacy, and Equal Protection." *Yale Law Journal* 95(3): 599–625.

———. 1987. "A New Threat to Pregnant Women's Autonomy." *Hastings Center Report*, August, 33–40.

Johnson, John M. 1989. "Horror Stories and the Construction of Child Abuse." In *Images of Issues: Typifying Contemporary Social Problems*, ed. Joel Best, 5–20. New York: Aldine De Gruyter.

Johnson, Kirk. 1993. "Lawsuits Seek to Ban Smoking in Fast-Food Restaurants." *New York Times*, April 3, 28.

Jordan, Brigitte, and Susan Irwin, 1987. "A Close Encounter with a Court-Ordered Cesarean Section: A Case for Differing Realities." In *Case Studies in Medical Anthropology: A Teaching and Reference Source*, ed. Hans Baer, 185–199. New York: Gordon and Breach, Science Publishers.

Journal of the American Medical Association. 1929. "Current Comment: Lady Nicotine and the Ladies." 93(2): 122–123.

Kandel, Denise B., and J. Richard Udry. 1999. "Prenatal Effects of Maternal Smoking on Daughters' Smoking: Nicotine or Testosterone Exposure?" *American Journal of Public Health* 89(9): 1377–1383.

Kandel, Denise B., Ping Wu, and Mark Davies. 1994. "Maternal Smoking during Pregnancy and Smoking by Adolescent Daughters." *American Journal of Public Health* 84(9): 1407–1413.

Kaufert, Patricia A., and John O'Neil. 1993. "Analysis of a Dialogue on Risks in Childbirth: Clinicians, Epidemiologists, and Inuit Women." In *Knowledge, Power, and Practice: The Anthropology of Medicine and Everyday Life*, ed. Shirley Lindenbaum and Margaret Lock, 32–54. Berkeley: University of California Press.

Kaufman, Nancy J. 1994. "Smoking and Young Women." *JAMA* 271(8): 629–630.

Kempe, C. Henry, Frederick N. Silverman, Brant F. Steele, William Droegenmueller, and Henry K. Silver. 1962. "The Battered-Child Syndrome." *JAMA* 181:17–24.

Kendrick, J. S., S. C. Zahniser, N. Miller, N. Salas, J. Stine, P. M. Gargiullo, R. L. Floyd, F. W. Spierto, M. Sexton, R. W. Metzger, J. W. Stockbauer, W. H. Hannon, and M. E. Dalmat. 1995. "Integrating Smoking Cessation into Routine Public Prenatal Care: The Smoking Cessation in Pregnancy Project." *American Journal of Public Health* 85(2): 217–222.

Klebanoff, M. A., J. D. Clemens, and J. S. Read. 1996. "Maternal Smoking during Pregnancy and Childhood Cancer." *American Journal of Epidemiology* 144(11): 1028–1033.

Klein, Richard. 1993. *Cigarettes Are Sublime.* Durham, N.C.: Duke University Press.

Kleinman, J. C., and A. Kopstein. 1987. "Smoking during Pregnancy, 1967–80." *American Journal of Public Health* 77(7): 823–825.

Klemesrud, Judy. 1971. "Women's Revolt? Harris Poll Detects 'Real Storm Signals.'" *New York Times*, January 19, 32.

Klonoff-Cohen, H. S., S. L. Edelstein, E. S. Lefkowitz, I. P. Srinivasan, D. Kaegi, J. C. Chang, and K. J. Wiley. 1995. "The Effect of Passive Smoking and Tobacco Exposure through Breast Milk on Sudden Infant Death Syndrome." *JAMA* 273(10): 795–798.

Kluger, Richard. 1996. *Ashes to Ashes: America's Hundred-Year Cigarette War, the Public Health, and the Unabashed Triumph of Philip Morris.* New York: Alfred A. Knopf.

Knopf Elkind, Andrea. 1985. "The Social Definition of Women's Smoking Behaviour." *Social Science and Medicine* 20(12): 1269–1278.

Kogan, Michael D., Milton Kotelchuck, Greg R. Alexander, and Wayne E. Johnson. 1994. "Racial Disparities in Reported Prenatal Care Advice from Health Care Providers." *American Journal of Public Health* 84(1): 82–88.

Kolata, Gina. 1990. *The Baby Doctors: Probing the Limits of Fetal Medicine.* New York: Delacorte Press.

Kolbert, Kathryn. 1989. "Webster v. Reproductive Health Services: Reproductive Freedom Hanging by a Thread." *Women's Rights Law Reporter* 11(3–4): 153–162.

Kolder, Veronika E. B., Janet Gallagher, and Michael T. Parsons. 1987. "Court-Ordered Obstetrical Interventions." *New England Journal of Medicine* 316(19): 1192–1196.

Koop, C. Everett. 1988. "Keynote Remarks." In *Nicotine Replacement: A Critical Evaluation*, ed. Ovide F. Pomerleau and Cynthia S. Pomerleau, xiii–xiv. New York: Ian R. Liss.

Ladd-Taylor, Molly, and Lauri Umansky, eds. 1998. *"Bad" Mothers: The Politics of Blame in Twentieth-Century America.* New York and London: New York University Press.

Ladimer, Irving. 1959. "Legal Protection for Unborn Children." *Parents' Magazine*, October, 44.

Landsman, Gail H. 1998. "Reconstructing Motherhood in the Age of 'Perfect' Babies: Mothers of Infants and Toddlers with Disabilities." *Signs: Journal of Women in Culture and Society* 24(1): 69–99.

Lando, Harry A., and Ellen R. Gritz. 1996. "Smoking Cessation Techniques." *JAMWA* 51(1–2): 31–32.

Lawson, Erma Jean. 1990. "Smoking and Smoking Cessation among Low-Income Pregnant Adolescents." Ph.D. dissertation, University of Kentucky, Lexington.

———. 1994. "The Role of Smoking in the Lives of Low-Income Pregnant Adolescents: A Field Study." *Adolescence* 29(113): 61–79.

Layne, Linda. 1990. "Motherhood Lost: Cultural Dimensions of Miscarriage and Stillbirth." *Women's Health* 16(3–4): 69–98.

———. 1997. "Breaking the Silence: An Agenda for a Feminist Discourse of Pregnancy Loss." *Feminist Studies* 23(2): 289–315.

———. 1999a. "'I Remember the Day I Shopped for Your Layette': Consumer Goods, Fetuses, and Feminism in the Context of Pregnancy Loss." In *Fetal Subjects, Feminist Positions*, ed. Lynn M. Morgan and Meredith W. Michaels, 251–278. Philadelphia: University of Pennsylvania Press.

———. 1999b. "'True Gifts from God': Motherhood, Sacrifice, and Enrichment in the Case of Pregnancy Loss." In *Transformative Motherhood: On Giving and Getting in a Consumer Culture*, ed. Linda L. Layne, 167–214. New York: New York University Press.

———, ed. 1999c. *Transformative Motherhood: On Giving and Getting in a Consumer Culture.* New York: New York University Press.

———. 2000. "Baby Things as Fetishes? Memorial Goods, Simulacra, and the 'Realness' Problem of Pregnancy Loss" In *Ideologies and Technologies of Motherhood*, ed. Helena Ragoné and Winddance France Twine. New York: Routledge. 111–138.

LeFevre, M. L., J. K. Evans, and B. Ewigman. 1995. "Is Smoking an Indication for Prenatal Ultrasonography?" *Archives of Family Medicine* 4:120–123.

Lerner, Sharon. 1995. "If We've Come Such a Long Way, Why Are We Still Smoking?" *Ms. Magazine*, May/June, 22–27.

———. 1996. "Tobacco Stains." *Ms. Magazine*, November/December, 47–55.

Lesser, Arthur J. 1985. "The Origin and Development of Maternal and Child Health Programs in the United States." *American Journal of Public Health* 75(6): 590–598.

Levin, Myron. 1999a. "Tobacco Firms Face Spate of New Suits." *Los Angeles Times*, January 7, A3.

———. 1999b. "Group Faults Use of Tobacco Case Funds." *Los Angeles Times*, April 29, C4.

Lewin, Tamar. 1997. "Abuse Laws Cover Fetus, a High Court Rules." *New York Times*, October 30, A17.

Lewis, Oscar. 1959. *Five Families*. New York: Basic Books.

Lieberman, E., I. Gremy, J. M. Lang, and A. P. Cohen. 1994. "Low Birthweight at Term and the Timing of Fetal Exposure to Maternal Smoking." *American Journal of Public Health* 84(7): 1127–1131.

Lieff, S., A. F. Olshan, M. Werler, R. P. Strauss, J. Smith, and A. Mitchell. 1999. "Maternal Cigarette Smoking during Pregnancy and Risk of Oral Clefts in Newborns." *American Journal of Epidemiology* 150(7): 683–694.

Litt, Jacquelyn, and Maureen McNeil. 1994. "'Crack Babies' and the Politics of Reproduction and Nurturance." In *Troubling Children: Studies of Children and Social Problems*, ed. Joel Best, 93–113. New York: Aldine de Gruyter.

Lock, Margaret. 1993. *Encounters with Aging: Mythologies of Menopause in Japan and North America*. Berkeley: University of California Press.

———. 1998. "Breast Cancer: Reading the Omens." *Anthropology Today* 14(4): 7–16.

Locker, Hilary. 1996. "Abuse and Pregnancy." *American Baby*, February, 14.

Longino, Helen E. 1990. *Science as Social Knowledge: Values and Objectivity in Scientific Inquiry*. Princeton: Princeton University Press.

Lopez, Iris. 1997. "Agency and Constraint: Sterilization and Reproductive Freedom among Puerto Rican Women in New York City." In *Situated Lives: Gender and Culture in Everyday Life*, ed. Louise Lamphere, Helena Ragoné, and Patricia Zavella, 157–171. New York: Routledge.

Louden, Jennifer. 1995. *The Pregnant Woman's Comfort Book*. San Francisco: Harper SanFrancisco.

Luker, Kristin. 1978. *Taking Chances: Abortion and the Decision Not to Contracept*. Berkeley: University of California Press.

———. 1984. *Abortion and the Politics of Motherhood*. Berkeley: University of California Press.

———. 1997. *Dubious Conceptions: The Politics of Teenage Pregnancy*. Cambridge: Harvard University Press.

Lumley, Judith, and Jill Astbury. 1989. "Advice for Pregnancy." In *Effective Care in Pregnancy and Childbirth*, ed. Iain Chalmers, Marc Murray Enkin, and J.N.C. Keirse, 1: 237–254. Oxford: Oxford University Press.

Lupton, Deborah. 1995. *The Imperative of Health: Public Health and the Regulated Body*. London: Sage Publications.

MacArthur, C., and E. G. Knox. 1988. "Smoking in Pregnancy: Effects of Stopping at Different Stages." *British Journal of Obstetrics and Gynaecology* 95(6): 551–555.

Mackay, Judith. 1996. "Women and Tobacco: International Issues." *JAMWA* 51(1–2): 48–51.

Manning, F., and C. Feyerabend. 1976. "Cigarette Smoking and Fetal Breathing Movement." *British Journal of Obstetrics and Gynecology* 83:262–270.

March of Dimes Birth Defects Foundation. 1993. *Healthy Babies, Healthy Business: An Employer's Guidebook on Improving Maternal and Infant Health.* White Plains, N.Y.

———. 1994a. "Be Good to Your Baby before It Is Born." Pamphlet.

———. 1994b. "Give Your Baby a Healthy Start: Stop Smoking." Pamphlet.

———. 1999a. "Rubella." http://www.modimes.org/HealthLibrary2/factsheets/Rubella.htm.

———. 1999b. "Birth Defects Information." http://www.modimes.org/HealthLibrary2/BirthDefects/Default.htm.

Marcus, Sharon. 1993. "Placing Rosemary's Baby." *Differences: A Journal of Feminist Cultural Studies* 5(3): 121–153.

Marcus, George E. 1995. "Ethnography in/of the World System: The Emergence of Multi-Sited Ethnography." *Annual Review of Anthropology* 24:95–117.

Mariner, Wendy K., Leonard H. Glantz, and George J. Annas. 1990. "Pregnancy, Drugs, and the Perils of Prosecution." *Criminal Justice Ethics* (Winter/Spring): 30–41.

Markens, Susan, Carole H. Browner, and Nancy Press. 1997. "Feeding the Fetus: On Interrogating the Notion of Maternal–Fetal Conflict." *Feminist Studies* 23(2): 351–372.

Marks, J. S., J. P. Koplan, C.J.R. Hogue, and M. E. Dalmat. 1990. "A Cost–Benefit/Cost–Effectiveness Analysis of Smoking Cessation for Pregnant Women." *American Journal of Preventive Medicine* 6:282–289.

Martin, Emily. 1991. "The Egg and the Sperm: How Science Has Constructed a Romance Based on Stereotypical Male–Female Roles." *Signs: Journal of Women in Culture and Society* 16(3): 485–501.

———.1992 [1987]. *The Woman in the Body: A Cultural Analysis of Reproduction.* Reprint. Boston: Beacon Press.

———. 1994. *Flexible Bodies: The Role of Immunity in American Culture from the Days of Polio to the Age of AIDS.* Boston: Beacon Press.

Martin, S. L., K. T. English, K. A. Clark, D. Cillenti, and L. L. Kupper. 1996. "Violence and Substance Use among North Carolina Pregnant Women." *American Journal of Public Health* 86:991–998.

Martínez, Elizabeth. 1997. *De Colores Means All of Us: Latina Views for a Multi-Colored Century.* Cambridge, Mass.: South End Press.

Martinez, Fernando P., Anne L. Wright, and Lynn M. Taussig. 1994. "The Effect of Paternal Smoking on the Birthweight of Newborns Whose Mothers Did Not Smoke." *American Journal of Public Health* 84(9): 1489–1491.

Maynard-Moody, Steven. 1995. *The Dilemma of the Fetus: Fetal Research, Medical Progress, and Moral Politics.* New York: St. Martin's Press.

McNeil, Maureen, and Jacquelyn Litt. 1992. "More Medicalizing of Mothers: Foetal Alcohol Syndrome in the USA and Related Developments." In *Private Risks and Public Dangers,* ed. Sue Scott, Gareth Williams, Stephen Platt, and Hilary Thomas, 112–132. Aldershot, UK: Avebury.

McNulty, Molly. 1988. "Pregnancy Police: The Health Policy and Legal Implications of Punishing Pregnant Women for Harm to Their Fetuses." *New York University Review of Law and Social Change* 16: 277–319.

Mehren, Elisabeth. 1995. "They're Experts on 'What to Expect.'" *Los Angeles Times,* March 5, E1, 4.

Meier, Barry. 1998a. "Files of Reynolds Tobacco Show Effort on the Young." *New York Times,* January 15, A10.

———. 1998b. "Philip Morris Censored Data about Addiction." *New York Times,* May 7, A14.

———. 1998c. "Politics of Youth Smoking Fueled by Unproven Data." *New York, Times,* May 20, A1, 16.

————. 1998d. "Remaining States Approve the Pact on Tobacco Suits." *New York Times,* November 21, A1, A12.

Mikhailidis, D. P., E. S. Ganotakis, J. A. Papadakis, and J. Y. Jeremy. 1998. "Smoking and Urological Disease." *Journal of the Royal Society of Health* 118(4): 210–212.

Minkler, Meredith. 1989. "Health Education, Health Promotion and the Open Society: An Historical Perspective." *Health Education Quarterly* 16(1): 17–30.

Missouri Department of Health–Centers for Disease Control. N.d. "Becoming Smoke-Free: Baby and Me Smoke Free." Pamphlet.

Montagu, M. F. Ashley. 1964 [1961]. *Life before Birth.* Reprint. New York: Signet Books.

Moore, Keith L. 1988. *The Developing Human: Clinically Oriented Embryology.* 4th ed. Philadelphia: Saunders.

Morgan, Lynn M. 1989. "When Does Life Begin? A Cross-Cultural Perspective." In *Abortion and Fetal "Personhood,"* ed. Edd Doerr and James Prescott, 97–114. Long Beach, Calif.: Centerline Press.

————. 1996. "Fetal Relationality in Feminist Philosophy: An Anthropological Critique." *Hypatia* 11(3): 46–70.

————. 1997. "Imagining the Unborn in the Ecuadoran Andes." *Feminist Studies* 23(2): 323–350.

————. 1998. "Ambiguities Lost: Fashioning the Fetus into a Child in Ecuador and the United States." In *Small Wars: The Cultural Politics of Childhood,* ed. Nancy Scheper-Hughes and Carolyn Sargent, 58–74. Berkeley: University of California Press.

Morgan, Lynn M., and Meredith W. Michaels, eds. 1999. *Fetal Subjects, Feminist Positions.* Philadelphia: University of Pennsylvania Press.

Moss, Kary. 1990. "Substance Abuse during Pregnancy." *Harvard Women's Law Journal* 13:278–299.

Mother Jones. 1996. "The Tobacco Wars." May/June, 40–49.

Mullen, P. D., J. P. Carbonari, E. R. Tabak, and M. C. Glenday. 1991. "Improving Disclosure of Smoking by Pregnant Women." *American Journal of Obstetrics and Gynecology* 165(2): 409–413.

Mullen, P. D. 1999. "Grant Report. Substance Abuse: Test Markers for Smoking Cessation Efforts." Robert Wood Johnson Foundation. http://www.rwjf.org/health/fulltext/024584e.htm.

Multnomah County (Oregon) Tobacco Prevention Coalition. N.d. "Working toward a Tobacco-Free Community." Pamphlet.

Mungeam, Frank. 1998. *A Guy's Guide to Pregnancy.* Hillsboro, Ore.: Beyond Words Publishing Co.

Murphy, Patrick T. 1996. "Protect the Innocent." *New York Times,* July 30, A 17.

Murphy-Lawless, Jo. 1998. *Reading Birth and Death in Obstetric Practice.* Bloomington: Indiana University Press.

Nathanielsz, Peter W. 1996 [1992]. *Life before Birth: The Challenges of Fetal Development.* Reprint. New York: W. H. Freeman and Company.

————. 1999. *Life in the Womb: The Origin of Health and Disease.* Ithaca, N.Y.: Promethean Press.

Nathanson, Constance A. 1991. *Dangerous Passage: The Social Control of Sexuality in Women's Adolescence.* Philadelphia: Temple University Press.

————. 1996. "Disease Prevention as Social Change: Toward a Theory of Public Health." *Population and Development Review* 22(4): 609–638.

————. 1997. "Analysis of U.S. Tobacco Control Movement: A Final Report to the Association of Schools of Public Health and the Centers for Disease Control and Prevention." Johns Hopkins University, School of Hygiene and Public Health, Department of Population Dynamics, May 12.

———. 1999. "Social Movements as Catalysts for Policy Change: The Case of Smoking and Guns." *Journal of Health Politics, Policy and Law* 24(3): 421–488.

———. N.d. *Disease Prevention as Social Change: Society, Politics and Public Health in the U.S., Canada, Britain and France.* Forthcoming

Nelkin, Dorothy. 1989. "Communicating Technological Risk: The Social Construction of Risk Perception." *Annual Review of Public Health* 10:95–113.

———, ed. 1992. *Controversy: The Politics of Technical Decisions.* Newbury Park, Calif.: Sage Publications.

Nelson, Barbara J. 1984. *Making an Issue of Child Abuse: Political Agenda Setting for Social Problems.* Chicago: University of Chicago Press.

Neubauer, Deane, and Richard Pratt. 1981. "The Second Public Health Revolution: A Critical Appraisal." *Journal of Health Politics, Policy and Law* 6(2): 205–228.

New York Times. 1921. "Calls Grandmother Unfit." April 19, 8.

———. 1929a. "Editorial: Dispute Methodist Data on Tobacco: American Medical Journal Urges Morals Board's 'Voice' to Prove Evils It Cites." July 13, 18.

———. 1929b. "American Tobacco Is Pushed Abroad." July 28, III, 7.

———. 1935. "Heart Action of Unborn Babies Speeds up When Their Mothers Smoke, Tests Show." February 8, 23.

———. 1985a. "Smokers' Babies: Care Costs High." October 22, C12.

———. 1985b. "Surgeon General Predicts Isolation for U.S. Smokers." October 22, C12.

———. 1985c. "Panel Asks Action on Small Babies." February 26, C9.

———. 1986a. "Obstetricians Offer Discount to Patients Who Don't Smoke." January 12, 33.

———. 1986b. "Of Smoking and Pregnancy." October 19, A60.

———. 1988. "Penalty Is to Quit Smoking." May 29, A22.

———. 1989. "Tobacco Town Smoking Ban Laid to Shopper's Complaint." November 11, A13.

———. 1993a. "Mother Who Smokes Loses Custody of Asthmatic Girl." October 15, A22.

———. 1993b. "Asthmatic Taken from Home Because of Cigarette Smoke." November 7, A36.

———. 1996a. "Smokers 50% More Likely to Bear Retarded Children." April 10, B7.

———. 1996b. "Tobacco Chemicals Linger in Babies." April 23, C3.

———. 1997a. "Smokers' Babies Show Nicotine Level of Adults." March 21, A20.

———. 1997b. "Editorial: The Return of Thalidomide." September 24, A18.

———. 1997c. "Broad Gains Seen in American Health." September 12, A1.

Newman, Karen. 1996. *Fetal Positions: Individualism, Science, and Visuality.* Stanford, Calif.: Stanford University Press.

Newnham, J. P. 1993. "Effects of Frequent Ultrasound during Pregnancy: A Randomised Controlled Trial." *Lancet* 342:887–891.

Nichter, Mark, and Elizabeth Cartwright. 1991. "Saving the Children for the Tobacco Industry." *Medical Anthropology Quarterly* 5(3): 236–256.

Nieburg, Phillip, James S. Marks, Nancy M. McLaren, and Patrick L. Remington. 1985. "The Fetal Tobacco Syndrome." *JAMA* 253(20): 2998–2999.

O'Keefe, Anne Marie, and Richard W. Pollay. 1996. "Deadly Targeting of Women in Promoting Cigarettes" *JAMWA* 51(1–2): 67–69.

O'Neill, Anne Marie. 1996. "Under the Influence: Drunk While Pregnant, a Woman Is Charged with Trying to Kill Her Baby." *People Weekly*, September 9, 53–55.

O'Neill, Patrick. 1998. "Cash Incentive Could Help Pregnant Smoker Quit." *The Oregonian*, March 3. http://www.oregonlive.com/todaysnews/9803/st03038.html.

Oakley, Ann. 1984. *The Captured Womb: A History of the Medical Care of Pregnant Women.* Oxford and New York: Basil Blackwell.

———. 1989. "Smoking in Pregnancy: Smokescreen or Risk Factor? Towards a Materialist Analysis." *Sociology of Health and Illness* 11(4): 311–335.

———. 1992. *Social Support and Motherhood: The Natural History of a Research Project.* Oxford, UK, and Cambridge, Mass.: Blackwell Publishers.

Oaks, Laury. 1994. "Fetal Personhood and Fetal Spirithood: The Cultural Construction of Abortion in Japan." *Women's Studies International Forum* 17(5): 511–524.

———. 1998. "Irishwomen, Eurocitizens, and Defining Abortion." In *Reproducing Reproduction: Kinship, Power, and Technological Innovation,* ed. Sarah Franklin and Helena Ragoné, 132–155. Philadelphia: University of Pennsylvania Press.

———. 1999. "Irish Trans/national Politics and Locating Fetuses." In *Fetal Subjects, Feminist Positions,* ed. Lynn M. Morgan and Meredith W. Michaels, 175–198. Philadelphia: University of Pennsylvania Press.

Orleans, C. Tracy, and John Slade, eds. 1993. *Nicotine Addiction: Principles and Management.* New York: Oxford University Press.

Paltrow, Lynn M. 1990. "When Becoming Pregnant Is a Crime." *Criminal Justice Ethics* 9(1): 41–47.

Papazian, Ruth. 1991. "Family Health: Smoking Is Dangerous to Kids." *Parents' Magazine,* October, 178–182.

Parents Expecting Magazine. 1996. "FirstSounds Prenatal Listening Kit." Advertisement.

Parents' Magazine. 1980. "Parents Report: Smoking before Childbirth." January, 18.

Patton, Cindy. 1990. *Inventing AIDS.* New York: Routledge.

———. 1996. *Fatal Advice: How Safe-Sex Education Went Wrong.* Durham, N.C.: Duke University Press.

Patton, G. C., M. Hibbert, M. J. Rosier, J. B. Carlin, J. Caust, and G. Bowes. 1996. "Is Smoking Associated with Depression and Anxiety in Teenagers?" *American Journal of Public Health.* 86(2): 225–230.

PennSAIC. 1994 [1992]. "Pregnant? Don't Smoke!" South Deerfield, Mass.: Channing L. Bete Co. Pamphlet.

Pepper, Rachel. 1999. *The Ulitmate Guide to Pregnancy for Lesbians.* San Francisco: Cleis Press.

Perlez, Jane. 1997. "Fenced in at Home, Marlboro Man Looks Abroad." *New York Times,* June 24, A1, 16.

Petchesky, Rosalind Pollack. 1981. "Reproductive 'Choice' in the Contemporary United States: A Social Analysis of Female Sterilization." In *And the Poor Get Children,* ed. Karen L. Michaelson, 50–88. New York: Monthly Review Press.

———. 1985 [1984]. *Abortion and Woman's Choice: The State, Sexuality, and Reproductive Freedom.* Reprint. Boston: Northeastern University Press.

———. 1987. "Fetal Images: The Power of Visual Culture in the Politics of Reproduction." *Feminist Studies* 13(2): 263–291.

Pfohl, Stephen J. 1977. "The 'Discovery' of Child Abuse." *Social Problems* 24:310–323.

Pollitt, Katha. 1990. "'Fetal Rights': A New Assault on Feminism." *The Nation,* March 26, 409–418.

Porter, Theodore. 1995. *Trust in Numbers: The Pursuit of Objectivity in Science and Public Life.* Princeton, N.J.: Princeton University Press.

Prochaska, James O., and Carlo C. DiClemente. 1992. "Stages of Change in the Modification of Problem Behaviors." *Progress in Behavior Modification* 28:185–218.

Profet, Margie. 1995. *Protecting Your Baby-to-Be: Preventing Birth Defects in the First Trimester.* Reading, Mass.: Addison-Wesley Publishing Company.

Querido, Melissa. 1999. "Elevating the Legal Status of the Fetus: Pregnancy Prosecutions and Abortion Rights." *Reproductive Freedom News* 8(6): 1–3.

R. J. Reynolds Tobacco Company. 1995. "How You Can Help Discourage Kids from Smoking." Winston-Salem, N.C. Pamphlet.

Ragoné, Helena. 1994. *Surrogate Motherhood: Conception in the Heart.* Boulder, Colo.: Westview Press.

———. 1998. "Incontestable Motivations." In *Reproducing Reproduction: Kinship, Power, and Technological Innovation,* ed. Sarah Franklin and Helena Ragoné, 118–131. Philadelphia: University of Pennsylvania Press.

Rajan, Lynda, and Ann Oakley. 1990. "Low Birth Weight Babies: The Mother's Point of View." *Midwifery* 6:73–85.

Ramirez, Anthony. 1990. "New Cigarette Raising Issue of Target Marketing." *New York Times,* February 18, A28.

Rapp, Rayna. 1988. "Chromosomes and Communication: The Discourse of Genetic Counseling." *Medical Anthropology Quarterly* 2(2): 143–157.

———. 1990. "Constructing Amniocentesis: Maternal and Medical Discourses." In *Uncertain Terms: Negotiating Gender in American Culture,* ed. Faye Ginsburg and Anna Lowenhaupt Tsing, 28–42. Boston: Beacon Press.

———. 1991. "Moral Pioneers: Women, Men, and Fetuses on a Frontier of Reproductive Technology." In *Gender at the Crossroads of Knowledge,* ed. Micaela di Leonardo, 383–396. Berkeley: University of California Press.

———. 1997. "Real-Time Fetus: The Role of the Sonogram in the Age of Monitored Reproduction." In *Cyborgs and Citadels: Anthropological Interventions in Emerging Sciences and Technologies,* ed. Gary Lee Downey and Joseph Dumit, 31–48. Santa Fe, N.M.: School of American Research.

———. 1999. *Testing Women, Testing the Fetus: The Social Impact of Amniocentesis in America.* New York: Routledge.

Reid, Roddy. 1995. "'Death of the Family,' or, Keeping Human Beings Human." In *Posthuman Bodies,* ed. Judith Halberstam and Iva Livingston, 177–199. Bloomington: Indiana University Press.

———. 1997. "Healthy Families, Healthy Citizens: The Politics of Speech and Knowledge in the California Anti–Secondhand Smoke Media Campaign." *Science as Culture* 29:541–581.

Renne, Elisha P. 1996. "The Pregnancy That Doesn't Stay: The Practice and Perception of Abortion by Ekiti Yoruba Women." *Social Science and Medicine* 42(4): 483–494.

Robert Wood Johnson Foundation. 1999a. "Call for Proposals: Smoke-Free Families: Innovations to Stop Smoking during and beyond Pregnancy: Phase II." October. Princeton, N.J. Pamphlet.

———. 1999b. "An Evidence-Based Best Practice Intervention for Prenatal Smoking Cessation." http://smokefreefamilies.uab.edu.

Roberts, Dorothy. 1997. *Killing the Black Body: Race, Reproduction, and the Meaning of Liberty.* New York: Pantheon Books.

Robertson, John A. 1983. "Procreative Liberty and the Control of Conception, Pregnancy, and Childbirth." *Virginia Law Review* 69(3): 405–463.

Rosenberg, Michael J., ed. 1987. *Smoking and Reproductive Health.* Littleton, Mass.: PSG Publishing Company.

Roth, Rachel. 1993. "At Women's Expense: The Cost of Fetal Rights." In *The Politics of Pregnancy: Policy Dilemmas in the Maternal–Fetal Relationship,* ed. Janna C. Merrick and Robert H. Blank, 117–135. Binghampton, N.Y.: Harrington Park Press.

———. 2000. *Making Women Pay: The Hidden Cost of Fetal Rights.* Ithaca, N.Y.: Cornell University Press.

Rothman, Barbara Katz. 1986. *The Tentative Pregnancy: Prenatal Diagnosis and the Future of Motherhood.* New York: Viking.

———. 1989. *Recreating Motherhood: Ideology and Technology in a Patriarchal Society.* New York: W. W. Norton and Company.

———. 1998. *Genetic Maps and Human Imaginations*. New York: W. W. Norton and Company.

Royce, Jaqueline M., Kitty Corbett, Glorian Sorensen, and Judith Ockene. 1997. Gender, Social Pressure, and Smoking Cessation: The Community Intervention Trial for Smoking Cessation (COMMIT) at Baseline. *Social Science and Medicine* 44(3): 359–370.

Sadler, L., K. Belanger, A. Saftlas, B. Leaderer, K. Hellenbrand, J. E. McSharrey, and M. B. Bracken. 1999. "Environmental Tobacco Smoke Exposure and Small-for-Gestational-Age Birth." *American Journal of Epidemiology* 150(7): 695–705.

Saletan, William. 1996. "Sins of Omission." *Mother Jones*, May/June, 58–62.

———. 1997. "The Fetal Health Risk Pro-Lifers Don't Talk About." *Glamour*, January, 81.

Samuels, Susan Uttaro. 1995. *Fetal Rights, Women's Rights: Gender Equality in the Workplace*. Madison: University of Wisconsin Press.

Sandelowski, Margarete. 1993. *With Child in Mind: Studies of the Personal Encounter with Infertility*. Philadelphia: University of Pennsylvania Press.

Sasco, A. J., and H. Vainio. 1999. "From in Utero and Childhood Exposure to Parental Smoking to Childhood Cancer: A Possible Link and the Need for Action." *Human and Experimental Toxicology* 18(4): 192–201.

Sawicki, Jana. 1991. *Disciplining Foucault: Feminism, Power and the Body*. New York: Routledge.

Scales, Ann, and Wendy Chavkin. 1996. "Abortion, Law, and Public Health." In *Man-Made Medicine: Women's Health, Public Policy, and Reform*, ed. Kary L. Moss, 219–248. Durham, N.C.: Duke University Press.

Schachter, Jim. 1986. "Woman Accused of Contributing to Baby's Demise during Pregnancy." *Los Angeles Times*, October 1, Metro section, 1, 6.

Schell, Lawrence M., John H. Relethford, Mamta Maden, Paul B. Namon, and Ernest B. Hook. 1994. "Unequal Adaptive Value of Changing Cigarette Use during Pregnancy for Heavy, Moderate, and Light Smokers." *American Journal of Human Biology* 6:25–32.

Scheper-Hughes, Nancy. 1992. *Death without Weeping: The Violence of Everyday Life in Brazil*. Berkeley: University of California Press.

Schmeck, Harold M., Jr. 1971. "Surgeon General Urges Battle to Dissuade Women Smokers." *New York Times*, January 12, 17.

Schmidt, Roger W. 1977. "Non-Smokers' Rights: The U.S. Experience." In *Smoking and Health II: Proceedings of the ACS/NCI Conference* [held in 1975], ed. Department of Education, U.S. Department of Health and Welfare, 347–351. Washington, D.C.: Government Printing Office.

Schwartz, John. 1998. "Thalidomide Wins Limited Approval." *Washington Post*. July 17, A1.

Schwarz, Richard H. 1995. "Your Healthy Pregnancy: Planning Your Next Baby." *American Baby*, February, 26, 28.

———. 1996. "Your Healthy Pregnancy: The Expectant Father." *American Baby*, February, 8, 10, 14.

Shear, Marie. 1985. "The Pro-Death Lobby." *Women's Review of Books* 11(6): 6–8.

Shende, Suzanne. 1997. "Fighting the Violence against Our Sisters: Prosecution of Pregnant Women and the Coercive Use of Norplant." In *Women Transforming Politics: An Alternative Reader*, ed. Cathy J. Cohen, Kathleen B. Jones, and Joan C. Tronto, 123–135. New York: New York University Press.

Slotkin, Theodore A. 1998. "Fetal Nicotine or Cocaine Exposure: Which One Is Worse?" *Journal of Pharmacology and Experimental Therapeutics* 285(3): 931–945. Excerpts available at http://ash.org/june98/06–25–98–3.html.

Simonds, Wendy. 1996. *Abortion at Work: Ideology and Practice in a Feminist Clinic*. New Brunswick, N.J.: Rutgers University Press.

Simpson, Winea J. 1957. "A Preliminary Report of Cigarette Smoking and the Incidence of Prematurity." *American Journal of Obstetrics and Gynecology* 73:807–815.

Sobo, E. J. 1995. *Choosing Unsafe Sex: AIDS—Risk and Denial among Disadvantaged Women*. Philadelphia: University of Pennsylvania Press.

Sontag, L.W., and Robert F. Wallace. 1935. "The Effect of Cigaret Smoking during Pregnancy upon the Fetal Heart Rate." *American Journal of Obstetrics and Gynecology* 29:77–83.

Sontag, Susan. 1990 [1978, 1989]. *Illness as Metaphor and AIDS and Its Metaphors*. New York: Anchor Books.

Stabile, Carol A. 1994. *Feminism and the Technological Fix*. Manchester and New York: Manchester University Press.

State of Maryland Department of Health and Mental Hygiene–Centers for Disease Control. 1992. "Smoking Cessation in Pregnancy Report." March. Baltimore: Health Education Center, Local and Family Health Administration.

———. N.d.a. "Quit and Be Free! Nurse's Guide." Washington, D.C.: U.S. Department of Health and Human Services, Public Health Service, Centers for Disease Control. Booklet.

———. N.d.b. "Quit and Be Free! Health in Pregnancy." Washington, D.C.: U.S. Department of Health and Human Services, Public Health Service, Centers for Disease Control. Booklet.

Stebbins, Kenyon Rainier. 1990. "Transnational Tobacco Companies and Health in Underdeveloped Countries: Recommendations for Avoiding a Smoking Epidemic." *Social Science and Medicine* 30(2): 227–235.

———. 1991. Tobacco, Politics, and Economics: Implications for Global Health. *Social Science and Medicine* 33(12): 1317–1326.

Steinbock, Bonnie. 1992. *Life before Birth: The Moral and Legal Status of Embryos and Fetuses*. New York: Oxford University Press.

Steinfeld, Jesse L.. 1983. "Women and Children Last? Attitudes toward Cigarette Smoking and Nonsmokers' Rights, 1971." *New York State Journal of Medicine* 83(13): 1257–1258.

Stern, Sue Ellen. 1992. "Overconcerned Dad." *American Baby*, May, 18.

———. 1995. "Your Feelings: A Dad-to-Be Who Smokes." *American Baby*, May, 16.

Stokes III, Joseph. 1983. "Why Not Rate Health and Life Insurance Premiums by Risks?" *New England Journal of Medicine* 308(7): 393–395.

Stolberg, Sheryl Gay. 1994. "Fetuses Found Affected by Secondhand Smoke." *Los Angeles Times*, February 23, A1.

———. 1998. "Surgeon General Warns of Rise in Ethnic Smoking." *New York Times*, April 28, A16.

Stone, Deborah A. 1989. "At Risk in the Welfare State." *Social Research* 56(3): 591–633.

Stout, David. 1996. "Direct Link Found between Smoking and Lung Cancer." *New York Times*, October 18, A 1, 16.

Stryker, Jeff. 1999. " Fetuses as Persons." *California HealthLine: A News Service of California HealthCare Foundation*, October 11. http://www.chcf.org/features/index.html.

Sumartojo, Esther. 1993. "When Tuberculosis Treatment Fails: A Social Behavioral Account of Patient Adherence." *American Review of Respiratory Disease* 147:1311–1320.

Taylor, Janelle S. 1992. "The Public Fetus and the Family Car: From Abortion Politics to a Volvo Advertisement." *Public Culture* 4(2): 67–80.

———. 1998. "Image of Contradiction: Obstetrical Ultrasound in American Culture." In *Reproducing Reproduction*, ed. Helena Ragoné and Sarah Franklin, 15–45. Philadelphia: University of Pennsylvania Press.

Terry, Don. 1996. "In Wisconsin, a Rarity of a Fetal-Harm Case: Attempted-Murder Charges for Alcoholic." *New York Times*, August 17, A6.

Terry, Luther. 1981. "The Health Consequences of Smoking Today." In *National Conference on Smoking OR Health: Developing a Blueprint for Action*. Proceedings. Initiated and underwritten by the American Cancer Society. New York, November 18–20.

Tippins, Prudence, and Sherill Tippins. 1996. *The Two of Us*. New York: Henry Holt and Company.

Tolson, George C., Judy M. Barnes, George A. Gay, and Julia L. Kowaleski. 1991. "The Revision of the U.S. Standard Certificates and Reports." National Center for Health Statistics. *Vital Health Statistics* 4(28).

Treichler, Paula A. 1988. "AIDS, Gender, and Biomedical Discourse: Current Contests for Meaning." In *AIDS: The Burdens of History*, ed. Elizabeth Fee and Daniel M. Fox, 190–266. Berkeley: University of California Press.

———. 1999. *How to Have Theory in an Epidemic: Cultural Chronicles of AIDS*. Durham, N.C.: Duke University Press.

Trostle, James A. 1988. "Medical Compliance as Ideology." *Social Science and Medicine* 27(12): 1299–1308.

Troyer, Ronald J., and Gerald E. Markle. 1983. *Cigarettes: The Battle over Smoking*. New Brunswick, N.J.: Rutgers University Press.

Tsing, Anna Lowenhaupt. 1990. "Monster Stories: Women Charged with Perinatal Endangerment." In *Uncertain Terms: Negotiating Gender in American Culture*, ed. Faye Ginsburg and Anna Lowenhaupt Tsing, 282–299. Boston: Beacon Press.

Tye, Joe B. 1986. "Fetal Tobacco Syndrome: Letter to the Editor." *JAMA* 256(7): 862–863.

University of California, San Diego Cancer Prevention and Control Unit and the California Department of Health Services. N.d. "Smoking While Pregnant Can Cause." Fact sheet.

U.S. Department of Health and Human Services (DHHS). 1980. *The Health Consequences of Smoking for Women: A Report of the Surgeon General*. Washington, D.C.: Government Printing Office.

———. 1982. *The Health Consequences of Smoking, Cancer: A Report of the Surgeon General*. Washington, D.C.: Government Printing Office.

———. 1986. *The Health Consequences of Involuntary Smoking: A Report of the Surgeon General*. Washington, D.C.: Government Printing Office.

———. 1989. *Reducing the Health Consequences of Smoking: 25 Years of Progress: A Report of the Surgeon General*. Washington, D.C.: Government Printing Office.

———. 1990. *The Health Benefits of Smoking Cessation: A Report of the Surgeon General*. Public Health Service, Centers for Disease Control, Center for Chronic Disease Prevention and Health Promotion, Office on Smoking and Health. Washington, D.C.: Government Printing Office.

———. 1991. *Healthy People 2000: National Health Promotion and Disease Prevention Objectives*. Public Health Service. Washington, D.C.: Government Printing Office.

———. 1998. *Chartbook on Children's Insurance Status: Tabulations of the March 1998 Current Population Survey*. Office of Health Policy. December. http://aspe.os.dhhs.gov/health/98Chartbk/98–chtbk.htm.

———. 20000. *Healthy People 2010*. Conference ed. 2 vols. January. Washington, D.C. http://www.health.gov/healthpeople/Document/HTML/Volume1/Opening.htm.

———. N.d. "Girl Power!" http://www.health.org/gpower/index.htm.

U.S. Department of Health and Human Services (DHHS) and Public Health Service. 1989. *Caring for Our Future: The Content of Prenatal Care—A Report of the Public Health Service Expert Panel on the Content of Prenatal Care.* Washington, D.C.: Government Printing Office.

U.S. Department of Health and Human Services, U.S. Women's National Team, and U.S. Soccer. 1999. "Smoke Free Kids and Soccer." June 30. http://www.smokefree.gov/campaign.html.

U.S. Department of Health, Education, and Welfare (DHEW). 1964. *Smoking and Health: Report of the Advisory Committee to the Surgeon General of the Public Health Service.* Washington, D.C.: Government Printing Office.

———. 1973. *Prenatal Care.* Publication no. (OCD) 73–13. Washington, D.C.: Government Printing Office.

———. 1979a. *Smoking and Health: A Report of the Surgeon General.* Public Health Service, Office of the Assistant Secretary for Health, Office on Smoking and Health. Washington, D.C.: Government Printing Office.

———. 1979b. *Healthy People: The Surgeon General's Report on Health Promotion and Disease Prevention.* Washington, D.C.: Government Printing Office.

U.S. House of Representatives. 1969. *Hearings before the Interstate and Foreign Commerce Committees on PL 91–222, the Public Health Cigarette Smoking Act of 1969. Parts 1 and 2–Cigarette Labeling and* Advertising. 91st Cong., 1st sess.

———. 1982. *Hearings before the Subcommittee on Health and the Environment, Committee on Energy and Commerce, on the Comprehensive Smoking Prevention Education Act,* HR 5653 and HR 4957. 97th Cong., 2nd sess.

———. 1983. *Hearings before the Subcommittee on Health and the Environment, Committee of Energy and Commerce, on the Smoking Prevention Act,* HR 1824. 8th Cong., 1st sess.

Vaughan, Christopher. 1996. *How Life Begins: The Science of Life in the Womb.* New York: Times Books/Random House.

Ventura, Stephanie J. 1999. "Commentary: Using the Birth Certificate to Monitor Smoking during Pregnancy." *Public Health Reports.* 114(1): 71–73.

Ventura, S. J., J. A. Martin, S. C. Curtin, T. J .Mathews, and M. M. Park. 2000. Births: Final Data for 1998. National Vital Statistics Report 48(3). Hyattsville, Md.: National Center for Health Statistics.

Vigue, Doreen Indica. 1996. "Woman Booked for Drinking." *Boston Globe,* August 15, B1, 8.

Vine, Marilyn F. 1996a. "Smoking and Male Fertility." *Clinical Proceedings: A Publication of the Association of Reproductive Health Professionals* (October): 7.

———. 1996b. "Smoking and Male Reproduction: A Review." *International Journal of Andrology* 19(6): 323–337.

Wallerstein, Nina, and Edward Bernstein. 1988. "Empowerment Education: Freire's Ideas Adapted to Health Education." *Health Education Quarterly* 15(4): 379–394.

Warner, Kenneth. 1985. "Cigarette Advertising and Media Coverage of Smoking and Health." *New England Journal of Medicine* 312(6): 384–388.

Washington Post. 1994. "Secondhand Smoke Can Affect Even the Unborn, Researchers Find." February 23, A3.

Whelan, Elizabeth M. 1979. "Taking Care of Yourself and Your Baby during Pregnancy." *American Baby,* April, 20.

———. 1980. "Dr. Elizabeth M. Whelan Discusses Cigarettes and Your Baby's Health." *American Baby,* July, 33.

———. 1984. *A Smoking Gun: How the Tobacco Industry Gets Away with Murder.* Philadelphia: George F. Stickely Co.

Williams, Marjorie. 1991. "Tobacco's Hold on Women's Groups." *Washington Post*, November 14, A1, 16.

Windham, G. C., J. Von Behren, K. Waller, and L. Fenster. 1999. "Exposure to Environmental and Mainstream Tobacco Smoke and Risk of Spontaneous Abortion." *American Journal of Epidemiology* 149(3): 243–247.

Windsor, R. A., J. B. Lowe, L. L. Perkins, D. Smith-Yoder, L. Artz, M. Crawford, K. Amburgy, and N. R. Boyd, Jr. 1993. "Health Education for Pregnant Smokers: Its Behavioral Impact and Cost Benefit." *American Journal of Public Health* 83:201–206.

Winthrop, Anne. 1992. "Men, Cocaine, and Fetuses." *American Baby*, May, 10.

———. 1993a. "Smoking, Drinking, and Pregnancy." *American Baby*, July, 8.

———. 1993b. "More Reasons to Quit Smoking." *American Baby*, November, 14.

———. 1995. "If You Are Pregnant, Relax!" *American Baby*, August, 10.

Wolf, Naomi. 1995. "Our Bodies, Our Souls: Rethinking Pro-Choice Rhetoric." *New Republic*, October 16, 26–35.

Wolinsky, Howard, and Tom Brune. 1994. *The Serpent on the Staff: The Unhealthy Politics of the American Medical Association*. New York: G. P. Putnam's Sons.

Wood, Thomas D., and Zilpha Carruthers. 1930. "Can One Influence an Unborn Child?" *Parents' Magazine*, September, 19, 68.

Woodman, Sue. 1990. "Target." *Mirabella*, April, 81–84.

Wymelenberg, Suzanne. 1990. *Science and Babies: Private Decisions, Public Dilemmas*. Washington, D.C.: National Academy Press.

Yanagisako, Sylvia, and Carol Delaney, eds. 1995. *Naturalizing Power*. New York: Routledge.

Yoder, P. Stanley. 1997. "Negotiating Relevance: Belief, Knowledge, and Practice in International Health Projects." *Medical Anthropology Quarterly* 11(2): 131–146.

Zapka, Jane G., Lori Pbert, Anne M. Stoddard, Judith K. Ockene, Karin Valentine Goins, and Debra Bonollo. 2000. "Smoking Cessation Counseling with Pregnant and Postpartum Women: A Survey of Community Health Center Providers." *American Journal of Public Health* 90(1): 78–84.

Zelizer, Viviana A. 1985. *Pricing the Priceless Child: The Changing Social Value of Children*. New York: Basic Books.

Index

Illustrations indicated by italics.

About the Author

Laury Oaks is an assistant professor in the women's studies program at the University of California, Santa Barbara. Her research has focused on various dimensions of reproductive rights, including fetal personhood and fetal spirithood in Japan, Ireland's abortion politics since the 1980s, and the aims of the prolife feminist movement in Ireland and the United States.